HISTORICAL INSTRUCTIONAL DESIGN CASES

Historical Instructional Design Cases presents a collection of design cases which are historical precedents for the field with utility for practicing designers and implications for contemporary design and delivery. Featuring concrete and detailed views of instructional design materials, programs, and environments, this book's unique curatorial approach situates these cases in the field's broader timeline while facilitating readings from a variety of perspectives and stages of design work. Students, faculty, and researchers will be prepared to build their lexicon of observed designs, understand the real-world outcomes of theory application, and develop cases that are fully accessible to future generations and contexts.

Elizabeth Boling is Professor of Instructional Systems Technology in the School of Education at Indiana University Bloomington, USA.

Colin M. Gray is Assistant Professor in the Department of Computer Graphics Technology at Purdue University, USA.

Craig D. Howard is Assistant Professor of Educational Psychology & Counseling in the College of Education, Health & Human Sciences at the University of Tennessee Knoxville, USA.

John Baaki is Assistant Professor of STEM Education and Professional Studies in the Instructional Design and Technology Program at Old Dominion University, USA.

HISTORICAL INSTRUCTIONAL DESIGN CASES

ID Knowledge in Context and Practice

Edited by Elizabeth Boling, Colin M. Gray, Craig D. Howard, and John Baaki

NEW YORK AND LONDON

First published 2021
by Routledge
52 Vanderbilt Avenue, New York, NY 10017

and by Routledge
2 Park Square, Milton Park, Abingdon, Oxon, OX14 4RN

Routledge is an imprint of the Taylor & Francis Group, an informa business

© 2021 Taylor & Francis

The right of Elizabeth Boling, Colin M. Gray, Craig D. Howard, and John Baaki to be identified as the authors of the editorial matter, and of the authors for their individual chapters, has been asserted in accordance with sections 77 and 78 of the Copyright, Designs and Patents Act 1988.

All rights reserved. No part of this book may be reprinted or reproduced or utilized in any form or by any electronic, mechanical, or other means, now known or hereafter invented, including photocopying and recording, or in any information storage or retrieval system, without permission in writing from the publishers.

Trademark notice: Product or corporate names may be trademarks or registered trademarks, and are used only for identification and explanation without intent to infringe.

Library of Congress Cataloging-in-Publication Data
A catalog record for this title has been requested.

ISBN: 978-0-367-35259-2 (hbk)
ISBN: 978-0-367-35370-4 (pbk)
ISBN: 978-0-429-33099-5 (ebk)

Typeset in Bembo
by Wearset Ltd, Boldon, Tyne and Wear

CONTENTS

List of Illustrations viii
Notes on Contributors xiii

1 Setting the Cases in Historical Context 1
  Colin M. Gray and Craig D. Howard

2 Curators' Notes: Historical Design Cases 10
  Elizabeth Boling and John Baaki

3 The Rochester Method: An Innovation in its Time
  (1878–1970) 22
  Malinda Eccarius

4 Designed for Destruction: The Carlisle Design Model
  and the Effort to Assimilate American Indian Children
  (1887–1918) 35
  John R. Gram

5 A Lived Experience of the Tennessee School for the
  Deaf (1920–2000) 50
  Makhosazana L. Lunga and Craig D. Howard

6 *Supervising Women Workers*: The Rise of Instructional Training Films (1944) 62
Colin M. Gray

7 The Skinnerian Teaching Machine (1953–1968) 85
Jason K. McDonald

8 The Original SRA Reading System: Individualized Learning in a Box (1957–1964) 104
Elizabeth Boling

9 MPATI: The Midwest Program on Airborne Television Instruction (1959–1971) 123
Monica W. Tracey and Jill E. Stefaniak

10 Automated and Amplified: Active Learning with Computers and Radio (1965–1979) 134
Anne Trumbore

11 TICCIT: Building Theory for Practical Purposes (1971–1978) 152
Andrew S. Gibbons and A. F. O'Neal

12 *Bridge*: A Cross Culture African American Reading Program (1975–1977) 186
Patricia A. Young

13 Creating Minimalist Instruction (1979–Present) 236
John M. Carroll

14 Experts in a Box: Expert Systems and Knowledge-Based Engineering (1984–1991) 253
Jo Ann Oravec

15 "Making Alcatraz Amazing": The Alcatraz Cellhouse Tour (1987–1995) 271
Elizabeth Boling

16 SimCalc: Democratizing Access to Advanced Mathematics (1992–Present) 283
Deborah Tatar, Jeremy Roschelle, and Stephen Hegedus

17 Using Analytics for Activity Awareness in Learning
   Systems (2003–2013)   315
   James M. Laffey, Christopher Amelung, and Sean Goggins

   Index   340

ILLUSTRATIONS

Figures

1.1	A historical overview of the time period represented by cases in this book, spanning education, US history, and technology	2
3.1	Dr. Zenas Westervelt, superintendent of Rochester School for the Deaf	24
3.2	A class of RSD students practice fingerspelling with their teacher	27
3.3	Even speech is taught using the Rochester Method for instruction	29
4.1	The Albuquerque Indian School buildings, circa 1910, and staff of the Albuquerque Indian School, circa 1910	37
4.2	Young male students at the Albuquerque Indian School in military uniforms holding American flags, circa 1895	37
4.3	Daily routine from the Albuquerque Indian School, 1913 to 1914, and daily routine, bugle calls, and yearly calendar from the Chiloco School, 1912–1913, reprinted in *The Indian School Journal*	39
4.4	Female students at the Albuquerque Indian School, circa 1881	43
5.1	The TSD buildings that became other parts of Knoxville's cultural life	52
5.2	South Knoxville campus buildings that are now gone	53
5.3	TSD gymnasium under construction	54
6.1	Opening frame in the reel of *Supervising Women Workers*, indicating that this film was circulated by the Indiana University Audio-Visual Center	63

6.2	An advertisement for the "Problems in Supervision" series from a 1945 issue of *Business Screen Magazine*, alongside training-related advertisement ephemera of the era	64
6.3	Title screen for the film	66
6.4	The primary characters in the film	67
6.5	Women exiting the plant	69
6.6	Examples of mechanical knowledge on the plant floor, with the male worker shown as an expert, and women workers as in need of mechanical knowledge	71
6.7	Women pictured on the shop floor as in need of male support	73
6.8	Women workers completing tasks that require high dexterity	74
6.9	A depiction of domestic work by Joe's wife, Molly, and Molly comforts Joe as he comes to the realization that women work in two jobs	76
6.10	A male supervisor confronting a worker for not wearing a cap, and the worker responding to the supervisor	78
6.11	The supervisor points to a pin on his lapel known as the Army-Navy E Award	80
7.1	Skinner's first teaching machine	88
7.2	A Skinnerian machine to teach the matching of shapes or patterns	89
7.3	A student using a constructed response teaching machine	91
7.4	The exterior of a Skinnerian teaching machine that allowed for constructed responses	91
7.5	The interior of a Skinnerian teaching machine that allowed for constructed responses	92
7.6	A student using a commercialized version of Skinner's teaching machine, manufactured by IBM	93
7.7	A student using a branching teaching machine	99
8.1	SRA Reading Laboratory, 1957	105
8.2	Contents list for the 1957 SRA Reading Laboratory included at the start of the Teacher's Handbook, and Table of Contents for the Teacher's Handbook	107
8.3	Samples of Power Builder key card, Rate Builder card, and Key booklet for the Rate Builders	108
8.4	Three-page spread from the SRA Reading Kit Teacher's Handbook with a fold-out page showing the basic steps of the program with both the teacher and the student actions detailed step by step	109
8.5	Selected Power Builder cards from different levels of the 1957 SRA Reading Lab showing the titles, two-color illustrations, and initial portion of the story each contains	111
8.6	End of program evaluation from the 1957 SRA Reading Lab	113

x Illustrations

8.7	1957 SRA Reading Laboratory; author, contributor, and publisher credits printed on the outside of the box	115
8.8	Skills tables showing the skills covered in each Power Builder at each level in the 1957 and 1963 editions	116
8.9	Illustrations created by Leonard Everett Fisher for the orange-level Power Builders of the SRA Reading Kit	117
8.10	Profile of Althea Gibson, and morality tale	119
9.1	A DC-6 owned by Purdue University that was used to broadcast the MPATI curriculum	124
9.2	A DC-6, the same model pictured here, was fitted with a large antenna to broadcast the lessons while in flight	124
9.3	Broadcasting equipment stored on a DC-6	125
9.4	A class prepares to watch a televised broadcast	127
9.5	The Flying Classroom was an elongated TV station with 6.5 tons of equipment	128
10.1	Computer-Assisted Instruction. An elementary school student interacts with the artificial tutor	135
10.2	Elementary school students in Managua respond to a radio lesson in mathematics	138
10.3	Components of the artificial tutor	139
10.4	An artist in Nicaragua creates a worksheet for students to use during radio lessons	142
10.5	A PDP-1-powered CAI elementary math instruction	144
10.6	Record of a student–computer interaction on a teletype machine	146
10.7	Student feedback complete with summative score and personalized response given by the teletype machine	147
10.8	NRMP: An instructor fills in answers called out by students during a radio lesson	149
11.1	An early representation of the base frame concept that bridged computer logic concerns with instructional (display representation) logic concerns	161
11.2	The segmentation of computer logic (flowchart) into base frames that relate display content to interaction and computer logic	162
11.3	Early notes on strategy patterns produced by combination and recombination of basic elements derived from Merrill's concept learning research	164
11.4	Notes on an attempt to represent strategy patterns made up of definitions (G) and exemplars (eg) of different kinds into Algebra-like expressions	165
11.5	The basic display set obtained by crossing two assumed dimensions: expository/inquisitory and generality/instance	167
11.6	The custom controls for learner navigation of TICCIT segment displays	169

Illustrations **xi**

11.7	Navigational paths among TICCIT display types	170
11.8	Bunderson's assessment of the factors defining learners most compatible with TICCIT instruction	177
12.1	Dr. Gary A. Simpkins	188
12.2	Dr. Charlesetta Stalling	189
12.3	Book One	191
12.4	Reading Booklet One	194
12.5	*Shine* from Book One	201
12.6	*The Organizer* from Book One	201
12.7	*Stagolee* from Book One	202
12.8	*The Ghost* from Book One	203
12.9	*Old But Not Defenseless* from Book Two	206
12.10	*What I Got To Be Proud Of* from Book Two	207
12.11	*Dreamy Mae* from Book Three	208
12.12	*A Friend in Need* from Book Three	209
12.13	*Vibration Cornbread* from Book Four	211
12.14	*Little Big Man* from Book Four	212
12.15	*I'll Always Remember* from Book Five	215
12.16	*City Folks* from Book Five	216
12.17	*Dig And Be Dug* from Book Five	217
12.18	*What Folks Call Politics* from Book Five	218
12.19	Study Book Three—Teacher's Edition	220
12.20	Study Book Five—Teacher's Edition	221
12.21	Feedback Records, Study Book	225
13.1	Model using the IBM Displaywriter	238
13.2	IBM Displaywriter	239
13.3	Guided Exploration card addressing a basic user concern, with a set of hints, a checkpoint, and error information	240
13.4	The Minimal Manual incorporated design concepts from Guided Exploration cards but embodied them in a standard self-instruction manual design	242
13.5	The Training Wheels Displaywriter blocked the execution of advanced and problematic functions, producing a feedback message without changing system state	244
13.6	Guided Exploration cards for a telephone system	246
13.7	The View Matcher presenting coordinated views of the halted execution of a blackjack game	247
13.8	The Usability Case Studies library presents structured cases that can be analyzed and contrasted	248
14.1	Knowledge base example	264
15.1	View from the bay side of the lighthouse with the cellhouse immediately behind	272

xii Illustrations

15.2	"Broadway," the main corridor in cell block D down which a new prisoner walked at intake, and the starting point for the audio tour	274
15.3	James Quillen's voice is one of those included in the tour	274
15.4	Visitors peer into a cell, at the same moment of the tour and aware of each other, but each also experiencing it individually	279
16.1	A picture used to explain a SimCalc Mathworlds microworld in the 2010 article	291
16.2	An Early Envisionment of SimCalc Mathworlds, circa 1992	292
16.3	The "Alien Elevators" 1994 version of SimCalc created an interface that was game-like, based on a narrative, and involved high-quality graphics but which submerged the mathematics	294
16.4	Controls for the 1994 "Alien Elevator" version of SimCalc included a stylized position graph, a velocity graph, a clock, and an elevator	295
16.5	Timeline of the SimCalc project grants	297
16.6	Changes in velocity: different ways to move six meters	305
16.7	Piecewise graphs are easier for children to understand than continuous ones	306
17.1	A personal desktop in Shadow illustrating the Activity Monitor	316
17.2	Framework for Notification and CANS	320
17.3	CANS and Sakai	321
17.4	CANS e-mail digest	322
17.5	CANS Desktop Awareness Widget	323
17.6	CANS Social Comparison Digest	324
17.7	CANS Activity Monitor	326
17.8	Form for setting up an activity notifier	327
17.9	An e-mail digest which can be sent to a student each day for each class	328
17.10	Interactive web page for examining course activity	328
17.11	CANS widget data presentation in Sakai	330
17.12	Illustration of different levels of group cohesion derived from CANS data	332
17.13	Topic Model of online discourse in math news groups	334

Tables

7.1	Example frames from a constructed response teaching machine, along with the intended response	93
7.2	Principles of operant conditioning and design decisions they informed	94
7.3	Common student responses to Skinner's design decisions	101
17.1	The Principles of the Framework for Notification	319

CONTRIBUTORS

Christopher Amelung is the Assistant Vice Chancellor for digital strategy at Washington University in St. Louis and original author of CANS. He led efforts to design and develop the CANS implementation.

John Baaki is an Assistant Professor in the Instructional Design & Technology program at Old Dominion University in Norfolk, VA. He has research interests in both instructional design and human performance improvement. His research focuses on empathic design and how we have empathy for others, context, and oneself. He is interested in what a localized context of use means for both stakeholders and designers.

Elizabeth Boling is Professor of Education and has served as Associate Dean of Graduate Studies and Chairperson of the Instructional Systems Technology Department at Indiana University, Bloomington. She holds her BFA (Texas Tech University) and MFA (Indiana University) in Printmaking. Her research interests include design theory, practice, and pedagogy. She is co-editor of the *Handbook for Research in Educational Technology and Communications* (5th edition) and is currently Editor-in-Chief of the *International Journal of Designs for Learning*.

John M. Carroll is Distinguished Professor of Information Sciences and Technology at the Pennsylvania State University. His research interests include methods and theory in human–computer interaction, particularly as applied to Internet tools for collaborative learning and problem-solving, and the design of interactive information systems. His work on minimalist design was recognized with the ACM Joseph T. Rigo Award in 1994 and the IEEE Alfred N. Goldsmith Award in 2004. He has received many other honors and awards, including an honorary doctorate from Universidad Carlos III de Madrid in 2012.

Malinda Eccarius spent 45 years in the education of individuals who are deaf or hard of hearing, starting in 1971, including parent–infant education, itinerant teaching, state school consultation, with self-contained classes and collaboration with regular education elementary classrooms. Dr. Eccarius was an academic diagnostician at the Boys Town National Research Hospital, before beginning work at the University of Nebraska—Lincoln in 1994. As state schools for the deaf closed in the Great Plains and Midwest, Dr. Eccarius and colleagues at UNL designed an online instructional system to address the scarcity of rural educators with credentials to serve children with hearing loss returning to their local school districts. This design has been funded by the Federal Office of Special Education for five successive iterations. In 2016, Dr. Eccarius retired from UNL; she retains her emeritus status as Associate Professor of Practice in the Department of Special Education and Communication Disorders.

Andrew S. Gibbons completed his doctorate in Instructional Psychology at Brigham Young University in 1974. For 18 years he directed large-scale instructional design projects in industry. In 1993 he joined the Utah State University Department of Instructional Technology, and in 2003 he joined the faculty of the Instructional Psychology and Technology Department at BYU as Department Chair. Dr. Gibbons' book, *An Architectural Approach to Instructional Design* (Routledge, 2014), proposes a functional, layered, and modular theory of instructional design.

Sean Goggins joined the University of Missouri's iSchool faculty in 2013. He was previously on the faculty of Drexel's iSchool, from 2009 to 2013, and is leading efforts to conceptualize the use of context-aware activity data in learning analytics. Goggins moved to the Computer Science Department in 2016, where he led the creation of the University of Missouri's Masters program in Data Science. He is currently pursuing his research in the context of serious games and open source software.

John R. Gram is an instructor in the History Department at Missouri State University. He specializes in American Indian history, as well as the history of the American West and Southwest Borderlands. His first book, *Education at the Edge of Empire: Negotiating Pueblo Identity in New Mexico's Indian Boarding Schools*, was published by University of Washington Press in 2015. He has contributed chapters to multiple edited volumes, and his work has appeared in the *History of Education Quarterly* and *American Indian Quarterly*.

Colin M. Gray is an Assistant Professor at Purdue University in the Department of Computer Graphics Technology. He is program lead for an undergraduate major and graduate concentration in UX Design. He holds a PhD in Instructional Systems Technology from Indiana University Bloomington, a MEd in Educational Technology from University of South Carolina, and a MA in Graphic Design from Savannah College of Art & Design. He has worked as an art director, contract designer, and trainer, and his involvement in design work informs his research on design activity and how design capability is learned. His research focuses on the ways in which the pedagogy and practice of designers informs the development of design ability, particularly in relation to ethics, design knowledge, and professional identity formation. His work crosses multiple disciplines, including human–computer interaction, instructional design and technology, design theory and education, and engineering and technology education.

Stephen Hegedus is Dean of the School of Education at Southern Connecticut State University. Previously, he was founding director of the Kaput Center for Research and Innovation in Science, Technology, Engineering, and Mathematics at University of Massachusetts Dartmouth where he was also professor of mathematics and mathematics education. He also served as department chair in mathematics education from 2010 to 2013. His current work involves the study and development of dynamic software environments, with associated curriculum focusing on classroom connectivity and haptic (force-feedback) technology. This project includes the professional development of pre- and in-service teachers and the large-scale integration of innovative technologies into K-12 curriculum. Previously he held appointments as research fellow, educational consultant, and lecturer at the University of Oxford in England. Dr. Hegedus earned his PhD in Mathematics Education from the University of Southampton, England, where he earlier received a BSc with honors in mathematics and economics.

Craig D. Howard is an Assistant Professor at the University of Tennessee–Knoxville. He earned a PhD from Indiana University Bloomington and a Masters from Teachers College, Columbia University. Craig studies how we support and develop professional discourse in learners, and how we create, curate, and share design knowledge via instructional design cases.

James M. Laffey is Professor Emeritus of Learning Technology at the University of Missouri. He has led the research and development of numerous systems to improve online learning and social ability in online learning. He is currently leading a project funded by the U.S. Department of Education to develop a video game for science education called Mission HydroSci.

Makhosazana L. Lunga is currently pursuing a concurrent Master of Science in Instructional Technology and a PhD in Learning Design and Technology degrees at the University of Tennessee-College of Education, Health, and Human

Sciences (Department of Educational Psychology and Counseling). She started her career in South Africa where she served at the Development Bank of Southern Africa as an economic analyst. Makhosazana has also served at a South African-based market research organization as a quantitative research manager. She has an interest in investigating how culture influences the use of instructional technology within higher education.

Jason K. McDonald is an Associate Professor in the Department of Instructional Psychology and Technology at Brigham Young University. Following a career in the educational film and digital media industries, he returned to academics where he currently studies the practical resourcefulness of designers (particularly instructional designers), and the resourceful practices of design educators. He also teaches courses in instructional design, project management, learning theory, and design theory, and is coordinator of the Design Thinking minor at Brigham Young University.

A. F. O'Neal founded and directed the Kansas City Missouri Public Schools Computer-Assisted Instruction Laboratory from 1966 to 1971. From 1971 to 1974 he pursued his PhD at the University of Texas and Brigham Young University, consulting with Mitre and Hazeltine on TICCIT. Since 1974, when he directed the TICCIT-based S-3 aircrew training development in San Diego, he has consulted and developed instructional systems for academia, industry, and military and governments worldwide.

Jo Ann Oravec is a Professor in the College of Business and Economics at the University of Wisconsin–Whitewater in the Department of Information Technology and Supply Chain Management; she is also affiliated with the Holtz Center for Science and Technology Studies at the University of Wisconsin–Madison. She has been a visiting Fellow at Oxford and Cambridge Universities. She received her MBA, MS, MA, and PhD degrees at UW–Madison. She taught public policy at Baruch College of City University of New York, and also taught artificial intelligence in the Computer Sciences Department at UW–Madison. She chaired the Privacy Council of the State of Wisconsin, the nation's first state-level council dealing with information technology and privacy. She has written several books (including *Virtual Individuals, Virtual Groups: Human Dimensions of Groupware and Computer Networking*, Cambridge University Press). Her research has been covered in BBCNews.com and she was a featured speaker in Japan and Australia.

Jeremy Roschelle is co-Executive Director of Learning Sciences Research at Digital Promise. In his research, Roschelle examines the design and classroom use of innovations that enhance the learning of complex and conceptually difficult ideas in mathematics and science. Two running themes in his work are the study of collaboration in learning and the appropriate use of advanced or emerging technologies (such as component software and wireless handhelds) in education. His BS degree in Computer Science is from the Massachusetts Institute of Technology. His PhD in Learning Sciences is from the University of California, Berkeley. He is a Fellow of the International Society of the Learning Sciences.

Jill E. Stefaniak is an Assistant Professor in the Learning, Design, and Technology program in the Department of Career and Information Studies at the University of Georgia. Her research interests focus on the professional development of instructional designers and design conjecture, designer decision-making processes, and contextual factors influencing design in situated environments.

Deborah Tatar is Professor of Computer Science and Psychology at Virginia Tech, where she is also a Fellow in the Institute for Creativity, Art, and Technology, a member of the Center for Human–Computer Interaction, and a member of the program for Women and Gender Studies. She was previously a cognitive scientist in the Center for Technology in Learning at SRI International, a member of the Research Staff at Xerox PARC, and a senior software engineer at Digital Equipment Corporation. Her current interests are (1) designing classroom-based learning technologies that integrate technology, curriculum, and teacher professional development to address important learning issues, and (2) addressing, by design and analysis, the ways in which technology increasingly puts users in a passive position. Deborah Tatar received her doctorate in Psychology from Stanford University and her BA in English and American Literature and Language from Harvard.

Monica W. Tracey is a Professor of Learning Design and Technology in the College of Education at Wayne State University. Her teaching and research focus on design theory and design research of interdisciplinary design, including empathic design and developing professional designer identity. Tracey has worked for over 30 years in design and on numerous design projects. Her work includes designing internationally and across disciplines.

Anne Trumbore, EdD, is Executive Director of Digital Portfolios at The Darden School, University of Virginia. Previously, Anne established and currently led Wharton Online, a strategic, revenue-producing, digital learning initiative of The Wharton School, University of Pennsylvania. As an early-stage employee at Coursera, NovoEd, and Stanford's Online High School, Anne helped pioneer new forms of student-centered online education. Her work has resulted in a number of publications on online pedagogy and history, the future of higher education, and the future of work. She is currently working on a book on the history of technology in higher education (with Princeton University Press).

Patricia A. Young is an educational technologist, professor and software developer. As an Associate Professor at the University of Maryland Baltimore County, her research examines culture as a design construct in the development of culture-based information and communication technologies. She also investigates the history of educational technologies designed by and for African Americans. Dr. Young developed the Culture-based Model as a novel framework for building culture-based information and communication technologies. This model is documented in several articles, and her 2009 book *Instructional Design Frameworks & Intercultural Models* (Information Science Reference). She is the first woman and African American to serve on the editorial board of the internationally ranked journal *Educational Technology Research and Development*. Dr. Young also built Proticy, an original learning analytics software that improves teaching and learning in higher education. She is currently working on a new book focusing on human specialization.

1
SETTING THE CASES IN HISTORICAL CONTEXT

Colin M. Gray and Craig D. Howard

The cases contained in this book span the early 1880s to the early 2010s—a 130-year period that has produced profound changes in connectivity, social relationships, technological capability, equality and the role of citizenship, and the mode and outcomes of education in relation to all of these other shifts. While our goal in this chapter is not to fully describe or determine the historical framing of this lengthy period—indeed, many texts have and could be written on such a subject—we do believe there is value in setting the stage to aid the reader in stepping out of their own positions in time to identify, negotiate, and interact with the historical, social, educational, and technological contexts in which each of the designs described in this book arose. All the cases presented in this book share a US framing, so we will address this period from a US-centric perspective. In the following sections we will use a timeline of the period covered by this book (Figure 1.1) to present these contexts in a way that might support the reader's capacity for "making strange" their present reality (Bell et al., 2005) so that they can appreciate the social milieu in which many designers of learning materials in our past made decisions, shaped future realities, and adapted to—and even overcame—the technological constraints of their era.

1880 to 1900

Our cases of designs for learning begin at a time when scholars surmised that intelligence might be measured by the relative weight or size of one's head. And indeed, Darwin's theory of evolution—published in 1859—shaped numerous perspectives on intelligence and human development that laid the groundwork for movements in the twentieth century focused on eugenics. In the United States, the year 1877 marked the end of the project of reconstruction following the

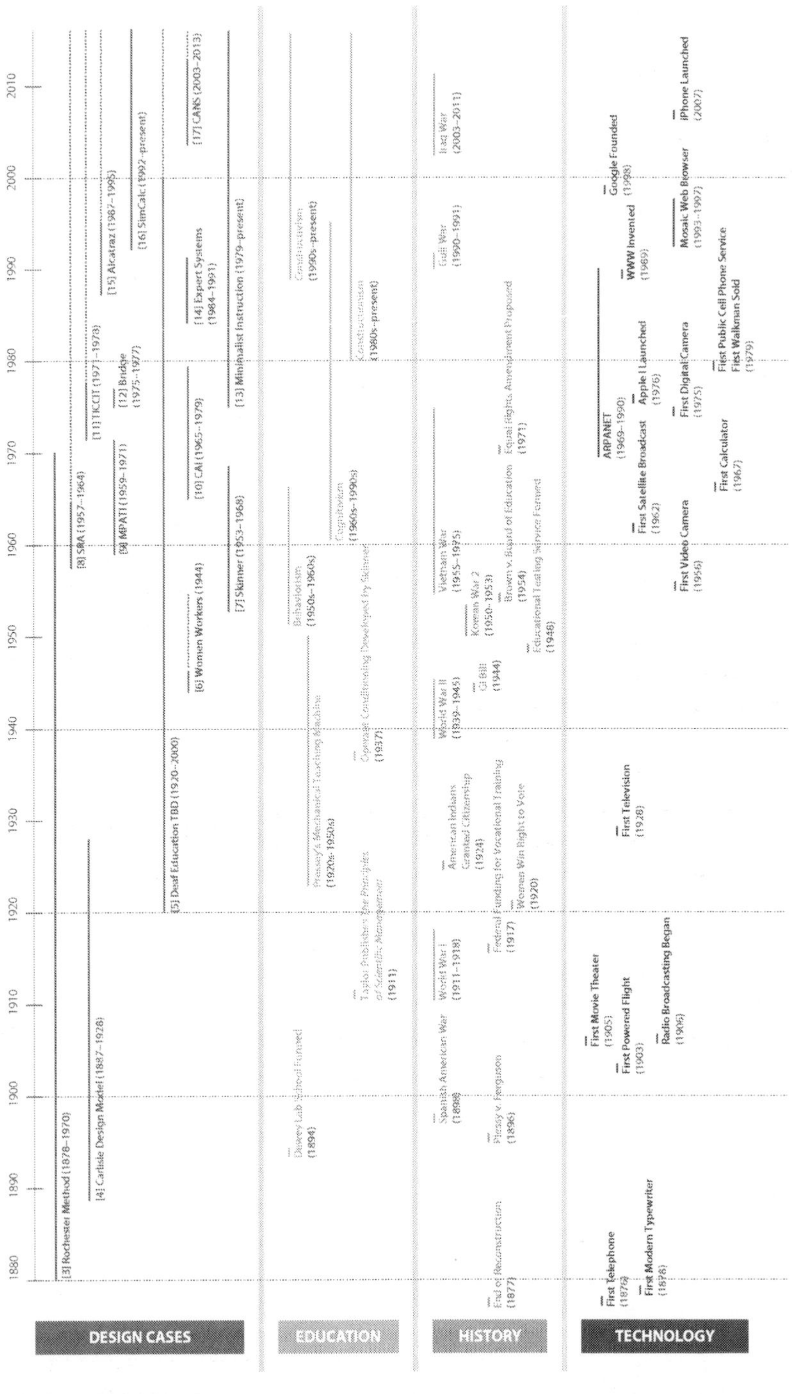

2 Colin M. Gray and Craig D. Howard

FIGURE 1.1 A historical overview of the time period represented by cases in this book, spanning education, US history, and technology.

American Civil War, setting into motion a century of failed integration, limited rights for Black Americans, and a desire for Americans of all origins to obtain higher levels of education.

This book begins with a case depicting this turbulent period of nation-building, where politicians and settlers alike sought to realize the racist ideology then known as "manifest destiny" which whitewashed violence against indigenous tribes across the plains and onto the west coast of the United States. And indeed, the Plessy v. Ferguson Supreme Court decision in 1896 made explicit the "separate but equal" doctrine that would remain until the 1950s. More than one case in this volume depicts interventions that intended to assimilate learners through prohibition of their native language.

In Chapter 4, Gram describes the implications of this nation-building and the choices made on a national and local level to strip tribes of their identity, culture, and language through the creation of schools as part of the "Carlisle Model" intended to assimilate American Indian children into the broader US population. Problems of assimilation were foregrounded during this period, with the East coast considering what was termed the "Irish problem," and on the West coast, Chinese immigration that led to the adoption of the Chinese Exclusion Act in 1882. In Chapter 3, Eccarius describes a different kind of exclusionary challenge—in this case, the creation of educational experiences for the deaf and hard-of-hearing community and the rise of bilingual education that could account for both speech and signing as a means of communication. These chapters present a contrast—one where indigenous rights are being systematically stripped away, and the other where the Rochester method is being introduced to encourage the eventual development of a deaf identity and culture. In Chapter 5, Lunga and Howard depict the lived experience of that same decision to ban American Sign Language as a language of instruction through an account of a student at the Tennessee Asylum for the Deaf and Dumb from when that ban was lifted.

At the end of this period, one of the first notable instances of intentional educational experimentation emerged—the formation of the Dewey Lab School in Chicago in 1894. This lab school facilitated the rapid testing of educational innovations which, when employed in similar lab schools across the nation, would inform much of the education developments of the twentieth century. This effort can be viewed in contrast to the social experimentation and hegemony of the Native American and Deaf schools of the era.

1900 to 1920

The first decades of the twentieth century led to many enduring technological and international developments which would define the era—and shape our present. The large-scale production of automobiles started to redefine local and national transportation, with Ford's Model T—sold from 1908 to 1927—resulting in 16.5 million orders, in a country numbering just over 100 million.

Other technological developments related to communication, with the first radio broadcast and first purpose-built movie theater emerging in the first decade of the new century. In 1903, the first powered flight led to the possibility of new transportation speed, both domestically and internationally. However, despite the technological promise of this era, The Great War dominated this period of history, with the unprecedented engagement of troops, coalition-building among the US and European nations, and the use of technology to support wartime activities.

While no design cases in this volume are fully set during this period, it is important to note that Native Americans were not recognized as citizens throughout this period, only gaining the right to vote in 1924. The Carlisle school closed in 1918, and many of the other schools that sought to integrate American Indians into broader society closed before the beginning of World War II. In parallel to this decline in attempts to assimilate Indian tribes, women only gained the right to vote in 1920, after almost a century of organizing. That same year, The Tennessee Asylum for the Deaf and Dumb became the Tennessee School for the Deaf.

1920 to 1940

The post-World War I era resulted in substantial shifts in the status of the United States and its connectedness and role as a growing world power. From a technological perspective, the introduction of television encouraged the development of new kinds of content and foreshadowed the shift from theaters to home viewing that would take place over the latter half of the twentieth century. The implementation and shape of instructional interventions was far more mundane than previously, and slow in growth. While progressives renamed asylums to schools, the actual curriculum of these learning organizations still struggled to empower learners. More substantial strides in designing learning experiences began to appear, but these efforts were disrupted or slowed by an international economic downturn, which resulted in what is now known as the Great Depression. Pressey's first mechanical teaching machine, developed in the mid-1920s, demonstrated the potential of educational technologies in allowing for learners to progress at their own pace with the use of programmed instruction, and pointed to an era dominated by behaviorism, with the emergence of operant conditioning—developed by Skinner in 1937. Pressey's teaching machines set the stage for Skinner's programmed instruction work in the 1950s, discussed in Chapter 7.

1940 to 1960

This 20-year period was defined by war, with World War II, the Korean War, and the start of the Vietnam War framing international relations, the development of technology to support wartime activities and communication, and the role of training in supporting these efforts. Wartime readiness was framed around scaling up the American military, often cited as an early touchstone for the development of systematic instructional design models that could operate at scale (Reiser, 2001; Saettler, 2004). This era was especially impactful for the development of audiovisual communication, with the propaganda of Germany, Japan, and the United States used both as a training tool and a means of motivating participation in the war effort. Towards the end of this period of history, the Supreme Court decision on Brown v. Board of Education laid the groundwork for integration efforts—rejecting the "separate but equal" decision of 50 years before and creating a space for the potential of racial equality.

In Chapter 6, Gray describes the wartime effort through the lens of societal norms and human performance, analyzing and describing a film developed by the US Office of Education to support the onboarding and integration of women into the manufacturing workforce during World War II. This chapter points to the social shifts brought about by war, and in relation to new power gained through women's suffrage, showing the use of audiovisual communication in addressing complex challenges that are part training, part social engineering. In Chapter 7, McDonald describes the rise of behaviorism in education, showing the natural consequences of Pressey's mechanical teaching machine in promoting learning, resulting in the famous "Skinner Box" which inspired mass-market "teaching machines." And indeed, the role of behaviorism in conjunction with the instructional systems work of the US military heralds an era of education and training *at scale*, with the passage of the GI Bill in 1944 that guaranteed access to education and training for almost 8 million veterans, leading to record enrollments in higher education, and the formation of the Educational Testing Service in 1948 which (perhaps problematically) framed educational achievement in relation to a set of standardized tests. These chapters, taken together, demonstrate the growing dominance of instructional design activities—although instructional design was not yet a defined discipline—in informing education and training experiences. The late 1940s saw the development of the Indiana University instructional film lending library, which then supported the development of audiovisual specialists that would define the next era of instructional design.

1960 to 1980

The post-war period resulted in a rapid expansion of the US population which, when coupled with the continued technological development, set the stage for the mass-market adoption of audiovisual and other communication technologies. This growth in technological capacity is the focus of many of the cases in this book focused on designs that originated during this era—ranging from the "flying satellites" used by the MPATI program to deliver instruction to rural students, to the use of teletype to support computer-assisted instruction in Nicaragua, to the development of home-based instruction through TICCIT that enabled interactive instruction over cable and touch-tone telephone systems.

While the Vietnam War overshadowed much of this period, impacting domestic and international politics, the "space race"—culminating in the first landing of men on the moon in 1969—defined the era. This broad and deep expansion of engineering capacity and technological capability informed the creation and mass-market awareness of many other technologies, such as the first integrated video camera in 1956, the first satellite broadcast in 1962, and the first digital camera in 1975. International concern relating to the development and proliferation of nuclear weapons by the United States and the USSR also led to an interest in developing resilient communication technologies that had no single point of failure—inspiring the development of ARPANET in 1969, the direct parent of the modern Internet. Finally, a growing interest in democratizing access to technologies and expanding their reach informed the development of the first commercial cell phone network in 1979 and the creation of the Apple I in 1976. Meanwhile, *Sesame Street* aired its first episode in 1969.

Two strands of designing for learning dominate in the cases from this period. First, cases on the SRA Reading toolkit, Bridge program, and Minimalist Instruction approach point towards new ways of engaging learners in controlling their own learning and appealing to learners with a range of backgrounds and previous knowledge. In Chapter 8, Boling describes the development and use of the SRA Reading toolkit, a fixture of many classrooms from the 1960s onward, and still in use in digital form to this day. This toolkit allowed a range of learners to evaluate and build their skills in an independent manner, relying on a set of learning materials which were intentionally scaffolded through a programmed instruction perspective. In Chapter 12, Young describes the creation, use, and eventual failure of an instructional approach that leveraged students' skill in Black English to engage them in the development of Standard English skills. The Bridge toolkit, while not ultimately successful in its aims due to the sociopolitical climate of the time, reflects the desire to build upon and maximize the lived experience of the learner—pointing towards social constructivist approaches to learning that would rise in prominence in the 1980s and 1990s. In Chapter 13, Carroll describes the development of a new approach to structuring and scaffolding learning, valuing failure and error recovery over traditional modes of sequencing learning experiences. This instructional design approach, born in the era of early software development, informed the development of onboarding experiences that allowed learners more autonomy and agency, while also pointing towards an era when software manuals would no longer be relevant.

Second, cases on the Midwest Program on Airborne Television Instruction (MPATI), learning experiences through radio, teletype, and computers in the United States and in Nicaragua through early computer-assisted instruction, and the home-based learning potential of the TICCIT system show the potential of new remote learning technologies in creating new possibilities for learning experiences. In Chapter 9, Tracey and Stefaniak describe the use of DC-6 aircraft to broadcast instructional content to learners across the midwest, showing the emerging potential of audiovisual instruction and the early attempts to mitigate rural/urban divides in access to educational content. In Chapter 10, Trumbore describes the pioneering work of Patrick Suppes in developing computer-assisted instructional approaches that leveraged a bricolage of technologies available at the time—implementing teletype terminals, early mini-computers for processing, and recorded lessons to allow learners to receive tailored content based on their assessed capabilities the previous day. This targeting of individualized learning experiences points towards the rapid adoption of personal computers in the late 1970s and 1980s, and more broadly to the use of the Internet to create self-paced e-learning content. Finally, in Chapter 11, Gibbons and O'Neal describe the creation of an instructional system that would allow multiple learners to access interactive content through the use of a touch-tone telephone and cable broadcast system, which then managed the delivery of content through a networked mini-computer. This project built on the success of programmed instruction in other contexts, while also allowing the learner almost unprecedented control over the pacing of their learning experience.

1980 to 2000

The post-Vietnam era brought new social, environmental, public health, and technological challenges to the United States. The impacts of integration, including methods such as redlining, caused the collapse of integrated city centers, and precipitated the movement of the affluent White population to the suburbs. However, the growth of technology during this period became a defining aspect of the era—from the domination of cable television (MTV launched in 1981), to the growth of personal media devices such as the Walkman (1979), to the increasingly common ownership of personal computers. This represented a substantial shift from a handful of channels on a family's single TV to a range of media and connectivity options across many devices, with the expanded promise of personal computers, game consoles, and pre-Internet versions of remote interaction. Educational environments began to take advantage of the technology of the era, with the distillation of constructionism through Papert's Mindstorms in 1980; this approach to learning endeavored to facilitate mathematical thinking and programming skills by controlling a LOGO turtle, laying the foundations for constructionist approaches to learning designs in ways that would foreshadow the "maker movement" of the twenty-first century.

Perhaps the technological innovation that shaped this era the most was the shift from a federally managed ARPANET to a publicly available "worldwide web." The creation of browsers, such as Mosaic—which later transformed into Netscape and then Mozilla—allowed everyday people to access web resources, which later precipitated the "read/write" web that allows most of our modern Internet communities to exist. The broad availability of Internet access facilitated wholly new opportunities for educational engagement, including online degree programs, spaces for informal learning, and the documentation of shared educational resources. From an educational perspective, technology was used to more substantially engage and empower learners. The rise of constructivist and constructionist approaches to learning gave learners more control and agency in their learning, and inquiry-based approaches that these learning theories informed allowed for new configurations of classroom and extracurricular learning. In tandem with formal learning environments, organizations increasingly used instructional approaches to empower workers, creating upskilling opportunities to retain and promote the workforce.

The three chapters set in this era represent the diversity of learning experiences that instructional design could address. In Chapter 16, Tatar et al. describe the creation of new instructional approaches to encourage mathematics learning, relying upon the visualization opportunities afforded by a new generation of personal computers. This constructivist approach to learning mathematics allowed learners to have increased agency as they saw mathematics in action and informing real-world behaviors, rather than only a series of abstract concepts. In Chapter 14, Oravec describes the use of knowledge-based engineering to empower workers at the Campbell Soup Company with just-in-time instruction, using computer systems to support and augment the expertise of workers. Finally, in Chapter 15, Boling describes the use of audio to enrich and redefine the experience of visiting Alcatraz, using soundscapes to encourage certain kinds of learning, while also pointing towards a heightened and aesthetic role that instructional design could play in informal learning experiences.

2000 to the Present

The final era leads us to within a decade of the present day. Technology plays an increasingly dominant role in shaping our daily lives, with the promise of the Internet in democratizing access to information and encouraging communication now impacting our everyday lives in profound and increasingly invisible ways. While cell phones were common by the year 2000, the introduction of the iPhone in 2007 signaled a change in technological consumption and access to interactive services. The growth of personal informatics devices, such as smartphones, and later smartwatches and other Internet of Things devices, increased the spread and possibility of technological engagement, as well as the potential privacy and security risks of participating in these data ecosystems. The Internet served as a central point of communication for a new generation of educational technology systems, including the birth of modern learning management systems (Blackboard launched in 1997), the proliferation of virtual online communities (Second Life launched in 2003), the creation of online communities to track and share knowledge (Wikipedia launched in 2001), and the tools to blog and share personal communication (Blogger and LiveJournal launched in 1999). In parallel with this growth, many tech companies that have come to define the modern era had their birth in the late 1990s and early 2000s, such as Google (1998), Facebook (2004), and Amazon (1994). These companies, among others, launched a wide range of products that have expanded the reach of designs intended for learning which would have been unthinkable a generation ago, including free access to a publicly edited encyclopedia (Wikipedia launched in 2001) and real-time access to billions of videos on every subject imaginable (YouTube launched in 2005).

These technological forces, when applied to educational technology, inform our final case. In Chapter 17, Laffey et al. describe the use of learning analytics to identify new means of engagement with learners. By capitalizing on the data already tracked through learning management systems, the context-aware activity notification system (CANS) allowed learners and instructors to gain better insights into learning activity, including ways of contributing to community—as well as individual—learning. The technological issues faced by the developers of CANS—and its eventual abandonment—also represents the challenges of fast-moving data and software ecosystems.

References

Bell, G., Blythe, M., & Sengers, P. (2005). Making by making strange: Defamiliarization and the design of domestic technologies. *ACM Transactions on Computer-Human Interaction*, *12*(2), 149–173. https://doi.org/10.1145/1067860.1067862

Reiser, R. A. (2001). A history of instructional design and technology: Part I: A history of instructional media. *Educational Technology Research and Development: ETR & D*, *49*(1), 53. https://doi.org/10.1007/BF02504506

Saettler, P. (2004). *The evolution of American educational technology*. Charlotte, NC: Information Age Publishing.

2

CURATORS' NOTES

Historical Design Cases

Elizabeth Boling and John Baaki

Design cases afford their readers a critical form of design knowledge—the vicarious experience of designs created by others. These vicarious experiences augment the direct experiences designers also collect, and together both forms of experience create a reservoir from which ideas, inspiration, design schema, and potential moves for approaching design problems are drawn. Every designer relies on this form of knowledge, known as precedent. In some fields of practice there has been a long tradition of sharing precedent, but in others, like instructional design, there has not. Consequently, designers creating materials, systems, and environments for learning may have limited experience of current designs in their field and almost no chance for an experiential understanding of designs from earlier decades. This collection of cases provides the chance for readers to expand their design knowledge backward in time, adding multiple vicarious experiences to their reservoirs.

While a designer or a scholar might read many individual design cases, benefitting from each, reading a curated collection of design cases offers extended value by virtue of the connections and disparities present in the collection, and the opportunities for reflection that a collection provides. Curators' notes are intended to assist the reader, pointing out connections between and disparities among the cases, and suggesting perspectives that may guide the reading or illuminate points of interest in the cases.

Part of the collection in this volume was originally assembled as a special issue of the *International Journal of Designs for Learning* focused on historical designs under the editorial direction of Craig Howard and Colin Gray. We have now augmented those with an additional half-dozen cases. For that special issue "we actively encouraged a representative sample, taking into account both breadth of topics and the genres of designs represented" (Howard & Gray, 2014). In expanding that collection, we have also made an effort to include several much older cases and to harness the interests of case writers willing to write from a journalist perspective; that is, not having been involved in, or connected to, the original design effort. The cases are arranged along an approximate timeline. The starting points are generally known, but the end of a design is not always easy to pinpoint. Some ended definitively, while others faded away, or were subsumed into other designs, or even still survive in revised form.

For a reader who is interested primarily in the historical journey from 1878 to 2003 as represented in these cases, you can read straight through in chronological order. Or it is, of course, always appropriate to begin with the cases that appeal to you first because of their titles or their topics. Alternatively, it may be productive to consider reading the cases (or rereading them) selectively looking for elements they have in common, or that contrast from one case to another; in other words, reading from a focused perspective. As editors we offer these notes, organized as four lenses, to facilitate this last method of experiencing the design cases in this volume.

Lens 1: Relationships between technology and designs

Multiple forms of technology are featured in these design cases. Often these are the technologies of the day, already available for use to designers hoping to achieve educational or informational goals. In others, designers are pushing the boundaries of the technologies available to them or extending conceptions of how those technologies might be able to support learning.

Using the materials and technologies at hand. The teaching machines described by McDonald (Chapter 7) in his case focused on learning machines may illustrate the use of materials and technologies at hand most clearly; simple technologies like levers, rollers, and dials mounted into wooden boxes serve to automate the presentation of lesson elements and selection of answers. The machines were, of course, handmade proof of concept designs rather than mass-production items, but those disseminated more widely also relied on traditional mechanical configurations. Other designs rely on professional-grade, but still traditional and analog, technologies, like the paper systems described in Young's chapter on the Bridge reading program (Chapter 12), Boling's on the SRA reading program (Chapter 8), and Gray's on the 1944 instructional film, *Supervising Women Workers* (Chapter 6).

The chapters in which Tracey and Stefaniak (Chapter 9) discuss the MPATI program and Trumbore (Chapter 10) discusses active learning with computers and radio show designers who pressed existing technologies into service. The MPATI team used aircraft and television transmission, two technologies that were well established by the time they were designing, to deliver the televised math lessons they provided across multiple locations in the US midwest states where schools did not have the resources to offer those lessons. In the process, delivering the lessons was stretched to the point that the overall design could not be sustained. Where television in the MPATI case was stretched to a point where it could not be sustained, Lunga and Howard (Chapter 5) share in the Tennessee School for Deaf case that in the 1970s there was very limited open captioning on television. By the 1980s there were improvements, and by the 1990s captioning became universal. Instructors used open captioning on television to teach via a bilingual approach. Similarly to using the technology at hand, a program that began as Computer Assisted Instruction in Elementary Mathematics in Palo Alto, and used comparatively high-end, experimental computer technology in the Trumbore case, was translated into a radio-based design when it was adapted for widespread use in Nicaragua. For a time the program also used paper forms for assessments in these classrooms; these forms were transferred to punch cards and then magnetic tape for a while, cycling back through newer technologies, before being sent by traditional postal service back to California for analysis. This design, in its principle and methods although not with the punch cards, magnetic tape, or Stanford analysis components, has persisted and continues to be used by millions of students in primarily poor countries.

"Using the technologies at hand" can involve using readily available technologies to meet the goals of a design in a practical way, only to find those technologies changing—or gone. Laffey, Amelung, and Goggins describe the design of CANS (Chapter 17) which was integrated into the Sakai Learning Management System, well established at the time but changing too fast for the grant-funded development team to keep up. Ultimately, therefore, CANS was discontinued in favor of future, and sustainable, Open Source development. In Carroll's case (Chapter 13) describing minimalist instruction, on the other hand, the design was developed in an environment where personal computing was just becoming widespread. The technologies at hand in this case were not "at hand" because they were traditional or well established, but because they were the reason for the design to be undertaken. This design yielded an understanding of how people behave as they are learning new technologies, and an alternative to step-by-step instruction for supporting that learning. While these ideas have endured, any of the original digital designs resulting from those ideas are gone, rendered permanently inaccessible because the systems of storage and delivery required to use them have disappeared, to be replaced in rapid succession by newer, and incompatible, ones.

Capitalizing on and Extending Emerging Technologies

When the creators of these designs have used emerging technologies, those have ranged from the simple, like the Walkman ™ in the "Alcatraz Cellhouse Tour" case (Chapter 15), to the more complicated—like those used for the expert systems described by Oravec (Chapter 14)—which, arguably, are still emergent. In a project like TICCIT, described by Gibbons and O'Neal (Chapter 11), almost everything was an experiment on the cutting edge, from a delivery system to bring digital lessons into private homes at a time when personal computers were non-existent, to the innovation of procedural technologies for lesson development, presentation, and interaction. This was not a matter of using what was available so much as pushing the edge of technology forward. SimCalc (Chapter 16) (described by Tatar, Roschelle, and Hegedus), which broke more conceptual than technological ground, nevertheless includes an interesting detour into the technologies of gaming which were then, as they are now, rapidly evolving. Interestingly, they assessed this aspect of the project to be a "dead end," and they describe the use of more established, although still current, means to implement the design. Laffey, Amelung, and Goggins (Chapter 17) describe a complicated relationship between a forward-looking conceptual design in learning analytics and the effort required to keep chasing the integration of emerging and evolving Learning Management System technologies. A striking feature uniting these cases is that the exciting new technologies the designers have used are viewed as a means to create learning experiences not previously considered possible.

What if These Designers Could Have Used the Technologies of their Futures?

Through this lens a reader does not focus on what is actually said in each case but imagines what might have been said if these designers had been able to take advantage of the technologies that arose after their time. It is not difficult to imagine this for the SRA Reading System (Chapter 8) or Alcatraz (Chapter 15) audio tour projects; both still exist in updated forms, incorporating new technologies as they have become available. Likewise, instructional film (Chapter 6), as represented in Gray's chapter, has evolved with advances in technology to become, by and large, instructional video. However, other designs—now disappeared—might have been quite different if the technologies to realize them had been available at the time. Teaching machines, as described by McDonald (Chapter 7), are a prime example; they might have advanced quickly and in quite a different way than later designs which did incorporate some of Skinner's ideas. What would the MPATI project (Chapter 9) have looked like if wireless towers and the Internet had been available when it was conceived? And would the Rochester Method described by Eccarius (Chapter 3) have existed at all if Zenas Westervelt had been able to use the technologies which later contributed to its discontinuation? And the availability of video conferencing and close captioning, had they been available sooner, might have brought ASL and Signed English side by side for the Tennessee School for the Deaf much more quickly, perhaps without as much stress in the user experience.

Lens 2: Relationships between designs and their users

Each of these cases makes clear, in one way or another, the goals of the design being described, and by extension, who was intended to use that design. Adopting the lens of these intended users can yield interesting perspectives on the cases, particularly when either the author or the reader, or both, can discern a gap between how the designs were intended to relate to learners and how they may actually have done so.

Agency versus Control

Design of the SRA Reading System (Chapter 8) was intended to offer teachers a form of control in their classrooms by offloading routine reading instruction, giving time back to the teachers which they could use as they saw fit to engage in teaching that required their unique expertise. The design did, however, strive to control tightly the way in which teachers would introduce and use the materials. In order to achieve its primary goal, the design provided—possibly without direct intentionality—a form of agency to learners by giving them choices of reading material and requiring that they assess their own performance independently. Over time, entropy may have reversed these relationships from those originally intended. A student assigned to "go read something from the SRA box until the others finish their work" is probably not experiencing the same sense of agency as one who is working her way systematically up the levels in the box. And the teacher who, without a full kit of materials allowing the system to work as designed, is free to use it any way he sees fit, but will not reap the promised bonus of offloaded instructional effort that it promises.

In the schools established on the Carlisle Model described by Gram (Chapter 4) complete control of the students was intended, but learner agency exerted itself, and students found ways to advocate for themselves. Some students ran away, while other students secretly shared home cultures in their prohibited native languages. Students often adapted their lessons in ways that valued their home communities and cultures. In the end, students did not stop being Indians just because the school told them they should. Lunga and Howard (Chapter 5) describe a different manifestation of agency regarding the culture of learners in their chapter on the Tennessee School for the Deaf, wherein community organizations exerted pressure in concert with learners exerting their agency to force a gradual acceptance of students' native language into the pedagogy.

Minimalist instruction (Chapter 13) may represent the best example of supporting agency and minimizing control over learners from the inception of a design. The key factor in this case was viewing learner activity as a positive component of learning. People's goals and efforts to experiment and to make sense of processes are seen in this design as actions to be encouraged, facilitated, and further strengthened by the design rather than channeled towards one desired path.

Knowing Who the Learner Really Is

Eccarius (Chapter 3) and Gram's (Chapter 4) chapters, or Lunga and Howard's chapter (Chapter 5), present designs that were focused on specific learners, but it is not clear that the designers they discuss knew entirely for whom they were designing. Were they designing for children who happened to be Native American, deaf and hearing-impaired, or for the socially constructed categories of *the deaf* and *American Indians*. Did it make a difference? In the first instance, designers presumably would have foregrounded the culture and knowledge students brought with them into the learning experience, whereas in the second instance, learners' identities were largely ignored—or were actively suppressed, or targeted for eradication. In schools designed on the Carlisle Model, we can see clearly that learners are working against the overt intention of the design, and that they understand the design is working against their best interests. The focus on using education to solve an "Indian problem" led these designers to look at these students as a category, and not to question their own understanding of who they were.

Designers' Views of Instructors

The Bridge (Chapter 12) and SRA (Chapter 8) programs both provide detailed, even rigid, guidance on how instructors are to implement the systems. A designer of Bridge, interviewed by Young, is very explicit about how the designers wanted to ensure that teachers could not implement the design otherwise than intended. And for the Rochester Method (Chapter 3), the designers strictly regulated teachers' mode of communication. Various designs documented here are intended, in one way or another, to replace functions previously assumed to be those of the teacher or instructor. In some cases this replacement is framed as offloading effort, as in the SRA system, or supplying resources not otherwise available to teachers, as in MPATI (Chapter 9), instructional film as discussed by Gray (Chapter 6), and by Trumbore (Chapter 10) on computers and radio. The purpose of MPATI was to provide students with access to learning that they may not have otherwise experienced. For example, a Spanish teacher with just two years of training might be required to teach advanced Spanish. Using MPATI, an expert Spanish teacher could provide the teacher with classroom assistance by exposing students to advanced Spanish concepts. Trumbore describes how some teachers gave students recorded lessons as pre-work to prepare them for the teacher's instruction, while other teachers used recorded lessons as drill and practice for lessons already taught; teachers determined the best way to use the recorded lessons. In others, the teacher is sidelined for the sake of a presumably more effective theoretical or technical approach to support learning; this can be seen in the chapters on learning machines (Chapter 7), SimCalc (Chapter 16), TICCIT (Chapter 11), and expert systems (Chapter 14). Laffey, Amelung, and Goggins (Chapter 17) describe how analytics offer support to instructors by augmenting the instructors' understanding of how learning is progressing, signaling a positive view of instructors, whereas Carroll (Chapter 13) makes it clear that minimalist instruction reframes the instructor (in the form of printed and digital materials) as a hands-off provider of basic guidance and occasional rescuer when learners get into serious trouble by exercising almost total agency.

Lens 3: A Critical View of Designing

The point of reading with a critical lens is not to pose categorical questions regarding each design case. "Was learning gain established?" "Did the design win an award?" "Did the design survive to the present day?" "Was the design actually implemented in the first place?" The value of a design case does not depend on whether questions like these can be answered with a "yes," or even whether a case addresses questions like this at all. Some do and some do not. However, a case like Bridge (Chapter 12), in which the design is acknowledged never to have been implemented, or one like MPATI (Chapter 9), in which the design was ultimately unsustainable and discontinued, are nevertheless assumed to yield value to readers at an unspecified but certain point in the future because they add to that reader's store of vicarious design experience. Using a critical lens to add a layer of appreciation to the experience of these designs can render them especially memorable, and therefore potentially useful, and enrich the store of affordances they may yield to a reader at that unknowable moment in the future.

When "Of Their Time" Is, Or Is Not, a Design Failure

All designs are "of their time" because of course they must be, and some age better than others. Readers may note this phenomenon in the illustrations for the SRA reading system (Chapter 8); they are distinctly identifiable by their 1950s style, which holds up well at present in part because their creator was a talented artist of the day, and in part because their "mid-century modern" look is in vogue at the time of this volume's publication. These illustrations may have been viewed less positively 20 years ago and perhaps will be again 20 years, or 5 years, hence—just as the consciously hip-1970s style of the Bridge materials (Chapter 12) is likely to strike modern readers as more or less appealing, depending on what style is *au courant*, signals social-historical significance to them, or serves as a nostalgic blast from the past at the time the case is read. Response to the visual and dramatic style of the instructional film *Supervising Women Workers* (Chapter 6) and others like it, on the other hand, is likely to remain persistently ambivalent. A mix of recognizable production techniques imported by their creators from mainstream, often classic, dramatic films with the inescapably pedantic, mundane subject matter—not to mention the unavoidably explicit expression of outdated social values—renders them to the modern eye as falling somewhere along a spectrum ranging from cringeworthy (possibly unworthy) specimens, to laughable memes.

Apart from the failure to hold up over time, some aspects of designs are open to legitimate critique in the present. In this collection it is worth noting in Gram's chapter on the Carlisle Model (Chapter 4) that the designers' goals were subject to ethical questions in their day, not just recently as a matter of changing mores, and that the goal of eradicating a people's culture through its children is subject to ethical questions in any era. For comparison, the chapter on the Rochester

Method (Chapter 3) also describes a design in which children leave home to live in a residential school where their method of communication is strictly monitored. Strong views on communication held by members of the Deaf culture provide an interesting opinion on the concern for the academic achievement of the students, not only in this case but in Lunga and Howard's chapter on the Tennessee School for the Deaf (Chapter 5). A similar dynamic holds for the Bridge case (Chapter 12) in which the intentions of the design ran counter to the desires of the community intended to benefit from it, but the design itself cannot be seen as wholly unethical.

Variability in Benefits to Learners

The SRA (Chapter 8) and TICCIT (Chapter 11) designs yielded their best results for a narrow profile of the learners using the design; in the first case those already performing well and in the latter case those termed "logical" learners. For the SRA system this disparity in outcomes is clearly considered to be expected by the designers; the materials point out that for the lowest ability learner only "a little improvement is promised together with satisfaction at being included in the program, but no long-term (lifetime) expectation of a reading level above 5th- or 6th grade." In fact, for this design, once a number of studies of its effectiveness had been conducted, its benefit to any individual learner can be seen to vary from the benefit claimed. Rather than improving reading skills across the board (no significant difference being the most frequent finding for those using versus those not using the system), the system seems to have promoted motivation and satisfaction, largely as a by-product of the decision to offload some tasks to students.

Design cases are not chosen, or valued, on the basis of the demonstrated success of the designs they describe. In fact, effectiveness data are neither expected nor provided for most design cases. A reader choosing the critical lens, however, may want to query any number of these cases with regard to how well they might serve a reasonable range of learners intending to use them. The designs described in the analytics and expert systems chapters, for example, seem to rest on an underlying assumption, from two different perspectives, that their users will all have equivalent abilities with regard to perceiving and applying appropriate patterns of knowledge. Will this be the case? Will all the students using an LMS be able to perceive equally well meaning in the data they are being shown about their own learning behaviors, or apply that meaning to adjust their behaviors? Will repair specialists be uniformly skilled in conceptualizing new problems in terms that can be used to request help from an expert system? Would ancillary training be required, and has that been a feature discussed in the case? Likewise, the "Alcatraz Cellhouse Tour" (Chapter 15) did not serve every possible visitor to the site equally well as originally designed. Rework was required to account for users with sensory differences, very young users, and non-English-speaking users—and the design may yet fail to serve equally well visitors who bring varying perspectives on privilege and social justice to the site.

Lens 4: How Designs Come to Life, How They Die, and How They Are Reincarnated

This lens for reading design cases may be most interesting to those whose interests include the processes of designing, and how designs are situated in their contexts, over and above experiencing the designs themselves. In discussing this lens, we appreciate that no single factor usually drives the creation, or the demise, of a design; consequently, some of the cases will appear in more than one section.

How Designs Come to Life

Theory and research play a large role in the stories behind many of these designs. Teaching machines (Chapter 7) may serve as the canonical example of design that came to life born directly of theory, but other cases involve theory-building as a component of the design process (as in minimalist instruction), and design as a vehicle for exploring theories of teaching and learning (as in SimCalc, analytics, and Bridge).

Design is frequently, however, a pragmatic response to existing in the world and to the conditions of our existence. Readers can see that the SRA system (Chapter 8), for example, sprang originally from the lived experience of a teacher concerned about the realities of student learning problems in his classroom, although that teacher did then develop and apply theory during its creation. In other cases like MPATI (Chapter 9) and the Alcatraz tour (Chapter 15), while there may be academic theories that describe or explain designs, the designs themselves have sprung from the confluence of practical needs and available means.

Social factors drive designs into existence as well. In 1957, Sputnik created an urgency to explore educational applications of technology. In both TICCIT (Chapter 11) and SimCalc (Chapter 16), Sputnik was an early spark that drove educational form, and in the case of SIMCALC helped incite thinking about the future of mathematics education. Bridge (Chapter 12) was an explicit response to alleviate inequality in the conditions of learning, and the Indian Schools (Chapter 4) were explicit instruments of social change through suppression of culture. Both the Rochester Method (Chapter 3) and pedagogy design at the Tennessee School of the Deaf (TSD) (Chapter 5) were responses to the Milan Conference in 1880. In the case of TSD, a bilingual approach of American Sign Language and English resulted in integrating technology, first television and then smartboards, Internet, and videoconferencing, into how students learn and collaborate.

How Designs Die, or Fade Away

Varied though the genesis of designs may be, myriad are the ways in which they may cease to exist. Several designs discussed under the lens of the relationship between designs and technology died in large part because technologies available at the time either could not sustain the weight of those designs (as in MPATI), or because the technologies they used changed or disappeared (as in the chapters on analytics, and minimalist instruction). For others, newer technologies emerged and altered the context so that the design was no longer required, as with the Rochester (Chapter 3), MPATI (Chapter 9), or computers and radio cases (Chapter 10)—or technologies simply changed too fast for the design to keep up, as with CANS in the analytics chapter (Chapter 17). In other cases the technology is available but human psychology itself presents obstacles to its persistence, as with learning machines in which the psychology of learning proves to be too complicated for the design to address, or expert systems and analytics in which the psychology of performance presents ongoing challenges to design. Likewise, diffusion of innovation is not simple; in the SimCalc case (Chapter 16) the premise of representation change meant changing the sequence of learning and how learning is measured, which did not necessarily match curricular expectations and end-of-year examinations. In other words, slow adoption stemmed from a disconnect between long-term societal change versus short-term requirements to increase test scores now. And societal factors can prevent a design from being adopted, as with Bridge (Chapter 12), erode support for it, as with the Rochester Method (Chapter 3), or cause it to implode through learner revolt, changing mores, or both, as with the Carlisle Schools (Chapter 4). And a design like the SRA Reading System (Chapter 8) that persists to the present day may also fade away in some aspects, as when parts of a design are used up, mixed up, or lost; the remaining materials may be used in any number of ways that do not match the intentions of the designers. To all of these we can add lack of funds to sustain designs, a cause of demise that can stand alone, as with the computer implementation in MPATI (Chapter 9) where the costs of equipment and airplanes was eventually insupportable, or add to other problems, as when the Computer Assisted Instruction in Elementary Mathematics project (Chapter 10) lost funding, continued with its analytic component to support the Nicaraguan Radio Mathematics Project (NRMP), but eventually had to end that support because of cost. Perhaps experimental projects, like TICCIT, will always end when the funding dries up. Whether foregrounded or not, a reader might consider likely the financial dimensions of other cases. For example, in the case of instructional film (Chapter 6), while production costs of instructional film might be justified for the sake of quality, the expense of the infrastructure for shipping film to and from Indiana University and that of maintaining film projectors at instructional sites could not be rationalized once cheaper technology, like video, appeared and even cheaper distribution via digital means became available.

Reincarnation

It is interesting to note that designs for learning considered to be current, even cutting edge, at any given time, can be viewed in part as reincarnations of earlier designs. Without attenuating this metaphor too badly, one aspect of reincarnation may be seen to hold; the design idea that has returned in a new form may, indeed, be very different from its earlier incarnation—perhaps unrecognizable on the surface. This is partly because its return is not based on an orderly progression from one design to the next, but on the persistence of the spirit that animated earlier designs. A reader familiar with computer documentation and help systems, for example, will recognize that minimalist instruction (Chapter 13) animates current designs for online help systems and quick-start instructions for commercial technologies, even though these do not resemble the original. We do not mean to argue that the mere existence of one design has led directly to the creation of another. Neither do we mean to argue that abstract principles guiding designs, or abstracted from them, are *not* involved in perceptible similarities between designs separated in time. It may be surprising, however, when reading through this lens, to appreciate the specifics of how these ideas have manifested in concrete products and systems, and user conventions, long before the current reader encountered those ideas.

Current designers with an interest in augmented reality learning experiences may want to read Boling's Alcatraz chapter (Chapter 15) to consider how comparatively simple technology was used in 1987 at the Alcatraz National Park site to merge the auditory and visual senses with multiple physical locations for an augmented reality lesson in the history of that infamous prison site. The spirit of such a design is concerned with bringing information to location, deepening or enriching the experience of place, and recognizing the importance of geography to the salience of information. Proponents of immersive learning may recognize in the Carlisle Model schools (Chapter 4) and the Rochester Method (Chapter 3), where students' entire lives were rendered indistinguishable from the learning design, the spirit of an approach in which the power of total experience is harnessed towards a desired outcome. Likewise, project-based learning as an approach finds a strong prequel in minimalist instruction (Chapter 13) which is fundamentally oriented to the existence of a compelling goal and envisioned as support ("training wheels") and guidance (recovery from error). In fact, this design will also interest those who focus on scaffolding as a design strategy for learning. And those who have followed the emergence, ebb, flow, and current morphing of MOOCS will want to check Trumbore's description (Chapter 10) of Computer Assisted Instruction in Elementary Mathematics to consider the aspirations of that project to massively scale up access to learning.

Considering the total upheaval of schooling during a global pandemic when millions of students are learning from home, designers may want to read the SRA chapter (Chapter 8) to reflect upon how Achieve3000 or IXL use similar learning elements to assist students in exploring their own learning, or MPATI (Chapter 9) to consider the uses of—and stresses on—available technologies (like Zoom™) to meet a population's needs for learning in places where those needs could not otherwise be met. When instructional designers in higher education are struggling to help faculty take courses online, Trumbore's design case (Chapter 10) on Computer Assisted Instruction in Elementary Mathematics and the Nicaraguan Radio Mathematics Project (NRMP) demonstrates that moving a learning design from one mode to another, and to a mode offering very different affordances, is a challenge reborn.

The number of designs in this collection that include some form of goal focused on individualizing learning will be interesting to readers using the reincarnation lens. In fact, it may be most efficient to list the designs focused on scaling up learning through generalized solutions rather than individualizing learning. Arguably, instructional film (Chapter 6), MPATI (Chapter 9), the Carlisle Model school (Chapter 4), and the Rochester Method (Chapter 3) fit this description, but all the rest, to one degree or another, aim to differentiate learning either for a group (as in the Bridge and SimCalc chapters), or for each learner interacting with the design. Even in the "Alcatraz Cellhouse Tour," in which each visitor hears exactly the same audio tour, is geared to creating a unique experience for each of them as they merge their own life world with what they are seeing and hearing. What may seem to be inflexible designs (e.g., learning machines) are intended to create a learning experience responsive to the individual in terms of pacing, if not content.

In Summary

Multiple additional lenses may be used through which to view these design cases, including those fully particular to the individual reader. We recognize, however, that the primary purpose of the cases is to offer an experiential glimpse of designs for learning from the past that can no longer be experienced directly in their original form. We have encouraged authors to offer as much as they can in the way of story and media in order to fulfill this purpose, as well as what they can discover, or reconstruct interpretively, from the designs regarding the decisions that went into creating them. A reader who approaches the cases looking for these aspects will, we believe, come away from the collection with an extended understanding of the field through designs they did not know about previously, and a concrete, textured appreciation of those they may have only heard about before. The lens of experience is the one we recommend most highly. Approach each case as an opportunity to add one more vicarious experience to your store of memories, available to you in the unknowable future as a tool for designing.

Reference

Howard, C. D., & Gray, C. M. (2014). Introduction to the Special Issue on Historic Design Cases. In C. M. Gray & C. D. Howard (Eds.), *International Journal of Designs for Learning* [Special Issue on Historic Design Cases], 5(2), i–iv. https://doi.org/10.14434/ijdl.v5i2.13257.

3

THE ROCHESTER METHOD

An Innovation in its Time (1878–1970)

Malinda Eccarius

In 1971, in my Introduction to Deaf Education course, I saw an educational film of a classroom of teenagers using the Rochester Method (RM), a communication system designed to support learning of English by children who were deaf. Practitioners of the method simultaneously fingerspelled and spoke every word, and wrote and read English wherever possible. I don't remember what they were studying, perhaps because I could not understand either the students' speech or their rapid fingerspelling. It was clear, however, that students and teacher were actually communicating about ideas, not just participating in the rote speech drills I had seen in other films during this course. Yet, at the moment when I was seeing this film as part of my preparation to teach children who were deaf or hard of hearing, the Rochester Method was experiencing its death throes. At this time, it is likely that college students majoring in Deaf Education no longer see this film, and almost certain that designers of educational systems more broadly defined do not have even this vicarious experience of what the Rochester system was like when it was in use.

Context for the Design of the Rochester Method

In the late 1870s, the widespread use of signs for communication in schools for the deaf was gradually being replaced by the speech-only communication advocated by Alexander Graham Bell. In 1880, attendees at the Conference of Milan, a turning point in the history of Deaf education, met to decide on the best philosophy for educating children who were deaf or hard of hearing. Specifically, these gentlemen, highly respected educators of their time, from across North America and Western Europe, were determined to decide what mode of communication should be used in educating *all* children who were deaf or hard of hearing: spoken language, or the use of manual signs and gestures. Nine out of 12 speakers, led by Alexander Graham Bell, among others, strongly advocated the use of speech and speech reading alone. The resolutions passed by the delegates were uniformly in favor of oral education. However, a minority, led by The Reverend Thomas Hopkins Gallaudet, argued that the use of visual communication was both natural and accessible—and that indigenous sign systems were already used by the Adult Deaf community in most countries participating in the conference.

Within a few years of the Milan Conference, oral-only educational systems rapidly became the majority, especially in private schools, throughout the United States and most Western European countries. However, compromise instructional systems soon began to appear. Some professionals estimated that fewer than one in ten children born deaf, and lucky enough to be in classrooms, proved to be even minimally successful using only speech and speech reading to communicate with hearing individuals. Children who were forbidden to sign developed their own gestural systems to use in the dormitories and out of sight of hearing adults, even at the risk of severe punishment.

Almost from the moment that delegates from the Milan Conference, including both Bell and Gallaudet, returned to the United States, Deaf Education, composed of a somewhat fragmented system of residential institutions (many using a form of signed language at the time and employing Deaf teachers), and private programs, usually focused on speech development, became highly polarized. Several factors contributed to the polarization:

- Historically, educators assumed a causal link between the ability to speak and the ability to think in any abstract way. How could someone, for example, converse about any event outside the here and now without symbolic language?
- The hearing population in general assumed that the language of signs (ASL) was *not* a symbolic language. It was, in their minds, only a set of gestures, useful for concrete instructions in the here and now. You had to be able to see what you were trying to "talk" about.
- Ninety-five percent of children who were deaf had hearing parents. Hearing parents wanted their children to be like them, to learn as they, the parents, had learned. The parents wanted their children to have hearing friends and to communicate easily within the Hearing community. As Deaf teachers were forced out of the educational system by oral educational designs, the hearing educators who replaced them agreed with hearing parents.
- Deaf parents, however, also wanted their children to communicate with them, and with their Deaf friends, and to learn easily using their natural language of signs. Some Deaf adults with children who were deaf came from generations of Deaf parents, grandparents, and great grandparents. Deaf adults, especially those in Deaf Communities, knew that they could communicate any idea using signing. The Deaf parents of children at school in

24 Malinda Eccarius

FIGURE 3.1 Dr. Zenas Westervelt, Superintendent of Rochester School for the Deaf.

the 1870s, however, often had a very limited education themselves, and were sometimes isolated from other Deaf individuals, especially in rural areas. The very first formal classroom education of two children in America who were deaf did not take place until 1817, and the first schools for the deaf were founded in the mid- to late 1820s. Very few children attended them, relative to the actual population of children who were deaf or hard of hearing. Graduates of schools for the deaf tended to remain in the area of their school, forming communities. Other individuals who were deaf often remained in rural settings, isolated from sources of natural and easy communication.

Administrators of schools for the deaf were also the designers of instructional systems for the deaf in their own institutions. Their personal philosophies, whether for signing or for spoken language, heavily influenced their decisions. Zenas Westervelt, the young principal of the prestigious Rochester School for the Deaf (RSD) in Rochester, New York was not satisfied with the outcomes of other systems of educating children who were deaf or hard of hearing, including speech-only systems. In contrast to his peers, he believed that every child who was deaf possessed the ability to develop in the same way, and to the same extent, as children with typical hearing.

At the Convention of Educators of the Deaf in Columbus, Ohio in 1878, even before the Milan Conference, Westervelt proposed a drastic, groundbreaking, and controversial design. At RSD, *all communication, in every setting,* would consist of English presented in three ways: fingerspelling, speaking and speechreading, and extensive use of reading and writing. Westervelt believed that, with all three sources constantly available, idiomatic English would be fully transparent to RSD students. Westervelt's abrupt mandate to implement the Rochester Method at RSD is an excellent example of how the decisions of a single administrator could determine the instructional system of an individual school for the Deaf during that time period.

Westervelt's primary goal was that students would comprehend and use spoken and written English to think and to reason, also the goal of the oral-only systems dominant at the time. However, his was, in fact, a compromise system, the compromise being the use of fingerspelling to make spoken English visually transparent to students, who were free to access any or all of the three modes available to them (fingerspelling, speaking, and speechreading) as needed.

Part of Westervelt's motivation for his design was the need to continue the education of adventitiously deafened children, i.e., children who had lost their hearing after birth, especially those who had already acquired spoken English. In the 1870s, many children entered RSD after losing some or all of their hearing due to diseases, such as meningitis, measles, whooping cough, or scarlet fever, or after experiencing head trauma. Such children often had fully established spoken English skills at the time of entry. Westervelt described these individuals as declining cognitively after becoming deaf; at the time, cognitive ability was judged by an individual's use of clear, spoken English to communicate abstract ideas. Westervelt noticed both a gradual deterioration of speech clarity, and the tendency of students to plateau in their academic and conversational development. Westervelt decided that adding fingerspelling would make instruction and communication transparent, allowing students to resume their academic progress.

Congenitally (born deaf) deaf children of Deaf[1] parents usually acquired naturally, and entered school with, what we now know to have been a fully formed language of signs, now recognized as American Sign Language (ASL), a complete language independent of spoken English, studied and described by linguists since the 1970s. (In ASL, some signed words contain handshapes similar to those of fingerspelling; sometimes a fingerspelled English word is part of an ASL expression but signing and fingerspelling are not the same form of communication.) Clayton McLaughlin, in a presentation to the Convention of American Instructors of the Deaf, noted in 1920 that the children with Deaf parents in an RSD classroom often competed successfully with children with partial hearing, even when not allowed to use their native signed language.

The most challenging students in the late 1870s were the congenitally deaf children living in an inaccessible oral language environment with hearing parents until coming to school at age 5 or 6. Because the children did not hear, and very few spoken sounds are unambiguously visible on the lips, deaf children with hearing parents rarely learned a first language naturally in their home environment. In fact, hearing loss was often not detected; many children were considered mentally defective outside, or even within, their immediate family.

Westervelt believed that the educational system he was designing would facilitate the spoken English language development of *all* the children in an RSD classroom, by making idiomatic English transparent in all environments. He also declared that individuals who were deaf were as cognitively able as individuals who were hearing, and that graduates of his educational system would demonstrate their competence through the clear and natural use of English using fingerspelled, written, and spoken forms. Some "backward children," mentioned in several of my sources, probably children with multiple challenges or children who entered school without any first language, did receive specialized education. However, even in those classes, the specially prepared teachers used the RM for communication at all times and were admonished to check carefully to make sure that the children were not just lazy and unwilling to apply themselves (Scouten, 1942).

Westervelt, although hearing, was a fluent signer himself, but he believed that signing interfered with acquisition of English because it was not synchronized with speech. He also noted that writers who used only natural signed language did not reflect the structure of English in their writing. (American Sign Language has its own visual grammatical structure and does not have a written form generally accepted by the Deaf Community). He also believed that the use of signs was a distraction for the children of Deaf families while they were trying to learn English; he did not allow them to use signs during the years they attended RSD, although he assumed that they would resume their use of signed language with Deaf friends and family after leaving school, as well as interacting with the hearing community.

Students at RSD, according to the reports of many participants and outside observers, did, in fact, communicate in fluent, idiomatic English using at least the written mode, and in many cases used spoken English as well under certain circumstances. They met regularly and exceeded the achievement levels of the best schools for the deaf in the country, according to contemporary observers and evaluators. The Rochester Method remained in use at RSD for 70 years following its initial implementation.

What Did the System Look Like, and How Did It Work?

To add detail to my original impression, gained from the educational film I saw in 1971, of how the Rochester Method (RM) worked as a system for Deaf Education, I turned to sources from the time that this system was in actual use. Fortunately, a primary and authentic source of information about educational designs for children who are deaf and hard of hearing is available. Published beginning in 1847, *The American Annals of the Deaf and Dumb* (becoming, in 1886, the *American Annals of the Deaf*) contains articles and presentations from a primary professional organization, the Convention of American Instructors of the Deaf—the voices of contemporary practitioners sharing, at various conferences, the latest in instructional systems designed for a group of learners that have challenged educators for centuries. Here in the *Annals* I found a clear description of the

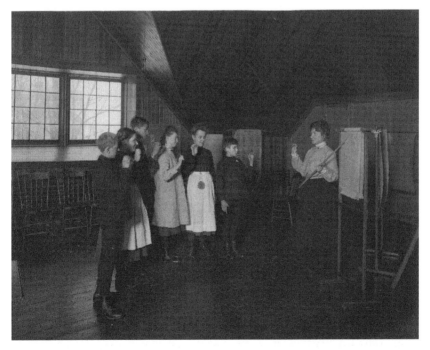

FIGURE 3.2 A class of RSD students practice fingerspelling with their teacher.

RM classroom, written by Clayton L. McLaughlin (1920), at the height of RM use. McLaughlin was obviously a strong advocate of the Rochester Method, but other first-hand observers suggest that his description is essentially accurate. The McLaughlin article appeared 42 years after Dr. Westervelt, as superintendent of Rochester School for the Deaf (RSD) first mandated in 1878 the use of RM in all aspects of student life—including classrooms, vocational workshops, playgrounds, cafeterias, and dormitories. Twenty years after McLaughlin wrote his description, Edward L. Scouten, a teacher at RSD from 1938 through 1940, assembled and commented on reviews of the school and the system, and evaluations of RSD graduates, each review conducted by a professional in the field based on first-hand observation. In these reviews, descriptions of the implementation of the RM are virtually identical to McLaughlin's explanation.

RSD staff members implement the Rochester Method in all settings, including dormitories, playgrounds, cafeterias, and chapel; however, a classroom is a convenient example. A classroom consists of a teacher and six to ten students who live in a residential school. Students are seated or standing in a row or a half-circle, with a direct line of sight to the teacher, writing surfaces, and, ideally, each other. The students standing in this classroom differ from each other in significant ways. The first major difference which would influence educational achievement and their participation in this classroom would be the age of onset of hearing loss for a given individual. The adventitiously deafened student lost hearing after birth, at any age. The congenitally deaf student might be born deaf to Deaf parents, or the congenitally deaf student might be born deaf to hearing parents. The second major difference influencing access to communication for students in any of these three categories would be the amount of usable hearing they retained (residual hearing).

The teacher for this class, assuming that it was a typical classroom at RSD, does not have preparation in education specifically designed for children who are deaf or hard of hearing, other than learning how to fingerspell and synchronize the three modes. To facilitate his design, Westervelt required the presence of instructors who could teach academic content effectively in English. He deliberately chose to use teachers prepared for regular classrooms rather than specially trained teachers in most cases. The teacher in this classroom has, in fact, periodically gone back to teach in a Hearing school for a year or more at a time; by moving back and forth, the teacher keeps in touch with modern methods of teaching children who can hear. The teacher also learns about recent changes in state grade level standards and renews his or her expectation that students who are deaf will interact in the same way as typically hearing children at the same grade level.

If this is a high school classroom, the teacher is a specialist in a content area such as mathematics, social studies, science, art, literature, or speech. In the winter 2002 issue of the journal *Rochester History*, I saw pictures of classrooms from around the turn of the century, showing classroom walls and chalkboards covered with content area material—the same materials that might have been seen in Hearing classrooms of the period (Rosenberg-Naparsteck, 2002).

The Rochester Method (1878–1970)

A Speech Class

FIGURE 3.3 Even speech is taught using the Rochester Method for instruction. Students here are using special symbols to cue mouth movements, but the teacher explains the symbols using speech, fingerspelling, and writing.

In this requirement, Westervelt was ahead of his time. Only in the twenty-first century have teachers at schools for the deaf and public school classrooms for children who are deaf or hard of hearing been mandated by state and Federal law to have teaching credentials in the content area and grade level they teach (mathematics, elementary education, early childhood, general special education, and so on), in addition to a specialization in education of children who are deaf or hard of hearing.

Because the hearing adults working with the RSD students only needed to know English, how to write, and how to fingerspell, the design for the RM made it highly portable to various environments at the school. Other pictures in the *Rochester History* article showed children meeting outdoors for art classes, on the school farm learning to grow vegetables, in the kitchen helping to cook, and in dormitories with staff supervisors, making beds. The requirement to use fingerspelling at all times was absolute; school staff seen using the language of signs were dismissed. Students who signed at school were sent to the Superintendent's office to be shown how to communicate their ideas using fingerspelling and spoken English. The pictures in this article come, with permission, from the

RSD Archives collection, and show children and teachers communicating via the Rochester Method in speech and fingerspelling classes.

Besides the classroom, the one environment mentioned in every description of RSD and the Rochester Method is the chapel. Westervelt agreed with virtually all his colleagues of the period that a primary purpose of education was to promote the ability to understand English. From an educational perspective, English, as a "true language," was considered to be an essential part of the thought process. Thinking, in turn, permitted the development of moral values and religious understanding. In designing a way for children to receive religious instruction, Westervelt would achieve the highest educational goal in Deaf education at the time.

The curriculum content the children are learning in the RM classroom would be at a specific grade level, and consistent with the regular state curriculum, which was designed to allow students to pass the New York Board examinations at the end of high school, an almost unheard-of achievement for congenitally deaf individuals at the time. In his positive review of the program, McLaughlin (1920) admits that not all students at RSD were expected to pass the Boards, or even to finish the high school content, but contends that the system provided adequate resources to allow bright and hard-working children to do so. Some of the students did just that. One student apparently left the school to attend a Ladies' Academy with typically hearing students, although after a year she came back to RSD, saying that she could communicate freely with the hearing students, but that learning new academic content through speechreading and printed language alone was difficult and exhausting.

McLaughlin also notes, almost in passing, that the children in this classroom would, of course, be several years older than Hearing students learning the same content. That age difference resulted from the late age at which hearing loss was detected, and typical school entry at age 5 or 6. Edward L. Scouten (1942), a former teacher at RSD, in his literature review of the origin and development of the Rochester Method, quoted Westervelt's plans for children entering the "infant program" at the age of 5. Westervelt planned for two years of language preparation using pictures and real experiences accompanied by typical English, prior to beginning formal academic instruction. His directions included the rate of speech and spelling to be used (approximately 80 to 100 words per minute), in complete sentences rather than single words, even to children with no previous language experience of any kind. In fact, in providing what he perceived as complete and accessible language, Westervelt was attempting to replicate the experience of most typically hearing infants, who gradually acquire the language of their communication environment. We now know that a child's mind is most open to that natural acquisition process from birth to perhaps age 3. Westervelt's infant class students were much older; however, RSD students excelled academically when compared with most of their peers from other institutions, who had also started school at age 5 or older.

At the time, many instructional designs for students who were deaf were based on the assumption that the children could not acquire language in a natural way. Typically, oral educational systems for deaf students required that English be taught through what was, ironically enough, called the "natural method," memorizing and applying grammatical rules of English, a practice still in general use in the 1970s and 1980s, with a notable lack of success in producing free, idiomatic use of English.

Limited Use and Eventual Disappearance of the Rochester Method

In continuous use at RSD for 70 years, the Rochester Method was attempted for short periods elsewhere, including the Louisiana School for the Deaf and the Florida School for the Deaf. However, without the driving force of Dr. Westervelt's personality, the faculty and administrators of these centers of Deaf Culture were not convinced that ASL should be abandoned entirely, and the RM was not adopted in its "pure" form. Their doubts were shared by even some students and teachers at RSD, who recognized that fingerspelling was slow and cumbersome, and that it distorted the fluency of speech. There is, however, one additional important factor; the lives of children who were deaf were changing. By the time other schools attempted to partially implement the system in the 1970s, some of the changes listed below had already taken place. For example, pictures of children at the Florida School for the Deaf fingerspelling in the 1970s show them wearing personal hearing aids. The accompanying article includes data showing promising student achievement in spelling and mathematics computation but also notes the times when Total Communication (which might mean ASL or signed English, or both) was used for improved fluency, such as dramatic presentations or social settings (McClure, 1975).

Over the 70 years of its use, outside educators and researchers would periodically review and evaluate the process and the outcomes of the RM design. Changes in their conclusions clearly reflected changes in cultural perceptions of Deaf individuals, progress in listening technology and cognitive research, and recognition of American Sign Language as a legitimate language independent of English. If I combine my 45 years of widely varied experience in Deaf Education from 1971 to 2016 with the literature contemporary with the full implementation of the RM, I see at least four changes in perceptions and educational practices that may have contributed to the disappearance of the instructional system known as the Rochester Method.

The characteristics of the learners changed. Children in the late twentieth and early twenty-first centuries have often survived illnesses that were fatal for children in the late nineteenth century. Survivors tend to present with multiple challenges, placing them in the category of special needs or "backward" students that McLaughlin and Scouten said required teachers with special training.

Listening technology improved. Westervelt did not have access to tools for amplification (making sounds louder). However, listening aids evolved from the ear trumpet in the 1800s to wearable hearing aids in the 1940s and 1950s. FM listening systems, introduced in the 1960s, moved the teacher's voice directly into each student's ear. In the past two decades we have seen expanding use of rapidly improving personal hearing aids and cochlear implants (C.I.s) by some children. (Not all children benefit from cochlear implants, and C.I.s are not generally acceptable in parts of the Deaf Community.) Accessibility to instruction now often includes viable auditory as well as visual input.

Neurological research identified an optimal window of language acquisition. Connected and functional language is naturally acquired most easily beginning at birth, whether the language is spoken or signed, so long as it is accessible in the environment. Universal hearing screening at birth has allowed increasing involvement of hearing parents as partners in providing an accessible environment for their infants' language acquisition from birth. Laws mandating public education for children with sensory disabilities ages 0 to 3 had begun in individual states by the 1980s, and similar laws were eventually passed at the Federal level. Hearing parents were increasingly reluctant to send their young children away to residential schools, although many Deaf parents, whose children had acquired a first language at an appropriate age, still valued schools for the deaf as centers for cultural development, where ASL was used for instruction and general communication as part of Deaf Culture.

American Sign Language was generally accepted by the Hearing Community. ASL is now studied by linguists as a complete and separate language. Total Communication, especially using manual codes attempting to represent English in the late 1960s and early 1970s, and Bilingual-Bicultural Education separating and teaching both ASL and English, in the 1980s, were broad movements that replaced individual compromise designs such as the Rochester Method. Many universities teach ASL as a World Language, along with French, German, Chinese, etc. Tactile fingerspelling became an important aspect of instruction for individuals who are both deaf and blind, but classroom application of the RM in its original form faded away.

Did the Rochester Method Leave an Imprint?

For a perspective on the influence of the RM on current educational designs in this field, I read the Communication Philosophy Statement on the website of the Rochester School for the Deaf, the place where the Rochester Method began—the place where it was implemented in all of its aspects. Here is their statement:

Our Communication Philosophy
RSD recognizes the right of its students to have full and ongoing access to language and communication, both incidental and planned. Optimal

access to all communication is vital to our students' academic and social development. American Sign Language (ASL) and English are the languages used at RSD for communication and instruction.

RSD is fully committed to ensuring that our students reach their maximum potential in ASL and English, while also supporting their individual communication needs. Recognizing that ASL and English are unique, distinct separations and clear boundaries between both languages are not only ideal but crucial and necessary also. To that end, RSD will serve as a language-rich environment for our deaf and hard of hearing students.

(Rochester School for the Deaf, n.d.)

Dr. Westervelt's design for educating children who were deaf and hard of hearing in the 1870s was powerfully influenced by his goals and beliefs. We know that he believed that a child who was deaf was able to acquire language, and to learn to think, in the same way as a child who was typically hearing. At the time, some contemporaries ridiculed him for that belief, but today, educational system designs for children who are deaf are virtually all based on that assumption.

Dr. Westervelt strongly believed in the need for transparent access to communication in all environments, and especially in the classroom, where in the 1880s auditory-oral instruction (far from transparent to a child without usable hearing) was likely to be the only mode allowed. He chose to add fingerspelling to speech, speechreading, reading, and writing as an unambiguous visual form of English, the only language accepted at the time as complete and therefore capable of reflecting complex thought. Today, RSD is committed to Bilingual-Bicultural education, a design where English and American Sign Language are taught as separate but equally transparent languages, and where individual students also have access to listening technology, speech development, and birth through preschool parent–infant learning opportunities.

Dr. Westervelt believed, with his peers, that his students should learn to interact with typically hearing individuals and be able to function independently in work environments. However, unlike his peers, he recognized the need for his students, especially those with Deaf families and friends, to be comfortable throughout life in many settings, within both the Hearing and Deaf communities. RSD clearly embraces that broader view, although not all other modern educational systems are designed for that purpose or share Westervelt's belief. The city of Rochester has one of the largest and most active Deaf Communities in the United States.

Rochester School for the Deaf today remains a prestigious center for Deaf Education in the United States. The school has proudly embraced Dr. Westervelt's search for transparency and cognitive growth, but now RSD accomplishes his goals by providing instruction in ASL and in English, access to sound through amplification, and Deaf adult role models in teaching, administrative and staff positions as well as access to a vibrant outside community. While Westervelt's original design for the instructional system referred to as the Rochester Method has disappeared, its essential goals remain. I suspect that Dr. Westervelt would approve.

Note

1. Use of a capital D indicates individuals who consider themselves to be members of a cultural community. Not all persons with hearing loss identify with the Deaf Community; in this chapter, such individuals would be described using "person first" language, such as "children who are deaf or hard of hearing."

References

Gannon, J. R. (1981). *Deaf heritage: A narrative history of Deaf America*. Silver Spring, MD: National Association of the Deaf.

McClure, W. J. (1975). The Rochester Method and the Florida School. *American Annals of the Deaf, 120*(3), 331–340. Retrieved from www.jstor.org/stable/44388536.

McLaughlin, C. L. (September 1920). The Rochester Method. *American Annals of the Deaf, 65*(4), 403–413. Retrieved from www.jstor.org/stable/44462466.

Rochester School for the Deaf (n.d.). www.rsdeaf.org/ (accessed February 17, 2020 and March 13, 2020).

Rosenberg-Naparsteck, R. (2002). The Rochester School for the Deaf. *Rochester History, 64*(1). Article pdf. Retrieved from https://4.files.edl.io/63c1/02/11/19/221524-ad429462-848c-4720-9d60-ad1f392c4011.pdf.

Scouten, E. L. (1942). *A re-evaluation of the Rochester Method*. Rochester, NY: The Alumni Association of Rochester School for the Deaf.

4
DESIGNED FOR DESTRUCTION

The Carlisle Design Model and the Effort to Assimilate American Indian Children (1887–1918)

John R. Gram

Background

As the Indian Wars drew to a close at the end of the nineteenth century, the federal government faced two interrelated "problems" in respect to the surviving indigenous populations still living in the territory it now claimed. First, it needed to incorporate American Indians into the larger US population but did not believe it could do so without "de-Indianizing" them first. Second, it needed to extinguish remaining indigenous claims to what the federal government said was now US land.[1]

One solution to both of these problems was the Dawes Allotment Act of 1887. The Act forcibly broke up reservations into individual landholdings, then put allotment owners on a long path towards US citizenship. This freed up "excess" Indian lands for sale to white settlers. It also meant that members of sovereign tribal nations with whom the United States had signed treaties would eventually be forced to interact with the federal government as individual American citizens—unable to call upon the sovereign status or treaty-guaranteed rights of their indigenous polities (Hoxie, 2001; Genetin-Pilawa, 2012; Elinghaus, 2017). Until individual American Indians were deemed ready for citizenship, they would be treated as wards of the federal government.[2]

The other major solution was the creation of a new network of federal Indian schools. The United States government had already been involved in the assimilation of American Indians through Western models of education for most of the nineteenth century through its financial support of various sectarian schools. Starting with the Civilization Fund in 1819 and ending with President Ulysses S. Grant's "Peace Policy" in the 1860s, the federal government had relied on Catholic and Protestant mission organizations to lead the struggle to "civilize" American

Indians (Mardock, 1971; Prucha, 1976; Keller, 1983). However, the government became more directly involved as the century drew to a close. Eventually, the Bureau of Indian Affairs ran a three-tiered system of government schools, largely located in the trans-Mississippi West. In theory, students attended a day school in their home community for several years before transferring to a nine-month boarding school located at reservation headquarters. After this, they would travel to one of two-dozen-plus off-reservation boarding schools, where they would spend a minimum of five years completing their American education, as well as their transformation into productive members of American society.[3]

In reality, not all American Indian students advanced through the school system in this manner. For example, some off-reservation schools maintained primary grades for some considerable time, despite the fact that students who attended these schools were supposed to be ready for advanced school work (see, e.g., Gram, 2015) In fact, if there is one thing that roughly three decades of scholarly attention to the government schools have taught us, it is that there was no truly "universal" experience for American Indian children. No school functioned exactly as it was supposed to, and the experiences of various tribal nations with the schools could vary significantly.

Still, it is easy enough to talk about how the various schools were *supposed* to operate, even if none met this ideal. For the purposes of this chapter, I will be focusing on the off-reservation boarding schools that sat at the top of the government system. There is limited scholarship on day schools and on-reservation boarding schools for those who are interested (start with McBeth, 1983; Ellis, 1996; Lawrence, 2011). The goal of the off-reservation boarding schools and their feeder schools was simple: transform American Indian children into Americans. These children would then return home as civilizing agents that could uplift their entire community. Thus, the United States would finally solve its "Indian problem" within a relatively short period of time. At least one Commissioner of Indian Affairs believed it could be done in a generation (Ellis, 1996).

The Carlisle Model

Off-reservation boarding schools took their design model from Carlisle Indian Industrial School, which opened in unused army barracks in Carlisle, PA in 1879. Carlisle's creator was an army officer named Richard Henry Pratt. He based Carlisle on his experiences working with adult Indian prisoners of war, as well as time spent working with American Indian children at Hampton Institute, a school created to serve primarily African American children (Lindsey, 1994; Adams, 1995; Fear-Segal, 2009). Pratt summed up his philosophy of Indian education in his famous phrase "Kill the Indian ... save the man" (Pratt, 1892). In other words, the purpose of the Carlisle model was to utterly destroy indigeneity. It was nothing short of a government-sponsored campaign of cultural genocide.[4]

FIGURE 4.1 (L) The Albuquerque Indian School buildings, circa 1910. (R) Staff of the Albuquerque Indian School, circa 1910.

Source: Courtesy National Archives #292879.

FIGURE 4.2 Young male students at the Albuquerque Indian School in military uniforms holding American flags, circa 1895.

Source: Courtesy National Archives #292868.

The assault on indigeneity began as soon as students arrived on campus.[5] By the end of their first day, students had lost up to four important markers for identity. Most lost their name, as school personnel assigned a new one. Often, this was a fairly standard American name, such as "John" or "Mary." At times, students received new names dripping with American meaning, such as "Ulysses Grant," "William Sherman," or "Noah Webster." Students with long hair, an important cultural marker for many tribal nations, had it cut. Students were also immediately stripped of whatever clothes they had worn to the school. In their stead, students received military uniforms that would become their daily attire. Indeed, military culture was an important aspect at most off-reservation boarding schools until well into the twentieth century (more below). Finally, students lost their languages; speaking in native tongues was forbidden at the boarding schools, though punishment for this infraction varied from school to school.

Having received these new important American cultural identity markers, students entered a highly regulated routine designed to reorient them to a new way of seeing themselves and the world. Daily routines could vary from school to school, but below is a fairly representative one. It comes from Albuquerque Indian School, an off-reservation boarding school in Albuquerque, New Mexico (Gram, 2015).

Daily Routine for Albuquerque Indian School (1913–14 School Year)

6:00AM	Rising Bell
6:20	Athletics and Drill
7:00	Breakfast
7:30	Care of Rooms and Dormitories
7:30	Instructive Work, Industrial Departments
7:30	Productive Work, Industrial Departments
7:30	Athletics for Morning Pupils
8:45	Academic Departments Open
11:30	Academic Departments Close
12PM	Dinner
1:00	Instructive Work, Industrial Departments
1:20	Productive Work, Industrial Departments
1:15	Academic Departments Open
4:00	Academic Departments Close
4:10	Athletics for Afternoon Pupils
5:00	Industrial Departments Close
5:30	Supper
6:00–7:00	Band Practice
7:00–7:45	Evening Work
8:00	Taps

We will turn to academic and industrial instruction in a moment. But first, there are several things to glean from the daily routine in terms of the school's focus on the assimilation of American Indian children.

First, notice the extent to which the Carlisle model borrowed from the military experiences of its founder; this went beyond simply dressing students in military uniforms. Students started each school day drilling with their assigned units. The day ended with Taps. For some school routines, the military structure is even more obvious. For example, Santa Fe Indian School's daily routine included bugle calls at various points of transition during the day (Gram, 2015). Reformers hoped that the emphasis on military training and discipline would help transform

70   THE INDIAN SCHOOL JOURNAL—ABOUT INDIANS

tion in the U. S., Dutton and Snedden; Special Methods in Geography, McMurray; Special Methods in History, McMurray; Special Methods in Language, McMurray; Special Methods in Arithmetic, McMurray; Crayon, Chalk and Pencil Drawing, Clayton.

HEALTH.

Care and Feeding of Children, Holt; Practical Points in Nursing, Stoney; Health Index of Children, Hoag; Rural Hygiene, Ogden; Conquest of Consumption, Hutchinson; Euthenics, Richards; Prevention of Infectious Diseases, Doty; Body and Its Defense, Gulick; Body at Work—Emergencies—Good Health—Control of Body and Mind, Gulick.

MISCELLANEOUS.

A Mother's List of Books for Children, Arnold; One Hundred Books for Children, Coussens; Fingerposts to Children's Reading, Field; The Book Lover, Baldwin; Up From Slavery, Booker T. Washington; Making of An American, Riis.

DAILY ROUTINE OF AN INDIAN SCHOOL.

No doubt, to the many readers of THE JOURNAL who have never visited an Indian school, a synopsis of the daily routine of one of Uncle Sam's big schools for the Native American would be interesting. The following is taken from the School Calender for 1912-1913 of the Chilocco School and will give a good idea of how our valuable time is spent, and also, how the work of the instruction is systematized and controlled.

SUNDAY.

8:00 a. m. Services for Catholic Students in Auditorium.
9:00 a. m.   General Inspection
10:00 a. m.—Sunday School for Non-Catholic Students in the Academic Building.
3:00 p. m.—General Undenominational Service in Auditorium—Sermon by a Minister of Arkansas City, or Visiting Clergyman.
7:30 p. m.—First, Second and Third Sunday of each month Meetings of the Young Women's and Young Men's Christian Associations; Fourth and Fifth Sundays, General Assembly, Auditorium.

MONDAY.

7:30 to 11:30 a. m., and 1:00 to 4:00 p. m., Industrial Departments in Session.
1:30 to 11:30 a. m., and 1:00 to 4:00 p. m., Academic Department in Session.
7:30 a. m. Academic Teachers' Meeting
7:00 to 8:00 p. m. Study Hour in Class Rooms or Homes

TUESDAY, WEDNESDAY, THURSDAY.

Academic and Industrial Departments in Session as on Monday.

7:30 p. m. Tuesday Industrial Teachers' Meeting

FRIDAY.

Academic and Industrial Departments in Session as on Monday.
7:00 p. m. Meetings of Literary Societies

SATURDAY.

Industrial Departments in Session as on Monday.
11:35 a. m. to 5:15 p. m., Students' Day in Town—Second Saturday in Month, Boys; Third Saturday, Girls.
7:00 p. m.—Last in Month, Academic Department Entertainment in Auditorium; the other Evenings, Social Gatherings in Gymnasium, or Assembly in Auditorium.

Mechanical Drawing Classes meet from 10:00 to 11:30 every School Day.
Domestic Science Classes 7:30 to 11:30 a. m., and 2:00 to 5:00 p. m. every School Day; on Serving Days time extends to 12:30 and to 6:00 p. m.
Domestic Art Classes, every School Day 7:30 to 11:30 a. m. and 1:00 to 5:00 p. m.

BUGLE CALLS.

A. M.

5:30	Reveille
6:20	First Call for Breakfast
6:25	Assembly
6:30	Mess Call
8:20	School Call
8:25	Assembly
11:25	Recall from School
11:50	First Call for Dinner
11:55	Assembly
12:00	Mess Call

P. M.

1:55	School Call
1:10	Assembly
4:00	Recall from School
5:20	First Call for Supper
5:25	Assembly
5:30	Mess Call
6:30	Study Call
6:55	Assembly
8:00	Recall from Study
9:00	Call to Quarters
9:05	Assembly
9:15	Taps

YEARLY CALENDAR.

Monday, September 16	Opening of Academic Dept
Thursday, November 28	Thanksgiving
Wednesday, December 25	Christmas
Friday, December 27	Open Session Hiawatha Society
Friday, January 3	First Term Ends
Monday, January 6	Second Term Begins
Friday, January 17	Open Session Sequoyah Society
Saturday, February 22	Washington's Birthday
Friday, February 28	Open Session Minnehaha Society
Sunday, March 23	Easter
Friday, April 11	Open Session Soangetaha Society
Friday, May 16	Second Term Ends
Sunday, May 18 to Wednesday, May 21	Commencement
Thursday, May 22	First Term 1913-1914 Begins
Friday, May 30	Memorial Day
Friday, June 20	Summer Vacation Begins

FIGURE 4.3 (L) Daily routine from the Albuquerque Indian School, 1913–1914. (R) Daily routine, bugle calls, and yearly calendar from the Chiloco School, 1912–1913, reprinted in *The Indian School Journal*.

Source: Courtesy National Archives #35812192.

children they saw as "wild" and "uncivilized." It remained part of the routine at most boarding schools until well into the twentieth century.[6]

With the installation of military discipline came corporal punishment. The majority of students' home nations did not rely on corporal punishment. Even those that occasionally used corporal punishment did so far more seldom and far less severely than contemporary American society. Corporal punishment may have been the single greatest culture shock for American Indian students (Morey & Gilliam, 1974; Collier, 2006). Punishments could be extraordinarily severe. For example, one school superintendent recorded in his diary that he wore out two brand new buggy whips punishing two runaways. The Commissioner of Indian Affairs forbade the use of corporal punishment early in the twentieth century but at some schools the practice seems to have survived sporadically (Gram, 2015).

Beyond the military overtones of the schedule, simply adjusting to a strict, clock-managed routine was a drastic adjustment for many. In his analysis of Indian boarding school autobiographical accounts, Andrew Krupat (2018) finds that adjustment to clock time appears so frequently that he labels it as one of several "topoi" central to the genre. Indigenous educational methods did not tend to rely on such regimentation, nor were they usually so location-specific; they tended to incorporate education into daily life and relationships (Sakiestewa Gilbert, 2010; Reyhner & Eder, 2017; King, 2018).

A second thing to notice about the daily routine is the important role extracurricular activities played in the Carlisle model. The daily routine above specifically mentions athletics and band. It is important to remember that the home cultures of these students already had both sports and music. However, the Carlisle model did not value these indigenous traditions, instead training students in American sports (such as basketball and football) and on American instruments (such as piano or brass instruments). Boys and girls participated in both athletics and music, though certainly boys had more opportunities to play sports. But this was in keeping with American views on education for boys and girls in general during this period (DeLuzio, 2007; Sakiestewa Gilbert, 2018).

Athletics and music were not just an integral part of "Americanizing" students; they were also a powerful publicity tool for the boarding schools—an opportunity to demonstrate the "success" of the boarding schools to a larger American audience in a way to which they could easily relate. For example, the Carlisle football team regularly competed against (and beat!) powerhouse American university teams. This is how many Americans first became aware of one of the greatest athletes of the twentieth century, Jim Thorpe. Teams at other boarding schools also successfully competed against white teams, in football and other sports (Bloom, 2000).

The third thing that readers should notice are moments that might seem rather mundane in a school's daily routine: "breakfast," "dinner," and "supper." However, here, too, students felt the pressure of assimilation. Not only the segregation, but also the food itself would have been relatively novel for students. The off-reservation boarding schools served food designed for an American diet. Many students had a hard time adjusting to these new food items. In addition, both the quantity and quality of the food suffered greatly at many schools because of financial shortages (more below). Though hunger may not have been a universal experience for all off-reservation boarding schools, small portions of poor-quality food crop up in the memories of many students (see, e.g., Coleman, 1993; Krupat, 2018). Students also ate in segregated lunchrooms, where boys and girls sat apart from one another; at a few schools it seems that they even ate at separate times. Indeed, keeping boys and girls separate as much as possible was a key component of the Carlisle model. Outside of the classroom and limited extracurricular moments, such as school dances, boys and girls spent little time together—which is not to suggest that male and female students accepted this segregation without question. Romances among students certainly blossomed from time to time (Krupat, 2018).

Though not referenced in the daily routine above, there is one more aspect of students' school days that is worth mentioning briefly: religious instruction. Though officially non-sectarian (in that they did not support one Christian denomination over another), the federal boarding schools were not secular institutions. For most Americans in the nineteenth and early twentieth centuries, being Christian (by which they meant Protestant) was a key aspect of being American and being "civilized." Boarding school students were required to attend Sunday School and Sunday services, either on campus or at a nearby church. Some schools also required religious instruction during the week. Most students received Protestant instruction; however, students who identified as Catholic could receive Catholic instruction instead, though it was up to the Bureau of Catholic Indian Missions and local clergy to provide the funding and personnel required for such instruction.[7] Students' home communities had rich spiritual and ceremonial lives; however, most reformers and school officials did not see these beliefs and practices as legitimate religion. Thus, part of "de-Indianizing" students was attempting to replace their indigenous spirituality with Christian instruction.

Estelle Reel's Course of Study

As one would expect, the majority of the daily routine above is devoted to classroom instruction. In 1901, Superintendent of Indian Schools Estelle Reel released a "Course of Study for Indian Schools"—the government's first attempt to provide a uniform course of study for all grade levels. In her introduction, Reel states that:

> This course [of study] is designed to give teachers a definite idea of the work that should be done in the schools to advance the pupils as speedily as possible to usefulness and citizenship. The aim of the course is to give the Indian child a knowledge of the English language, and to equip him with the ability to become self-supporting as speedily as possible.
>
> *(Reel, 1901, p. 5)*

She ends the introduction by expressing her "hop[e] that better morals, a more patriotic and Christian citizenship, and ability for self-support will result from what this course of study may inspire" (Reel, 1901, p. 6). What follow are nearly 300 pages of text covering a multitude of different topics that should be included in students' education: agriculture, arithmetic, blacksmithing, carpentry, geography, history, housekeeping, shoemaking, and spelling—just to name a few. Both academic and industrial training were necessary to produce "useful" Indians (more on this below).[8]

But what exactly did Reel's Course of Study look like in practice? Academic classroom instruction (in theory) would not look that much different than what happened in schools for white children at the time. American Indian students learned the basics of reading and writing in English, and they engaged in course materials and civic lessons designed to detribalize children and convince them of the "superiority" of American culture so that they could become "good" American children. Classes were conducted in English, despite the fact that most students had little to no mastery of the language when they first arrived; as mentioned above, speaking in native languages was forbidden, both inside and outside the classroom. Students' limited English, as well as limited access to classroom supplies, meant that teachers in boarding schools faced significant obstacles at times in delivering even the most basic instruction called for in Reel's Course of Study. One year, Santa Fe Indian School reported that they were delaying students' matriculation to the next grade because of how long it took for materials to arrive that school year (Gram, 2015). To make matters worse, many of the boarding schools suffered from a chronic shortage of qualified teachers. For a variety of reasons, recruitment of necessary personnel (and not just teachers!) proved a constant difficulty. For all these reasons, academic classroom instruction at the off-reservation boarding schools seldom resembled what Reel envisioned.

The other half of the school day was devoted to industrial education. Instruction for boys and girls was very different during this part of the day. Boys received training in a variety of trades, depending on what individual boarding schools offered: cobbling, tailoring, blacksmithing—just to name a few. Eventually trades like automotive repair appeared at some schools (Gram, 2015). Male students also received extensive training in agriculture. For some western tribal nations, agriculture was the responsibility of women. However, for a nation still in love with Jefferson's ideal of the republican yeoman farmer, teaching young men how to raise crops as independent agriculturalists was one of the most important lessons in masculinity that they could receive. It should be noted, of course, that many western tribal nations already had extensive experience with both agriculture and livestock; however, reformers and schools officials often looked down on indigenous techniques—an irony driven home even further by American struggles to bring agriculture to the West and Southwest, while indigenous communities had successfully lived in the region for countless generations. Training for boys reflected reformers' belief that Native Americans could be incorporated into the economic life of the nation, but only as members of the working class. Thus, the boarding schools were also designed to help solve the nation's new voracious unskilled labor demands brought on by the Second Industrial Revolution (Lomawaima & McCarty, 2006). This, more than anything else, is what Reel meant by creating "useful" Indians.

While some school later offered nursing training to female students, the vast majority of industrial training for girls was really domestic training. As reformers attempted to force Native Americans to shift from communitarianism to the primacy of the individual household, they knew that those households would need to be run by "civilized" Indian mothers and wives. In many ways, then, girls were the lynchpin for the entire assimilation project (Trennert, 1982). Girls spent their afternoons learning how to "properly" keep a house, how to cook "proper" meals, and how to raise a "proper" American family. At least one school went so far as to build cottages on campus where girls could practice playing house (Lomawaima, 1995).

A constant lack of necessary resources made industrial training even more important for the boarding school course of study. The boarding school experiment would never have lasted as long as it did without its ability to rely on student labor. Student sewing supplemented the limited supply of military uniforms and

FIGURE 4.4   Female students at the Albuquerque Indian School, circa 1881.

Source: Courtesy National Archives #2745522.

bedding. Students repaired and built school facilities when budgets inevitably fell short. Students labored in school fields and gardens in order to stock the schools with fresh produce. The list goes on. In short, boarding school students were first expected to provide the labor necessary to keep instruments of their assimilation operational before then being expected to play their part in providing the manual labor necessary to keep the American economy humming. This was yet another aspect of being "useful" Indians.

But the crown jewel of the Carlisle model, and something Reel's Course of Study expected every school to replicate, was the outing system. During the summer months, students could not return home (some schools made exceptions; see, e.g., Gram, 2015). Instead, they were hired out to local families as workers. In theory, this would allow students to make a little money, but the real purpose of these outings was to serve as a sort of cultural apprenticeship for students. Immersed in American families, students would receive the final polishes on their education by spending time incorporated into the very model they were supposed to reproduce back home. Despite being the lynchpin of the Carlisle model in many ways, it was consistently the point of greatest failure for the off-reservation boarding schools that tried to implement that model. For one, the outing system was largely voluntary at the western off-reservation boarding schools. Not all students chose to participate. Another significant problem was that there were simply not enough "proper" white American families living near most of the off-reservation boarding schools. This made a cultural apprenticeship virtually impossible. Most male students who participated in the outing system ended up working as agricultural laborers on nearby large farms. There they worked alongside other boarding school students and temporary laborers while receiving minimal supervision from the schools—and certainly nothing resembling a cultural apprenticeship. Most female students worked as domestic servants in local households—something closer to what the Carlisle model envisioned, perhaps, but still functioning largely as hired help.[9]

Why the Model Failed

By replicating the Carlisle design model and implementing the Reel Course of Study (and later modifications), reformers and government officials hoped to quickly assimilate the American Indian population (and lands!) into the larger nation. However, the federal boarding schools failed in their mission. Despite reformers' optimism concerning the Carlisle model, the off-reservation boarding schools established in the American West did not destroy indigeneity among the western tribal nations. Carlisle closed in 1918. Most of the off-reservation boarding schools modeled on it did not survive past the 1930s. A few continued to operate after post-World War II, but by then the harsh vision of assimilation represented by the Carlisle design model had been significantly modified—replaced by a federal vision of education which, though it certainly continued to struggle to understand, value, and base instruction on tribal cultures, still looked quite different from what had come before (Szasz, 1999). Today, most of the off-reservation boarding schools have closed; tribal nations actually run several of them now.

Why did the Carlisle design model fail? We can focus on three overarching reasons

First, we should give credit for the schools' failure to Native American students, parents, and communities. Most of the schools did not effectively isolate students from their home cultures. Parents and community leaders visited many of the schools to check on the treatment of their children. Many parents and communities had little say over whether or not to relinquish their children to the federal boarding schools; but they never forgot about them. As they had power and opportunity, they demanded that the government take the treatment of their children seriously.

Students also advocated for themselves in various ways. Sometimes students ran away from the schools. Though this did not necessarily result in a permanent escape from the school (often runaways were found and returned), school officials had to use limited funds to track down students—funds that could not then be used to cover other school operations. Because of this, sometimes superintendents decided that older runaways were not worth the effort to track down. Students could resist in other ways as well. Students talked in forbidden languages or discussed their home cultures in secret. They also used resistance techniques we might see children use in any school model, such as pretending to not understand instructions or working as slowly as possible. Finally, students often managed to adapt their academic and industrial lessons in ways that still valued and supported their home communities and cultures. In other words, they did not cease to be Indian just because the schools told them they should. Several scholars who have studied student agency at the boarding schools refer to this as students "turning the power" of the schools for their own indigenous ends (Trafzer et al., 2006; Sakiestewa Gilbert, 2010).

Beyond Indian agency, the second greatest factor in the failure of the schools was a habitual lack of resources. Congress never sufficiently funded the federal boarding school system. As mentioned above, this lack of resources affected every facet of boarding school life. It inhibited classroom instruction. It resulted in poor quality and insufficient quantity of food. Several consequences not discussed as yet involved student health. Because Congressional funding was based on the number of students attending a school, federal boarding schools habitually overcrowded their campuses, exacerbating shortages and leading to unsanitary conditions. And a lack of resources meant that the boarding schools also seldom had the necessary medical supplies or personnel to protect students from the consequences of living in such conditions (see, e.g., Keller, 2002). One of the most tragic legacies of the federal boarding schools are the tiny tombstones that dot so many of the campuses.

We saw how the boarding schools turned to student labor to try to bridge the gap between what was needed and what was provided for school operations. However, the boarding schools also turned to American Indian personnel to tackle the habitual shortage of employees. Across the federal boarding schools, American Indians served as teachers, disciplinarians, matrons, campus security—nearly every vital role (Cahill, 2013). What this meant practically was that most students could count on having at least one American Indian school employee. This provided yet another potential avenue from resisting and undermining the assimilative mission of the Carlisle model.

Finally, changes in the philosophical approach to Indian education also helped undermine the mission of the federal boarding schools. While tracing the evolution of American Indian education policy over the nineteenth and twentieth centuries is beyond the scope of this chapter, it is worth mentioning the drastic shift in policy that starts in the late 1920s and matured as part of the "Indian New Deal" in the 1930s. At the heart of this shift was a growing conviction that American Indians should be allowed to remain Indian. This is not to say that American Indian educational policy ceased to be ethnocentric. Reformers still believed they knew what Indians needed in order to have a successful future; however, they were at least willing to let them enter that future as Indians now (Philp, 1977; Kelly, 1983; Szasz, 1999).

A Final Word

There are two things I would like to add in closing.

First, as many readers of this volume are likely aware, education is not universal. It is a culturally conditioned process designed to form students into successful members of a specific society. For the reformers who designed the Carlisle model and for the school officials who implemented it, however, education was part of the boundary between civilization and savagery. Because they regarded American Indians as "backward," they also believed they did not value education. This was, of course, utter nonsense. American Indian communities continue to prepare their children for the future as best they can, as they always have. The transmission of knowledge, values, and social expectations continues in an unbroken line in these communities. Today, American Indian educators and tribal leaders remain at the forefront of efforts to adapt both indigenous and Western models of education to the needs of American Indian youth and their communities.

Second, American Indian success in surviving, navigating, resisting, and adapting ("turning the power" of) the boarding school experiment should not cause us to take lightly what the reformers and school personnel hoped would happen. Again, this was state-sponsored genocide. Other countries, such as Canada, have begun to come to grips with their own boarding school legacies; the United States largely has not—although the efforts of organizations such as the National Native American Boarding School Healing Coalition are starting to change this. Related, we should take seriously the very real damage the boarding school experiment did to generations of American Indian children and their communities. Just because the schools failed does not mean they did not leave behind generational scarring and trauma. In fact, this generational trauma is something that American Indian communities are continuing to struggle with today (Child, 2018).

Notes

1. Scholars of indigenous history use the term "settler colonialism" to describe US expansion across the continent. In a settler colonial model, the settler society legitimizes its occupation of conquered territory by eliminating distinct indigenous societies and by extinguishing indigenous land claims. This allows the settler society to create the myth that they are the true indigenous people—that the conquered territory is actually their homeland. The literature on settler colonialism is vast, but readers could start with Wolfe (2006) and Jacobs (2011) in the reference section at the end of this chapter. Wolfe and Jacobs also discuss how the federal boarding schools helped further the aims of the US settler society.
2. Over the course of the twentieth century, tribal nations have made extraordinary strides in regaining their sovereignty and in holding the federal government responsible for honoring its treaty obligations. The story of that struggle is beyond the scope of this chapter, but I did not want to leave readers with the impression that neither reservations nor sovereign tribal nations exist today.
3. The literature on the federal Indian schools has exploded in recent decades. The best place for readers to begin is probably still Adams (1995).
4. Many scholars use "cultural" or other modifiers as a way of distinguishing what happened at the boarding school from more popular understandings of genocide, such as the Holocaust. Other scholars (e.g., Woolford, 2015) argue that the term "genocide" should be used without a modifier in order to underscore the severity of what happened at the schools. Certainly, genocide is not limited to the physical destruction of bodies, and the boarding schools do meet several provisions of the United Nations' 1948 definition of genocide.
5. Virtually any of the works on the individual boarding schools will cover aspects of what follows in this paragraph. Again, readers could start with Adams (1995).
6. Interestingly, quite a few boarding schools ended up serving in the national guard or the army during World War I, drawing upon their boarding school military training.
7. Most studies of individual boarding schools cover how religious instruction functioned at that particular institution. For the instruction of Catholic students, readers could start with Prucha (1979).
8. Readers who would like a more in-depth analysis of Reel and her Course of Study should begin with Lomawaima (1996).
9. For readers interested in further understanding how the outing system functioned outside of Carlisle, the best single study is Whalen (2016).

References

Adams, D. W. (1995). *Education for extinction: American Indians and the boarding school experience, 1875–1928*. Lawrence, KS: University Press of Kansas.

Bloom, J. (2000). *To show what an Indian can do*. Minneapolis, MN: University of Minnesota Press.

Cahill, C. D. (2013). *Federal fathers and mothers: A social history of the United States Indian Service, 1869–1933*. Chapel Hill, NC: University of North Carolina Press.

Child, B. J. (2018). The boarding school as metaphor. *Journal of American Indian Education*, 57(1), 37–57.

Coleman, M. C. (1993). *American Indian children at school, 1850–1930*. Oxford, MS: University of Mississippi Press.

Collier, B. S. (2006). "St. Catherine Indian School, Santa Fe, 1887–2006: Catholic Indian education in New Mexico." PhD dissertation, Arizona State University.

DeLuzio, C. (2007). *Female adolescence in American scientific thought, 1830–1930*. Baltimore, MD: Johns Hopkins University Press.

Elinghaus, K. (2017). *Blood will tell: Native Americans and assimilation policy*. Lincoln, NE: University of Nebraska Press.

Ellis, C. (1996). *To change them forever: Indian education at the Rainy Mountain Boarding School, 1893–1920*. Norman, OK: University of Oklahoma Press.

Fear-Segal, J. (2009). *White man's club: Schools, race, and the struggle of Indian acculturation*. Lincoln, NE: University of Nebraska Press.

Genetin-Pilawa, C. J. (2012). *Crooked paths to allotment: The fight over federal Indian policy After the Civil War*. Chapel Hill, NC: University of North Carolina Press.

Gram, J. R. (2015). *Education at the edge of empire: Negotiating Pueblo identity in New Mexico's Indian boarding schools*. Seattle, WA: University of Washington Press.

Hoxie, F. E. (2001). *A final promise: The campaign to assimilate the Indians, 1880–1920*. Lincoln, NE: University of Nebraska Press.

Jacobs, M. D. (2011). *White mother to a dark race: Settler colonialism, maternalism, and the removal of indigenous children in the American West and Australia, 1880–1940*. Lincoln, NE: University of Nebraska Press.

Keller, J. (2002). *Empty beds: Indian students' health at Sherman Institute, 1902–1922*. East Lansing, MI: Michigan State University Press.

Keller, R. H. (1983). *American Protestantism and United States Indian policy, 1869–1882*. Lincoln, NE: University of Nebraska Press.

Kelly, L. C. (1983). *The assault on assimilation: John Collier and the origins of Indian policy reform*. Albuquerque, NM: University of New Mexico Press.

King, F. (2018). *The Earth Memory compass: Diné landscapes and education in the twentieth century*. Lawrence, KS: University Press of Kansas.

Krupat, A. (2018). *Changed forever: American Indian boarding school literature, Vol. 1*. Albany, NY: State University of New York Press.

Lawrence, A. (2011). *Lessons from an Indian day school: Negotiating colonization in Northern New Mexico, 1902–1907*. Lawrence, KS: University Press of Kansas.

Lindsey, D. F. (1994). *Indians at Hampton Institute, 1877–1923*. Champaign, IL: University of Illinois Press.

Lomawaima, K. T. (1995). *They called it Prairie Light: The story of Chilocco Indian school*. Lincoln, NE: University of Nebraska Press.

Lomawaima, K. T. (1996). Estelle Reel, Superintendent of Indian Schools, 1898–1910: Politics, curriculum, and land. *Journal of American Indian Education*, 35(3), 5–31.

Lomawaima, K. T., & McCarty, T. L. (2006). *To remain an Indian: Lessons in democracy from a century of Native American education*. New York: Teachers College Press.

Mardock, R. W. (1971). *The reformers and the American Indian*. Columbia, MO: University of Missouri Press.

McBeth, S. J. (1983). *Ethnic identity and the boarding school experience of West-Central Oklahoma American Indians*. Lanham, MD: University Press of America.

Morey, S., & Gilliam, O. L. (Eds.). (1974). *Respect for life: The traditional upbringing of American Indian children*. Garden City, NY: Waldorf.

Philp, K. R. (1977). *John Collier's crusade for Indian Reform, 1920–1954*. Tucson, AZ: The University of Arizona Press.

Pratt, R. H. (1892). *Official Report of the Nineteenth Annual Conference of Charities and Correction*. Reprinted in Richard H. Pratt, *"The advantages of mingling Indians with Whites," Americanizing the American Indians: Writings by the "Friends of the Indian" 1880–1900* (Cambridge, MA: Harvard University Press, 1973), 260–271. http://historymatters.gmu.edu/d/4929/ (accessed March 24, 2020).

Prucha, F. P. (1976). *American Indian policy in crisis: Christian reformers and the Indian, 1865–1900*. Norman, OK: The University of Oklahoma Press.

Prucha, F. P. (1979). *Churches and the Indian schools, 1888–1912*. Lincoln, NE: University of Nebraska Press.

Reel, E. (1901). *Course of study for the Indian schools of the United States: Industrial and literary*. Washington, DC: Government Printing Office.

Reyhner, J., & Eder, J. (2017). *American Indian education: A history* (2nd edn). Norman, OK: University of Oklahoma Press.

Sakiestewa Gilbert, M. (2010). *Education beyond the Mesas: Hopi students at Sherman Institute, 1902–1929*. Lincoln, NE: University of Nebraska Press.

Sakiestewa Gilbert, M. (2018). *Hopi runners: Crossing the terrain between Indian and American*. Lawrence, KS: University Press of Kansas.

Szasz, M. C. (1999). *Education and the American Indian: The road to self-determination since 1928* (3rd edn). Albuquerque, NM: University of New Mexico Press.

Trafzer, C. E., Keller, J. A., & Sisquoc, L. (Eds.). (2006). *Boarding school blues: Revisiting American Indian educational experiences*. Lincoln, NE: University of Nebraska Press.

Trennert, Jr., R. A. (1982). Educating Indian girls at nonreservation boarding schools, 1878–1920. *Western Historical Quarterly, 13*(3), 271–290.

Whalen, K. (2016). *Native students at work: American Indian labor and Sherman Institute's Outing Program, 1900–1945*. Seattle, WA: University of Washington Press.

Wolfe, P. (2006). Settler colonialism and the elimination of the Native. *Journal of Genocide Research, 8*(4), 387–409.

Woolford, A. (2015). *This benevolent experiment: Indigenous boarding schools, genocide, and redress in Canada and the United States*. Lincoln, NE: University of Nebraska Press.

5
A LIVED EXPERIENCE OF THE TENNESSEE SCHOOL FOR THE DEAF (1920–2000)

Makhosazana L. Lunga and Craig D. Howard

Design cases are often told from the perspective of the designer, but what is needed for a case is simply an intimate knowledge of the design and how it came to be as it is (Smith, 2010). In the case of the Tennessee School for the Deaf (TSD), once known as the Tennessee Deaf and Dumb Asylum, intimate knowledge of the total instructional design rests in the experiences of the students, teachers, and administrators who each shaped the school through their interactions, learning, and community-building. It is from this perspective that we address the case. This design case is channeled entirely through someone who experienced the design.

The first-hand experience that informed this case is from someone who attended the school, taught at the school, and had a father, a grandfather, and a son who attended the school as well. We interviewed TSD teacher Barry Swafford, who graduated from the TSD in 1971; his experiences with the school are informed by perspectives from before his time and through a lens that came after his own. His grandfather's and father's experiences are part of his context of knowing, and his awareness of how this design has come to be. We further informed this discussion with what we could construct from archival documents in local libraries. These together tell a complex story of the TSD from 1921 when the state broke ground to build the school to 2020, which we endeavored to make sense of through a user perspective. The complexity of this narrative arises out of the school's relationship with the hearing world. In the words of our interviewee, "We live among those in the hearing world every day. We interact with the hearing world daily." That is precisely what brought us to the case. The first author had an interaction with a deaf learner, which sparked curiosity, triggered more questions, and an interest to know more about the TSD, its community, and the long history of teaching and learning. Our interviewee stated plainly that he wanted to act as a bridge between the two worlds.

This is not an attempt to tell the history of deaf education. We attempted to uncover, as best as we could, the experience of the TSD for what it might tell us about the evolution of this community's school as a design. The narrative of the school as a single case of designed learning contains parallel histories of the physical spaces, events, influential associations, and technology. The physical spaces are the easiest to recount because buildings, unlike pedagogical practices and technologies, have clear beginnings and ends. We start with the buildings.

Physical Spaces

To gain an understanding of how the physical spaces of the school reside in the experiences and memories of those who experienced the school, we showed archival pictures of the school to Swafford and documented his recollections when he viewed the pictures. This part of the interview happened towards the end of our session together. We expected the histories of the TSD's buildings to reflect the changing purposes and direction of the school in an evolving context and suggest paths that we see elsewhere in the story of the school. Some buildings have been repurposed for service outside of the school, some are now gone, and some remain in uses close to how they were originally intended, although modified. We showed Swafford one of each.

When shown the pictures in Figure 5.1, Swafford recounted, "That is the old campus. It is now LMU—The Lincoln Memorial University Law School. That is where my grandfather graduated." Although repurposed, these spaces remain part of the identity of the school and were well documented in the literature we found in the archive. However, we had already discussed some more critical aspects of the growth of the pedagogy at the TSD and the experiences of his grandfather, so the archival pictures did not spawn much more elaboration in our interview.

The literature about the school paints a rather dry history from these early days. The original campus buildings now serve a different section of the Knoxville community. These structures are now the campus of Lincoln Memorial University in Knoxville (see Figure 5.1). While founded in 1844, the school's foundation and the front of the first buildings of the Tennessee Asylum for the Deaf and Dumb were constructed in 1848 near what is now downtown Knoxville; these were expanded in 1874 (Scott, 1857; Poore, 1929; Farlow, 1981). Despite initial worry about families unable to afford board and tuition fees, Scott (1857) notes that most families who had deaf children were interested in enrolling their children at the school. Scott (1857) discusses a tuition plan that supported those who would not otherwise be able to attend, enabling the school to grow. The school's physical structure doubled in size when buildings such as chapels (1879), auditorium (1879), hospital (1899), and north façade (1904/1905) were added (Farlow, 1981). By the time the school had grown to this larger size, the Tennessee Asylum for the Deaf and Dumb was one of the most recognized specialized schools in the country (Farlow, 1981). The school continued to experience a steady increase in

FIGURE 5.1 The TSD buildings that became other parts of Knoxville's cultural life: 1890–1920 Tennessee Asylum for the Deaf and Dumb.

Source: Used by Permission: Knox County Public Library Calvin M. McClung Historical Collection: http://cmdc.knoxlib.org/cdm/singleitem/collection/p265301coll9/id/1333?fbclid= IwAR203ipKRwBGzmzIuzmY9LDkrzN36WR_JjmRVXmlmPax_HKiB95p16E_4vc.

the number of applicants and enrollments,[1] and subsequently moved a couple of blocks away (Osborne, 2012).[2] Having outgrown its space, the school relocated to the current campus in South Knoxville in 1920, and the "old campus" began service for other purposes. Figure 5.1 shows images of the school while it was in use as the Tennessee Asylum for the Deaf and Dumb.

The next picture we showed Swafford was of buildings that no longer exist. The school moved to South Knoxville in 1924, and some of the buildings from that time are completely gone. The school changed its name from the Tennessee Asylum for the Deaf and Dumb to the Tennessee School for the Deaf at this time. Some of the original buildings on the South Knoxville campus have been demolished. When shown this picture (see Figure 5.2), Swafford remarked, "That is the present-day campus. That's TSD but that building has been torn down. Both of those buildings were the girls' dorm, since they were not used anymore, they were torn down."

FIGURE 5.2 South Knoxville campus buildings that are now gone, image taken from the Tennessee Historical Society showing the school's cottages A and B in the early 1920s during construction.

Source: Used by Permission: Courtesy of the Tennessee State Library and Archives: https://teva.contentdm.oclc.org/digital/collection/p15138coll11/id/22/rec/19.

Some buildings are still in use from that time, albeit in slightly different ways. As shown in Figure 5.3, the gymnasium was under construction in 1928. While someone new to the school might not recognize the structure at all, when shown the photo Swafford recollected, "That building is used in a different capacity. The E. Conley Akin gym was built in the 1970s with a swimming pool and is used for PE classes as well as various sports. The 'Old Gym' was renovated and the girls' volleyball team uses it when they have games because it has air conditioning."

Our discussion of physical spaces was relatively light, and the simple pictures brought quick yet unelaborated recollections from our interviewee. What we have here is only a fraction of the movement, demolition, and repurposing of the TSD's physical spaces. Like other American institutions that spanned this time period, the TSD also dealt with segregation, which drew restructuring of the physical spaces to match the hearing world's conventions of the times (Osborne, 2012). The pictures did not inspire those conversations. His recollections about the physical spaces were in stark contrast to the more elaborate recollections that

FIGURE 5.3 TSD gymnasium under construction. From this image, only the brick front wall of the lowest floor and foundation can be seen. Our interviewee still recognized the space but did not elaborate.

Source: Used by permission: Courtesy of the Tennessee State Library and Archives: https://teva.contentdm.oclc.org/digital/collection/p15138coll11/id/19/rec/18.

our interviewee shared about major events and key changes in pedagogy and technology that impacted the teaching and learning at TSD.

Events Experienced Through Their Legacy

Our semi-structured interview consisted of five questions; the fourth asked about important events (see the Appendix for the e-mail we sent prior to the interview). Swafford had come prepared, with notes. This part of the interview was perhaps the longest and most complex. We did not go into this expecting any particular answers; both authors are completely new to deaf education. Swafford started with events that happened well before his grandfather's time and recalled how they directly impacted the experience his grandfather would have had at the TSD:

> And like I said recently, during my grandfather's time, you know, that's when TAD [Tennessee Association for the Deaf] was really established

because there was a lot of complaints about Alexander Graham Bell and they had that Milan conference. Are you aware of the Milan conference that took place?

Swafford described events in the hearing world regarding deaf education that had played out over decades and over 100 years prior. In 1880 the Second International Congress on Education of the Deaf was held in Milan (Brill, 1984), and the ramifications of the attendee's resolutions impacted deaf education at TSD for years to come. At the Milan Conference, Alexander Graham Bell and others resolved to ban sign language, placing emphasis on oralism (Brill, 1984). Swafford highlights the impact of this event on TSD:

> And that [the Milan Conference] caused a big uprising in the Deaf community, and that's when the Tennessee Association of the Deaf really started. My grandfather didn't have the opportunity to have that. Deaf teachers at that time started to be removed from classrooms. Deaf teachers were looked over and hearing teachers started to take their place. As the years went by, like during my father's time, he was lucky, they started hiring Deaf teachers back into the field of deaf education. They still had an emphasis on speech, but manual communication [American Sign Language] was increasing during the years my father was at TSD.

Swafford's first-hand accounts tell us about the real impact these large events around the world had on the local community in Knoxville. While all deaf students may not have first-hand knowledge of these major events, their impact is still felt by those living in the community. Through his remarks, we see Swafford recognizing that his position as a Deaf teacher cannot be taken for granted, and thus his presence in the school is in some ways progress in itself because there once was a time at the TSD when deaf educators did not teach.

Swafford also connected these events to his own experience of school-based learning. The Milan Conference drew the complaints. The Tennessee Association of the Deaf was formed to support Deaf individuals and their right to the use of their native language in their process of learning. The Tennessee Association of the Deaf emerged out of tensions that brought the introduction of the Rochester Method of instruction to TSD (see Eccarius, Chapter 3, this volume). Swafford's personal recollection of actually using the Rochester method frames the experience as unfavorable: "During my last two years at TSD, I was forced to use the Rochester Method." TSD introduced the use of the Rochester Method which emphasized fingerspelled words in English and de-emphasized the use of a Deaf individual's native language, later known as American Sign Language. Swafford described the Rochester Method as an approach to force English-language acquisition and communication through fingerspelling, and he described the experience of the method: "I did have experience with that [Rochester Method],

And that's where you fingerspell everything and that really wasn't helpful. It is just a time waster. [Fingerspelling] is very time consuming." These events, while taking place almost a century before Swafford graduated from the TSD in 1971, impacted his experience of deaf education at the TSD, and were easily recalled in his memories of his father's experience as well. These events also overlapped with the institution's name change. Understanding the institution as a school rather than as an asylum coincided with this more ambitious, albeit nascent, pedagogy for deaf education that was felt intimately in the experience of learners at TSD.

Swafford recalled of his early experiences at TSD and his early experiences at Gallaudet University, "there wasn't really that much technology at the time and there wasn't a lot required … and at that time, people really did not recognize sign language as a language. It was a teaching tool for deaf children, but it was not recognized as a language." One might imagine this experience to reflect the experiences of TSD students prior to this time, but Swafford depicted a very different experience for those TSD students who came before him, just when ASL was beginning to be recognized as a language in its own right. This contrasts sharply with the stories told in primary source materials from his grandfather's time. Newspapers depict new pedagogies and practices in use. H. T. Poore, the school's superintendent from 1921 to 1951 (Knoxville News Sentinel, 1951), was lauded for introducing a number of new technologies and practices at the school, including, but not limited to, report cards, extending the years of study, teaching registers, a number of textbook updates, and even a "movie machine" (Osborne, 2012). All these practices and tools were introduced at a time prior to American Sign Language being recognized as a language in its own right. For Swafford, the recognition of American Sign Language as a language in its own right dwarfed any discussion of other changes.

Swafford described the lack of recognition of American Sign Language in tension with other desires to modernize the TSD. A Special Act of Legislation transferred administration of the school to the Tennessee Department of Education in 1935; all grades above the fourth were departmentalized and intensive programs with mental, aptitude, and achievement tests were implemented (Osborne, 2012). Swafford described the Deaf community's response to how deaf education is legislated from outside.

> There are two well-known organizations in the Deaf community, Tennessee Association of the Deaf and The TSD Alumni Association. They are very supportive and get very involved in deaf education. They want to make sure that deaf children have the appropriate education. And like I said recently, during my grandfather's time, you know, that's when TAD, the Tennessee Association for the Deaf, was really established.

In the context of these tensions, the pedagogy slowly adapted to better incorporate American Sign Language as a medium of instruction and learning.

Swafford recounted his direct experience in the 1960s: "During my time, students were grouped by their use of manual communication or oral speech. And when I was middle school age, the school decided to bring both groups of students together for instruction." In retrospect, important events like the acceptance of American Sign Language as a language in its own right might appear sudden, but that is not the lived experience that Swafford expressed. "So, in 1980, there was a nationwide recognition of ASL as a language. That was a very important tool in communication, so by that time Signed English was really starting to fade away, and they were using a mixture." What we noticed in reviewing the transcript was that this sudden change actually happened slowly, over at least 20 years in the lived experience of this member of the TSD school community.

As writers of this design case, what struck us about this development in the experience of the TSD is how lightly the recognition of a language can be taken in a casual conversation, when, in fact, its significance cannot be overstated. Swafford recounted,

> I had several Deaf teachers who could sign during that time and I really learned the most from them. You know because that's our native language. American Sign Language is my native language.

It is a matter of course that learning is facilitated far easier in the learners' first language, but the deaf or hard-of-hearing learners did not demand this affordance until much later at the TSD. Swafford recounted,

> In 1987, when I was a young teacher, the students started rebelling and wanted more American Sign Language in the classroom and not the Signed English. The Tennessee Association for the Deaf became involved and went to the state legislator which made the law that said ASL is the language of the Deaf ... with the support of TAD, and the Tennessee School for the Deaf Alumni Association, the Deaf community was very involved with deaf children, deaf education and what education deaf children receive.

This change set the stage for a bilingual approach to learning at the TSD later on. American Sign Language and English began to be taught separately, as is now done in other bilingual educational contexts relatively recently.

The Experience of Technology at the TSD

With the gradual increase of ASL and Signed English being used side by side in instructional interventions, technology use increased at the TSD. Swafford recalled the experience, and importance, of open captioning in the early 1970s. He recalled that at the time, open captions were used on television screens but "only at specific times, on specific days and a very limited number of programs offered that technology for the Deaf." While there were some improvements in the use of captioning seen in the 1980s, it wasn't until the 1990s that closed captioning became universal. Swafford recounted that captioning was "a huge tool and a huge part of technology that has been an asset to Deaf people." TSD learners still experience captioning in their learning in school.

In recent times, other technologies have entered the experience of TSD. However, Swafford experienced these technologies from the other side of the desk. Smartboards and Internet-connected media players have offered him opportunities to switch between ASL and English to expand his teaching strategies. Swafford describes a teaching intervention similar to those that take place in other bilingual educational settings such as Spanish-English, French-English or Chinese-English contexts around North America:

> I might have a Deaf actor in a movie, and I'll turn the captions off in English, and I'll ask the kids to tell me what they said, write it in English and then we turn the captions back on, and they're like, Oh, so that meant this and that can make that correlation and see the concept. Sometimes I like to play with the students, you know, and kind of trick them I'll say, how do you say this in English? How do you say this in ASL? And so, we'll do a little play on languages that way.

Swafford also mentioned websites, learning management systems, and video conferencing tools that he uses to facilitate learning. This depiction of deaf education is very different from the depictions of his experience relying on blackboard writing to grasp the message in a lesson. There is a cautious appreciation when he recounts the differences in the experiences that deaf children experienced in the past.

> Education for deaf kids now is so much better than it was in my time … and you know, technology has changed our lives.… Like this morning because of COVID-19, I had a meeting with some of my students. We use [web conferencing], you know.… So, it doesn't stop, learning doesn't stop. I am still teaching even from my home.… So now with technology coming into the classroom, the use of computers, there's more the need for American Sign Language being incorporated in the classroom.

The recognition of American Sign Language as a language in its own right had a direct impact on Swafford's lived experience of TSD. American Sign Language did not represent division from the hearing world but rather access to it. It enabled many other things to happen. In his descriptions, he included anecdotes from outside TSD, emphasizing how fortunate he was to use American Sign

Language at home, how others may not have been so fortunate, and how quickly his son learned to switch between the two without help while watching captioned movies.

Unintended Consequences of the Introduction of Technology

While Swafford celebrated technology, he also hedged regarding its benefits. He was quick to note the costs to the Deaf community by an uncalculated absorption into the hearing world. The term he used reminds one of cultural assimilation fears of immigrant groups; he warned about loss to the "hardcore Deaf" community.

> Millennials, their culture is a little different than the people, like of my generation of a long time ago.... You know, when I say hardcore ... their culture should be the same, but technology has influenced Deaf culture. In my day, technology influenced deaf children as well, but in a different way. Today's young people, they keep their distance. They use video relay service on the phone. They use computers, they use video conferencing ... back in the old days, we used to have Deaf clubs. We had Deaf softball teams; we had Deaf basketball teams. We had all these clubs where Deaf people in the community would gather to share information. In the past we also had captioned movie night, you know, where Deaf people would come together, you know, to support each other. Long ago there wasn't captioning on the TV like there is now.... We don't have softball teams, basketball teams anymore. We live more remote. You know, we don't get together and play cards. You know, Deaf people don't gather at people's homes like they used to. It's just interesting how technology has affected that. We have more choices like people who can hear now we have that communication access, where before in my time we didn't have that access, like people who can hear. So that's why I say hardcore. There's a hardcore group of Deaf, you know, it's not so much anymore.

In analyzing the interview, it was difficult to separate these notions of community from the experience of the TSD. The blurring of those lines of what is and is not one community or another was purposive. Swafford commented towards the end of the interview:

> The Deaf and hearing have bridged the gap. So, it's the same within our community. You know, you have to belong to the Deaf community, and the hearing community. I'm just a member of the community in general, you know, my local community. You know, I have hearing people all around me.

Conclusion

At the heart of the interview with Swafford was a telling comment, almost an aside. He recounted the appointment of a superintendent that supported bilingual American Sign Language and English education. Therein lies the crux of his generational experiences, and the pivot. Swafford's comment might have slipped by us had we not slowed our reading of the transcript of the interview as we did. Swafford recounted his reaction at the prospect of an advocate of bilingual education in the superintendent position: "And I thought, mhh, here we are now." We interpreted this as the notion that an acceptance of American Sign Language-English bilingual education unlocked opportunities he had struggled to obtain for years, that had eluded his father and grandfather, but had ushered in a new experience of the TSD for his son as well. The school, it seems, is not the buildings. Those held relatively little consequence in his recollections. However, the choice to accept or prohibit a bilingual approach to education was a critical design decision that made possible a range of other affordances, technologies, and experiences. This narrator had experienced being a bilingual learner where half of his linguistic proficiency was off limits at times. He had experienced being a bilingual teacher where half of his resources were off limits at times. Now he was a bilingual teacher and designer of bilingual learning who experienced what it is like to have the affordances of bilingual education opened up during his career and to watch the impact that this decision had on his learners, and on his son.

Acknowledgments

The authors would like to thank Barry Swafford of the Tennessee School for the Deaf for the interview and the preparation he brought to it, and his interpreter Charis Davis. We would also like to thank Alaina Eck and Jennifer Culbertson who provided edits to an early draft of the chapter.

Notes

1. Increase in enrollment was as follows: 10 students (1845–1846), 13 (1846–1847), 19 (1847–1848), 25 (1848–1849), 27 (1850), 31 (1851–1852), 34 (1852–1853), 43 (1853–1854), 57 (1844–1855), 62 (1855–1856) (Scott, 1857). When the school moved to Broadway and Summit Hill Drive in the 1920s, the number of enrolled students had increased to over 200. The move also coincided with the school name change: *Deaf and Dumb Asylum* replaced with *Deaf*. According to the hundredth Anniversary of the Tennessee School for the Deaf, 1845 to 1945, efforts led by Mrs. H.T. Poore's administration in 1922 helped educate the public that the deaf are not dumb (Tennessee School for the Deaf, 1945).
2. The original building was used as a school from 1846 to 1924. The City of Knoxville purchased the school in 1922 and occupied it in 1925 (McNabb, 1972). It served as the Knoxville City Hall up until 1980 (Osborne, 2012) and is currently used as the Lincoln Memorial University School of Law. They then moved to Broadway and Summit Hill drive before moving to the current buildings in South Knoxville.

References

Brill, R. G. (1984). *International congresses on education of the deaf: An analytical history, 1878–1980*. Gallaudet University Press.
Farlow, G. (1981). *City of Knoxville*. Department of Community and Economic Development, City of Knoxville. http://lcweb2.loc.gov/master/pnp/habshaer/tn/tn0100/tn0177/data/tn0177data.pdf.
Knoxville News Sentinel. (1951, November 10). *Mrs. H. T. Poore Resigns at TSD*. Retrieved from https://infoweb-newsbank-com.proxy.lib.utk.edu.
McNabb, W. R. (1972). History of the Knoxville City Hall. *Tennessee Historical Quarterly, 31*(3), 256–260.
Osborne, A. (2012). Tennessee School for the Deaf's 1884 graduate designed S. Knoxville campus. *Knoxville News Sentinel*. Retrieved from http://archive.knoxnews.com/news/local/tennessee-school-for-the-deafs-history-lives-through-photographs-ep-361006515-357099801.html.
Poore, H. T. (1929). The Tennessee School. *American Annals of the Deaf, 74*(3), 221–223.
Scott, A. (1857). History of the Tennessee School for the Deaf and Dumb. *American Annals of the Deaf and Dumb, 9*(2), 117–122.
Smith, K. M. (2010). Producing the rigorous design case. *International Journal of Designs for Learning, 1*(1), 9–20.
Tennessee School for the Deaf. (1945). *100th anniversary of the Tennessee School for the Deaf, 1845–1945*. Knoxville, TN: n.p.

Appendix: Interview Questions

Here is basically what we will be asking you:

1. What brought you to deaf education as a career?
2. Can you describe some of the more innovative spaces, teaching tools, or strategies that have entered the TSD for the deaf in the past or in your career?
3. Had there been particularly impactful technologies that have changed how we educate the Deaf and hard of hearing in Tennessee?
4. In your recollection, were there any major events that changed the school in significant ways?
5. What role has the Deaf community played in the ways we go about deaf education in Tennessee?

We are not at all attempting to critique deaf education. What we are doing is trying to capture the knowledge embodied in deaf education's tools and spaces. Documenting the struggles and advances, and celebrating the change and evolution, is more like what we are trying to do.

6

SUPERVISING WOMEN WORKERS

The Rise of Instructional Training Films (1944)

Colin M. Gray

In the early 1940s, large portions of the world were at war. Americans were spread across the globe engaged in conflict on two fronts, with a volume of manufacturing and deployment of troops powerful enough to pull the United States out of the lasting effects of the Great Depression. Over 16 million troops were deployed, and over 10 million US workers were displaced due to this deployment, resulting in the need for many new workers who had not traditionally been part of the workforce—namely women. This surge in the workforce led to a rapid change in the US economy, with the war effort shifting the unemployment rate from 17.2 percent in 1939 to 1.2 percent by 1944. Women joined the workforce in large and unprecedented numbers—by the beginning of 1942, already 2.8 million strong—holding jobs traditionally carried out by men as part of the effort to manufacture needed goods during World War II when many men were serving in the military and unavailable.

Beyond the obvious lasting historical impact of World War II, the systems engineering required to train and deploy millions of troops and workers left an impact on educational processes as well (Reiser, 2001; Saettler, 2004). Some instructional design scholars place the emergence of systematic instructional design practice at the heart of military training, which, while first mediated through industrial training using Dale's "Cone of Experience," later led to lasting impacts on formal educational programs.

In the early 1940s, many filmmakers were drafted to serve in the war effort to engage the public and build morale. While many Americans were exposed to these filmmaking efforts through newsreels at the movie theaters, watching films developed by some of the leading directors of the era (cf. the 2014 book and 2017 TV series *Five Came Back*), numerous efforts, less transparent to the general public, were made to advance training for members of the military to give them a sense

Supervising Women Workers (1944) **63**

of the geopolitics that led to the war (e.g., the seven-part documentary series *Why We Fight*, directed by Frank Capra). However, numerous films were also produced to inform work on the home front, many of which have likely been lost to history. I will seek to describe and interpret the design and instructional messaging of one such film in this chapter, focusing on the adaptation of work practices when supervising women in a manufacturing setting.

Instructional Film Distribution and the Audio-Visual Center

Prior to World War II, there was no significant infrastructure for instructional media development in the United States. I will tell the parallel story here, in brief, of the birth of the instructional film movement, and the role of Indiana University (IU) and instructional film pioneer L.C. "Ole" Larson in bringing large-scale instructional film development and distribution to the United States, serving a primary role in the craft-based, audiovisual roots of instructional design.

While the specific film I analyze and describe here did not originate within the Audio-Visual (AV) Center at IU, it was later archived there (Figure 6.1), and is accessible to this day due to the digitization efforts of IU Libraries ("About the IU Audio-Visual Center", n.d.). This instructional film archive began with the

FIGURE 6.1   Opening frame in the reel of *Supervising Women Workers*, indicating that this film was circulated by the Indiana University Audio-Visual Center.

FIGURE 6.2 (L) An advertisement for the "Problems in Supervision" series from a 1945 issue of *Business Screen Magazine* alongside (R) training-related advertisement ephemera of the era.

Source: Archival materials supplied by the Internet Archive (at archive.org) in association with Prelinger Archives.

goal of Larson to "*integrate* photo and film production, rental of educational films, and researching, teaching about, and promoting the use of audiovisual media" (Molenda et al., 2020). Larson's effort led to the formation of the Educational Film Library, which launched in 1947 and created the infrastructure for renting instructional films to schools, colleges, and other organizations. The proceeds of these rentals then supported the instructors who taught in the AV program and created a budget for the production of other instructional films. At the height of the film library in 1969, 392,000 reels of film were circulated around the country, and the AV Center included over 30 staff members who taught courses in educational media (Molenda et al., 2020). The archival and preservation effort to document the extent of this instructional film library is ongoing (Bertin, 2019), and these contemporary digitization efforts and their accompanying curation notes—in part—allow us to tell our story here.

The Context of Wartime Film Production

The film at the heart of the analysis found in this chapter was archived by Indiana University staff as part of the Indiana University Libraries Moving Image Archive (IULMIA). This film, entitled *Supervising Women Workers*, was part of a series of films on "Problems in Supervision" produced by the US government during the war era (Figure 6.2, left), at least some of which have been preserved by the IULMIA. Other titles in this series on workplace training during wartime include *Maintaining Workers' Interest* (1944), *Discipline Part 1: Giving Orders* (1943), and *Placing the Right Man on the Job* (1944) ("Problems in Supervision", n.d.). The IULMIA archive describes this series as follows:

> Eleven short films from the U.S. Office of Education produced Problems In Supervision series provide a detailed look at the wartime factory shop floor and assembly line in their mini-dramatizations of workplace conflict. A workforce of men and women (portrayed by a small cast of actors reappearing throughout the series) are seen operating the lathes and drill presses, assembling machines, and confronting conflict between worker and supervisor. These government sponsored training films attempt a timely response to the thousands of new workers entering the wartime industrial workforce.
>
> *("Problems in Supervision," n.d.)*

The film *Supervising Women Workers*, part of this larger series, was made in 1944 by the United States Office of Education and directed by Herbert Kerkow (*Supervising Women Workers*, n.d.). The Office of Education was responsible for producing educational materials for schools and organizations across the country, and, under the auspices of the U.S. Office of Education's Division of Visual Aids for War Training, "457 units were produced, consisting of 457 16mm sound motion pictures and instructor's manuals, and 432 35mm silent filmstrips" ("Division of Visual Aids for War Training", n.d.). In describing the role of the Office of Education during the wartime effort, C. F. Klinefelter, listed as the Committee Chair in the ending credits of the film I am focusing on, positions the U.S. Office of Education as "the only Federal Government Bureau that deals with education as such." Klinefelter describes "professional and administrative lines"—by which he means taking information being developed in other government bureaus and "adapting them for instructional use in the schools" (U.S. Congress, 1940, p. 23).

The Design of *Supervising Women Workers*

The framing of the film begins immediately (Figure 6.3); it is part of a series entitled "Problems in Supervision," signaling that supervising women is problematic—to be considered alongside many less-gendered issues such as leadership, productivity, motivation, and engagement. And likely the notion of supervising women did represent real challenges in that day—both from the perspective of its unfamiliarity and the evident sexism with which the problem is approached, which was then likely to provoke problems that might not have arisen otherwise.

In the almost 11-minute film, a series of scenes set in the foreman's office (Figure 6.4) signals approximately 7 primary sequences that communicate the purpose of the film. Each of these sequences is framed in relation to cultural

FIGURE 6.3 Title screen for the film.

Supervising Women Workers (1944) **67**

FIGURE 6.4 The primary characters in the film; (L) the supervisor who is providing advice, and (R) the foreman, Joe, who is learning how to supervise women in his plant.

expectations of women at the time and communicates the foreignness which the employment of women likely fostered to a male audience. I will summarize these sequences below, and then walk through each sequence in more detail with attention to the cinematic and scriptwriting qualities alongside a description of the learning content. All content is dealt with first "on its own terms" without an analysis of the appropriateness of the gendered claims being made, recognizing that this film was created in a time when these gendered norms were commonly accepted, even while also being problematic.

1. **[0:35–1:35]**
   The framing of the film strongly implies that women need different supervision than men because they come in with an objective deficit in know-how and because their psychology is presumed to be fundamentally different.
2. **[1:35–2:34]**
   Women need more explanation in the production workplace than men because they do not come in with knowledge of tools common in an industrial manufacturing setting, and this lack of knowledge extends to how these tools are used or relevant vocabulary.
3. **[2:45–3:43]**
   There is a need for women to be better supported in this kind of work, particularly in breaking down complex tasks and using appropriate vocabulary.
4. **[3:43–5:55]**
   Women bring a particular value to the job, particularly a facility with tasks requiring dexterity and accuracy. Assumptions of women's knowledge and responsibilities in the home are used to problematize the needs of women in the workplace.
5. **[5:57–7:24; 9:30–10:10]**
   Male supervisors are warned not to be overly familiar with women workers because other women will be jealous. General principles of working with women are identified.
6. **[7:24–9:30]**
   Male supervisors are advised not to correct or admonish women as they would men because women will deflect the criticism and react emotionally unless they are told why they have to follow rules/procedures.
7. **[10:10–10:24]**
   When a situation arises with women, it must be dealt with quickly or it will escalate; this advice is given in a way that suggests it does apply both to men and to women.

1. Women Need Different Supervision Than Men

The film begins with an implicit assumption that the presence of women in the workplace required different norms and means of management than in the past.

From the beginning, Joe, the foreman, is positioned as a competent manager, with his supervisor telling him: "You know how to handle men, and you know how to keep the line moving.... You work hard, Joe. You're a good foreman." However, this knowledge is deemed insufficient for the present situation, as the supervisor claims: "Yes, women workers do present problems, Joe. It's tough, I know, but there are thousands of others just like you all over the country facing the same problems." As he states this, there is a visual of the boss looking through a window at a large group of women exiting a nearby building; the women are all wearing skirts, several women are wearing heels, with their hair and makeup done (Figure 6.5). This is presented in such a way that it feels women are almost "invading" the plant, implying that business is no longer "as usual." This sequence concludes with a juxtapositioning of management approaches that may be considered to apply both to men and to women, and some concern that women present unique challenges that may impact the supervisor emotionally, as well as managerially:

SUPERVISOR: I think that we can say that the broad principles that are involved in the supervision of men apply equally well in the case of women.
FOREMAN: That ain't what I learned about women.... Women scare me—at least they do in a factory.

FIGURE 6.5   Women exiting the plant.

In this opening sequence, the focus is on framing the human performance problem rather than imparting specific instructional wisdom. The dominant presence of women is considered as a management challenge, with claims that perhaps some broad management principles are ungendered, while new principles may also need to be considered. This series of scenes lays out the purpose of the film and foregrounds the idea of women workers as a problem that needs to be dealt with by male management.

2. Women Do Not Have Necessary Knowledge

After framing women workers as being problematic, the first issue the supervisor directly engages with is a lack of knowledge about working in a manufacturing environment. This knowledge deficit is then extended in two directions: a lack of knowledge of common industrial tools; and a lack of relevant vocabulary. As the supervisor explains in a voiceover while women attempt to use industrial machinery on screen (Figure 6.6): "Many of them are working on their first industrial job … it's a totally unfamiliar world." To demonstrate this knowledge deficit in more detail, a scene showing a group of male workers communicating in informal-yet-professional jargon about tools and procedures is shown; the voiceover interprets this situation in relation to the purpose of the film as follows: "You see, they're not naturally familiar with mechanical principles, nor machines. Even language applying to common processes and tools are new to them."

In this sequence the language of deficit is most common, with the implicit assumption that a lack of tool knowledge and vocabulary is due not only to the lack of industrial experience but also to the female gender of the workers. This deficit is presented as something that can be overcome, however, with the supervisor claiming: "I know it takes time to make them feel at home, but it can be done." The sequence finishes with a wry exchange between the supervisor and foreman, perhaps an attempt to bring a metacognitive reflection on how this specific performance concern relates to the topic of gender more broadly:

FOREMAN: You talk like a man that knows women.
SUPERVISOR: We'll see, Joe.

3. Women Need Support in Learning New Tasks

This sequence begins back in the foreman's office as the supervisor states: "You know, women workers can be surprisingly good producers. And it helps a lot to get them off to a good start."

In doing so, the supervisor frames the situation as a human performance problem, laying the groundwork to allow the foreman to help these women *become* "good producers," with a focus on how to make complex work processes

Supervising Women Workers (1944) **71**

FIGURE 6.6 Examples of mechanical knowledge on the plant floor, with the male worker (L) shown as an expert, and (R) women workers as in need of mechanical knowledge.

more attainable and understandable for women workers, presumably with the support of male supervisors (Figure 6.7). The supervisor provides several specific suggestions for encouraging women workers to build their skills:

SUPERVISOR: When breaking in any new worker, and of course especially a woman, you've got to explain every angle of the process down to the last detail. Since most of them lack mechanical background, means you've got to study every job and subdivide it into simple operating steps.

SUPERVISOR: It's a good idea not to use trade terms, except of course when you must. And then explain in plain language exactly what these terms mean.

SUPERVISOR: And no matter what the job, he fits the tools and the work arrangements to suit the worker.

In this sequence instructional language is foregrounded, with a description of how to evaluate tasks ("explain every angle of the process down to the last detail"), build an understanding of the tacit and explicit knowledge needed to execute a task ("study every job and subdivide it into simple operating steps"), and avoid using jargon ("explain in plain language exactly what these [trade] terms mean"). At the conclusion of this instructional guidance, the supervisor moves away from more general ways of depicting job knowledge to place the focus on the learner—perhaps an unusual perspective at the time. While showing a woman carefully working with ball-bearings on screen (Figure 6.8, right), the supervisor suggests that "the tools and the work arrangements [should] suit the worker," reframing the potential skills women may bring and foreshadowing the focus of the next sequence.

4. Women Bring Valuable Skills

After framing women as problematic and lacking knowledge, this sequence reminds the audience that women do bring a skillset that may be seen as desirable, and that they may have additional complicating factors that impact their work. In particular, the value of dexterity is highlighted, alongside a closeup of a woman (clearly indicated by the presence of nail polish) drawing thread through an item attached to a small vise (Figure 6.8, left) with a voiceover of the supervisor claiming that "women workers don't mind routine and repetitive work" with particular skill in tasks that require "high finger dexterity … or [tasks with] an *unusual* sense of accuracy."

At this point the location shifts from the plant to the home of the foreman, where his wife is pictured making an apple pie—linking the workplace and the home in a way that foregrounds the unique situation of many women workers, while also expressing a common image of the 1940s housewife. Through the voiceover, this change in location is situated within a broader framing of expertise. As the narrator notes: "What's old stuff to you and me is brand new to them," he

Supervising Women Workers (1944) **73**

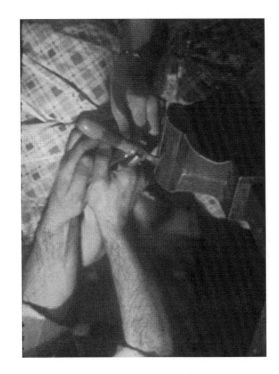

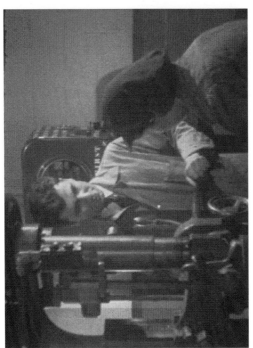

FIGURE 6.7 Women pictured on the shop floor as in need of male support.

FIGURE 6.8 Women workers completing tasks that require high dexterity.

explains that there are things outside of the factory that might be unfamiliar to men, but are very familiar to women, like baking a pie.

Following this situating of a woman in a domestic setting is perhaps the most incisive cultural critique of gendered labor and work practices offered in the film. Joe makes a connection between his wife's busy domestic life and the time off his female employees were asking for, which he had previously considered excessive. "Perhaps they have two jobs, one at work and one at home," he muses, and his wife graciously—perhaps out of social necessity of the time—allows him to think this was his own idea. This scene starts with Joe's wife, Molly, listening to him talk about his day (Figure 6.9, left):

MOLLY: Are you troubled about something?
JOE: You know, everything went alright, Molly, but you know I had seven requests for time off today. Well I guess women don't realize what it means to stick on the job.
MOLLY: Maybe they don't.
JOE: How was your day?
MOLLY: Pretty quiet. I did the washing this morning, cleaned the house, took Junior to the dentist. Did the shopping; I put up sixteen jars of jam this afternoon. Then I went to work on Junior's clothes. Joe, I'm sorry supper's late.
JOE: Nice going, old lady.
[...]
JOE: You know, Molly. I've been thinking.
MOLLY: Yes, Joe.
JOE: Maybe some of those women and girls coming into the plant—maybe they have home responsibilities too.
MOLLY: Could be.
JOE: Maybe they really do need time off. Perhaps I could rearrange their work schedule.
MOLLY: I'm sure they'd like that. So many of them have two jobs, Joe. One in the home, one in the plant.
JOE: Gee, I'm glad I thought of that!
MOLLY: Yes, dear.

In this exchange, the hidden domestic labor expected of women at the time—and even in the present day—is exposed and used to justify different ways of assessing loyalty, what it means to "stick on the job," and provide additional flexibility to workers based on other factors beyond their technical capabilities. While raising the issue of gendered work practices and responsibilities, this scene also sardonically addresses the privilege ascribed to cisgender males at the time, with Joe claiming credit for the epiphany that Molly had framed for him (Figure 6.9, right).

76 Colin M. Gray

FIGURE 6.9 (L) A depiction of domestic work by Joe's wife, Molly. (R) Molly comforts Joe as he comes to the realization that women work in two jobs.

5. Women Are Jealous and Principles Are Needed to Guide Interactions

Following on from the cut-scene to a domestic context, in this sequence Joe and the supervisor are back in the office. Joe is holding a printed manual, which is used as a prop to dig more deeply into what is purported to be fundamental knowledge about women. Joe seems to struggle with the application of some of the information contained in this manual, and hands it to the supervisor, who then leafs through it and begins by quoting some of its contents:

SUPERVISOR: [quoting from manual] "Women are individualistic by nature and are apt to make a personal application of any action, rule, or regulation."
JOE: You're telling me.
SUPERVISOR: [quoting from manual] "The supervisor should scrupulously avoid spending too much time with any individual woman worker, holding everyone to the same standards of performance and avoiding any appearance of favoritism."
JOE: That's a neat trick, if you can do it.
SUPERVISOR: Well, Joe, this all boils down to four things to remember:

1. Don't mix pleasure with business.
2. Women can be awfully jealous of each other.
3. Avoid undue familiarity.
4. Women are more sensitive than men.

These claims about women workers are expressed in totalizing language, with two "principles" addressed directly to the foreman ("don't mix pleasure with business" and "avoid undue familiarity") and two "principles" making claims about women regardless of context ("women can be awfully jealous of each other" and "women are more sensitive than men"). This set of principles is used to frame the remainder of the film, and points directly towards the next sequence where aspects of these principles are investigated in more detail.

6. Women React Emotionally When Criticized

These principles are activated as Joe retells a story of an experience one of his workers had with a woman worker on the factory floor. This experience is shown through a cut to a scene from the factory floor, where a worker (Mary) is operating a drill press without a proper cap to protect her long hair from being caught in the equipment. As the male supervisor on the floor confronts her (Figure 6.10, left), Mary's immediate reaction is emotional in support of the primary narrative: "Well, why pick on me; the other girls aren't wearing their caps." The male supervisor then directs Mary's attention to the rulebook which states the need to wear safety caps, after which Mary silently acquiesces, putting on her cap (Figure 6.10, right).

78 Colin M. Gray

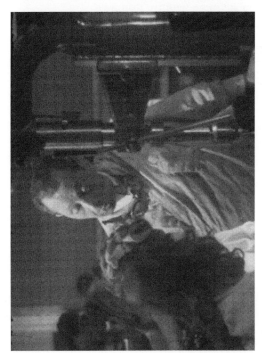

FIGURE 6.10 (L) A male supervisor confronting a worker for not wearing a cap, and (R) the worker responding to the supervisor.

In the debrief of this experience back in the office, Joe assesses this worker's reaction as follows: "they give you an argument, and a crazy one at that." To describe this experience from a gendered perspective, the supervisor then comes to the conclusion that a male worker would be more reasonable and individualistic: "the man probably would have kept the argument about himself and not trapped the foreman the way she did." This "trapping" is then elaborated upon by the supervisor as "an old stunt": "You go after a women worker on one point, and she switches the issue."

SUPERVISOR: If she had been a man, he wouldn't have laid down a safety rule so arbitrarily. You know, Joe, you've got to tell them the why of every rule—particularly women. Now suppose he had handled it in this way: [scene cuts to shop floor]
FOREMAN: Mary, your hair was just about two inches away from this drill chuck. And that's why we ask you to wear a cap, so that your hair don't get caught.
MARY: Well, gee. [stammering]
FOREMAN: You see, rules are here to protect you and the other girls working around you.
MARY: Well gee, I saw some of the other girls, and they weren't wearing any caps.
FOREMAN: That's right, but they're not working with machines. They just sit at a bench and assemble things. Nothing dangerous to them or the people nearby.
MARY: You know, I never thought of it that way before.
FOREMAN: You have your cap with you, haven't you?
MARY: Yeah. [laughs] Okay, I get it.

This sequence focuses primarily on the purported sensitivity and seeming irrationality of women from a male perspective, rather than addressing any of the four principles from the previous sequence at length. Near the end of this sequence these behaviors are linked to what the supervisor states is the role of the "eternal feminine"—a gender-essentialist term that conveniently framed the lack of gender equality in the early 1900s. In extending this notion further, the supervisor advises Joe to "watch the little things," noting that the "eternal feminine is very conscious of them." This construction of gendered expectations as the film begins to close seems to point towards an ongoing fracture in working relations due to the presumed inherent stability in both male and female worker profiles, and the notion that the "eternal feminine" is not something that has the potential to impact or change male-dominated work practices, but is rather something to "contend with."

7. Situations Should be Dealt with Quickly

In the closing sequence of the film, the supervisor advises that situations such as those addressed in this film should be dealt with quickly or they may escalate. This

80 Colin M. Gray

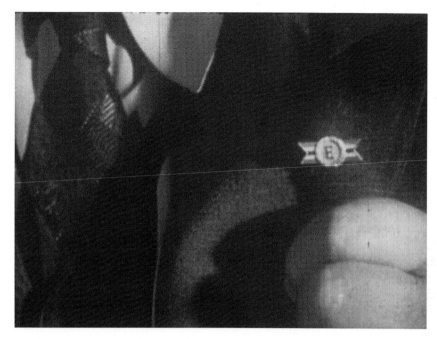

FIGURE 6.11 The supervisor points to a pin on his lapel known as the Army-Navy E Award. This award was an indication of "Excellence in Production" of war equipment, won by only 5 percent of all companies that produced equipment for the war ("Army-Navy E Award", n.d.).

advice is given in a way that suggests it does apply both to men and to women, and is linked directly to success in the war effort: "Remember, Joe; we couldn't have won this [pointing to a VE pin on his lapel] without the help of the women in this plant" (Figure 6.11).

Training and Human Performance Support in the Film

In this short training film, we gain access to early perceptions of human performance support, ways of articulating educational goals through audiovisual means, and the effort of these filmmakers to address large societal changes in relation to their training goals. In this concluding section I will describe the intersection among audiovisual qualities, training and human performance qualities, and the social milieu the designers used to shape the dominant themes of the film.

Demonstration through Drama vs. Direct Instruction

This is a training film, but its narrative mode is familiar both from drama and from other instructional films of the day. An older and wiser character—apparent both in visible age and organizational status—guides a younger one with less experience; in this case, Joe is positioned as having less experience supervising women in the workforce.

The supervisor character dispensing wisdom uses a tone by turns avuncular, conspiratorial, and pragmatic. Due to the dim lighting of the office in which these scenes are filmed, he may even appear somewhat creepy, such as when he discusses "the eternal feminine" in an oddly personal tone at the conclusion of the film. Joe, the younger and presumably less wise counterpart of the supervisor, is somewhat less emotive. However, he listens to his advisor attentively, and is expressive when he has an insight (offered by his wife) later in the film. In these interactions between Joe and his supervisor, a rhythm generated by the scenes first of the manager and his boss in an office setting and scenes from out on the shop floor or in the worker's home generates a sense of familiarity with the subject matter, and a sense of closeness to Joe's character. This seems to embody Kerkow's stated goals as a film director in a publication two years after this film was produced, where he explained: "We tried quite definitely to make the listener feel as if a friend were sitting next to him explaining what is happening on the screen." Ultimately, these interactions have a felt personal quality that gives the experience of the film an emotional character it would not have if it were staged as a plain lecture.

Production Design

The look of the film also follows a dramatic mode, not quite noir—a style in its early heyday at this time that valued rich contrast in lighting and attention to form alongside a more cynical and pessimistic view of reality—but not comparatively bright like a western of the time. There are relatively few recognizable production sets beyond what might already be accessible in the plant, with only the office scenes and a scene in a home setting to buffer the B-roll of plant interactions. The effect given is a complete separation between the voice of the supervisor and foreman and the work that happens "on the ground" on the plant floor, with only voiceovers to cut between the instructional mode (in the office) and the implementation mode (on the plant floor). It is also interesting to note that only one instructional example is placed in context—the instance of the woman unsure of why she needed to wear a cap in Sequence 6—with all other film of the plant floor serving to supplement the main dialogue, rather than serve as a point of interest in its own right. These aspects of the production design could be intentional decisions to impact the instructional quality of the film, but may just as easily have been a function of the lower budget allocated to government films versus Hollywood productions, which would have impacted the lack of use of set decoration, payment of extras to fill in scenes, and the use of dark lighting to obscure minimal sets where possible.

Perspectives on Human Performance Technology

The content of the film provides vivid stereotypes of attitudes and language apparently acceptable at the time but likely repugnant to most in the current day. However, beyond the pervasive language of sexism, a key principle of human performance technology is demonstrated. Namely that multiple factors contribute to effective performance in the workplace (Bichelmeyer & Horvitz, 1999), many of which exist beyond traditional notions of "training" or "education." Despite the director and writer's positioning the supervision of these women—repeatedly called "girls"—as a *problem*, an underlying awareness is evident that if these women do not know the specialized jargon of the workplace or functions of the tools they are expected to use they will not be able to do their jobs, and that it is the responsibility of the organization to provide knowledge and skill to their workers. While much of this awareness is cast in primarily or solely gendered terms through tropes such as "women are emotional" or "women are jealous," there are several moments where a genuine understanding of how to translate complex skills and performances to be accessible to new workers is effectively communicated. Straightforward approaches such as "study every job and subdivide it into simple operating steps" or "explain in plain language what terms mean"—now commonplace in instructional design practice—are used effectively to encourage better onboarding practices, while perhaps also occluding the fact that these same approaches are also relevant for male members of the workforce. Beyond these forms of instructional awareness, a social barrier to performance is also given a nod when the supervisor realizes that his female workers have intrusive demands on their time owing to domestic responsibilities falling differently on them compared to their male counterparts. While this barrier does not rise to the level of social critique, the knowing glance of the housewife and the growing awareness of the foreman of the factors that may influence the capability and capacity of the workforce do point towards a larger potential for engaging human potential.

Design Concerns

This film was one of many produced in the 1940s and 1950s, and many of these films are now available online in various collections. However, given the uniquely targeted subject matter of the film I have analyzed here, I wish to provide some additional words of caution that point critically towards the diversity of characters represented, the social norms they are positioned to reproduce or extend, and the ways in which training films such as this are complicit in this reproduction of societal norms.

Given the age of this film, it is very easy to lampoon the characters and messaging, and this makes the films difficult to take seriously when values have (purportedly) changed markedly since they were created, but yet are so clearly communicated by them. On the one hand, it is hard to fault a designer for being of his time, but it is possible to view this film and others as embodying the oppressive viewpoints of a dominant and unreflective social group. As pointed out in my previous work, identifying and becoming critical of these viewpoints and societal norms is as much the role of the instructional designer as is making visible the opportunity for learning (Gray & Boling, 2016). It is clear in this film that the treatment of female characters is complex and unresolved; women are presented as subservient, yet rebellious; jealous and emotional, yet bringing valuable skills; without recognizable technical skills, yet mysterious and terrifying. These tropes draw upon perceptions of women that dominated in the 1940s, and in some ways continue to the present day.

Instructional films like this one strongly suggest a belief in the efficacy of media-based instruction and of narrative to convey concepts and principles. It is doubtful that this belief is fully supported by this film, in which the key ideas are dependent on a shared cultural perspective and orientation on the part of the developers and the audience. Use of the dramatic format requires this because some key information is communicated through facial expression and body language (as with the female worker who resists following the rules or the foreman who gives a knowing grin), visual symbol (the *Army-Navy E Award* button), and the use of an expression such as "the eternal feminine." However, despite the dramatic format of the film, the scenes rely on thinly drawn characters who serve largely to state explanatory content and sometimes to illustrate examples through very short scenes, or vignettes, that do not build or develop. In other words, whatever power drama and production value might lend to the instruction is watered down, making the presumed value of film as the medium for this instruction questionable.

Acknowledgments

I gratefully acknowledge the efforts of the Indiana University Libraries Moving Images Archive, and their permission to reproduce still images from *Supervising Women Workers*. In addition, I express my thanks to Elizabeth Boling and Tiffany Roman for their insights on early drafts of this chapter, along with Barb Bichelmeyer who inspired the study of the IU film archive.

References

About the IU Audio-Visual Center. (n.d.). Indiana University Libraries Moving Image Archive. Retrieved May 5, 2020 from https://collections.libraries.indiana.edu/IULMIA/about-iuavc.

Army-Navy E Award. (n.d.). Naval history and heritage command. Retrieved May 5, 2020 from www.history.navy.mil/research/library/online-reading-room/title-list-alphabetically/a/army-navy-e-award.html.

Bertin, A. (12/2019). Attack of the cardboard box: A story of intracollegiate collaboration between the Indiana University Libraries Moving Image Archive and University

Archives—Indiana University Libraries Moving Image Archive. *Indiana University Libraries Moving Image Archives.* https://blogs.libraries.indiana.edu/filmarch/2019/12/10/attack-of-the-cardboard-box-a-story-of-inner-collegiate-collaboration-between-the-indiana-university-moving-image-archive-and-university-archives/.

Bichelmeyer, B. A., & Horvitz, B. S. (1999). Comprehensive performance evaluation: Using logic models to develop a theory-based approach for evaluation of human performance technology interventions. In J. Pershing (Ed.), *Handbook of Human Performance Technology* (pp. 1165–1189). San Francisco, CA: Jossey-Bass Pfeiffer.

Division of Visual Aids for War Training. (n.d.). United States Office of Education. SNAC (Social Networks and Archival Context). Retrieved May 5, 2020 from http://n2t.net/ark:/99166/w6z37r26.

Gray, C. M., & Boling, E. (2016). Inscribing ethics and values in designs for learning: A problematic. *Educational Technology Research and Development: ETR & D, 64*(5), 969–1001. https://doi.org/10.1007/s11423-016-9478-x.

Molenda, M., Appelman, R., & Boling, E. (2020). IST's Historical Mission: Helping People Learn through Multi-sensory Experiences. Presentation at IST Conference 2020.

Problems in Supervision. (n.d.). *World War II propaganda films and IU.* Indiana University Libraries Moving Image Archive. Retrieved May 5, 2020 from https://collections.libraries.indiana.edu/IULMIA/exhibits/show/world-war-ii-propaganda-films/problems-in-supervision.

Reiser, R. A. (2001). A history of instructional design and technology: Part I: A history of instructional media. *Educational Technology Research and Development: ETR & D, 49*(1), 53. https://doi.org/10.1007/BF02504506.

Saettler, P. (2004). *The evolution of American educational technology.* Charlotte, NC: Information Age Publishing.

Supervising Women Workers. (n.d.). Media Collections Online. Retrieved May 5, 2020 from http://purl.dlib.indiana.edu/iudl/media/653702t657.

U.S. Congress Senate. (1940). Committee on Education and Labor. *Division of Aviation Education. Hearing Before a Subcommittee ... on S. 4041.... July 9, 1940. (76th Cong. 3rd Sess.).* https://play.google.com/store/books/details?id=Et0aiOsOGdkC.

7

THE SKINNERIAN TEACHING MACHINE (1953–1968)

Jason K. McDonald

This design case describes B. F. Skinner's teaching machine, an educational technology developed in the mid-twentieth century, commonly viewed as a precursor to later innovations such as computer-based instruction (Niemiec & Walberg, 1989) and eLearning (McDonald et al., 2005). The value of this case is not only as historical precedent, however. Although it does provide insight into the design of later approaches, Skinner's device was only one antecedent of modern educational technologies, and, in fact, was not even the first mechanical apparatus that could be referred to as a teaching machine (Benjamin Jr., 1988). An additional benefit of the case, then, is found by examining how Skinner made design decisions to intentionally apply his behavioral theory of operant conditioning in the development of his machine. Even today, despite how Skinner and his behaviorist approaches have fallen out of favor, his work is still an important illustration of how a psychological theory has been operationalized for practical implementation in a specific technology.

Background

Recognized as the most eminent psychologist of the twentieth century (Haggbloom et al., 2002), B. F. Skinner is largely remembered as the foremost advocate of the theory of operant conditioning. For a time a leading theory purporting to explain a wide range of human behaviors—including learning—operant conditioning's success lay both in its descriptive components, that attempted to show how the future behavior of animals changes as they experience the consequences of past behavior, as well as its prescriptions about how this natural process could be harnessed to shape a behavior towards an intended end (for detailed explanations of operant conditioning, including how it differs from other forms of behaviorism, see McSweeney & Murphy, 2014). In Skinner's view (as well as that of behaviorists generally), the conditioning process was ultimately responsible for the complex activities and interactions typically explained by theories in the other human sciences, not only in psychology but also in fields such as economics, political science, sociology, and, relevant for this case, education (Skinner, 1963). From this perspective, learning is not the result of some invisible mental process, but, rather, is due to a person (or other animal) experiencing the right kind of consequences in the environment (called reinforcers) that results in a type of observable response that has historically been called knowledge or understanding (Skinner, 1954).

But while he was deeply committed to the theoretical and experimental work that led to his explanations for human behavior, Skinner was no ivory tower academic. He was not content to only research the conditioning process, and throughout his career drove his theories towards practical application, believing that the proper role of psychology was to make a tangible impact on the quality of life available to people everywhere (Skinner, 1953). In addition, Skinner was an inventor, and often created his own mechanisms to first test his theories and later translate them into serviceable forms (Ferster, 2014). This included exploring ways in which the conditioning process could be applied to classroom education.

While there were likely many antecedents leading to Skinner's interest in education, including a general concern in mid-twentieth-century America about the state of the educational system (Saettler, 1990), in his autobiography he pointed to a personal reason. He recalled an instance in late 1953 when he observed a class in which one of his daughters was a student:

> I sat in the rear of [my daughter] Debbie's fourth-grade arithmetic class. The students were at their desks solving a problem written on the blackboard. The teacher walked up and down the aisles, looking at their work, pointing to a mistake here and there. A few students soon finished and were impatiently idle. Others, with growing frustration, strained. Eventually the papers were collected to be taken home, graded, and returned the next day.
>
> *(Skinner, 1983, p. 64)*

As Skinner watched, he became frustrated with how inconsistent the students' experience was with the principles of conditioning:

> Possibly through no fault of her own, the teacher was violating two fundamental principles: the students were not being told at once whether their work was right or wrong (a corrected paper seen twenty-four hours later could not act as a reinforcer), and they were all moving at the same pace regardless of preparation or ability.
>
> *(p. 64)*

As he concluded his account, Skinner compared this experience to his experimental work:

> But how could a teacher reinforce the behavior of each of twenty or thirty students at the right time and on the material for which he or she was just then ready? I had solved a similar problem in the laboratory. When I was a graduate student, almost all animal psychologists watched their animals and recorded their behavior by hand. They could only make a few observations, many of them not too reliable. Mechanization had made a great difference. Charlie Ferster [a fellow researcher] and I could have done only a small fraction of our work [in operant conditioning] if we had not used instruments.
>
> *(pp. 64–65)*

Based on what he had learned in his lab, then, Skinner proceeded to design a machine that would allow students to learn in a manner consistent with the principles of operant conditioning.

While the scope of this case is limited to exploring Skinner's designs, it is useful to note that using machines for educational purposes was not without precedent. Although the actual phrase "teaching machine" does not appear to have entered into widespread usage until Skinner's work became popularized, there were clearly other educational technologies available before his time, including notable examples like radio or motion picture. However, both Skinner and many of his contemporaries did not consider these to actually be teaching machines because while they were aids for learning they were not seen as carrying out the most essential functions of a teacher (Benjamin Jr., 1988). Other antecedents, in contrast, included features that Benjamin noted were commonly identified as essential in mid-twentieth-century definitions of true teaching devices: "a teaching machine is an automatic or self-controlling device that (a) presents a unit of information ... (b) provides some means for the learner to respond to the information, and (c) provides feedback about the correctness of the learner's responses" (p. 704). The most widely known precedent that met this definition was a machine developed by Sidney Pressey in the 1920s that could be used to both test students on material they learned as well as to teach them new material (Pressey, 1960). Skinner (1983) later claimed, however, that he was unaware of Pressey's work before he began his own, and that his machine was primarily based on what he had learned in his laboratory research about using mechanical devices as tools to apply the conditioning process.

The Design of Skinnerian Teaching Machines

Skinner's first attempts to design a teaching machine were, by his own account, "primitive" (Skinner, 1983, p. 65). But they were functional and demonstrated his core techniques. Within a few days of his experience in his daughter's class he created his first prototypes to teach simple math:

> Problems in arithmetic were printed on cards. The student placed a card in the machine and composed a two-digit answer along one side by moving two levers. If the answer was right, a light appeared in a hole in the card. In a second model, the student moved sliders bearing the figures 0 through 9, a figure on each slider appearing through a hole in the card. If a composed answer was correct, lights appeared in a corresponding row of holes when a level was pressed. (To make sure that the student would not move the sliders to search for the right answer, pressing the level locked them in place.)
>
> *(p. 65)*

Little other detail is available about the physical design of Skinner's first prototypes. But a few months after designing them, in early 1954, he described a later iteration of his machine as being "about the size of a small record player,"

FIGURE 7.1 Skinner's first teaching machine. Students manipulated the machine by moving sliders to choose a response, then turning a dial to lock in their response.

Source: Reprinted from "Programmed Instruction Revisited", by Skinner, B. F. (1986). *The Phi Delta Kappan, 68*(2), 104.

with a "top surface [that included] a window" through which students could see instructional materials "printed on a paper tape." The sliders remained for students to choose the numbers that would solve the problem, at which point they turned a knob that punched their answer into the paper. If correct, "the knob turns freely and can be made to ring a bell or provide some other conditioned reinforcement.... A further turn of the knob engages a clutch which moves the next problem into place." But if incorrect the knob would not move, and students were required to try again (Skinner, 1954, p. 95). A photograph of this teaching machine, the first that Skinner demonstrated publicly, is found in Figure 7.1.

Additional teaching machines followed. In the same presentation where he described his arithmetic machine, Skinner referred to a variation that used sliders to choose letters instead of numbers, to teach spelling and verbal reasoning (Skinner, 1954). He also designed a machine for young children that taught shapes, colors, and the relationship between pictures and simple words (see Figure 7.2). Students would match what they saw in a top frame with options

FIGURE 7.2 A Skinnerian machine to teach the matching of shapes or patterns. Students were prompted to press a picture, then press a second picture that corresponded in some way to the first picture.

Source: Reprinted from *The Technology of Teaching*, by Skinner, B. F. (1968). New York: Meredith Corporation, p. 75.

presented in a lower frame, making their selections by touch. Versions of this machine also included audio material for students to compare with visual material (Skinner, 1965b). Whereas his previous machines were purely mechanical devices, working solely through manual manipulation of dials, sliders, and knobs, this machine apparently included some electrical components, since Skinner described how each touch would close a circuit to record the student's response (Skinner, 1961).

While these teaching machines accommodated a range of media representations—pictorial, aural, and visual-verbal—they limited students' input options to either the manipulation of sliders and dials, or touch. To broaden the range of input possibilities, in the later 1950s Skinner designed a machine that allowed students to write their response to a prepared prompt. In the terminology of the teaching machine movement, these prompts were called frames, presumably because of how the window through which students viewed the prompt framed the material (see Stack, 1973). After viewing a frame and writing their response, students used a lever to move from the initial frame to another that provided the solution (both being printed on a rotating disk). Moving the lever also advanced the paper tape on which they wrote so that their response was under a plastic pane, to prevent them from changing their answer. Students then compared their answer to the solution, and, if their response was correct, they slid the lever in another direction to punch a hole in their paper to record that the material on the frame had been mastered. The device continued on a loop, skipping the frames that had been marked correct, until the entire disk had been learned (Skinner, 1958, 1986; see Figures 7.3 to 7.5). As Skinner designed them, frames were very small, sometimes asking students to write only one or two letters. Table 7.1 illustrates the intended progression through a sample set of frames Skinner wrote, showing how each frame attempted to solicit a certain kind of answer that was meant to culminate in students' developing the ability to respond without guidance.

After experimenting with a number of designs, Skinner began work to commercialize his teaching machine. To provide them to schools as quickly as possible he relied on connections available through Harvard (the university at which he was employed) to contact an employee of IBM. Executives at IBM, in turn, were persuaded enough by Skinner's vision that they contracted with him to create models that could be mass produced (Skinner, 1983). Figure 7.6 illustrates one of these models. This iteration, however, included sliders for both numbers and letters, allowing it to serve a dual purpose of teaching mathematics as well as spelling or other material that required the construction of a verbal response. It also included a larger, raised display to increase viewability. Concurrent to his work at IBM, Skinner patented his first teaching machine design in 1955 (Skinner, 1955), then continued to patent other designs throughout the 1950s and 1960s (e.g., Skinner, 1957, 1965a), working with additional corporations like Rheem Manufacturing and Meredith Publishing to make machines available to the public.

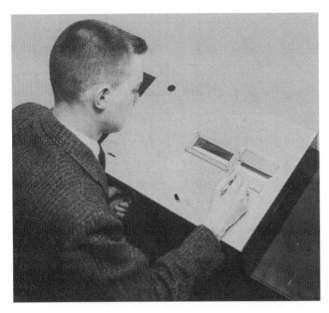

FIGURE 7.3 A student using a constructed response teaching machine. Student wrote their responses to a prompt, then advanced the machine to compare their response to the correct answer.

Source: Reprinted from "Programmed Instruction Revisited", by Skinner, B. F. (1986). *The Phi Delta Kappan, 68*(2), 107.

FIGURE 7.4 The exterior of a Skinnerian teaching machine that allowed for constructed responses. This is the same machine described in Figure 7.3.

Source: © User: Silly rabbit/Wikimedia Commons/CC-BY-3.0.

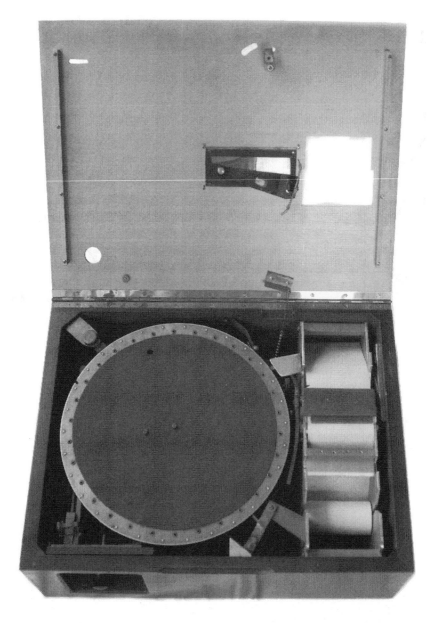

FIGURE 7.5 The interior of a Skinnerian teaching machine that allowed for constructed responses. This is the same machine described in Figure 7.3.

Source: © User: Silly rabbit/Wikimedia Commons/CC-BY-3.0.

TABLE 7.1 Example frames from a constructed response teaching machine, along with the intended response. Students wrote their response on a paper tape located next to the frame, advanced the frame to uncover the desired solution, then compared their response to the correct answer.

Frame	Intended response
Manufacture means to make or build. *Chair factories manufacture chairs.* Copy the word here: _ _ _ _ _ _ _ _ _ _	M A N U F A C T U R E
Part of the word is like part of the word **factory**. Both parts come from an old word meaning *make* or *build*. m a n u _ _ _ _ u r e	F A C T
Part of the word is like part of the word **manual**. Both parts come from an old word for *hand*. Many things used to be made by hand. _ _ _ _ facture	M A N U
The same letter goes in both spaces: m _ n u f _ c t u r e	A A
The same letter goes in both spaces: m a n _ f a c t _ r e	U U
Chair factories _ _ _ _ _ _ _ _ _ _ _ _ **chairs**.	M A N U F A C T U R E

Source: adapted from Skinner, 1958, p. 972.

FIGURE 7.6 A student using a commercialized version of Skinner's teaching machine, manufactured by IBM. Students manipulated the machine using sliders and dials, similar to that in the machine described in Figure 7.1.

Source: Reprinted from "Programmed Instruction Revisited", by Skinner, B. F. (1986). *The Phi Delta Kappan, 68*(2), 106.

Operant Conditioning and the Design of Skinnerian Teaching Machines

Skinner's reports often provided details that indicated how his teaching machine designs were influenced by the principles of operant conditioning. Before summarizing some of these, I note that while numerous criticisms have been levied against Skinner's assumptions, techniques, and results (e.g., McDonald et al., 2005; Schnaitter, 1999; Taylor, 1964; Virués-Ortega, 2006), it is not my purpose to review those here; analyzing why operant conditioning fell out of favor is beyond the scope of a design case. So while I acknowledge that teaching machines are not currently considered an effective educational technology, and, likewise, that operant conditioning is generally not considered a defensible learning theory, I present Skinner's explanations without judgement in an attempt to better understand his design decision-making. The principles of conditioning that Skinner reported as the basis of his designs, along with features of his teaching machine that applied these principles, are shown in Table 7.2. Detailed explanations of each are found throughout this and the following section.

One frequently recurring principle Skinner discussed was that of immediate, positive reinforcement (or a desirable consequence an animal or person experienced for a behavior, resulting in an increased likelihood that the same behavior would be exhibited again). Beginning with his first teaching machine

TABLE 7.2 Principles of operant conditioning and design decisions they informed

Conditioning principle	Design decisions
Reinforcement—an immediate, desirable consequence for displaying the correct behavior	Small frames
	Small responses
	Pleasant rewards like ringing a bell, given immediately upon answering correctly
	The contentment that followed from self-pacing
	Easy steps—minimize/eliminate wrong responses
Shaping—reinforcing simple behaviors that approximate a desired outcome, then reinforcing those until they incrementally build into more complex behavioral structures	Small frames
	Begin with existing behaviors
	Incremental progression
	Mechanization (machines are required)
	Hiding future frames until current frames have been attempted
	Carefully arranged material
	Linear presentation of material
	Constructed responses, not multiple-choice
Vanishing—incrementally removing external supports until a terminal behavior could be exhibited independently	Remove letters, words, or other prompting details from a frame and have students fill-in-the-blank

publication (entitled *The Science of Learning and the Art of Teaching*), Skinner devoted considerable space to describing how his invention facilitated the kinds of reinforcers he thought were important for learning (Skinner, 1954). He first argued that effective learning is the result of experiencing large numbers of reinforcers. He then observed how:

> The most serious criticism of the current classroom is the relative infrequency of reinforcement. Since the pupil is usually dependent upon the teacher for being right, and since many pupils are usually dependent on the same teacher, the total number of contingencies which may be arranged during, say, the first four years [of school], is of the order of only a few thousand.
>
> *(p. 91)*

But Skinner estimated that for an introductory subject, such as the mathematics his first machine was designed to teach, somewhere between 25,000 and 50,000 reinforcers were required to learn, covering not only basic math facts but "the alternative forms in which each item may be stated," along with "hundreds of responses" to teach more advanced concepts, practical tips for solving problems, and the drawing together of discrete behaviors into a "whole mathematical repertoire" (p. 92).

Skinner then described specific features of his machine that allowed for these large numbers of reinforcements to be achieved (Skinner, 1954). First, each frame presented only one, very small mathematical detail, eliciting a similarly small, targeted student response. By tying some kind of positive consequence to each response (such as the ringing of a bell), Skinner presumed that students working the teaching machine at a reasonable rate would be reinforced multiple times a minute, rather than only receiving occasional and sporadic reinforcement from their teachers. Also, the bell or other reinforcer immediately informed students of the accuracy of their response; they did not have to wait minutes or hours for a teacher to evaluate their answers for them. In addition, since students used the machine individually, Skinner believed that the fact that they were able to work at a pace they were comfortable with would provide further reinforcement. Finally, Skinner also speculated that even "the mere manipulation of the device will probably be reinforcing enough to keep the average pupil at work for a suitable period each day" (p. 95). In a later publication, Skinner calculated that instead of the few thousand reinforcements students received over the entire length of their schooling (a number, he reminded, that was much too small for even one subject, let alone cumulatively for every content area), his teaching machines could provide the proper number of reinforcers in as little as 15 minutes a day per subject (Skinner, 1958).

Closely connected to Skinner's descriptions of reinforcement were his explanations of how teaching machines shaped students' behavior. Shaping was a conditioning technique that began with the simple, and often random, behaviors that an animal exhibited. By reinforcing these behaviors when they even approximated the first step of a desirable outcome, the animal would exhibit them more frequently. Then, when they spontaneously exhibited the next step they received another reinforcement, and so on until the desired terminal behavior was achieved. For instance, when Skinner trained pigeons to turn in a circle, he first fed them a food pellet when they happened to take one step to the left. Soon this behavior was conditioned, and the pigeons were consistently stepping left, instead of the random movements typically seen in birds that had not been conditioned. Skinner would then offer another pellet when the pigeons took a second step, and after a time this two-step cycle also became a conditioned behavior. This pattern was repeated until the pigeons consistently turned an entire circle, or even two and three circles, before being offered food (Skinner, 1948).

Skinner believed his teaching machines were designed to shape students' behavior in a similar manner (Skinner, 1954, 1958, 1968a). Instruction began by reinforcing behaviors students could already exhibit, such as copying a word letter-for-letter when they were asked to do so. Then, by presenting frames that approximated a desired terminal behavior, the students were instructed to complete this task until they exhibited it consistently. For example, if the end goal was to spell a word from memory, after the student copied the word the next frame might remove a letter and ask them to fill-in-the-blank (a process called vanishing). Additional letters were removed in subsequent frames, until at some point the student could print the entire word without any written prompt. In Skinner's view this was an additional value of each frame including only one, very targeted detail (Skinner, 1958). In fact, he was skeptical that a frame could ever be considered too easy, because every right response was another positive reinforcer, and so in that sense the smaller the steps (and the easier it was for students to complete each step), the more effective the frame would be, while also having the benefit of eliminating the negative conditioning effects that might accompany fear of failure (Skinner, 1958). Even though each frame was only an incremental change, over time the cumulative effect of these changes could produce complex actions, not limited to single words but eventually extending to the recitation of long poems, or speaking another language (Skinner, 1961).

Skinner also made an interesting argument for the necessity of using a machine itself to teach, by referring to its role in operationalizing the conditioning process. In response to people who asked, "cannot the results of laboratory research on learning be used in education without machines?" (Skinner, 1958, p. 976), Skinner responded that while certainly any educational strategy or technology could be improved by aligning it as much as possible with the principles of conditioning, to really take advantage of what conditioning offered, "some sort of device is necessary" (p. 976). He further asserted that while some advocates might suggest that the principles of conditioning were independent of any particular manifestation, and so could just as easily be implemented in a book or other form, doing so would almost certainly violate some important step in the process. He illustrated by describing how it would be difficult to design a book so that "one frame [would not reveal] the response to another" (p. 976), which would interfere with both shaping and reinforcement. At another time he argued that teachers or books could not fully implement conditioning "because many contingencies [in conditioning] are too subtle and precise to be arranged without instrumental help" (Skinner, 1961, p. 380). So, somewhat in contrast to common arguments that technology is merely a vehicle that offers no independent value for learning (e.g., Clark, 1994), Skinner thought the actual technology of the teaching machine was more than a convenience that perhaps made learning more efficient but was not required to make it effective. While he did not think "elaborate instrumentation" was required (Skinner, 1968a, p. 405), he continually asserted that some form of mechanized apparatus was, for all practical purposes, a necessity to apply the conditioning process successfully. Other interventions—human or otherwise—were just not able to successfully "arrange many of the contingencies of reinforcement which expedite learning" (Skinner, 1965b, p. 430; see also Skinner, 1968a).

Comparisons to Other Educational Technologies

Skinner's critiques of other educational technologies reveal alternative ways he thought his design decisions properly applied operant conditioning in his version of the teaching machine. His most basic critique was that most educational technologies were "simply devices which mechanize functions once served by human teachers," and actually contributed little or nothing to human learning (Skinner, 1965b, p. 427). To illustrate, Skinner described a number of common technologies that, while perhaps having some place in education, were not teaching machines in the sense of actually controlling learning (as was the result when conditioning was applied). Testing machines, for instance, could be a convenient timesaver during the assessment process, but despite claims that "a student learned something when told whether his answers are right or wrong" (p. 427), Skinner did not view such a possibility as a true application of operant conditioning: "holding a student responsible for assigned material is not teaching, even though it is a large part of modern school and university practice. It is simply a way of inducing the student to learn without being taught" (pp. 427–428). Skinner had similar criticisms of technologies "designed primarily to attract and hold attention" (p. 428), such as television. He concluded that these were activities "which should never have been served by teachers in the first place, and mechanizing them is small gain" (p. 428). In contrast, a teaching machine, in Skinner's view, must arrange "contingencies ... favorable to the shaping and maintaining of behavior" (Skinner, 1968a, p. 406). This implied more than only presenting information or even requiring the student to interact with learning material in some way. Rather, properly applying conditioning demanded that the teaching machine also arrange the learning material, and require students to respond, in manners that activated processes that properly reinforced the desired behavioral change.

Skinner also critiqued educational approaches he thought appealed to mistaken understandings of operant conditioning. He was highly critical, for example, of a common analogy drawn between conditioning and Socratic teaching (e.g., instructing students through a series of leading questions). He called the Socratic method, in fact, "one of the great frauds in the history of education" (Skinner, 1965b, p. 428). A major problem with Socratic approaches, in Skinner's view, was that they only asked students to respond to questions being asked, but did not apply techniques such as vanishing, where prompting statements are incrementally removed in a process of shaping so that students become more independent in displaying the proper responses on their own (Skinner, 1968a). Skinner was similarly critical of teaching machines that only exposed students to material multiple times, or only required them to practice. Such exposure or practice was not effective for its own sake, Skinner thought, and only worked if it was informed by principles such as reinforcement and shaping (Skinner, 1965b). Teaching machines, however, did properly reinforce, shape, and vanish according to schedules determined by rigorous analysis, and so could be relied on to apply conditioning in a complete manner (Skinner, 1958).

Skinner also argued against a competing form of teaching machine that applied a technique known as branching (also called intrinsic programming). In the terminology of the time, Skinner's machines became known as "linear" because each student completed the same material in the same sequence: "whether the answer given at any particular step is right or wrong, the *next* item of information to which the student is 'exposed' is normally the same" (Goodman, 1962, p. 7, emphasis in original). Many researchers believed this technique was, at best, inefficient because it could waste students' time on material they may have already mastered. But other observers also believed linear machines could be ineffective, since if students made an error at some point during instruction it could be evidence that they required additional remediation not needed by students giving the right answer. To correct this perceived deficiency, they designed a variation on the teaching machine that routed students down different paths depending on how they responded to a given frame. To make the number of paths manageable, these machines most often presented material in the form of multiple-choice questions (Crowder, 1959). An example of such a machine is found in Figure 7.7.

Skinner was dissatisfied with the branching approach for two reasons. First, he thought that unless the desired end behavior was to select or match, students should somehow construct their response (either through writing or moving dials to select an answer) rather than choose an answer from a list, as in the multiple-choice mechanisms of most branching machines. If students only selected a response, this could not be shaped into the desired end of constructing a response on their own, because selecting was not an incremental step

FIGURE 7.7 A student using a branching teaching machine. This machine functioned similar to a multiple-choice test, where students pushed a button to select an alternative in response to a given stem.

Source: Reprinted from *Programmed Learning and Teaching Machines*, by Goodman, R. (1962). London: The English Universities Press, p. 15.

along the way towards constructing (Skinner, 1961). Second, even presenting incorrect options "violated a basic principle of good [conditioning] by inducing the student to engage in erroneous behavior" (Skinner, 1961, p. 393). This was not only due to them possibly selecting a distractor but even being shown the options held the potential to inadvertently reinforce the wrong ones. He illustrated:

> Consider an item such as the following, which might be part of a course in high school physics: *As the pressure of a gas increases, volume decreases. This*

is because: *(a) the space between the molecules grows smaller; (b) the molecules are flattened; (c) etc....* Unless the student is as industrious and as ingenious as the multiple-choice programmer, it will probably not have occurred to him that molecules may be flattened as a gas is compressed.... If he chooses item (b) and is corrected by the machine, we may say that he "has learned that it is wrong," but this does not mean that the sentence will never occur to him again. And if he is unlucky enough to select the right answer first, his reading of the plausible but erroneous answer will be corrected only "by implication"—an equally vague and presumably less effective process. In either case, he may later find himself recalling that "somewhere he has read that molecules are flattened when a gas is compressed." And, of course, somewhere he has.

(pp. 393–394, emphasis in original)

The power of reinforcement was so strong, Skinner believed, that if the wrong option was conditioned, "neither the vigorous correction of wrong choices nor the confirmation of a right choice will free the student of the verbal and nonverbal associations thus generated" (p. 394).

The Student Experience of Using Teaching Machines

Most research studying the teaching machine examined their effect on student performance; generally, early experiments tended to generate positive outcomes (Schramm, 1964), with more negative results occurring as machines began to be implemented in classrooms uncontrolled by researchers (McDonald et al., 2005). Beyond these studies of student performance, and of particular interest for this case, some research was also conducted that provided insights into the student experience of using teaching machines, including how students reacted to design features that implemented conditioning principles (see Table 7.3). Reporting on a college psychology course that was taught through machines, Skinner and Holland (1960) reported that while some students thought it was "fun and challenging" (p. 171), others were bored by the ease of the material. They also reported some dissatisfaction with the linear progression of the course, wanting to go back and review frames they had previously mastered. Others seemingly experienced "anxiety" during their experience, possibly because "it was inconvenient to have to come to a special room to study," they thought some of the frames were "ambiguous," or "the machine encouraged incorrectly reporting a response as right" (p. 171).

Fine (1962) reported similar experiences from younger (K-12) students. Some students described their satisfaction with self-pacing, with one girl representatively stating, "I go as fast as I want and I don't have to worry about keeping up with somebody else" (p. 94). Another added that "the best thing" about teaching machines was "being able to work at my own speed" (p. 95). Students also

TABLE 7.3 Common student responses to Skinner's design decisions.

Conditioning principle	Design decisions	Common student responses
Reinforcement	Small frames Small responses Pleasant rewards like ringing a bell, given immediately upon answering correctly The contentment that followed from self-pacing Easy steps—minimize/eliminate wrong responses	Some reports of fun and challenge Enjoyment of self-pacing Boredom; material was too easy
Shaping	Small frames Begin with existing behaviors Incremental progression Mechanization (machines are required) Hiding future frames until current frames have been mastered Carefully arranged material Linear presentation of material Constructed responses, not multiple-choice	Desire to review material already mastered Material could be ambiguous or encourage reporting incorrect answers as right
Vanishing	Remove letters, words, or other prompting details from a frame and have students fill-in-the-blank	Desire to do more than only provide information in response to vanishing prompts

liked the immediate, positive reinforcement they received: "you find out your mistakes right away, so you can correct them yourself.... Everybody wants to know whether he's done right or wrong. When I get the right answer, it makes me feel good" (p. 94). Others, however, described more challenging experiences. One student told Fine that it was difficult "not being able to go back and review what you've done.... I guess we're supposed to remember everything we've read" (p. 95). This student also noted that there was more to teaching than asking students to respond to prompts and then vanishing those cues: "there are still some subjects where I'd want a teacher.... Mostly social studies, where there's a lot of discussion. I like a course where you can talk about what's going on, with the teacher" (p. 96).

Conclusion

Skinner's teaching machines have a mixed legacy. Despite his vigorous defense of his theoretical purity, schools generally adopted a pragmatic approach of using machines that mixed linear and branching techniques, as well as using non-mechanized (and therefore usually cheaper) applications of Skinner's techniques that became known as programmed instruction (Casas, 1997). But even at their peak popularity, "it appears that universities and school districts used the technology on an experimental basis only … [and] on a minor scale" (p. 16). And while Skinner noted a higher level of enthusiasm in corporate training settings (Skinner, 1968b), even in this context teaching machines quickly faded from use.

Skinner never abandoned his commitment to operant conditioning, however, and continued to advocate that educational technology would only become a true teaching tool when it correctly implemented conditioning processes. While late in his life he did observe that his original teaching machines had become "museum pieces" (Skinner, 1986, p. 104), he did not mean this in a derogatory sense. He merely thought the mechanical devices he originally designed could be replaced by modern instruments that took advantage of improvements in computing technology. And he continued to insist that proper application of conditioning was more than an aid to learning; it actually controlled the teaching process, saying that if a computer "teaches by arranging contingencies of reinforcement … it is not functioning as a computer, of course; it is teaching. It should be called a teaching machine" (p. 110). Skinner, then, was remarkably consistent for over 30 years in how he tried to apply operant conditioning to the problems of classroom learning. As he explained how his design choices aligned with the principles of conditioning, and as he critiqued other educational technologists who (in his view) misunderstood conditioning or who compromised its effectiveness in the designs of their own machines, one can see the translation of his theoretical constructs into specific design decisions that had a practical impact on the features of the teaching machine he developed. So, regardless of the reluctance modern observers might have about using Skinner's actual theory or techniques as precedent in their own designs, his process can serve as an example of how theory can be operationalized for implementation into specific forms of educational technology.

References

Benjamin Jr., L. T. (1988). A history of teaching machines. *American Psychologist, 43*(9), 703–712.

Casas, M. (1997). "The history surrounding the use of Skinnerian teaching machines and programmed instruction (1960–1970)." Doctoral dissertation, Harvard University.

Clark, R. E. (1994). Media will never influence learning. *Educational Technology Research and Development, 42*(2), 21–30.

Crowder, N.A. (1959). Automatic tutoring by means of intrinsic programming. In E. Galanter (Ed.), *Automatic teaching: The state of the art* (pp. 109–116). John Wiley & Sons.

Ferster, B. (2014). *Teaching machines: Learning from the intersection of education and technology.* Baltimore, MD: Johns Hopkins University Press.

Fine, B. (1962). *Teaching machines*. New York: Sterling Publishing.
Goodman, R. (1962). *Programmed learning and teaching machines: An introduction*. London: The English Universities Press.
Haggbloom, S. J., Warnick, R., Warnick, J. E., Jones, V. K., Yarbrough, G. L., Russell, T. M., Borecky, C. M., McGahhey, R., Powell III, J. L., Beavers, J., & Monte, E. (2002). The 100 most eminent psychologists of the 20th century. *Review of General Psychology, 6*(2), 139–152.
McDonald, J. K., Yanchar, S. C., & Osguthorpe, R. T. (2005). Learning from programmed instruction: Examining implications for modern instructional technology. *Educational Technology Research and Development, 53*(2), 84–98. https://doi.org/10.1007/BF02504867.
McSweeney, F. K., & Murphy, E. S. (2014). *The Wiley Blackwell handbook of operant and classical conditioning*. New York: John Wiley & Sons.
Niemiec, R. P., & Walberg, H. J. (1989). From teaching machines to microcomputers: Some milestones in the history of computer-based instruction. *Journal of Research on Computing in Education, 21*(3), 263–276.
Pressey, S. L. (1960). A simple apparatus which gives tests and scores—and teaches. In A. A. Lumsdaine & R. Glaser (Eds.), *Teaching machines and programmed learning: A source book* (pp. 35–41). National Education Association of the United States.
Saettler, L. P. (1990). *The evolution of American educational technology*. Libraries Unlimited.
Schnaitter, R. (1999). Some criticisms of behaviorism. In B. A. Thyer (Ed.), *The philosophical legacy of behaviorism* (pp. 209–249). New York: Springer Science+Business Media.
Schramm, W. (1964). *The research on programmed instruction: An annotated bibliography*. U.S. Department of Health, Education, and Welfare, Office of Education.
Skinner, B. F. (1948). "Superstition" in the pigeon. *Journal of Experimental Psychology, 38*, 168–172.
Skinner, B. F. (1953). *Science and human behavior*. New York: The Free Press.
Skinner, B. F. (1954). The science of learning and the art of teaching. *Harvard Educational Review, 24*(1), 86–97.
Skinner, B. F. (1955). *Teaching machine* (Patent No. US 2,846,779A).
Skinner, B. F. (1957). *Teaching and testing aid* (Patent No. US 2,987,828A).
Skinner, B. F. (1958). Teaching machines. *Science, 128*, 969–977.
Skinner, B. F. (1961). Why we need teaching machines. *Harvard Educational Review, 31*(4), 377–398.
Skinner, B. F. (1963). Behaviorism at fifty. *Science, 140*, 951–958.
Skinner, B. F. (1965a). *Method and devices for teaching writing skills* (Patent No. US 3,363,337A).
Skinner, B. F. (1965b). The technology of teaching. *Proceedings of the Royal Society, 162*, 427–443.
Skinner, B. F. (1968a). Reflections on a decade of teaching machines. In R. A. Weisgerber (Ed.), *Instructional process and media innovation* (pp. 404–417). Skokie, IL: Rand McNally.
Skinner, B. F. (1968b). *The technology of teaching*. Meredith Corporation.
Skinner, B. F. (1983). *A matter of consequences: Part three of an autobiography*. Nwq York: Alfred A. Knopf, Inc.
Skinner, B. F. (1986). Programmed instruction revisited. *Phi Delta Kappan, 68*(2), 103–110.
Skinner, B. F., & Holland, J. G. (1960). The use of teaching machines in college instruction. In A. A. Lumsdaine & R. Glaser (Eds.), *Teaching machines and programmed learning: A source book* (pp. 159–172). National Education Association of the United States.
Stack, C. W. (1973). How to name our baby. In L. Lipsitz (Ed.), *Using programmed instruction* (pp. 40–43). Englewood Cliffs, NJ: Educational Technology Publications.
Taylor, C. (1964). *The explanation of behaviour*. Humanities Press.
Virués-Ortega, J. (2006). The case against B. F. Skinner 45 years later: An encounter with N. Chomsky. *Behavioral Analysis, 29*(2), 243–251.

8

THE ORIGINAL SRA READING SYSTEM

Individualized Learning in a Box (1957–1964)

Elizabeth Boling

In 1966 as a fifth-grade student and Air Force dependant in a Department of Defense School in Japan, I was pulled out of my class and sent to Mr. Cass's sixth-grade room for reading period. I couldn't say now whether this went on for the entire school year or for only part of it, but I can say that the SRA Reading Lab (Science Research Associates Reading Lab) which I encountered there quickly became my favorite part of school—then, and for some years afterward in memory. The Lab was a big box, longer than my arm could span, sitting in the back of the room on a shelf. I seem to recall that Mr. Cass instructed me individually on how to use the Lab. Take a large, illustrated card from the box, starting at the front with the easiest ones, and read the story or article printed on it. Then get an answer sheet and use that to record my answers to the questions on the back of the card. Use a key to score my answers and record the score myself. And take another card when I am done, moving forward through the rainbow of sections marking increases in difficulty.

What was the allure of this experience? Considering this question, I note that I was scolded in first grade for reading ahead and revealing to the class, "Oh, look. Look and see. A kitten is in the box!" And while we had many books at home, I also remember being restricted to the children's room in the library where *Cherry Ames: Student Nurse* (Wells, 1943) and *The Secret of the Old Clock* (Adams, 1959) featuring Nancy Drew, were fun, but repetitive and soon finished. So, reading at my own pace and level, reading about science, adventure, and world culture, and checking *myself* to see how well I understood—all these were a revelation to me as experiences in school. Autonomy, variety, trust—all had been in short supply during my school experiences so far. The thought of the SRA induces an upwelling of positive feeling whenever I think about it, even now, decades later.

The Design

So, what was the early SRA Reading Lab? Since I consider the Reading Lab *as a design*, I realize that the only details I can recall are a few of the stories, those thick, color-coded cards with bold illustrations, and that long box in the back of the classroom. In order to describe this design fully, therefore, I had to travel to the University of Illinois library to see first-hand the one 1957 edition identified within our institutional lending system. I was able to review the 1963 and 1964 editions there as well; given their dates of publication, it could have been any of these that I used in Mr. Cass's class. This kit, labeled IIIA, was intended to be used in "above-average sixth grade" or in grades 7 to 12.

I recalled the box very much as it appeared on the storage shelf in the library, although it had seemed a great deal larger to me in 1966 (Figure 8.1). Opening it,

FIGURE 8.1   SRA Reading Laboratory, 1957; color-coded reading cards on the left with the instructor booklets behind them, self-assessment materials are stored on the right. Close-up of assessment materials (R).

I was surprised at how compact it actually is, and how much more complicated than I had appreciated. The main compartment contains 10 sections divided by color-coded tabs with 15 single-fold reading cards in each one, starting with third-grade reading level (orange) through college freshman level (purple). These cards fit tightly into the largest section, leaving a space behind them for the booklets instructing teachers how to use the Lab and providing tracking sheets for students. Two compartments to the right hold test cards, scoring guides, record booklets, and something I had not recalled: colored pencils matching the color codes on the reading cards. I suspect that my class was using a kit that had been in stock for some time, or had been donated to this overseas school second-hand without the pencils, because those pencils would have been very attractive to me and therefore memorable. Something else I did not recall, because I would not have seen them, were the teachers' handbooks containing detailed instructions for using the Lab.

The Teacher's Handbook for this kit is over 50 pages long, and it outlines a detailed, highly prescribed program for using the materials, beginning with a diagnostic session to determine where each student stands in reading skill and what advancement might be expected (Figure 8.2). A chart is provided for this purpose, matching each student's score to a starting point in the materials. Combining this diagnostic exam plus an I.Q. score, potential for improvement is also predicted using three profiles expressed in the terminology of the day: mentally retarded, emotionally retarded, and educationally retarded. For the first, a little improvement is promised together with satisfaction at being included in the program, but no long-term (lifetime) expectation of a reading level above fifth or sixth grade. The second profile is assumed to make real gains in reading performance, credited to satisfaction at immediate success in the program and motivation-based improvement in mental health, but not ever to be expected to reach college level. The third profile is described as "superior" and "highly gifted," but not having been challenged previously by schoolwork and therefore anticipated to make substantial gains with high satisfaction and go on to college, becoming "a source of much needed manpower to the nation." Gains of two to three grade levels from current grade level in reading are stated to have been achieved by students using this system usually in the first year, but possibly not until the second.

The program outlined for using the SRA Reading Lab is described as, ideally, 50 periods (length not specified) across 12 weeks, tapering from 20 per week in the first month down to 5 per week in the third month. Across these weeks the order of activities is specified, along with scripts for explaining the program to students and leading them through the activities. These activities include using the Power Builders (the story cards that I recall so vividly) and their associated assessments the Skill Builders, which are shorter articles read aloud by the teacher from the Teacher's Handbook before students attempt assessments on their own, and the timed Rate Builders, also self-assessed through a Key (Figure 8.3).

THE MATERIALS OF THE SRA READING LABORATORY

The Box Contains:
150 POWER BUILDER Cards, 15 at each of 10 grade levels, each level designated by a color
A key card for each POWER BUILDER
150 RATE BUILDER Cards, 15 at each of 10 grade levels, each level designated by a color
40 Key Booklets for the RATE BUILDERS, each booklet containing *all* the answers for the 150 RATE BUILDER comprehension checks
1 STUDENT RECORD BOOK
1 TEACHER'S HANDBOOK
2 SETS OF COLORED PENCILS

The STUDENT RECORD BOOK Contains:
1 STARTING LEVEL GUIDE, a separate four-page folder (to be removed from the center of the book) to help place the student at the right starting grade level in THE SRA READING LABORATORY
The POWER BUILDER Starter Selection, which everyone in the class uses to become acquainted with procedures
Record Blank pages on which the student will record all of his work
Graphs and Charts for recording both daily work and progress from day to day
Six LISTENING SKILL BUILDER comprehension checks

The Teacher's Handbook
This is the book now in your hands. Note that on pages 35–45 it provides six LISTENING SKILL BUILDER selections to be read to the class, with a copy of the comprehension checks and their keys.

TABLE OF CONTENTS

INTRODUCTION	1
MATERIALS OF THE SRA READING LABORATORY	2
TO GET ACQUAINTED WITH THIS HANDBOOK	2
TIME ALLOTMENTS AND SCHEDULES	4
TACTICS AND STRATEGY	8
PROCEDURES	13
1. Goal-Setting	13
2. Using the Starting-Level Guide	15
3. Discussing Individual Differences	18
4. Introducing the Student Record Book	19
5. Presenting the Survey Q3R Method	21
6. How to Use the Power Builder Starter Selection	22
7. Presenting the Power Builder Starter Selection	23
8. How to Use the Power Builders	27
9. Presenting Multi-Level Work with the Power Builders	28
10. Teaching the Use of the Rate Builders	30
11. How to Use the Rate Builders	31
12. Beginning Multi-Level Work with the Rate Builders	32
13. Presenting SQ3R for Use in General Reading	34
14. Introducing the Listening Skill Builders	35
THE LISTENING SKILL BUILDERS	36–45
EVALUATION, INTERPRETATION, AND GUIDANCE	46
Individual and Class Progress to Date	46
Some Student Problems at This Stage	47
How Far and Fast Should Students Progress in the Power Builders?	49
How Far and Fast Should Students Progress in the Rate Builders?	51
Example of Reading Levels in an Average 7th Grade Classroom	52
Final Evaluation	56

FIGURE 8.2 (L) Contents list for the 1957 SRA Reading Laboratory included at the start of the Teacher's Handbook. (R) Table of Contents for the Teacher's Handbook.

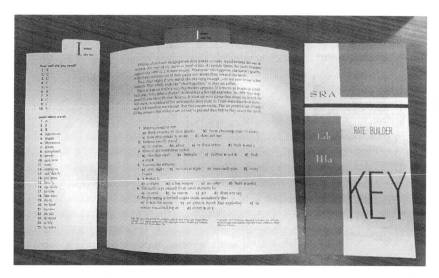

FIGURE 8.3 Samples of Power Builder key card, Rate Builder card, and Key booklet for the Rate Builders.

The degree to which this experience is intended to be programmed, that is, carried out in a prescribed sequence according to instruction, is notable. In addition to pages of directions, charts, and graphs, and the forms by which each activity is structured, a quick guide is provided (Figure 8.4). In viewing this chart, picture the mid-twentieth-century classroom with rows of desks, bookshelves at the back, chalkboards along the sides, and a teacher at the front reading out loud to perhaps 20 sixth-grade students. They listen and then complete an assessment that will determine which color tab they will begin with when they are later invited to remove their first Power Builder cards from the SRA box, return to their seats, and begin to read. At this point the silence in the room is only disturbed as, at varying intervals, one student or another rises to retrieve a quiz card, and later an answer key, from the box. Pencils scratch as they mark their answers and record their progress in the Student Record. Those working the most quickly may return twice to the box for another Power Builder during this session. At prescribed points during the 12-week program, the teacher uses the Rate Builders and Listening Skill Builders. Rate Builders are short texts for timed silent reading with questions to answer afterward. The Listening Skill Builders are similar to the initial diagnostic sequence in that the teacher reads a text aloud and students complete a quiz over the meaning of that text immediately following the reading. These texts, unlike those in the Power Builders, are focused on explanations of positive reading and learning habits.

From a student's point of view (as evidenced by my experience of this program, and the memories of who used it and have discussed it with me), the Power

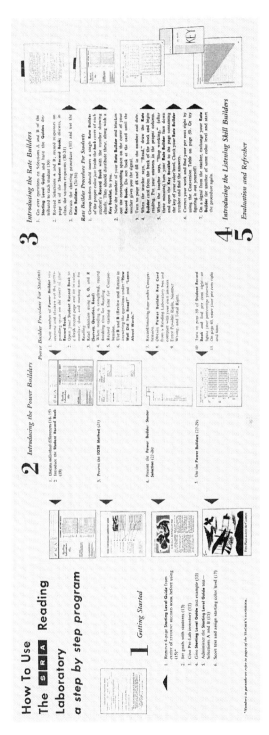

FIGURE 8.4 Three-page spread from the SRA Reading Kit Teacher's Handbook with a fold-out page showing the basic steps of the program with both the teacher and the student actions detailed step by step.

Builders are the salient component. Each bifold card is substantial, measuring around eight inches square and printed in two colors on heavy, coated cardstock. Pulling one from the box, a student sees a title in large type and an evocative image on the front face, framing the subject of the article this card contains (Figure 8.5). The articles were almost all factual, including biographies, science and social science stories, and notable historical and cultural stories, with a few branching out into myths and fictional stories with moral messages. Because the program calls for students to progress from one level to the next based on their performance on assessments completed after reading each Power Builder, most will not be expected to read every card at every level. This means that a student can review the title and illustration on a card and pass over it in favor of one that looks more interesting. Sometimes there is a short line at the box while students wait for one of their peers to select her next choice for maximum potential interest.

Carried out as prescribed, this is primarily an internal learning experience. Externally it is intended to be quiet and orderly, despite repeated trips by individuals to and from the SRA box, and even if some students are struggling with reading and others are elated over being allowed to read as much and as quickly as they like.

Design Decisions in the SRA Reading Lab

Don H. Parker, creator of the SRA, was a designer who worked from his experience as a classroom reading teacher (Holloway, 2000) and from a theoretical perspective regarding education and learning, which he called the "multilevel philosophy' (Parker, 1963, p. 21). His philosophy held that each person should have "the opportunity to start where he is and move ahead as fast and as far as his learning rate and capacity will let him" (p. 9), which requires, therefore, a "vertical curriculum" wherein children in the same classroom would be studying at different levels and rates (p. 223). Distinguishing between training, which he defined as *skill-building*, and education, which he defined as *skill-using*, Parker described a future for education in which these two would be taught differently. He did not subscribe to the idea that teaching machines would replace teachers, but did posit that "self-programmed, laboratory-type instructional materials can free the teacher from the drudgery involved in teaching the skill disciplines" (p. 21), by which, in reading, he meant speed, vocabulary, and comprehension. Without naming it directly, he points to the SRA Reading Lab, in development 13 years and published 6 years before, as an example of such material.

Design Philosophy

Popular accounts of the origins of this design stress the engaging narrative of his experience as a reading teacher who, noticing the differences in the speed with

Original SRA Reading System (1957–1964) **111**

FIGURE 8.5 Selected Power Builder cards from different levels of the 1957 SRA Reading Lab showing the titles, two-color illustrations, and initial portion of the story each contains.

which his students learned, developed folders of educational materials at different levels to support each of them, carried them to school in an orange crate (Allen, 2017), and later struggled to get them published in a form usable by other teachers. Looking at the materials themselves and reading *Schooling for Individual Excellence* (Parker, 1963), however, it is clear that the influence of his graduate education permeates this design. The multi-level philosophy leads directly to the envisioned situation in which individual children will be reading different material at the same time and will be assessed differently at the same time. A teacher may not be able to manage this variability in skill learning effectively, especially while also attending to what Parker sees as the central, and different, core of education—skill-using. The decision to have the students handle their own choice of readings and their own assessments therefore solved a critical procedural problem in the design of this system. Arguably, as discussed below, this decision resulted in the single most positive feature of the design which was the autonomy it afforded to students.

The System

As already noted, the SRA Reading Lab is presented as a complete, and prescribed, system of reading skills instruction. Everything required to make it work is provided, including: precise directions for teachers on scheduling the program; full scripts for teachers to use with students; charts and graphs for calculating assessments; record-keeping sheets; all content materials; and the means to determine how and how much students could be expected to learn while using the system. The comprehensive nature of the system suggests a critical design decision—while the system affords autonomy to the students, it does not do the same for the teacher, except for a limited flexibility in scheduling. The decision to call it a "laboratory" signals the kind of precision with which it was expected to be used. It may also signal the assumption that, as in a laboratory, if an experiment is entered correctly into a lab notebook anyone should be able to take those instructions "to the bench" and carry out that experiment without making any more decisions. In other words, the teacher should not have to think in order to use the system. This is consistent with Parker's notion that teaching skills is a routine drudgery to be taken out of the teacher's way.

The system is designed to generate evaluation data (Figure 8.6). In addition to the records of student assessments generated during use of the program, end-of-term evaluations ask for perceptions of learning, reactions to the materials, and an explicit question about how the system could be improved. Nothing in the materials indicates how this information could be returned to the Science Research Associates, but clearly it was intended to be and perhaps the representatives who sold the materials solicited the evaluation results later. Results of preliminary evaluation carried out during development of the system are reported in the Teacher's Handbook as 112 percent higher gain in skill across

Post-Lab. Evaluation of _____ **Date** _____
                                    Last Name   First Name   Middle Initial

Teacher _____ **School** _____ **Grade** _____

Give your frank and honest opinions on the questions below:

1. Do you like the reading improvement work you have been doing with The SRA Reading Laboratory? .... ____Yes ____No

2. What have you gained from this work so far? _____
   _____
   _____

3. Has your reading work helped you in doing other school work? If so, how? ___
   _____
   _____

4. What did you like best about your work with The SRA Reading Laboratory? ___
   _____
   _____

5. What particular thing did you like least about this work? _____
   _____

6. What suggestions can you give for making The SRA Reading Laboratory program even better?
   _____
   _____

FIGURE 8.6   End of program evaluation from the 1957 SRA Reading Lab.

almost 500 students compared to those not using the system, although I did not find a published article describing the method of the study or details of the results. The decision to extend this evaluation beyond development and into implementation underscores both the scholarly and the scientific orientation of the design team. Although it is not a literal machine, the designers seem to have envisioned it being used as one, according to the detailed instructions; therefore, its results are presumed to be measurable and its function subsequently refined.

Physical Materials

The choice to package the Reading Lab in a single large box was likely related to cost, as decisions regarding physical materials always are. However, two-color printing—while economical for the time—was not the most economical option available, and including custom-printed pencils with a different label for each color (see Figure 8.1) was clearly not a decision made in the interest of keeping costs down. There is a kind of completeness to the kit; everything needed is in one place (at least until the fourth-graders get into it) and therefore the learning system can be implemented as intended without relying on anything additional.

Reviewing the credits on the side of the box (Figure 8.7), it is evident that a credentialed team was assembled to guide the design. The list of Power Builder titles for each of the three early editions of the SRA Reading Lab demonstrates that care was taken to assemble materials of both variety and quality; an easily discernible decision that this was a key requirement for the design. Articles are credited to the writers and publications from which they were sourced and adapted; given the direct author credits just under each title, it appears that each author adapted their own material. A good deal of effort must have gone into this work because the Handbook in each kit details the skills covered by readings at each level (Figure 8.8), and overall reading level is controlled across the sections of the kit. It is unlikely that the original texts were conveniently written to these specifications. To ensure that the readings covered appropriate skills at specific levels of difficulty, multiple rounds of detailed review and revision must have taken place. This supposition is supported by inference from a published account of the Pacific Horizons Reading Scheme (Anderson, 1972), a multi-level reading instruction program in Papua New Guinea modeled largely on the SRA Reading Lab. This account describes the multiple, complex considerations that went into gauging readability and appealing to readers' interest.

Likewise, the illustration credit is to Leonard Everett Fisher, showing that the decision was made to hire an artist who had already been awarded the Pulitzer Award for Painting (1950) and who would go on to a distinguished career as illustrator, painter, and author, to produce images for this and subsequent kits. In fact, the original plan was to seek an artist for each level in the kit. However, when I contacted him, Fisher, now 96 years old, recounted to me that while he was turning in his first samples he argued it would be simpler to work with 1 artist than with 15 and thereby won the entire contract from editor Lee Deighton, who would go on to become president of Macmillan Publishers. That contract lasted 4 to 5 years and covered over 1000 illustrations and 1000 more color overlays for multiple editions of the Reading Lab, not counting "do overs because Don Parker had a different visual idea" (L. E. Fisher, personal communication, March 30, 2020). Fisher's story suggests to me that there was a strong investment in the appeal of these materials. I was decidedly *not* a Pulitzer Award winner when I created illustrations for a digital reading series developed by a national publisher 35 years ago, but recall that the editor I worked with was deeply committed to the appeal of those materials for the children who would use them—and I lost track of the number of "do overs" on that project. Later in my career when I managed a graphics group for a global technology company, we needed a current and engaging look on a high-profile project; we sought out and hired an award-winning illustrator to create those images.

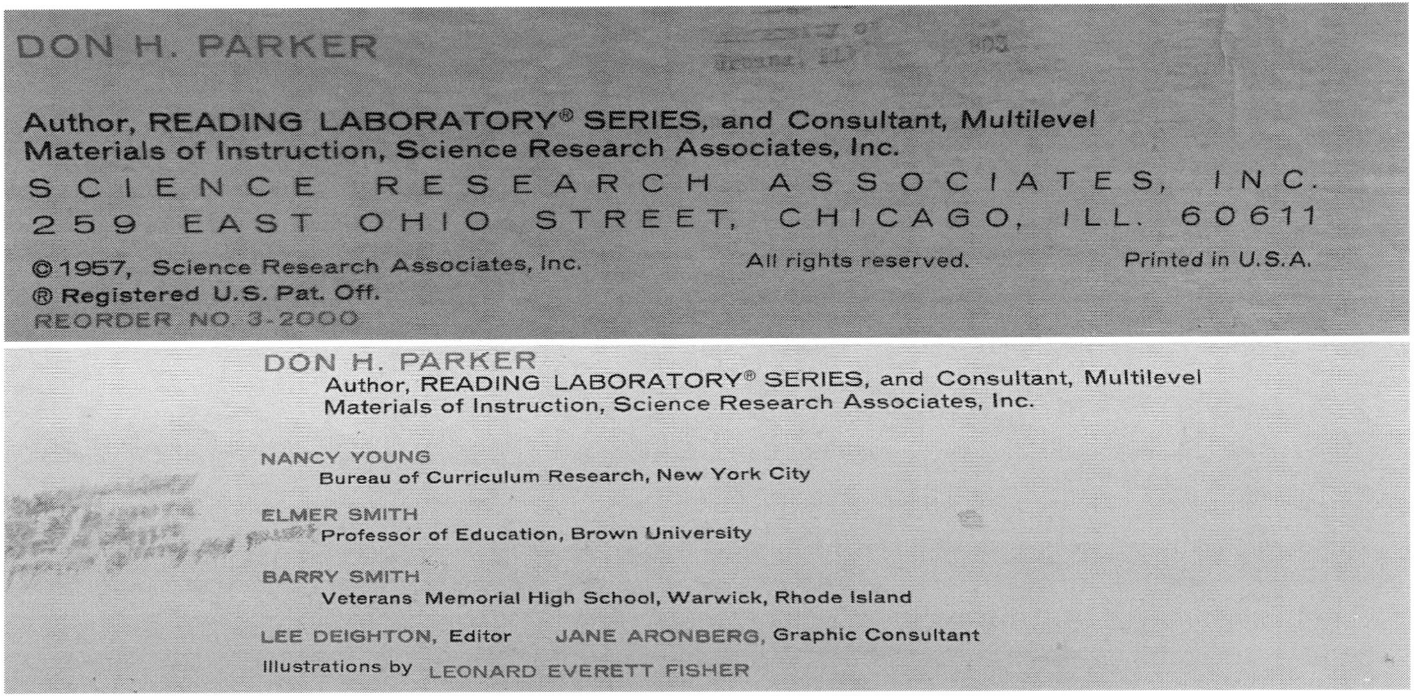

Original SRA Reading System (1957–1964) **115**

FIGURE 8.7 1957 SRA Reading Laboratory; author, contributor, and publisher credits printed on the outside of the box.

Word Analysis Skills	COLOR LEVEL: Orange	Olive	Blue	Brown	Green	Red	Tan	Gold	Aqua	Purple
Prefixes	5,8		10,12	4,9,11, 12,13	1,5,7,9, 11,13,15	13,15	6,7,9, 12,15	3,4,5,9, 10,12,14	8,10,11, 14	7,10,11
Suffixes	2,10	11	6,9,10, 14,15	1,2,3,4, 9,12,13, 15	1,2,8,9, 11	3,12	1,2,3,5, 7,8,10, 15	1,3,5,6, 7,8,9, 10,11,12, 13,14,15	1,5,6,7, 9,12,15	1,2,3,4, 5,6,9
Base Words	7,9,13, 14,15	4,12,13, 14,15	2,3,5, 7,8,15	2,4,7, 10,13,14	1,4,6,8, 12,14	4,7,10, 15	2,3,15	5,7,9, 11,15	2,3,4,7, 11,12,13	1,4,10, 12,13,15
Roots					6,12,13	6,10,14	8,12, 13,14	1,4,8, 12,14	1,2,3,4, 10,11, 13,14	3,7,8, 10,11, 12,13
Syllabication		1,8,11, 12	1,6,9, 10,12	1,2,3,6, 7,10,12, 13,15	1,9,10, 14	1,2,7,9, 13,14,15	5,7,11, 13,14,15	3,9,10, 11,14,15		2,3,10, 12
Consonant recognition	1,2,3, 6,8,9, 10,15	5,9,14	3,4,5, 15		11					
Consonant blends	1,2,3,6, 7,8,9,10, 12,15	4,5,7,9, 10,14	3,4,5, 10,15	1,2,12, 13	9,10,14	2,9	7,11			
Silent consonants	4,5,12	4,5,9,15	5,15							
C and *G* sounds	4,5,7	3,7,15								
Vowel sounds	1,3,5,8, 9,10,11, 13,14	2,6,8,10, 11,12,13, 15	2,3,7,8, 13	3,5,6,7						
Silent vowels		2,6,7,10, 11,13,15	2,7,11,14	3,5,6,11						
Final *e*			8,9,14	1,7,8,9, 10,14	4,7,8,11, 12	3,8,11	2,10,15	1,2,10, 12	6,7,9	2,9
Changing *y* to *i*	10	3,4,13		4,7,8,9, 14	2,11,15	5,6,8	1,3,4,9, 12	6,13	13,15	1,5,12
Doubling final consonants (1 syllable)	14		14			14	1,2,3,6, 13	2,5,8,12	1,9,12	2,8,14
Doubling final consonants (2 syllables)			13	2,10,12, 15	3,5,8,15	1,7,13	5,9,13, 14	11,14,15	4,11,13	3,10,12, 15
Contractions			4,5,6	4,5,10						
Spelling hints						3,10,11	4	4,7	2,5,10, 14	1,6,7, 11,13

BROWN (6.0)
Distribution of Skills in "Learn About Words" Sections

		POWER BUILDER NUMBER: 1, 6, 11	2, 7, 12	3, 8, 13	4, 9, 14	5, 10, 15	SECTION
Word Meaning	Vocabulary: word meaning from context of story	•	•	•	•	•	A
Word Meaning	Vocabulary: semantic variations (from story)	•	•	•	•	•	B
Phonic and Structural Word Analysis	Dictionary skills: alphabetical order 1st letter	•					C
	Base words + endings: *s, ed, ing; er, est*		•				C
	Prefixes: *in, re*			•			C
	Silent, *g*, or *f* sound of *gh*: *f* sound of *ph*				•		C
	Vowel Pattern 5: special sound of *a, e, o* + *u, w*					•	C
	Dictionary skills: alphabetical order 2d letter	•					D
	Changing y to *i* to add ending		•				D
	Suffixes: *ful, less*			•			D
	Vowel Pattern 5: long and short sound of *ea, oo*				•		D
	Homonyms					•	D
	Dictionary skills: alphabetical order 3d letter	•					E
	Contractions		•				E
	Three sounds of *ch*: *ch, sh, k*			•			E
	Syllable Rule 3: words ending in *le*				•		E
	Syllable Rule 4: words ending in *ed*					•	E

FIGURE 8.8 (L) Skills table showing the skills covered in each Power Builder at each level in the 1957 edition. (R) Skills table showing the skills covered in each Power Builder at each level in the 1963 edition.

Original SRA Reading System (1957–1964) **117**

FIGURE 8.9 Illustrations created by Leonard Everett Fisher for the orange-level Power Builders of the SRA Reading Kit. In addition to their distinctive mid-century look, they feature a consistent visual style, details relevant to the stories, and a dramatic light/dark treatment that suggests each text will include some element of drama or excitement.

Critical Design Concerns

As an admitted fifth-grade SRA Reading Lab enthusiast, one whose experience with the SRA persists over half a century later as a high point in my education, I approached this design case prepared to re-encounter and describe the design that provided that positive experience. In addition, of course, I encountered aspects of the design not apparent to me when I was a student.

Consumables and Coherence

While not the most significant of concerns, I reviewed the materials several times looking for how the consumable elements would be replaced in pre-photocopier 1957, and without the inclusion of spirit masters (originals to be used for solvent-based duplicates). Even given the smaller class sizes of the day, the system could only be used at most twice before new record sheets would be needed—although regular pencils could be substituted for the original multi-color ones. There could, of course, have been an arrangement whereby schools would contact the salesperson, or the Science Research Associates, to replenish portions of the kit. Coherence is another matter; even when it is complete, this kit includes multiple components that must work together if the program is to function as intended. I remember Mr. Cass's classroom as orderly and expect that I would have tried to get anything I used back in the right place. But who knows how much work Mr. Cass had to do before, or after, class to keep everything where it belonged and make sure all the bits stayed together? And at $37.95 in 1957 (Larrick, 1957), or almost $350 in 2020 dollars, these materials were not cheap. Even when they were missing parts, therefore, they were likely to be kept around the classroom but they would no longer be used as intended because they *could* no longer be used as intended. Anecdotally, I have heard friends' recollections of being told to use materials from a defunct kit when they were finished with the rest of their work in class, which is certainly not what the designers intended.

Currency and Cultural Awareness

The decision to use primarily informational, non-fictional content in the Power Builders resulted in some inevitable limits on the currency of the program. Science and biographical topics for example, will always go out of date in ways that fictional readings would be less liable to do. In the absence of direct information regarding why this decision was made, it might be linked to the framing of the program as a teaching machine for skill-learning (versus skill-using)—in other words, practical and factual rather than interpretive or fanciful. The selection of topics was of its time and reflected the majority status and the biases of the designers. These selections were not exclusively or entirely negative. Profiles of successful minority figures were included, as with the article on Althea Gibson who was a recent success story at the time and who went on to have an illustrious career in sports and philanthropy (Figure 8.10). Materials relevant to girls as well as boys were also included (Figure 8.10), although close readings of all the Power Builders reveal in more than one case sexism, systemic bias, and lack of cultural awareness. These may not have been fully avoidable for those designers, but they do limit the design—and not just from the perspective of 50 years later.

Complexity of the System

The 1957 SRA Reading Lab, and the editions published over the subsequent ten years, were rigidly prescribed in terms of how they were expected to be used. In a 1966 study of the effectiveness of the system it was noted that the Lab shared common characteristics with teaching machines (Pont), and we know this to have been intentional (Parker, 1963). In order to use the Lab as designed, therefore, teachers had to set aside a substantial portion of class time over 12 weeks, follow multiple instructions to the letter, and, paradoxically, turn over a rather complicated set of assessments to their students. I am not able to recall whether Mr. Cass used the SRA Reading Lab as the Teacher Handbook dictated, but I have been told by friends who also experienced the SRA that their teachers

FIGURE 8.10 (L) Profile of Althea Gibson, who was at the time a sports champion early in her career, written by biographer Aylesa Forsee and essentially consistent with contemporary information. (R) Morality tale with the positive message that confidence is more attractive and valuable than surface beauty; the framing of the story leans heavily on sexist stereotypes.

did not—up to and including using the reading materials just to keep students busy if they finished their work before the rest of the class. It is possible to see in published accounts that the system was adapted in more or less significant ways for ESL/EFL learning (Robb & Susser, 1989; Kharma, 1981), professional development (Kokes, 1977), and adult literacy (Hicks, 1970). This may be because the system was hard to follow, or was difficult to fit into a class schedule, or because it afforded variations in use; it is not possible to tell and is likely different in different situations. And neither strict prescription nor open-endedness are objective design flaws. However, given some of the studies conducted with the SRA Reading Lab, discussed below, it may be that the open-ended nature of the system was ultimately more of its strength than its carefully calculated contribution to skill-building.

Variable Studies of Effectiveness

While the contribution of a design case does not hinge on proving that the design was effective, questions of effectiveness may reasonably be discussed when such claims are made as part of the design itself and studies have been carried out. The 112 percent comparative gains in skills claimed in the Teacher's Handbook for students using the system, compared to those who did not, were not the results achieved in other studies of the system. These included: no improvement on any measure when the system was used as an add-on or as a full reading program and SRA students learning less than others (Waldrip, 1966); no contribution of the SRA to reading improvement, but positive motivation of students and offloading effort from teachers (Pont, 1966); no significant difference in reading proficiency but a positive novelty effect (Gurney, 1966); and no significant difference between the SRA and another reading program, but students reporting boredom with an SRA-only program among college undergraduates in Malaysia (Boey, 1975). Mixed results were also reported, including a dissertation study of effectiveness in which, as Parker did claim would happen, 3600 fourth-, fifth-, and sixth-graders were tested and those of high ability were found to benefit more than those of low ability (Adamczyk, 1959). In 1961, Jones found that among 104 fourth-, fifth-, and sixth-graders, those of high ability gained in vocabulary and those of low ability gained in comprehension within the group using the SRA, but no significant difference overall in learning between the groups using the SRA and those not using the SRA. Kellaghan (1969) reported positive results in reading speed and accuracy among 219 fifth-grade students in an Irish boys' school. More generally, Cawley and co-authors (1965) studied the use of several reading programs with junior high school students and reported that concentrated and individualized instruction can improve performance. No study, however, except those carried out during the development of the program, showed the results claimed by Parker for the system. Notably, however, multiple studies, including those previously mentioned in which the system was adapted, discuss the motivating effect on students of choosing their own materials, advancing from one level to another, and assessing their own performance. Considering the system as a design, it might be fair to speculate that the decisions made in order to offload tedious instruction from teachers resulted in materials the strength of which lay in the autonomy offered by individualized instruction.

Acknowledgments

The author expresses gratitude to Julie M. Frye, Education Library Head at Indiana University, and to Nancy P. O'Brien, Professor and University Library Head, Social Sciences, Health, and Education Library, University of Illinois at Urbana–Champaign, for their assistance in locating and arranging for my access to the SRA Reading Laboratory materials.

All photos and scans credited to and used by permission of the author.

References

Adamczyk, M. M. (1959). "The relative effectiveness of a multi-level reading program at the intermediate level." Unpublished thesis.
Adams, H. S. (1959). *The secret of the old clock*. New York: Grosset & Dunlap.
Allen, E. (2017, May 4). *A box of nostalgia: The SRA Reading Laboratory*. Retrieved from https://bookriot.com/2017/05/04/a-box-of-nostalgia-the-sra-reading-laboratory/.
Anderson, J. (1972). The development of a reading laboratory for second language learners. *RELC Journal*, 3(1–2): 50–59.
Boey, L. K. (1975). The SRA Reading Laboratory and reading comprehension. *RELC Journal*, 6(1): 14–16. https://doi.org/10.1177/003368827500600103.
Cawley, J. F., Chaffin, C., & Brunning, H. (1965). An evaluation of a junior high school reading improvement program. *Journal of Reading*, 9(1): 26–29.
Gurney, D. (1966). The effect of an individual reading program on reading level and attitude toward reading. *The Reading Teacher*, 19(4): 277–280.
Hicks, G. (1970). Methods and materials used in teaching functional illiterates in a correctional institution. *Journal of Correctional Education*, 22(2): 17, 23–24.
Holloway, L. (2000, July 1). Obituary. Donald H. Parker, 88, Inventor of self-paced reading program. *The New York Times*, Section A, p. 11.
Jones, R.L., & van Why, E. L. (1961). The SRA Reading Laboratory and fourth grade pupils. *Journal of Developmental Reading*, 5(1): 36–46.
Kellaghan, T. (1969). An experimental investigation of the use of an SRA Reading Laboratory in Irish schools. *The Irish Journal of Education*, 3(1): 22–28.
Kharma, N. N. (1981). An attempt to individualize the reading skill at Kuwait University. *English Language Teaching Journal*, 35(4): 398–404.
Kokes, L. B. (1977). Reading program helps employees step ahead. *Journal of Reading*, 20(5): 364–367.
Larrick, N. (1957). The clip sheet. *The Reading Teacher*, 11(2): 121–123.
Parker, D. H. (1962). Reading rate is multilevel. *The Clearinghouse: A Journal of Educational Strategies, Issues and Ideas*, 36(8): 451–455. https://doi.org/10.1080/00098655.1962.11475901.

Parker, D. H. (1963). *Schooling for individual excellence*. London: Thomas Nelson & Sons.

Pont, H. B. (1966). An investigation into the use of the S.R.A. Reading Laboratory in the three Midlothian schools. *Educational Research, 8*(3): 230–236.

Robb, T. N., & Susser, B. (1989). Extensive reading vs skills building in an EFL context. *Reading in a Foreign Language, 5*(2): 239–251.

Waldrip, D. R. (1966). An experiment with the SRA Reading Laboratory at grade two. *The Journal of Educational Research, 59*(9): 419–423.

Wells, H. (1943). *Cherry Ames: Student nurse*. New York: Grosset & Dunlap.

9

MPATI

The Midwest Program on Airborne Television Instruction (1959–1971)

Monica W. Tracey and Jill E. Stefaniak

Introduction

The Midwest Program on Airborne Television Instruction (MPATI) was a bold experimental program attempting to disseminate instruction to areas where educational television was not readily available. To enrich educational programming, MPATI provided standardized educational programming to elementary and secondary school students in rural areas. Aircraft flew for 6 to 8 hours a day over Montpelier, Indiana (Figure 9.1) to transmit educational offerings across a range that was 200 miles in diameter (Perlman, 2008).

Instructional videos pre-recorded on videotape at several educational television facilities in the Midwest were aired from the MPATI planes (Figure 9.2). This allowed for instruction to be shared via telecasts to students in Indiana, Illinois, Kentucky, Ohio, Michigan, and Wisconsin. Teachers were provided with instructor guides to help facilitate lessons and assist students during activities.

Although a novel approach to distributing instruction, MPATI officially ended after ten years in 1971 due to an inability to raise enough money to fund the maintenance of the aircraft. This design case will highlight how the novel concept of MPATI was the first form of satellite television transmission, utilized principles of programmed instruction to educate elementary and secondary school students in the Midwest, and moved the audiovisual movement of instructional design forward. In addition, to support the case, an interview was conducted with an end learner, a student participant of MPATI. While MPATI did not experience long-term success, it helped researchers in our field better understand the use and constraints surrounding instructional media and the design of instruction (Gibson, 2001).

FIGURE 9.1 A DC-6 owned by Purdue University that was used to broadcast the MPATI curriculum.

Source: Purdue University Archives.

FIGURE 9.2 A DC-6, the same model pictured here, was fitted with a large antenna to broadcast the lessons while in flight.

Source: Public domain.

The Genesis of MPATI

Though experimentally launched in 1959, the MPATI program dates as far back as the mid-1940s when Westinghouse Engineer, Charles Noble, discovered that he could broadcast a television signal from an airborne aircraft. He maintained that this would eliminate the existing line-of-sight transmitting limitation. Noble called his invention Stratovision, a network of strategically placed aircraft flying in the skies that could transmit television signals to homes. Because the FCC placed a freeze on new television stations in 1948, Stratovision never materialized (Jajkowski, 2004).

In 1958, the Westinghouse Corporation approached Phillip Coombs, the Executive Director of the Ford Foundation, to discuss the possibility of using the Stratovision concept for educational television. Working with educators at Purdue University in Indiana, along with financial backing from the Ford Foundation and an FCC agreement for a three-year experiment, the Midwest Program on Airborne Television Instruction was officially formed. The board consisted of superintendents of schools from Ohio, Michigan, and Illinois. MPATI launched in 1959 and was housed at Purdue University. With a $16-million grant from the Ford Foundation, regular service began in 1961. This was the first use of satellite communication for distance education. Six tons of broadcasting equipment (Figure 9.3) were stored on a propeller-driven DC-6 aircraft that flew in a figure

FIGURE 9.3   Broadcasting equipment stored on a DC-6

Source: Southwestern Ohio Instructional Technology Association.

of 8 approximately 4.5 miles above Montpelier, Indiana to deliver a signal across a 200-mile radius (Jajkowski, 2004).

The broadcasting equipment allowed for 20 lessons to be broadcast every school day to students ranging from elementary school to college. Maintenance of televisions and antenna systems made television reception a dependable method for communication.

Developing the curriculum included soliciting the assistance of several universities to design and develop primary and secondary courses in English, foreign language, music, literature, science, the arts, and mathematics. A nationwide search was conducted to select teachers, and 20 teachers were hired to deliver the designed curriculum. Although engineers monitored the technical quality of the programming, course quality was assessed by educational academics.

MPATI in Action

The purpose of the MPATI instructional television program was to provide schools with access to learning about subjects their students may not have otherwise experienced. Airborne teachers recorded lessons that were broadcast to schools across the Midwest (Figure 9.4). These teachers were knowledgeable in their respective fields and were able to teach course material at a level much more advanced than the typical classroom teachers at these sites. Classroom teachers were provided with an instructor guide to help facilitate instruction and carry out activities following the televised broadcasts.

Schools interested in participating in the MPATI televised program were responsible for securing their own funding. In 1963, the cost to participate in the MPATI program was $1.00 per student; however, these fees rose to $2.50 per student by 1966 (University of Maryland Libraries, 2007). Their budgets determined how many lessons they could offer their students.

Principals and teachers reviewed the MPATI curricular offerings together to determine whether the televised instruction would meet the needs of their schools and students. Airborne courses were not considered to be a "one size fits all" and it was the school's responsibility to ensure that the lesson plans would complement their curricular standards as set by their school district and state. Lesson plans were also selected based on the teacher's educational background in the classroom. Sometimes, a teacher was required to teach advanced Spanish and may have had only two years of training themselves. Having an expert teacher facilitate the course not only provided the instructor with additional classroom assistance but also offered exposure to more advanced concepts for the students.

Each videotaped educational program was broadcast over UHF (ultra-high-frequency) channels 72 and 76 every school day during school hours (Gibson, 2001). The TV broadcast antenna was lowered from the plane once it reached an appropriate altitude. Coined "the flying classroom" (Figure 9.5), the MPATI airplanes served the largest geographic region in the world, 127,000 square miles,

FIGURE 9.4 A class prepares to watch a televised broadcast.

Source: Purdue University Archives.

FIGURE 9.5 The Flying Classroom was an elongated TV station with 6.5 tons of equipment.

Source: Southwestern Ohio Instructional Technology Association.

with one television transmitting facility. Dublin, Ohio was an example of one community served by "the flying classroom."

Dublin, northwest of Columbus, was once a rural community, but in 1964 it was becoming a suburban community. The focus of a documentary on MPATI (The Ohio State University, 1964), Dublin suffered from similar educational challenges to other schools across the country. The Dublin Superintendent looked to MPATI to provide his fifth-grade class instruction in introductory Spanish four days a week, as they faced increased enrollment and the need for additional teachers. The teacher prepared the class before the students watched the lecture using materials provided by the MPATI curriculum. She also served as a guide during the telecast. The Spanish teacher opened the program singing in Spanish wearing traditional Spanish attire. Elsewhere in the Dublin school district, another fifth-grade class received science instruction, also from MPATI. The principal explained that prior to this advanced science program and all of the support materials, 4 percent of the students chose science as their favorite subject. Following MPATI, 46 percent of the students chose science as their favorite subject. Students in an MPATI advanced math course in Dublin tested above average in algebra after one year of the MPATI course. The principal, providing this anecdotal evidence, stated that Dublin had a good educational program but the MPATI program added to the vitality of the curriculum. He further explained that educators must reorganize to determine how to meet the demand of the increased number of students and teaching students the additional things they have to know (The Ohio State University, 1964).

The film featuring Dublin, Ohio was created in part as an exemplar of MPATI to recruit additional participants. The Ford Foundation funded the first year of the three-year experiment, forcing the need to enlist ongoing financial support from member schools. The project was ultimately divided into 18 districts across the 6 states. Each district acted under the guidance of a selected college or university that also served the MPATI staff.

One Student's Experience

Rick was an excited 11-year-old fifth-grader in Indianapolis, Indiana. His class was informed that on this day they would not have their regular teacher but would watch television instead. The students were told that they would get instruction through the television at a designated time, when a plane was flying overhead. Rick and his classmates were very excited as they were ushered out of their classroom across the hall to the Music Room to sit in front of the only TV this private Lutheran school owned. After sitting down and waiting with great anticipation, the television teacher came on the screen. The students' excitement was palpable as their teacher dialed the TV into the channel and then made fine-tuning adjustments. Initially, the novelty of watching television at school and the promise of a different teacher captured the interest of the students. To the disappointment of the students and teacher in the long run, the image was static, and the television teacher mostly stood in front of a blackboard droning on, not making much sense to the students. Rick and the others enjoyed the new experience but missed their regular teacher. Upon reflection, he recalled that the class only watched the television teacher two or three times, and then stopped viewing the program altogether.

Rick explained that this private Lutheran school had a limited budget and his guess was that the school picked the program up for free. He had no memory of supplementary materials or special support activities for the broadcast. This was one problem with the MPATI program. Their broadcasts were not scrambled, so anyone with a UHF tuner could receive the programming, and this did not encourage schools to join and pay the required fees. Additional challenges plagued "the flying classroom" and ultimately caused its demise.

Challenges

Challenges contributing to the termination of the MPATI televised instruction program included technology and logistics. While television reception had been highly dependable, the maintenance on the broadcaster's side posed great difficulty for the technicians responsible for overseeing the equipment on the plane. Keeping in mind that this program took place in the early 1960s, all lesson plans were videotaped. The early videotape-recorders were subject to overheating and other malfunctions (Jajkowski, 2004). The technicians on the planes had great difficulty addressing maintenance issues with all of the equipment being stored in the plane. The 24-foot antenna was also an issue, as it was constantly moving. An innovative solution to this issue was discovered. When the aircraft reached its position, the 24-foot antenna mast was hydraulically extended in a straight down position and a gyroscope would keep it within one degree of the vertical position regardless of the position of the aircraft (Jajkowski, 2004). All of this equipment— the videotape players, the antenna, and the technicians—operated out of the back of the plane.

Retaining pilots was also a challenge for the MPATI program. Flying 2000 miles per day in the same figure-of-8 pattern proved boring and redundant for the pilots. Although MPATI attempted to fix this problem by hiring part-time pilots who worked infrequently, pilots were also challenged by the Midwest weather. Although there was little MPATI could do about the weather, it purchased a second plane so that if the first plane was grounded due to mechanical difficulty, a second plane was ready to fly to keep the educational programming flowing.

In the classrooms, not every television set had UHF receivers with individual channels listed. At this time there were only three major broadcast television stations, so finding the MPATI channels on the television sets was a challenge for the teachers. Scheduling lessons posed a logistical challenge for schools that participated in the MPATI program. The equipment on the airplane was limited to broadcasting 20 lesson plans every school day due to the number of channels to which MPATI had access. While the six states participating in the program were in the Midwest, they were spread across the Eastern and Central time zones, which made scheduling difficult. Class schedules varied from school to school which caused scheduling to be problematic and generated great levels of dissatisfaction among membership schools (University of Maryland Libraries, 2007).

MPATI was plagued by a lack of membership and the technical limitations inherent in the project at the time. The final blow for the program appeared to be in the mid-1960s when the FCC refused to grant additional UHF channels to the project. By this point advancements in satellite technology were being made, and by 1966 the FCC had stopped issuing any licenses for television stations above channel 69 (Jajkowski, 2004). MPATI, once thought of as a giant leap in technology advancement, was ultimately hurt by the advancements in technology. It became a tape library, returning the two DC-6 aircraft and surrendering its broadcast licenses to the FCC. It would serve as a library to its member schools for the next three years, before the entire project was dissolved in 1971.

Implications

While MPATI experienced success for a brief period, its greater contribution was that it pushed the boundaries of distance education by being the first form of satellite television transmission. Distance education is defined as being "institution-based, formal education where the learning group is separated and where interactive telecommunication systems are used to connect learners, resources, and instructors" (Schlosser & Simonson, 2009, p. 1). The videotape and televised instruction used by MPATI was a precursor for online instruction and the distance education that we are familiar with today. MPATI broke down the preconceived notions that students could only learn if they were in a face-to-face environment with their instructor.

MPATI was a novel and innovative approach to instructional technology because the program allowed for curriculum to be disseminated via television signals ten years prior to the Public Broadcasting Service being launched in 1969 (Jajkowski, 2004). By the late 1980s, interactive satellite distance learning had become commonplace both in education and in business. Since that time, distance education has evolved from MPATI to interactive satellite to the Internet. Students can now participate in synchronous and asynchronous learning with individuals located all across the world. MPATI existed at a time when instructional designers were not accustomed to using terms such as asynchronous versus synchronous, but these terms are now used frequently in many learning environments, particularly distance education, as instructors have a variety of instructional tools, activities, and strategies at their disposal. In this instance the practice of MPATI drove the development of the theory of distance education. While MPATI was an early attempt at disseminating curricula from a distance, we have seen the field of instructional design grow to include best practices for web-based instruction in part because of numerous iterations of distance education initiatives.

MPATI provided opportunities for schools in remote areas to stretch their curricular offerings and provide students with learning opportunities they would not have access to otherwise. While MPATI offered a variety of elementary and secondary lesson plans, the onus was placed on the school districts to identify what lesson plans would enhance their pre-existing curricula. This was an early example of how learner-centered design was being used in distance education.

Membership schools affiliated with MPATI were constrained by having to access televised broadcasts according to a dissemination schedule. In the 1960s, feedback regarding the effectiveness of MPATI instruction was collected once a year through teacher surveys and discussion groups. This prevented the instructor from recognizing when groups of students were struggling with course content and constrained their ability to customize the instruction to meet their individual needs. It also posed significant challenges for the designers to update the curriculum, as this too was done annually and based on feedback from all membership schools. Technologies today, however, allow the end user or learner to participate, have freedom and flexibility in their learning time, and provide timely feedback to the designers in an effort for continuous improvement. Applications such as chat rooms, blogs, journals, discussion boards, and e-mail allow students to communicate with their instructors and peers instantaneously and report any challenges they may experience with subject materials or other aspects of a course.

Much like MPATI, 50 years later we are still faced with similar design and curricular concerns. While technological applications appear to be growing at what seems to be an exponential speed, teachers, school districts, universities, and businesses must identify options that will enhance their specific needs. These technological innovations require instructional designers to continually approach design through a new lens. For example, interaction, as we have previously defined it, is no longer a descriptor of one form of communication. Technologies provide for numerous forms of interactions and designers must grapple with designing for different types and levels of interaction taking place between the learner, content, and the learning environment.

This design case highlights how the novel concept of MPATI was the first form of satellite television transmission, utilized principles of programmed instruction to educate elementary and secondary school students in the Midwest, and moved the audiovisual movement of instructional design forward. There is still a growing need for usable and affordable technology, well-designed instructional materials and resources, and people in and outside of the classroom available to facilitate learning (Gibson, 2001).

Summary

Although we look at the MPATI program now and see all of the challenges its designers faced, it was an innovative use of the airborne television technology available in the 1960s allowing school children to be educated in ways otherwise not available through their school. We learned through MPATI that distance learning via television was viable and could be effective if technology and human support were in place.

References

Gibson, D. (2001). The way we were ... Education on the fly. *Technos Quarterly, 10*(3). Retrieved from www.ait.nt/technos/tq_10/3gibson.php.

Jajkowski, S. (2004). MPATI: The flying classroom. *The Video Veteran*. Retrieved from www.chicagotelevision.com/MPATI.htm.

Perlman, A. (2008). *Flying classrooms in the Midwest: The MPATI's experiment in regional educational television*. Retrieved from http://mediacommons.futureofthebook.org/imr/2008/02/28/flying-classrooms-in-the-midwest-the-mpatis-experiment-in-regional-educational-television.

Schlosser, L., & Simonson, M. (2009). *Distance education: Definition and glossary of terms* (3rd edn). Charlotte, NC: Information Age Publishing.

The Ohio State University. (1964). *Airborne Television: Profile of a School*. A Series of Motion Picture Documents on Communication Theory and the New Educational Media.

University of Maryland Libraries. (2007). *Midwest Program on Airborne Television Instruction (MPATI) Records*, Special Collections, University of Maryland Libraries. Retrieved from http://hdl.handle.net/1903.1/1591.

10
AUTOMATED AND AMPLIFIED
Active Learning with Computers and Radio (1965–1979)

Anne Trumbore

Introduction

In 2012, Massive Open Online Courses (MOOCs) captured the attention and imagination of the public as a new educational technology that could promote learning on a massive scale. Yet the design for engaged learning using technology, including computer-mediated, individualized instruction and even the flipped classroom, can be found in two Stanford projects implemented in the early 1960s and 1970s. The first, Computer Assisted Instruction (CAI) in elementary mathematical logic began with a pilot in Palo Alto in 1965; its achievements and limitations led to the creation and implementation of the Nicaragua Radio Mathematics Project (NRMP), 1975 to 1979, which has become the model for Interactive Radio Instruction (IRI), a scalable methodology for active learning and the standardization of instruction. To date, over 20 million students worldwide have participated in IRI's active learning methodologies in a diverse set of subjects (Ho & Thukral, 2009). Like MOOCs, the goals of both CAI and NRMP were to improve educational quality, provide effective, low-cost access to education, and to deploy available technologies to enhance teaching and learning at scale.

Historical and Intellectual Location of CAI And NRMP

The US Department of Education (then the Office of Education) began funding research projects which explored the uses of computers in educational contexts in the late 1950s. By 1969, over 210 projects had been funded in the US across a variety of use cases, including programming, computer models, informational retrieval systems, administration, curriculum development, training, and computer-assisted and computer-managed instruction. Perhaps because the available technology was bulky, expensive, and not easily obtained, the most common use of the computer across these projects was for the organization, administration, and analysis of data.

Yet, despite limitations of access, a handful of researchers at institutions such as the University of Illinois at Urbana-Champaign, Penn State University, and Stanford University were pioneering efforts in computer-assisted instruction, where the student actively engaged with the computer to receive lessons and immediate response based on performance. Their efforts actualized a long-held vision of using technology to construct an "artificial tutor" to scale personalized and accurate instruction on demand. Although the technology was generally inaccessible, it was capable of interacting with the user; the early experiments focused on the expansion and adaptation of these capabilities.

One experiment notable for the boldness of its design and its demonstrated effectiveness was Computer Assisted Instruction in Elementary Mathematics by Professor Patrick Suppes at Stanford University. I worked at Stanford for Dr. Suppes from 2004 to 2012, and details about these projects emerged from conversations between us in 2014.

The project began in 1965 with elementary school students in Palo Alto (Figure 10.1) and was designed to see whether computers could help very young

FIGURE 10.1 Computer-Assisted Instruction. An elementary school student interacts with the artificial tutor.

Source: Suppes, 1966.

students learn mathematical reasoning. The initial school sites and the students were chosen based on proximity to the campus and the willingness of their teachers to participate in the experiment. Proximity was necessary to provide adaptive instruction: the machines the students used were connected by telephone lines to a central computer on the Stanford campus.

Each day, students listened to a recorded lesson and answered drill and practice questions to assess their understanding of the material. Their performance data was delivered to the central computer where it was analyzed each night, so that each student received a lesson tailored to their level of understanding the following day.

Some students were given these lessons as pre-work to prepare them for their teacher's instruction; other teachers used them as drill and practice for lessons already taught. In each case, the teacher determined how to best use the technology to blend the classroom so that it served student learning objectives.

Both students and teachers enjoyed working with the technology, and while the program was successful, expanding to schools in Mississippi, Kentucky, and Iowa in addition to the California schools over the next two to three years, it was ultimately too expensive and impractical to scale. Each participating location had access to a Programmed Data Processor (the PDP-8 mini-computer) which transmitted student data via telephone line to the PDP-1 computer at Stanford for nightly analysis. Most schools did not have access to these larger computers, and the PDP-8 was capable of being connected to only 60 teletype terminals (TTY) on which the instruction was primarily delivered. The high cost and limited availability of the hardware meant that the reach of computer-assisted instruction exceeded the grasp of easily available technologies by too wide a margin.

But the relative ease of implementation for schools which had access to the hardware, the improvement in learning outcomes, the standardization of high-quality interactive instruction, and the enthusiastic response from both teachers and students appealed to the US government as a method of providing access to effective educational content and practices to underdeveloped regions and/or underserved students around the world. The most significant hurdle to widespread implementation was the cost and availability of the technology.

The United States Agency for International Development (USAID) contacted Suppes and his team and asked if principal design elements of CAIs of adaptivity, interactivity, and effectiveness could be replicated using radio to help scale active learning practices globally. "We worked on computers, but then USAID asked if we could use radio, because it was cheaper," says Suppes (personal communication, June 12, 2014). Historically, one of the cheapest and most widely available technologies used for education was radio, yet education delivered via radio was broadcast-only, with none of the interactivity of CAI.

After an initial survey of several potential sites, Nicaragua was chosen because the government provided both facilities and local staff for the project, students would be taught in their native language, and there was no pre-existing radio instruction. Most importantly, the math curriculum developed by the Nicaraguan Ministry of Education closely resembled those of other developing countries; therefore, it was an ideal test case for which to pilot a mathematics curriculum developed for radio broadcast supported by teacher-directed activities. If proven successful, USAID hoped this model could then be easily localized to other regions around the world.

And so in 1975, 10 years after fourth-grade students in Palo Alto area schools completed daily drill-and-practice arithmetic lessons in their classroom on a teletype machine connected by telephone lines to a computer on the Stanford campus, first-grade students in 16 classrooms in the [District] of Masaya, outside Managua, Nicaragua, listened to a 20-minute mathematics lesson on the radio while responding verbally, physically, and by writing answers on a worksheet to questions posed during the broadcast (Figure 10.2).

Those worksheets were brought to a central location in Managua where they were entered into a computer using punch cards. Those cards were fed into the computer and their data stored on magnetic tape; those tapes were sent by international mail to Stanford where the data was analyzed on the computer there. This data was used to refine the lessons to be more effective. The data transfer from Nicaraguan schoolroom to Stanford campus took approximately one week; curriculum changes could be made during the course of the school year. It is interesting to note that during the years of operation no data was ever lost in the mail.

Growing political instability in Nicaragua in 1978 precipitated the withdrawal of US government funding for the project, and Stanford funding followed suit. Yet while the project lay dormant in Nicaragua, the principles and methodologies of NRMP were adapted and expanded over the next 40 years to include Interactive Radio Instruction (IRI) across a range of topics, including mathematics, language, science, and reading among others. To date, over 20 million learners in primarily poorer and/or densely populated countries, including Sudan, Mali, Indonesia, Haiti, and India, have used IRI in the classroom, and IRI continues to be a viable approach to reaching the estimated 72 million children worldwide who are not in school (Ho & Thukral, 2009).

Online, the design model of scalable, active learning introduced in CAI and developed in IRI is now seen in a number of popular educational technologies, especially adaptive learning programs, and MOOCs themselves. Just as importantly, these early projects helped pioneer the practice of collecting student data to measure effectiveness of instruction and allow for curricular changes during the instruction period as well as to individualize instruction based on performance. Most significantly, both CAI and NRMP identified the potential of technology to enhance teaching and learning by making them more effective and affordable. Fifty years later, we are using similar design principles of interactivity, engagement-based strategies, evidence-based design, and adaptive instruction and methods to achieve those same goals.

138 Anne Trumbore

FIGURE 10.2 Elementary school students in Managua respond to a radio lesson in mathematics.

Credit: Tom Tilson.

Describing the Designs of CAI and NRMP

The designs of CAI and NRMP answered two separate but related questions: is it possible for technology to provide interactive and individualized instruction, and if so, can that instruction be scaled effectively to those who need it most?

The design objective for CAI was to create an automated tutor–student relationship using the computer, an emerging and somewhat experimental technology in education in the 1960s. The computer played the role of the tutor, providing instant feedback to the student and adapting instruction based on the student's understanding. Individualized instruction in the form of student–tutor relationships has been considered an ideal method of learning in every aspect except for efficiency; the promise of combining the instructional effectiveness of the tutor with the cost-effectiveness of automating him or her served as the ideal for this project's design (Suppes, 1966), just as it continues to serve the purpose of many educational technologies of today.

The design of the tutor comprised three technologies: recorded lessons provided aural instruction, a cathode-ray screen displayed questions or problems, and a keyboard or stylus (light pen) enabled the student to respond to the machine by entering answers or solutions. Students were engaged aurally as they listened to lessons, visually as they read questions or problems, and physically as they typed on a keyboard or tapped the screen. In turn, the machine provided visual feedback to the students' physical responses to create an interactive learning experience (Figure 10.3).

The first technology used was audio instruction: students listened to recorded lessons delivered through headphones while seated at the terminal. These lessons

FIGURE 10.3 Components of the artificial tutor.

Source: Suppes, 1966.

were created to develop understanding of mathematical logic and reasoning and to fulfill explicit learning objectives created by teachers. Because the rich lessons could then be repeated as often as needed, their effect could be amplified to many students across classrooms and school locations.

Audio messages were felt to be preferable to solely visual ones because evidence showed that student understanding at elementary levels clearly increased when instruction was verbal and not written. Young children respond better to the spoken than to the written word, and when math instruction is presented verbally, comprehension of mathematical concepts is not dependent upon literacy or reading skills. Aural delivery in CAI was proven to be especially useful for underserved learners whose reading skills were not commensurate with their mathematical reasoning ability. And even adept readers at a young age are able to understand spoken directions at a far greater degree of complexity than written ones (Suppes, 1966). The effectiveness of audio instruction was expanded and examined more closely in the design and delivery of mathematics lessons via radio, as realized in the Nicaraguan Radio Mathematics project.

The second technology used in the design was the cathode-ray tube employed to display questions and problem sets. At the time, this technology was very new and was seen as desirable owing to its resemblance to the popular television screen. Younger students who could not yet read (or whose skills were emergent) could point to correct answers and see spatial relationships among figures as they listened to an explanation.

The third technology was either a light pen used to tap the cathode-ray tube or a modified keyboard: both allowed the students to communicate with the machine. The keyboard was the easiest and cheapest way for the student to transmit her response to the computer; one-keystroke responses were designed to lower the barrier for those unfamiliar with typing or the keyboard itself.

When students put on headphones and communicated with the machine, they created a closed circuit of learning between themselves and the technology. This closed loop allowed space for deliberate practice and for individualized instruction, but it separated the students physically from the learning community inside the classroom. The isolation had beneficial effects; it enabled students to focus exclusively on their own learning. Although this design of CAI with recorded lessons, cathode-ray tube, and keyboard or stylus was the most expensive implementation of the artificial tutor, it was also the most desirable for the most practical of reasons—it was quiet and did not disturb other students in the classroom. (A more widely available implementation, the teletype machine, was noisy and could be a distraction.)

CAI was first envisioned in three possible forms, dependent upon available technology. The least expensive and most widely available implementation employed teletype machines. Students read arithmetic problems, typed their answers, and received instant feedback from the machine. This model was used primarily for drill and practice sessions to test and reinforce understanding. The second implementation more fully realized human student–tutor interaction through recorded lessons, visual prompts and problems on a cathode-ray tube or teletype, and visual feedback to the student's physical response of typing or tapping an answer. While this approach required more sophisticated hardware, it was more suitable for younger children and others whose reading skills were not yet fully developed. The third model of interaction was designed to encourage verbal dialogue between the student and the machine: the student would listen to a recorded lesson and respond verbally to questions, and the computer would interpret the response as correct or incorrect. This vision was too advanced for the technological capabilities of 1965. But its potential would be realized and ultimately expanded in the Nicaragua Radio Mathematics Project ten years later.

NRMP amplified the possibilities of interactive audio instruction piloted in CAI. The objective of this design was to "use the voice transmitted by modern methods of radio rather than the classroom teacher," says Suppes (personal communication, 2014). The design goal for this project was to enhance teaching and learning by standardizing instructional delivery and expanding its reach at low cost, and its purpose was to improve education globally by providing access to effective educational materials to remote and/or underserved students and to correct for divergent levels of teacher preparation.

Due to the goals of cost efficiency and scale, the bulk of the design work for the NRMP was not performed with technology but with curriculum. Because the curriculum itself had been recently redesigned and the teachers retrained, the redesign work focused on delivery rather than content. The design team from Stanford felt that teachers would be less resistant to changes in how lessons were delivered rather than in what the lessons covered. Therefore, the key objectives of the design of these radio lessons were to implement the strategies of effective teachers: encouraging active response from children, distributing practice, reinforcing knowledge of results, and providing different pathways for children who learn at different rates.

Working with the official mathematics curriculum developed by the Nicaraguan Ministry of Education, curriculum designers worked with local experts and scriptwriters to create 20-minute interactive lessons (Figure 10.4) where students engaged with the radio 40 to 50 times by responding verbally, making a physical motion, or writing on their worksheet.

First, the curriculum designers broke the existing curriculum into smaller units on specific topics which could be reassembled into a lesson to provide distributed practice in several areas over a series of lessons. Then the scriptwriter created a draft of a radio script from these specifications which encouraged students to respond. This draft was then read to staff involved in classroom observation and teacher training to gain feedback on clarity, level of difficulty in language, and overall student interest in the characters and stories in the lesson. Third, an artist created a worksheet on which students could record their responses. The data from these worksheets was then analyzed by computer.

FIGURE 10.4 An artist in Nicaragua creates a worksheet for students to use during radio lessons.

Credit: Tom Tilson.

When the data indicated that a lesson was not effective, it was rewritten and re-recorded, and then re-broadcast to the students weeks later. Testing and analysis showed significant improvement following lesson revision and continued practice on the topic by students.

Each radio lesson script was written to implement the following effective teaching strategies: to give students multiple opportunities to actively engage with the lesson, to provide knowledge of correct results to increase the rate of learning, to encourage practice with concrete materials to make abstract concepts real, to distribute practice over multiple sessions, and to tailor instruction to individual learning rates when possible.

This last strategy proved difficult to implement using synchronous broadcast as the delivery method for instruction. "We recognized in designing NRMP that we could not individualize the radio responses to the individual responses of the students. The point of the project was to send a very high level of exposition, and the advantage was in the curriculum," says Suppes (personal communication, 2014). The other active learning strategies were realized through having the students respond to questions and prompts in the broadcast at a rate of two to three times a minute. A key finding of initial pilot projects was that students remained engaged with the lesson so long as they were asked to respond frequently; students were even more engaged than if the mathematical questions were embedded in an entertaining story.

These 20-minute lessons, followed by 20 minutes of instructor-led activities, provided all of the mathematical instruction for first-grade students. Each day, the lesson was broadcast to classrooms on the radio, during which students interacted with the radio; afterwards, the teacher directed additional activities designed to reinforce and deepen the students' understanding of the material. These activities were provided to teachers in a written guidebook developed alongside the curriculum. This shift in instructor role from content delivery to learning facilitator is enjoying a resurgence through the use of filmed content in "flipped classrooms" across a range of schools and institutions in the US. Nearly 40 years ago, NMRP pioneered the design of blending the classroom with interactive technology so that the instructor could devote more time to instruction and less to content delivery.

Experiencing the Designs

Computer-aided Instruction

By 1968, CAI had spread to schools in four states, selected for their willingness to experiment and their access to a master computer such as the PDP-8. Most students participated in drill and practice with the teletype machine. Schools in California had direct phone lines connecting the terminals or teletype machines to a PDP-1 (Figure 10.5) on the Stanford campus or an IBM 1500 system located nearby. In Kentucky and Mississippi, terminals and teletypes at the school were connected to a PDP-8 which was itself connected to the PDP-1 at Stanford.

The location of the instructional terminals varied by school. Schools that had multiple machines available for instruction, a separate room to house them, and teaching staff available to help with any technological difficulties grouped the machines in one room. Other schools distributed the machines one to a

FIGURE 10.5   A PDP-1-powered CAI elementary math instruction. Terminals at the school locations were connected by phone lines to a local PDP-8 which was connected via phone line to the PDP-1 at Stanford.

Credit: Marcin Wichary (www.flickr.com/photos/8399025@N07/2635003339).

classroom, and the teacher provided support if necessary. Teachers in the project had the opportunity to participate in a workshop where they created learning objectives which incorporated practice with the computer, and also received training in trouble-shooting technical difficulties, such as the ribbon breaking in a teletype machine.

Students were assigned to work with the machine once a day for five to ten minutes. This work consisted of practice exercises, and/or a recorded lesson and practice exercises chosen to fulfill learning objectives developed by the teacher. The content delivered to the student reflected what the teacher had previously introduced in the classroom and what the students had already practiced there: CAI lessons and drill and practice work served primarily to support and enhance the teacher's instruction.

Students took turns and sat at the machine one by one. They first typed in their name, which was often the most typing they had to do at any one time. The teletype whirred, the keys clacked, and the first question of a lesson chosen on the basis of the student's performance the previous day was presented for the student to answer. Students had 10 to 15 seconds to answer these questions such as "L.C.M is Least Common Multiple. ____ is the L.C.M of 4 and 9." If the student did not answer in time, the machine responded with the message TIME IS UP. If the student answered incorrectly, the machine typed WRONG. If the student answered incorrectly or failed to answer two times in a row, the answer was shown, and the student was given a chance to enter this correct answer to reinforce the experience of entering the correct answer. Figure 10.6 shows how CAI communicated these to the learners via teletype. After the third attempt the next question was shown, whether or not the student submitted the correct answer. Because a certain number of exercises were expected to be completed within a certain time, students were limited to three attempts per question.

At the end of the lesson the student received a paper printout of the session, including a summative grade and a cheery message (GOOD BYE O FEARLESS DRILL TESTER). Figure 10.7 shows feedback to learners at the end of their session. The immediate feedback on performance and a supportive, personalized message motivated students, made their progress visible, and personalized the interaction with the machine through acknowledgement of work completed and examined. The student then rejoined the class, or, if the machines were in a separate room, returned to the classroom.

The idea of individualized instruction was further reinforced by the student leaving the class or the classroom to interact with a machine. Students who listened to an audio lesson and responded to recorded prompts on either the teletype or by touching a light pen on a cathode-ray screen could have this isolating effect intensified. Wearing headphones separated them from the class aurally, and what they saw visually and responded to was individualized and not part of the classroom as a whole.

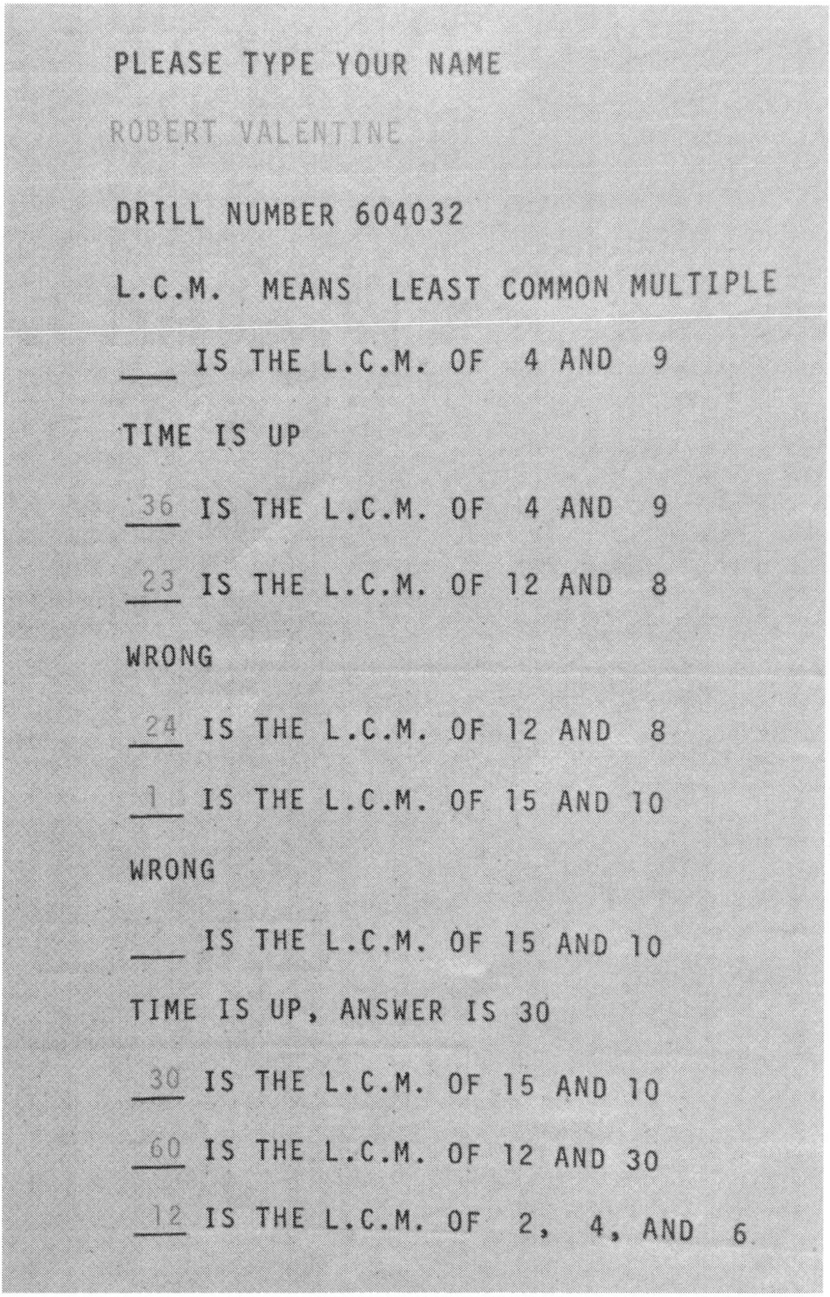

```
PLEASE TYPE YOUR NAME
ROBERT VALENTINE

DRILL NUMBER 604032

L.C.M. MEANS LEAST COMMON MULTIPLE

___ IS THE L.C.M. OF  4 AND  9

TIME IS UP

 36 IS THE L.C.M. OF  4 AND  9

 23 IS THE L.C.M. OF 12 AND  8

WRONG

 24 IS THE L.C.M. OF 12 AND  8

  1 IS THE L.C.M. OF 15 AND 10

WRONG

___ IS THE L.C.M. OF 15 AND 10

TIME IS UP, ANSWER IS 30

 30 IS THE L.C.M. OF 15 AND 10

 60 IS THE L.C.M. OF 12 AND 30

 12 IS THE L.C.M. OF  2,  4, AND  6
```

FIGURE 10.6 A record of a student–computer interaction on a teletype machine.
Source: Suppes, 1966.

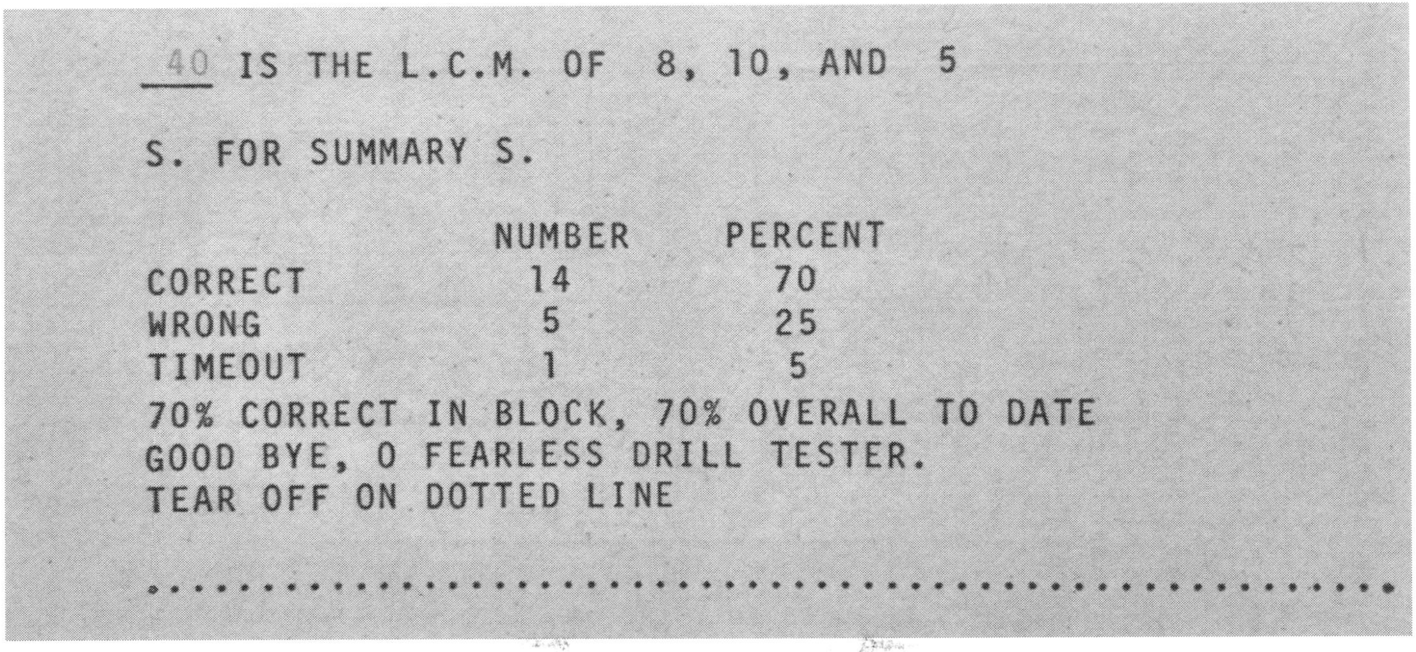

```
40  IS THE L.C.M. OF 8, 10, AND 5

S. FOR SUMMARY S.

            NUMBER   PERCENT
CORRECT       14       70
WRONG          5       25
TIMEOUT        1        5
70% CORRECT IN BLOCK, 70% OVERALL TO DATE
GOOD BYE, 0 FEARLESS DRILL TESTER.
TEAR OFF ON DOTTED LINE
```

FIGURE 10.7 Student feedback complete with summative score and personalized response given by the teletype machine.

Source: Suppes, 1966.

Nicaragua Mathematics Radio Project

Students in the NMRP, on the other hand, received their instruction collectively, since a primary goal of this program was low-cost quality instruction at scale. This proved potentially problematic to classrooms with a broad range of achievement. Collective instruction was individualized to some extent by distributing worksheets tailored to different levels of ability so that students followed the same instructions but were able to practice with materials suited to their individual level. Post-lesson materials to reinforce themes at differing levels were also considered, although ultimately worksheets were determined to be too expensive to provide to every student, and blackboards were used instead.

The day's lesson was broadcast to all participating classrooms, and students participated as a group. In each classroom, the teacher turned on the radio, music began, and a nationally known singer introduced the program with a song. (This song became a hit, and some objected that it made the study of math too popular.) Immediately, students were asked questions and expected to respond. The questions were posed in multiple forms to increase learning; for instance, an abstract question, "What is 5 plus 10?" was followed by the same question in concrete terms, "Juan earned five centavos yesterday, and ten centavos today. How much did he earn altogether?" Students were also asked to respond physically—tapping their knees a certain number of times, or holding up a number of fingers. Because many of the interactions were verbal or physical, students could learn from each other's responses; at other times during the first year (1975), they answered questions posed in the broadcast on worksheets, until these were deemed too expensive to supply daily. In subsequent years, teachers wrote down students' answers on the board (Figure 10.8) and used paper only once a week to take a test. The results of these tests were put on punch cards and transferred to magnetic tape in Nicaragua; the tape itself was sent to Stanford where the data was analyzed on the PDP-1.

The longevity of this curriculum design is notable; a 2009 report on IRI states: "Most of the principles of interactive instruction identified by the original Nicaragua project have proved durable, appropriate and relevant." Over 20 million students in over 37 countries have participated in IRI, and the principal elements of frequent opportunities for student response to recorded material are present in educational computer games, instructional videos with embedded quizzes, polling, and even the use of clickers in a live classroom. At the time that NRMP was designed, the idea that active learning promoted deeper learning was still in its infancy. In fact, Suppes published some of the first papers testing this hypothesis (Suppes & Ginsberg, 1962). The widespread adoption of the design of NRMP for IRI has proven to be a critical inflection point for active learning principles to be accepted and adopted broadly.

Failure Analysis

Both project designs were pedagogically innovative in promoting active learning techniques, and successful in improving student engagement and learning outcomes.

FIGURE 10.8 NRMP: an instructor fills in answers called out by students during a radio lesson.

Credit: Tom Tilson.

And both ultimately succumbed to financial pressures, although of different types. CAI was always intended as an experimental project, as access to the technology necessary to implement it was both expensive and scarce. Conversely, NRMP was developed to be cost-effective and broadly available, yet the sustainability of the project came under attack from political, financial, and organizational forces.

Pedagogically, both CAI and NRMP were successes. Students in NRMP classrooms reported learning gains approximately 20 percent higher in learning outcomes than their peers in traditional classrooms. Gains in oral topics such as oral addition, subtraction, and word problems were especially high. The most effective response was the delayed oral response: students were asked to think of an answer but not to say it aloud until prompted. Because the majority of the NRMP students lived in rural areas where most business or marketplace transactions were conducted orally, these learning gains reinforced the usefulness of interactive, oral mathematics education.

Initially, NRMP's lessons were well received by students and teachers; all the instructors who participated in the 1975 program asked to be included the following year. As the program continued, however, resentment developed among some teachers who felt they were being displaced as content experts by the radio lessons. Ultimately, the internal bureaucracy in Nicaragua, combined with lack of governmental control over teacher development, eroded support for the program.

Politically, the civil unrest and governmental instability of the late 1970s forced withdrawal; these events coincided with the financial pressure applied by USAID, which initially subsidized the project, insisting the Nicaraguan ministries assume half the cost of the program. When the ministries balked, both Stanford and USAID withdrew financial support for the project.

Conclusion

Just as the design and implementation of Computer Assisted Instruction (CAI) in elementary mathematical logic directly influenced and informed the design of the Nicaraguan Radio Mathematics Project (NRMP), so have both endeavors fundamentally expanded ideas of computer-mediated instruction to include providing multiple opportunities for active learning at scale. The commonalities of the instructional models of these projects are reflected in the design of many current educational technologies where students interact individually with a centralized curriculum. Each also identified the effectiveness and affordability of active learning practices enabled through technology. And while both projects explored the possibilities of technology to assume some of the work of instruction, both ultimately enhanced the role of teachers in the classroom by creating the conditions for new teaching practices to emerge.

Acknowledgments

The author wishes to thank Patrick Suppes for his support of this project and the work which inspired it, and Nancy Smith and Robert Smith for their assistance locating materials and references.

Further Reading on CAI and NRMP

Bakshi, S., & Jha, J. (2013). Interactive radio/audio interventions in elementary schools in Karnataka, India: A policy simulation exercise. Global Development Network, Centre for Budget and Policy Studies. Retrieved from www.gdn.int/admin/uploads/editor/files/GDN_PEMRP_CBPS_PS_Education.pdf.

Bosch, A. (1997). *Interactive radio instruction: Twenty-three years of improving education quality.* Washington, DC: World Bank Group.

Jamison, D. T. (1978). Radio education and student repetition in Nicaragua. World Bank Reprint Series, No. 91. Reprinted from Jamison, D. T. (1978). Radio education and student repetition in Nicaragua. In P. Suppes, B. Searle, and J. Friend (Eds.), *The radio mathematics project: Nicaragua, 1976–1977* (pp. 199–221). Stanford, CA: Stanford University, Institute for Mathematical Studies in the Social Sciences.

Jerman, M., & Suppes, P. (1969). A workshop on computer-assisted instruction in elementary mathematics. *The Arithmetic Teacher, 16*, 193–197.

Molnar, A., & Sherman, B. (1969). U.S. office of education support of computer activities. Retrieved from ERIC database at http://eric.ed.gov/?id=ED031959.

Searle, B. (1975). The Nicaragua radio mathematics project. Retrieved from ERIC database at http://eric.ed.gov/?id=ED112887.

Searle, B., & Suppes, P. (1978). Achievement levels of students learning primary-school mathematics by radio in Nicaragua. *Studies in Science and Mathematics Education (India), 1*, 63–80.

Searle, B., & Suppes, P. (1977). Computer usage in the Nicaragua radio mathematics project. In J. A. Jordan, Jr. and K. Malaivongs (Eds.), *Proceedings of the International Conference on Computer Applications in Developing Countries* (Vol. 1) (pp. 361–374). Bangkok, Thailand: Asian Institute of Technology.

Suppes, P. (1968). *Computer-assisted instruction: Stanford's 1965–66 arithmetic program.* New York: Academic Press. Retrieved from ERIC database at http://eric.ed.gov/?id=ED034432.

Suppes, P. (1978). *The radio mathematics project: Nicaragua 1976–1977.* Retrieved from ERIC database at http://eric.ed.gov/?id=ED167381.

References

Ho, J., & Thukral, H. (2009). Tuned in to student success: Assessing the impact of interactive radio instruction for the hardest-to-reach. *Journal of Education for International Development 4*(2), 34–51.

Suppes, P. (1966). The uses of computers in education. *Scientific American, 215*(3), 206–220.

Suppes, P., & Ginsberg, R. (1962). Experimental studies of mathematical concept formation in young children. *Science Education, 46*(3), 230–240.

11

TICCIT

Building Theory for Practical Purposes (1971–1978)

Andrew S. Gibbons and A. F. O'Neal

The Landscape and the Challenge

In 1970, one of the most pressing educational questions was, "Can the newly invented computer (barely 25 years old) carry out major instructional functions in a sustainable commercial-grade way?" In 1957, Sputnik had created a new urgency for exploring educational applications of technology. The goal was to improve instruction, distribute it to a wider audience, and at the same time lower development costs. Though today we take the instructional computer for granted, in 1970 this was an open question, and there were many doubters. Several problems had to be solved: computer cost, delivery cost, instructional development cost, and instructional quality.

Costs

Computers of the day in 1971 were large and expensive. A mainframe computer required special air-conditioned facilities and a team of trained technicians, programmers, and operators. Input–output systems were primitive—a teletype terminal, a deck of Hollerith punched cards, and a paper print-out or monochrome text display with keyboard. Vector graphics were a new technology requiring programming skills. Automated graphic and logic authoring interfaces were only just being developed and were not yet ready for general use. Connecting the computer to multiple users required the use of expensive high-quality telephone lines.

The costs of computerized instruction did not reside alone in equipment and delivery. The creation of instruction was expensive because each lesson was handcrafted. A lesson design team normally consisted of either a highly gifted individual with a special combination of skills and training, or a team of specialists consisting of a writer/editor, a programmer, and perhaps an artist. A subject matter expert was also needed to supply content knowledge. Specialized programming languages were tailored expressly for instructional purposes, but as expectations of lesson quality grew, new features had to be added to the languages, and they became quite large, detailed, and difficult to learn.

Instructional Quality

The quality of computerized instruction had to be seen in a future view, since no one, not even those who were creating it, knew quite what the instructional computer could do. The search for computer-based instructional quality was taking place on two levels: theoretical and applied.

During the 1960s and 1970s, experimental computer-based instructional styles grew up in great variety. Atkinson and Wilson (1969) featured reports of several high-visibility theoretical projects. Chapters outlined futuristic visions of intelligent, conversational instructional systems. Suppes (1969) envisioned a system that could "approximate the interaction [of] a patient tutor" (p. 43) and a dialogue system that could "recognize the spoken speech of a child" (p. 43). Stolurow (1969) proposed that "a CAI course of any magnitude should teach the student *how* to learn" (p. 90, emphasis in original).

Wenger (1987) conducted an extensive review of experimental intelligent tutoring systems dating from 1970. He distinguishes between "frame-based" and "intelligent" CAI, defining one as being fixed in its delivery sequence and the other as being a "communication" system that adapted its interactions to the moment-by-moment responses of the learner. This distinction became, and remains today, a major fault line between two schools of thinking about the core architecture of technology-based instruction, and it was a major issue in the design of the TICCIT system, as will be described below.

Wenger expressed his own vision of the future of computer-assisted instruction:

> Now imagine active books that can interact with the reader to communicate knowledge at the appropriate level, selectively highlighting the interconnectedness and ramification of items, recalling relevant information, probing understanding, explaining difficult areas in more depth, skipping over seemingly known material.
>
> (p. 6)

Below the level of these exalted visions, everyday designers were also experimenting with the new technology on a less formal, less theoretical, and more practical level. They too were struggling to envision what CAI should be. But their ideas had to be expressed in the immediate reality of the now. Using large experimental systems like Plato, designers wrestled with the difficulties of lesson creation within a confined and confining design space that was growing but still incapable of expressing far-out futuristic dreams. This work took place in an atmosphere of excitement and anticipation (see, e.g., http://platohistory.org/). This was the flavor of the time, and this was the context of the TICCIT project.

Origins of the TICCIT Project

During this period of great experimentation, every aspect of the technology was churning with rapid change much like what we are experiencing today. Specifically, hardware, software, instructional technique, design technique, and context of use were all fair game for experimentation.

TICCIT was one of two large-scale experimental computer-assisted instruction (CAI) projects; the other was PLATO. TICCIT and PLATO became contenders in a lopsided horse race sponsored by the National Science Foundation. The goal of the competition was to prove two very different configurations of the CAI system. TICCIT was a new development from the ground up. The PLATO system had been under development at the University of Illinois since 1960. By 1970, the system was mature, and in 1973 the university established the Computer-Based Education Research Laboratory (CERL) under the direction of Donald Bitzer. The configuration of the PLATO system included a powerful central computer communicating with hundreds of distant terminals communicating over telephone lines with smart terminals, which were themselves small computers.

In 1967, the National Science Foundation began supporting continued development of the PLATO system which had previously been funded mainly from military sources. Courseware authors programmed instructional materials using a specialized CAI language called TUTOR, which automated many functions common to instructional programming, such as answer processing, graphics, and data management. PLATO became popular among a loyal following, who found it easier to use for developing instruction than general-purpose computer systems with a weaker toolset. A number of experimental projects explored the system's capability for the creation of simulations, games, networked communications, and user-constructed virtual environments.

A major challenge for the PLATO system was cost: phone line costs and the cost per hour of instructional development. The creation of PLATO products required a programmer, often a subject matter expert who had taken the time to learn the TUTOR language. Development was by hand, and the specialized built-in TUTOR routines were cost-savers, but building every product from scratch was expensive. A second cost factor was the use of telephone lines for communication with far-flung terminals. At first, transmission quality was uneven, and as quality went up, so did the phone bill. This configuration was popular, but without outside support there was no business revenue plan to make it sustainable.

Emerging technologies were another important factor. Smaller, powerful, and less expensive mini-computers became available in the mid-1960s. Advances in peripheral technologies and equipment were rapidly changing the definition of the computer from monolithic and self-contained to smaller and modular. By 1970 the mini-computer technology was competing comfortably with the mainframe, and it was possible to test the new configuration for its capabilities for delivering instruction.

For this purpose, early in 1971, the National Science Foundation funded the TICCIT (Time-Shared, Interactive Computer-Controlled Information Television) project. This was the first part of a two-part experiment in alternative computer system configuration. The goal of Part I was a system that substituted a mini-computer and its multi-user operating system in place of the large mainframe computer. This system was designed to serve a smaller population (maximum 128 users), but it was designed to be adaptable for use in many local settings. An initial system was installed in Reston, Virginia using the community's cable TV system. It was used to deliver video, text, and audio information to television sets in homes, using for a control the keys of a touch-tone telephone. The smaller, more local, and portable design of the TICCIT system, compared to PLATO's large centralized system, allowed it to be installed in any setting wired with co-axial cable. This would eventually include schools, businesses, the military, and other public and private institutions. The physical learning stations of each of the two systems did not appear greatly different, but the invisible parts of the system—the engines under the hood, so to speak—were miles apart.

Experiment Part II took place following the launch of the "informational" configuration of the TICCIT system. NSF entered into an additional contract for the creation of an "instructional" version of the TICCIT system. This would allow instruction to take place in the home. The initial target for testing this concept was the creation of junior college-level courses in language, writing, and math instruction. This broadened the interpretation of the TICCIT acronym to include "Time-shared Interactive, Instructional Television." The equivalent of five courses were identified: three in introductory algebra, and two in English grammar, usage, and composition. The selection criteria were mainly economic. Since one of the main goals of the project was to demonstrate lower cost, high-volume junior college courses were chosen whose large enrollments would average costs over larger numbers of users. According to Alderman (1978), this coverage accounted for approximately one-fifth of the courses normally taken by a junior college student.

The goal of making the original TICCIT system instructional added a host of new hardware, software, instructional, and system design challenges. This design case describes how a large design team set about solving these problems, which included:

> To develop the process of courseware production to a level more comparable to that practiced in the engineering professions, and in the process

provide the student with powerful yet simple and consistent control over the instructional process.

(McWilliams, 1974)

This created seemingly conflicting goals:

- Full learner control over instruction
- "Engineered" courseware production
- Rapid production of a large volume of material

The goal of giving the learner control over instruction was very relevant at the time of the TICCIT project, as previously described, but it was considered beyond the reach of most designers. No such system had achieved commercial success.

In addition, the concept of "engineered" instruction was not particularly popular at the time of the TICCIT project, despite being promoted by influential theorist Richard C. Anderson (1961). For many educators and designers, the engineering term conveyed a mechanistic, robotic image. Recall that in the context of 1971 the programmed instruction method, which had an early association with the engineering of teaching machines, was only a few years in the past. But in the minds of many at the time, the mechanistic image was hard to shake, and it was growing less popular, not more.

What was meant by the "engineering" goal of the TICCIT project? This was not certain at the beginning, but the feature of learner control was what occupied the spotlight. However, given the volume of instruction to be created and the limited time, engineering that took advantage of the efficiencies of common structures could not help but be a critical part of the plan. Engineering came to mean that instead of hand-crafting each lesson as a unique creation there would be an underlying architectural concept that defined a pattern of behavior and operation common to all lessons. Built into this pattern would be a degree of underlying structure and discipline. It would provide for both exposition and practical application during learning. The evolution of this kind of a design and its impact on high-volume development is described in this chapter.

Stakeholders

The principal stakeholders of the TICCIT project were:

- The National Science Foundation (NSF)—Funding
- Educational Testing Service (ETS)—Evaluation services
- The MITRE Corporation—Hardware/Software system developer
- The TICCIT design research team
    - C. Victor Bunderson—Project lead
    - M. David Merrill—Design lead

- Primary implementation test sites
    - Northern Virginia Community College
    - Phoenix College

The authors of this design case were, in 1971, graduate students in the new Instructional Psychology program at Brigham Young University. Both were employed by the TICCIT project. In retrospect, it is amazing how much they were able to learn, but also how much they were able to contribute, given the right assignments and the confidence of their mentors.

For MITRE and NSF, what was at stake was proving an alternative concept of hardware and software deployment using mini-computers, color television displays, computer-controlled random-access video streams, and secure, high-bandwidth connections—a formula for lower cost and higher performance with a smaller footprint and a local range of operation. This would be an alternative configuration to the wide-range mainframe delivery system configuration pioneered by Bitzer and Johnson (1971) in the Plato system.

Bitzer's description of Plato is divided into two parts: the "science" of computer-based education, and the "engineering" of computer-based education. It is clear that engineering as Bitzer uses the term refers to the engineering of computers and peripheral hardware and software systems into a working delivery platform from which a great variety of instructional forms determined by individual designers could be delivered. This sense of the term engineering pertained also to the development of the TICCIT system. TICCIT involved a massive hardware and software integration effort, the details of which are not covered in this design case. However, the TICCIT project used the term engineering in a broader sense to refer to the structuring of the instructional experience, as noted above.

What was at stake for the TICCIT design team was the challenge of meeting goals similar to those being explored by intelligent tutoring system developers: (1) making possible instructional experiences adapted for or by the learner, (2) the engineering of an architecture that was scalable, and (3) high-volume production techniques that shortened development time. In 1971, this was an audacious goal.

The Context of Design Practice

The context of instructional design practice in the early 1970s was evolving. The empiricist approach of make-try-revise-repeat that characterized the programmed instruction movement (Markle, 1964) was sufficiently familiar and intuitive for most designers to accept. The concept of the instructional objective or goal was also well known, so it had become a standard tool of the designer's craft (Tyler, 1949).

But in 1971, the concept of instructional design as a formal process had not been defined, except within design communities involved in large cold war systems engineering projects such as the Pine Tree Line, the Mid-Canada Line, and SAGE—all complex air defense systems that combined radar, computers, and complex communications with human operators and maintainers. These projects called for more disciplined design processes that included detailed analyses of several kinds and the coordinated efforts of multiple design teams.

Robert Gagné participated in projects of this complexity, and he produced an edited volume dealing with the more involved systematic processes they entailed (Gagné, 1965). These ideas laid the groundwork for the systematic instructional design movement. Briggs also published a monograph for designers on media selection processes (Briggs, 1967), which he followed soon after with his first version of what he termed a "model" of procedures for instructional design (Briggs, 1970). Each military service promulgated its own instructional design process standards, but the Interservice Procedures for Instructional Systems Development (IPISD) that consolidated them and gave us the term ISD was not published until 1975 (Branson et al., 1975).

None of these works had acquired broad influence by 1971, when the TICCIT project was initiated, so the systematic design formalisms commonly known today as ISD or ADDIE did not provide a beginning point for the project. The design process guidelines that had more influence were related to Tyler's doctrine of the alignment of instructional goals, instructional activities, and instructional measurement (Tyler, 1949). Tyler's student, Bloom (Bloom et al., 1956), had published a system for categorizing learning outcomes, as had Gagné (1965, 1985). The taxonomic principle clearly did have an influence on the approach to TICCIT: certainly more than the then-emerging systematic design, or ISD, principle. This was generally the context of design practice among the principals of the design team at the time of TICCIT.

The Context of Design Theory

There was also a context of theory in 1971, and it was in a state of flux. At that time, interest in behaviorism was waning in favor of cognitivism. Publications by Bruner et al. (1956), Neisser (1967), and Simon and Newell (1971) and others had taken the discussion of human cognition and learning back inside the mind, to study its internal processes.

This was a critical point for the use of the term "theory" by designers. Up to that point, designers had been used to thinking exclusively in terms of scientific learning theory. Simon (1969) opened up new directions for thinking about theory by describing the importance of *technological theories* of design in contrast to scientific theories, as did Vincenti later (1990).

The phrase "instructional theory"—referring to technological theory applied to the creation of instructional experience—became increasingly common, beginning in the 1970s (Bruner, 1964, 1966; Gibbons & Rogers, 2009; Merrill & Twitchell, 1994; Reigeluth, 1983, 1987, 1999a; Reigeluth & Carr-Chellman,

2009; Snelbecker, 1974; Snow, 1977). Glaser and Resnick (1972) also wrote about theories of instruction in addition to theories of learning. It is interesting to note that, since then, *learning* theory has taken a direction that inclines it towards application to the point where it is getting harder to distinguish learning from instructional theory (see Bransford et al., 2000; Lave & Wenger, 1991; Richey et al., 2010).

The distinction among the kinds of theory is important because, in the course of the design of the TICCIT system and for many years afterward, instructional theories emerged from the project. These are described in the narrative of the design process below.

Solving the Design Problem

The most practical design problem of TICCIT was drawing together a number of disparate engineering concerns. On the one hand, there was the need to satisfy the computer programmers. They needed orderly, algorithmic structures to work with, because algorithms are the operational principle of computer programs. On the other hand, there were the demands of an effective instructional strategy to consider. This, it was clear, would be messy and non-algorithmic, but somehow it had to become more structured. On yet another hand, there was the need to create an interface or a mechanism that would unite these algorithmic and strategic concerns together in a way that allowed the learner to exert control over events. Finally, there was the requirement that the design be producible within time and resource constraints. This was perhaps the most difficult challenge, as the redesign of the original TICCIT system, the concept of the unique instructional approach of TICCIT, the design of lessons, the production and testing of five courses worth of lessons, and the installation of TICCIT systems on two junior college campuses had to be accomplished in just over three years (1971–1975), with none of the conveniences of the mouse, the touch panel, or the menu system of a user-friendly graphical interface.

This was the design problem, and it took some time for the large and diverse team to arrive at a unified understanding of it. The team grew quickly, striving to absorb the magnitude of the problem and their unique contribution to it in a short time.

There were several reasons why it was a challenge for individuals to adapt to this new environment: the diversity of the team, the depth of their expertise in their individual specialties, their intense focus on their own requirements, their own preconceptions about possible solutions, and their lack of understanding of the requirements and constraints of others. None of the team members had experienced a challenge the size of TICCIT, and most of them were used to the more relaxed pace of an academic setting. All of these factors turned the team at first into an effective Babel: everyone spoke a different, specialized design language. Of course, this was not apparent to the group at the time; people were focused on the design itself and not on the linguistic nature of designing: this "omigosh!" sunk in only years later. See, for example, how Rheinfrank & Evenson, (1986, 1996) brought formalization to the notion of design languages. See also Dubberly & Evenson, 2010.

How did work on the design proceed? Not systematically, it turned out, according to any particular design model. Things worked inward from different ends of the problem, beginning from two critical sub-problems that had to be solved right away: the programmer's logic problem and the instructional designer's strategy problem. Neither group had prior experience in team design, especially not team design that brought hardware and software engineers together to work with instructional designers. Bringing the two specialty worlds together was more difficult than anyone had imagined. Without realizing it, each group was solving its own sub-problem by creating its own design language that could eventually be integrated into a more inclusive and project-wide, shared design language that represented the needs of all design team members.

The Logic Problem

The logic problem was a programmer's problem. It turned out to be a problem of creating a language that both the computer and human beings could understand: one that directed the computer what to do under different circumstances. It was a matter of creating for the computer a language of things that needed to "happen" and a set of rules for determining when to make them happen.

None of us realized at the time that this is what we were doing. Mitchell (1990) describes a similar problem architects encounter when they try to create a common vocabulary for the computer as a partner in the design of buildings. Mitchell characterizes this problem as finding "the logic of architecture," and he proposes that this entails "both the practical and poetic uses of architectural languages" (p. ix). Any designer who engages the computer in designing encounters similar problems, including computer designers, computer chip designers, and computer network designers. Many design disciplines have encountered this problem and solved it successfully. Each case involved the invention of a design language that could be understood by both the computer and the human being. Simon (1999, pp. 153–154) refers to this as the problem of "representation," referring to the manner of representing the problem to the computer.

The solution to the logic problem was the invention of the "base frame." Figure 11.1 is taken from early work notes and shows the basic mechanism of a base frame.

A base frame was defined as a chunk of self-contained computer logic for governing changes to the display. During a single strategic exchange with the learner, the interaction might consist of multiple changes to the display, without a complete change of context (e.g., erasure). A base frame provided a way of defining the boundaries of a visual context. The concepts of window and overlay

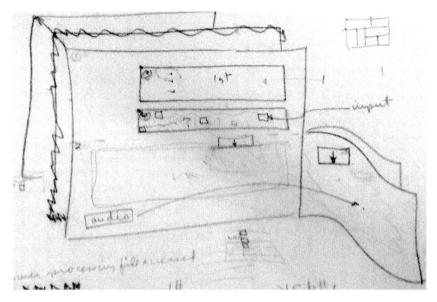

FIGURE 11.1 An early representation of the base frame concept that bridged computer logic concerns with instructional (display representation) logic concerns.

today make changing just a portion of the screen easy; at the time of TICCIT this was a more complicated challenge, especially because of the non-linear display sequences made possible by learner controls.

The base frame made it possible to maintain some elements of the display (such as a math graph related to a particular problem), while allowing other elements (such as explanatory or emphasis material, enhanced explanations, or practice-related feedback) to change, based on interactions with the learner. The base frame provided the interface between display (representation) content and the execution of strategic logic.

There were many styles of base frames. Base frames could be called and executed as needed, and new base frames could be created as needed. Instantiating a base frame with specific content was a matter of data entry, relieving lesson authors of the task of programming. Specifying screen coordinates identified changeable display areas; the various content elements that could populate an area were contained in one or more stored files. Figure 11.2 shows a page of designer notes exploring the partitioning of computer logic (the flowchart) into base frames (the boundaries shown by dotted lines). The computer did not have to know what content was already displayed: it only had to know what content file to place on the display at given coordinates at a given moment, defined by learner control sequences.

The base frame became a design language term that bridged the interests of different factions of our design team. It gave computer programmers a set of

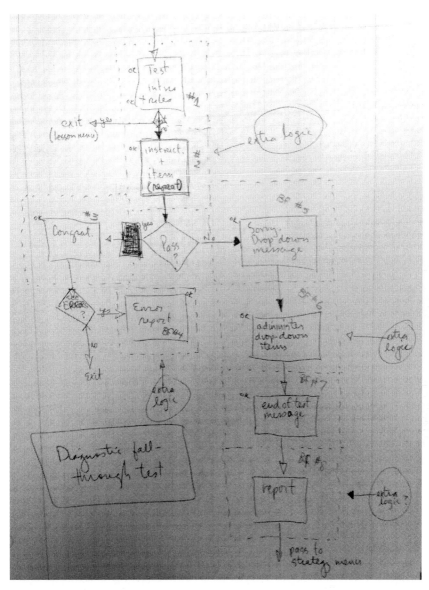

FIGURE 11.2 The segmentation of computer logic (flowchart) into base frames that relate display content to interaction and computer logic. For example, the "test intro rules" base frame might involve the presentation of multiple representation elements, but during their presentation and the interactions related to them, there would be an element that did not change (e.g., background, visual, etc.). Only upon exiting from one base frame to another did the entire display change and provide a new context for the display.

logical functions they could program, and it gave designers a way to describe media elements to activate based on the control operations of the learner, and it allowed the two groups to communicate across disciplinary boundaries.

The base frame from TICCIT is an early example of the "frame" concept that in later years became a fundamental structure in several authoring tools, including Authorware, Director, Flash, WICAT'S WISE, Allen Communications' Quest, and many others (Gibbons & Fairweather, 1998, ch. 4). It is doubtful that this was the first use of the frame (or window) concept; many people were experimenting with basic structures that could underlie instructional software designs. We just found it useful for our purposes. Later, the frame was also used as the fundamental construct underlying card systems such as Hypercard and Supercard. In the card systems, a "stack" of individual "cards" could each be populated with logic and display events selected from a menu. This was the equivalent of selecting an existing base frame and then populating it with content.

The Strategy Problem

The strategy problem was also a language creation problem. The language in this case was made up of terms that had meaning to the designer in the context of a coherent instructional plan. The solution of the strategy problem began with intense and sustained discussions, led by Dave Merrill, centered on research into concept instruction strategies he had conducted beginning with his dissertation study and extending through the period of the TICCIT project and beyond (see Tennyson et al., 1972; Merrill et al., 1992).

The two basic strategic structures in Merrill's research were: (1) the concept definition, and (2) the contrasting exemplar/non-exemplar pair. Merrill and his associates had learned through much research (Tennyson et al., 1972) that learning concept classification behavior was facilitated not only by the presentation of concept exemplars but also by the simultaneous presentation of very similar non-exemplars. This is called the matching principle. Moreover, it had been shown by this research that when building sequences of exemplar/non-exemplar pairs, successive pairs should be as different as possible from each other. This is called the divergence principle.

The strategy design team started to think of instructional strategy in terms of these basic elements: pairs of matched examples and non-examples and divergent sequences of these pairs that showed the broad range of exemplars. This was a good place to begin—with a design hypothesis that could be tested by building hypothetical prototypes and imagining what that would be like for the learner.

Many design sessions were spent experimenting with stringing combinations of these basic elements (definition, exemplar, non-exemplar) into fixed, algebra-like formulas. One might represent what we called an "all-American" strategy (one of everything); another might represent a "lean" strategy (minimum number of examples); yet another might be biased heavily towards "practice." There could also be different sequences of definitions and examples, and so the number of strategy pattern varieties could multiply through combination and recombination (see Figure 11.3).

From the list of strategy patterns, the idea was that a learner would choose a pattern they desired and the system would execute that pattern. It was not a great plan for learner control, since only a small number of options would end up being interesting, and they would be at a relatively large level of granularity. Over time a kind of symbol system evolved, where multiple repetitions of example/non-example pairs were represented with a "Δ" symbol and sequences of definitions and example sets were concatenated with "+" or "-" signs. Only "-" is shown in Figure 11.3. Figure 11.4 shows how long strategy sequences could be collapsed using a sub-index notation.

The problem with the solution at this stage was that we were thinking in terms of one type of learning objective (concept learning) and that the strategies consisted of long sequences of small events. Though this did give the learner choices to make, it did not seem to be a very good implementation of the ideal of learner control. This imperfect approach might have technically solved the problem, but it was not true to the spirit of creating a system for learner control. A more granular approach soon became apparent.

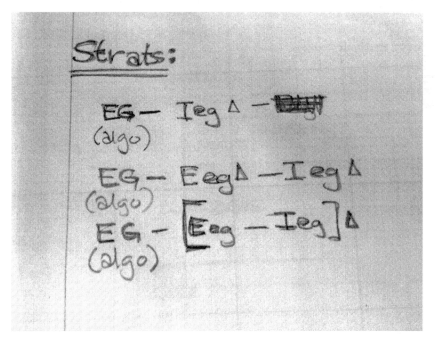

FIGURE 11.3 Early notes on strategy patterns produced by combination and recombination of basic elements derived from Merrill's concept learning research.

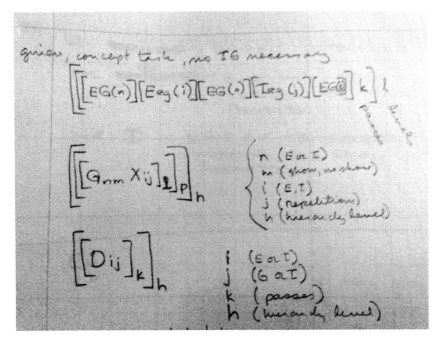

FIGURE 11.4 Notes on an attempt to represent strategy patterns made up of definitions (G) and exemplars (eg) of different kinds into Algebra-like expressions.

Dave Merrill arrived one morning in a state of high excitement and called together the TICCIT design team. He explained how the display types could be applied to a number of objective types at the level of the individual display. This not only provided the learner control at a much higher level of granularity but it could also be applied across multiple learning objective types. Dave was presenting what eventually became published as Component Display Theory. It was adopted as the fundamental strategic plan for the TICCIT system.

Component Display Theory, when combined with a typology of instructional objectives, created a language of instructional strategy elements that was needed to afford the TICCIT system a fine-grained form of learner control. It defined a system that was inert until the learner executed a control. To describe how these elements came together, it is necessary to briefly describe: (1) Component Display Theory, (2) the objective typology and its interaction with display types, and (3) the impact this had on the design of control system the learner would use to order up instruction. These are described in the following few sections.

Component Display Theory

The central premise of Component Display Theory (Merrill, 1983) is a combination of two assumptions: (1) that a given display is either expository (providing information) or inquisitory (requesting a response), and (2) that a given display may work at the content level of a generality or an instance. A basic set of displays is derived from crossing these dimensions (see Figure 11.5).

The design team used the following abbreviations for the display types:

- EG—Expository Generality
- IG—Inquisitory Generality
- Eeg—Expository Instance
- Ieg—Inquisitory Instance

Additional display types were added, but they were auxiliary types defined relative to this basic set. The complete set will be described below.

The Objective Typology

Assumptions were made: (1) that instructional strategies would correspond to instructional objective types, and (2) that TICCIT would support only a limited number of instructional objective types. Gagné (1965) had connected types of learning outcomes not only with strategic moves but also with "the implications…advances in knowledge have for the formation of what has come to be known as instructional theory" (Gagné, 1985, p. xi). Gagné realized that objective categories were based on informed assumptions:

> Eight different classes of situation in which human beings learn have been distinguished—eight sets of conditions under which changes in capabilities of the human learner are brought about…. From the standpoint of the outside of the human organism, they seem to be clearly distinguishable one from another in terms of the conditions that must prevail for each to occur. Might there actually be seven, nine, or ten, rather than eight? Of course.
>
> *(Gagné, 1965, p. 57)*

Figure 11.5 shows how the design team envisioned their selection of instructional strategies within Merrill's adaptation of Gagné's instructional objective types.

For the purposes of the TICCIT design, three instructional objective types were adopted: concept-using, procedure-using, and principle-understanding. The list of objective types deliberately excluded memory objectives in order to oppose the common tendency of computerized instruction designers to create drill and practice instruction instead of putting emphasis on more complex types of learning.

Why was this particular set of learning objective types chosen? Why not some other set? Gagné's statement above shows that the taxonomic principle

	EXPOSITORY	INQUISITORY
GENERALITY	(EG) Presentation of a generality	(IG) Request for the generality
INSTANCE	(Eeg) Presentation of an instance (example/non-example single or pair)	(Ieg) Request for a response (regarding an example or a non-example)

FIGURE 11.5 The basic display set obtained by crossing two assumed dimensions: expository/inquisitory and generality/instance.

Source: Merrill & Twitchell, 1994; Merrill 2008.

as practiced at the time (by a large number of taxonomists) was both subjective and objective. A review of Gagné's categories over the 20 years of the publication of *The Conditions of Learning* makes it plain that the learning objective categories he chose were sensitive to changes in the learning theory landscape. Over that period the categories evolved from behavioristic, to cognitive in their basis.

At the time of TICCIT, Dave Merrill, who was strongly influenced by Gagné, was experimenting with his own ideas, producing multiple versions of learning objective taxonomies over a period of years. His concern was to represent the influence of content separately from behavior. That is, he wanted there to be a concept, procedure, or a principle content that could be the subject of multiple types of behavior. This point of view led him over time to produce a version of his taxonomy that took the form of a matrix rather than a list. The taxonomy used in the TICCIT system was one version of this evolving idea.

Objectives Hierarchies

Subject matter experts and designers worked together to create TICCIT instructional goals using Gagné's learning hierarchies method (Gagné, 1968, 1977), an experimental method at the time that provided guidelines for analyzing intellectual skills. The result of learning hierarchy analysis—a specialized variety of task analysis—was a set of objectives organized in what was thought to be prerequisite order. Objectives lower down the hierarchy were considered necessary for the performance of objectives at higher levels.

Hierarchical analysis provided TICCIT designers with a systematic way to sequence objectives into "maps" that could be organized into Units, Lessons, and Segments. Lessons and Units were used as testing points. Instruction took place within Segments. TICCIT tests at the Unit and Lesson levels assessed mastery and were also diagnostic, pointing to remediation that might be needed at lower hierarchical levels. A color code was used on Course, Unit, and Lesson maps to indicate which tests had been passed at lower levels. This turned the Course, Unit, and Lesson maps into a status display. Learners were allowed to enter Segments and browse Units and Lessons at will. This constituted a form of learner control over content. "Mini-lessons" were created for each Segment to allow learners to survey content.

Designing the Full Set of Display Types and the Control System

Display types resided within Segments. The four basic display types were pared down to three, based on the assumption that the Inquisitory Generality (IG), a request for memory-level behavior, did not represent a desirable form of practice. It was a concern that designers might fall back to memory-level performance for concept definitions and rules, rather than asking the learner to make classifications and exercise their knowledge of procedures and processes.

Several display types were added to the basic set. These were logically derived from the basic display types to support learning in a variety of ways. It is easiest to explain the logical and consistent relationships among the displays by examining the controls provided to learners for navigation within a segment. These controls were located on a special keypad placed on the right side of the custom TICCIT keyboard (see Figure 11.6).

The **Rule**, **Example**, and **Practice** keys on the keypad correspond to the EG, Eeg, and Ieg display types respectively (refer to Figure 11.6).

When a learner entered a Segment, control keys provided access to the displays within the Segment. The basic displays included the following:

Rule: Expository Generality (EG)
    For concepts, the concept definition
    For rules, a statement of the rule
Example: Expository Instance (Eeg)
    For concepts, a medium-difficulty example or non-example
    For rules, a medium-difficulty demonstration of the procedure or process
Practice: Inquisitory Instance (Ieg)
    For concepts, a medium-difficulty classification problem
    For rules, a medium-difficulty request to apply the procedure/process

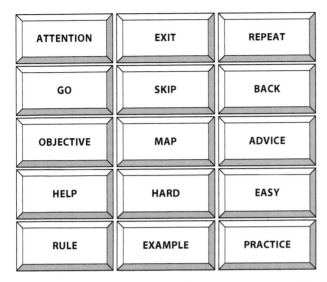

FIGURE 11.6 The custom controls for learner navigation of TICCIT segment displays. *Source*: after Merrill et al., 1980.

One set of controls regulated the technical level of explanations and the difficulty of practice items:

- **Hard**: A harder, more technical version of either the generality or the instance
- **Easy**: An easier, less technical version of either the generality or the instance
- (The **Easy** level of technicality was the default, pressing **HARD** or **EASY** ratcheted the level of difficult one level up or down)

The **Help** control provided expanded explanations for instances and practice items at every level of technicality.

The **Objective** control provided access to the instructional objective of the segment:

Several keys performed administrative functions, such as session control:

- **Attention**: Get the attention of the system or a monitor
- **Exit**: Leave the current session
- **Repeat**: Repeat the Segment just completed

Other controls were for navigation through topic hierarchies:

- **Map**: Move up one level of the hierarchy to view the map at that level
- **Go**: Enter Segment for instruction

170 Andrew S. Gibbons and A. F. O'Neal

- **Skip**: Skip an item
- **Back**: Go back an item

An **Advice** key offered learners access to strategic assistance. This function was partially implemented and was planned to grow into an intelligent coach. The Advisor function as implemented gave learners access to status information, strategy suggestions, and directions for using the system.

Figure 11.7 shows the major navigational paths through the displays of a TICCIT segment. Not all paths are shown because doing so would make the diagram unreadable.

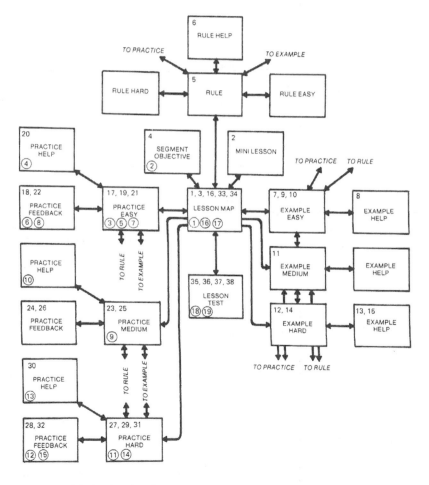

FIGURE 11.7 Navigational paths among TICCIT display types.

Source: Merrill et al., 1980.

For example: Learner #1, while looking at a lesson map:

1. Presses **GO** to automatically view the mini-lesson
2. Presses **MAP** to return to the lesson map
3. Presses a number and **GO** to highlight the segment box on the lesson map
4. Presses **OBJECTIVE** to view the segment objective and enter the segment
5. Presses **RULE** to view the generality (concept definition or rule expression)
6. Presses **HELP** to see a simplified explanation of the generality
7. Presses **EXAMPLE** to see an easy example (concept instance or worked rule)
8. Presses **HELP** to see a simplified explanation of the example. And so on....

This example shows that despite the complexity of Figures 11.2 to 11.4, from the learner's point of view, the keypad controls combined with the consistent definition of each display type created a simple language the learner could use to interrogate the system and chart a personal strategy. Control choices from the learner's point of view are best understood in the context of where the learner was at any given moment and the question the learner might have in mind, which would determine a useful next move. Learners did not advance until they requested a display with a keypress.

Integration of the Strategy and Logic Languages

The purpose of this design case is not to defend a particular choice of display types, objective types, or controls. Neither is it written in support of a particular style or philosophy of instruction. The purpose is to show how strategic design assumptions, and a set of logic primitives represented by base frames, created an engineering meta-language that made possible a unified, coherent design for TICCIT system instruction. This language allowed design team members from different specialties to discuss the design itself and create functional interfaces among conceptual strategic entities and practical software elements. We believe that a diverse design team must either implicitly or explicitly form such a language. We propose that design teams can come together more efficiently if they realize that language formation is an important aspect of design work.

The focal point of the different languages was the display. A display type, the basic atom of the TICCIT design, represented the integration point of: (1) the strategic design, (2) the goal structure represented by the objectives, (3) the content structure implied by the objectives, (4) the control structure, and (5) the message and representation structures, which will be defined in the following section.

The display functions chosen—which could easily have been a different set in a different designer's hand—made it possible to correlate the languages of all the functional areas of the design into a single design meta-language. The comprehensive TICCIT instructional design was expressed in terms from this meta-language. We feel this provides a testable design hypothesis: whether this concept of convergent languages might apply as well in the design of non-direct forms of instruction, such as intelligent tutoring, as well as it did to a direct form of instruction represented in TICCIT. We hypothesize that this is the case but that the size of the atomic unit in a more adaptive system will be smaller. In any design, regardless of the granular level of its adaptivity, certain functional decisions must be made (Gibbons, 2014), and the number of alternative paths ahead at any point during instruction cannot be assumed to be infinite, meaning that there is likely to be a finite, and perhaps not too large, number of design options at the heart of any design, around which other design decisions must center.

Authoring

The TICCIT design became firm over time, but that did not occur all at once. The best term to describe the firming up of the design might be "settling in." How the disparate parts of the TICCIT design came together in the minds of the entire design team—the subject matter experts who had to do the authoring described in this section, the programmers, the artists, the writers, the editors, the instructional designers, the quality control people, the data entry personnel, and the formative evaluators—may have been best described by Bucciarelli (1994, p. 159):

> Shared vision is the key phrase: The design is the shared vision, and the shared vision is the design—a (temporary) synthesis of the different participants' work.... Some of this shared vision is made explicit in documents, texts, and artifacts—in formal assembly and detail drawings, operation and service manuals, contractual disclaimers, production schedules, marketing copy, test plans, parts lists, procurement orders, mock-ups, and prototypes. But in the process of designing, the shared vision is less artifactual; each participant in the process has a personal collection of sketches, flowcharts, cost estimates, spreadsheets, models, and above all stories—stories to tell about their particular vision of the object.... The process is necessarily social and requires the participants to negotiate their differences and construct meaning through direct, and preferably face-to-face exchange.

The shared TICCIT design vision emerged through negotiation. Leading minds may have seeded and catalyzed the core concepts of the design, but independent specialists on the design team then had to give details to the design within their area of responsibility, and as conflicts in the details of the design occurred, team members had to negotiate a way through (see Baldwin & Clark (2000) for an extensive discussion of the idea of the setting of design rules, followed by negotiation of details in the computer design industry).

Just as the design process began from opposite poles of the problem (logic and strategy) it was finished beginning at the center and moving outward. The core of the design, once it was firm, began to discipline the details at the outer edges of the design. One of the areas where this had to happen was in a set of authoring standards that ultimately described in great detail what could and could not be included in each of the defined display types. Standards were created for artists, writers, editors, data entry personnel, and other production team members defining the points of quality for their step in the assembly process.

This was an engineering necessity owing to the large volume of instructional material that had to be created in a relatively short period of time at a high level of consistent quality. What was called for was an assembly line, and in order for that kind of production to take place, standards had to be set and maintained for each producible element. Moreover, as tweaks became necessary or as errors in the details of the production standard were spotted, changes had to be made and communicated to the entire production staff. The best description of what happened can be found in the *Lean* processes described by Womack and Jones (2003).

The assembly line metaphor, just like the engineering metaphor, communicates to some a cold, perhaps mechanical sense to most instructional designers, and it is not a popular topic in the design literature. However, the members of the TICCIT assembly line were intelligent, educated, and creative people. Their job was to work within a framework of constraints, producing a continuous flow of product, but to do so without giving up the creative edge of professionals. This requirement created a kind of living oxymoron: academics and knowledge workers defining their own mass-production machinery. As competitive forces from entrepreneurial and commercial organizations apply new standards of quality-at-volume to the design marketplace, the issue of volume production at high-quality levels will become increasingly important in the training of instructional designers. Stokes (2005) describes how a number of leading creative minds from a variety of design disciplines imposed constraints upon themselves specifically to challenge themselves to higher levels of creative insight. Perhaps in the future the competitive requirements of a mass educational market will have a similar effect.

Implementations and Evaluations

The subject of this case study is the evolution of the TICCIT design, not the specific courses implemented on TICCIT. However, the implementations and evaluations of TICCIT make it possible for us to speculate about the theoretical impact of the design.

Implementations

Several implementations of the TICCIT system design were made. These consisted of course, or partial-course, developments and productions, followed by field trials:

- Junior College courses in mathematics and English grammar were created and implemented with over 5000 Junior College students at Northern Virginia Community College and Phoenix College.
- Course materials for instruction in foreign languages, English, and general academic skills were developed and tested at the Model Secondary School for the Deaf at Gallaudet University.
- A course in oceanography was created by the U.S. Navy for use in the training of anti-submarine aircrews.
- An experimental course in aircraft systems operation was created and tested for use in S-3A sensor operator training at the Naval Air Station, North Island, California.
- Courses or partial courses were developed at Brigham Young University in critical reading, English as a second language, French grammar, Spanish grammar, and nursing. Segments were created and tested in German phonetics and Italian grammar. Much of the course development was in service to BYU's interest in language instruction, and smaller projects were carried out for research purposes. Pedersen (1985) notes that the BYU TICCIT system was still in use 12 years after its development, and the authors have ascertained that a version of TICCIT that has been ported to a new operating environment multiple times is still in regular use today.

Evaluations

Alderman (1978) reported an extensive evaluation of the TICCIT system in the Junior College implementations. Alderman and co-authors (1978) published a shorter report that describes the TICCIT and PLATO evaluations funded by the NSF. Evaluation reports from the private educational institutions and military organizations could not be obtained. A personal reminiscence about the TICCIT project by the project principal C. Victor Bunderson (2008) provides a valuable documentation of lessons learned from the TICCIT project. M. David Merrill (2008) also provides some insight into the impact of the TICCIT design.

The Junior College Evaluation

The implementation of TICCIT with 5000 students at the two Junior College sites in Virginia and Arizona was bumpy. It experienced almost every irregularity one would normally expect in a real-world environment. This might raise anxieties that the main effects would be hidden, but in fact this was the real environment in which the system was designed to operate, and if the desired real effects were strong enough, they should be detectable amid the noise. In the final analysis, two main effects seem to dominate the results of the trial: an instructor effect, and a practice effect.

The Instructor Effect

Instructors used the TICCIT instruction in ways that suited their own teaching style. They had their own views and expectations of how it would work, and they had never experienced computer-assisted instruction themselves. Therefore, they had no familiar usage patterns to fall back on. Teachers were inventing how to use TICCIT as they went. This unexpected—at least unanticipated—outcome underscores the importance of current research and training in the area of blended learning that can support an instructor in incorporating diverse media forms into an instructional plan.

A variety of usage patterns were observed. Byerly (1978) reports, "results were better when the programs were used as a supplement to class instruction. The effect on student morale was quite positive, and there was a 5% increment in student achievement in one English course" (p. 282).

Alderman (1978), the primary NSF TICCIT evaluator, expressed the opinion that the instructor effect was probably more powerful than the effect of the TICCIT instructional design. He observes:

> Instructor investment in these courses varied from direct supervision of all student work to supplementary assistance provided upon student request. In English courses instructors tended to choose the TICCIT lessons appropriate for their classes and to take an active role in assigning and correcting written exercises; instructors in mathematics courses, where department policy set the TICCIT coverage according to curriculum requirements, had responsibility for managing classes sometimes three times the size of usual lecture sessions.
>
> *(p. 41)*

Alderman reported that some college administrators used the TICCIT system as an opportunity to increase lecture course sizes, making comparison with traditional class sizes difficult. Alderman further notes that "most often, faculty indicated that they were unsure about the probable impact and significance of computer-assisted instruction" (Alderman, 1978, p. xxiv). However, he notes that "completion rates as well as student attitudes improved for the TICCIT program as the teacher's role under the program expanded" (Alderman et al., 1978, p. 45).

The Practice Effect

Alderman (1978, p. xxiii) also notes a PRACTICE key effect:

> PRACTICE was the one system feature that received high ratings by students both in comparison to its closest counterpart in lecture classes (i.e., homework assignments) and contrasted with ratings of other components of TICCIT's learner control. The practice problem appeared to be the cornerstone of the TICCIT system.

Students using the TICCIT system wanted to press the PRACTICE key early and often. There could be many different explanations. Perhaps they wanted:

- To see what the test was going to ask for
- To see if they already knew the subject matter
- To move sooner to a hands-on learner role
- To avoid being placed in a receptive role
- To obtain data for making strategy decisions

Whatever the reason a particular learner had, it is clear that the learners who used the TICCIT system wanted frequent interaction. Even within the structured world of TICCIT, this leads to speculation about the many possible alternative configurations of the display definitions and the controls that might have been designed, which could be focused more centrally on practice activities and the scaffolding of practice. We could ask: what would the control keys for such a TICCIT configuration look like? Current research literature provides many ideas ready-made for implementation in a learner-demand system that would allow the user to participate in determining the most useful control options, rather than the imagination of the designer alone. Koedinger's Knowledge-Learning-Instruction Framework (Koedinger et al., 2012) reviews practice-centered instructional methods from learning sciences literature. These methods suggest a range of learner controls that could be made available during instruction.

Early versions of the TICCIT control keys, some of which were dropped from the design, anticipated some of these initiatives: HELP at one point was to be augmented with SUPER HELP, which would have provided deeper explanations of concepts and processes; the NOTE key, which did survive, would have provided the opportunity for student reflections and insights to be recorded. At one point a SO WHAT? key was considered and then rejected. However, the most interesting key that never made it to the keyboard was the WHY? key, which "why?" Koedinger (2012) suggests is essential to the attainment of the highest and most complex forms of knowledge. A later section describes the WHY? key issue in more detail.

Who Profited Most from TICCIT?

In general, the results of the TICCIT trials in Junior Colleges (Alderman, 1978) showed that students who were self-directed and self-controlled users of the TICCIT system scored higher on independently administered post-tests, as did students who had prior familiarity with the subject matter.

Course completion rates were significantly lower for TICCIT classes than for their control group counterparts (16% versus 50% for math, and 55% versus 66% for English). However, those who did complete the TICCIT courses tended to score significantly higher on post-tests. The TICCIT design appears to have been effective for a portion of the learners.

Bunderson (2008) speculates that learners who were likely to feel most comfortable with the highly structured TICCIT instruction were those in the shaded portion of Figure 11.8, which includes learners who approach their task in a logical manner and who also prefer the predictability created by consistent, logical structuring of the courseware.

One significant finding came from a test of TICCIT at BYU subsequent to the formal evaluation at the Junior Colleges. A first trial of the BYU system placed no constraints upon students relative to semester boundaries. Students could finish when they wanted. In this trial the usual low completion rates were noted. However, Byerly (1978) describes the results of a second test conducted at BYU that constrained students to finish the course within semester boundaries, according to a set schedule:

> Not surprisingly, the TICCIT programs have been more apparently successful at Brigham Young University, the institution funded by the

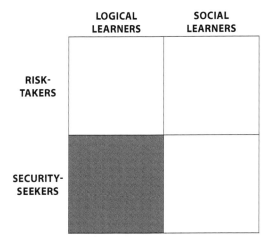

FIGURE 11.8 Bunderson's assessment of the factors defining learners most compatible with TICCIT instruction.

National Science Foundation to prepare them, where several hundred freshmen use the system each semester. The completion rates are 10–20% better than those of standard courses, and a survey found 9% more TICCIT than regular students passed a departmental achievement test.

(pp. 282–283)

The Orientation Effect

Bunderson (2008) has speculated about a potential negative effect of the hierarchical system of maps, which represented the subject matter to the learner in a fragmented manner:

> It is clear that the controls provided and the information displayed on the maps was not sufficient to achieve the broader vision of what learner control is all about. For one thing, it did not span an adequate range of preferences as shown in different models of thinking and learning preferences.

(p. 13)

Bunderson proposes that "what some of the students needed was to see the big picture more completely than the TICCIT map hierarchies conveyed." He cites as an alternative the concepts of "work models" and "elaborations" that grew out of TICCIT design discussions. Work models (Bunderson et al., 1981; Gibbons et al., 1995) progressively group performance goals into more complex performances for the integration of learning in increasingly challenging steps. This concept is closely related to the idea of increasingly complex microworlds described by Burton et al. (1984) and Vygotsky's Zone of Proximal Development (1978). Elaboration Theory (Reigeluth, 1999b) is also a direct response to the fragmentation of subject matter by the TICCIT hierarchical maps and it grew out of a search for an alternative.

The WHY? Key

Many discussions during TICCIT design centered on the WHY? control key, which was omitted from the final design but which existed in keypad designs up to the last moment. Discussions of the WHY? key always opened a Pandora's Box. This may have been due to the fact that it represented a watershed issue in the construction of adaptive, learner controlled, and intelligent instructional systems.

The classical approach to adaptive tutoring system design (See Wenger, 1987) relies for the most part on a semantic representation of the subject matter. In theory, such systems models of the learner, the learner's knowledge state, and the subject matter are used to inform instructional decisions, which are made using strategic rules that "understand" the semantic of the content and can therefore construct explanations on the fly.

In the TICCIT design, as with other frame-based designs, there was only a strategic semantic, which corresponded directly to the control keys. The system "understood" the categories of strategic frames, but the specific content and representation resources within those frames was pre-composed and fixed, sitting in a database, waiting to be called up. TICCIT did not have the ability to tailor the subject matter or message in response to a learner query. The learner was not allowed to ask "Why?" because the system had no way to understand and answer the question.

The WHY? key had to be abandoned because it represented a step too large for the architecture of the TICCIT system. But for many of us, it still poses a practical question about how tools for making adaptive, intelligent instructional designs can be placed in the hands of the average designer and how the instruction created can be placed under the control of the learner. If an instructional artifact can answer a "WHY?" question, then truly conversational instruction becomes a possibility.

Subsequent History of the TICCIT Design

The design of the TICCIT system was sold after the trial period to Hazeltine Corporation, then to Ford Aerospace, then to Loral, a French company. The turbulent computer and software landscape produced tectonic forces that over time shredded the original system. The mini-computer gave way to the microcomputer. Operating systems changed radically in their nature. Programming tools advanced and became more powerful, obsoleting their predecessors. The Internet became a distribution channel capable of exporting courseware easily and widely. In response to changes, the TICCIT system was ported several times to new hardware and software platforms, each time losing some of its functionality, including modifications to the control set. Today, the only known operating TICCIT system exists at Brigham Young University, where it is used to teach languages.

Conclusion

We believe the TICCIT project was revolutionary in its time and that its effects are still being felt in many ways. A project as visible, ambitious, and innovative as the TICCIT project was sure to leave behind a legacy of new learning about design. Ironically, the answer to the question of whether computer-based instruction could be used in a cost-effective way for instruction became a foregone conclusion, as prices for hardware, software, development, and delivery fell precipitously. The instructional computer was inevitable, but few realized it at the time of the TICCIT project. According to Suppes (1979, quoted in Bunderson, 2008, p. 8):

> It is rather as if we had had a similar test of automobiles in 1905 and concluded that, given the condition of the roads in the United States, the only thing to do was to stay with horses and forget about the potential of the internal combustion engine.

Today, when it is almost always assumed that the computer will play some part in instruction (even if only to project PowerPoint slides), the desperate struggle that filled our eyes with smoke and our ears with the noise of battle during TICCIT looks more like a dust devil on the far horizon. Today, horses are not allowed on the freeway, and the instructional computer is a fact of life.

As stated at the beginning of this chapter, the goals of the TICCIT system were:

- Full learner control over instruction
- "Engineered" courseware production
- Rapid production of a large volume of material
- Lower costs for development and delivery of computer-based instruction

Without quoting statistics, we will say that these goals were reached, and a design was produced that was applicable to a wide range of subject matters. Costs of development and delivery were drastically reduced (to about 10 percent of usual CAI costs), and a new computer system configuration was tested—a local-system concept that stood in clear contrast to the monolithic system style of the day. At the time of the project, these were major accomplishments, and they initiated a revolution in thinking smaller about the design and delivery of computer-based instruction. Ironically, the systems we use today are both local in the power they provide each user and monolithic in the access they provide to an immense worldwide network.

Other TICCIT outcomes included the following:

- The team design and production concept showed that it was possible to specialize development functions to achieve mass production of a quality product.
- The creation of specialized design languages and non-programming interfaces allowed a team of designers and producers to speak to the computer in a new human–computer pidgin.
- Control over instruction was placed in the learner's hands to an extent beyond the standard definition of "learner-controlled" at the time. Today, a similar, more advanced control system is available in the Web browser.

A new componentized definition of instructional strategy was originated that focused increased attention on the analysis of content structures, strategic structures, and the architecture of instructional designs in general at a whole new level of detail.

TICCIT was a bold departure from the existing norm. It generated new theory (e.g., component display theory, elaboration theory, work model theory). It laid the groundwork for several spin-off instructional design firms that carried the TICCIT ideas forward, changing and abstracting them to produce new concepts of design architecture (Gibbons, 2014).

The perspective of time has made it possible to see some things now that weren't apparent at the time. It was surprising, for example, the extent to which the strategic design was based on a number of key *assumptions* and that a number of assumptions together created a complete design hypothesis that could be (and was) tested. It has also become apparent that it was not a single theory that informed the design but many theories, each acting to inform a specific part of the design independently: theories of representation, of message structuring, of control optioning, of data management, and of system logic.

The making of these assumptions and the application of many engineering theories was an essential part of the design effort, without which design could not have proceeded. Anderson (1961, p. 377) points out the importance of engineering knowledge by stating that scientific study results are insufficient to produce a design:

> Engineering plays a critical role in the application scientific principles in any area. Take the development of rockets, for example. One could not deduce a rocket or even a blueprint for a rocket solely from the principles of physics or chemistry.... The product of basic research is a statement about the relationship among variables. It is my contention that these statements are never of very much direct value to practical educators, even when the statements are perfectly understood and every effort is made to apply them.

No amount of research and data could have told the TICCIT designers what to include in the design. Research and "science" can only inform designs. They cannot determine designs, because other kinds of knowledge are used during design that science does not provide (Vincenti, 1990).

The testing of the system by instructors showed that instructors with the proper vision could adapt TICCIT lessons within a larger instructional plan that enhanced the ability of the teacher and allowed instruction by teacher and computer to reach a higher standard of achievement than either one alone.

A language of strategic events was successfully mapped to a language of computer events in a seamless meta-design language that integrated computer and strategic functions into a coherent design. The concept of the internal structure of an instructional design at several levels became apparent, but only over time and with much additional experience. It should be noted that the assumptions made to form the basic display types and the instructional objective typology were arbitrary, even though they were based to some extent on a research foundation (generality and instance) and a reasonable premise (expository and inquisitory). It should be obvious that the four basic display types were just the core of a larger, abstract set of display types that could have been created by any combination of matrixed dimensions. The number of display types is not absolute, nor is the number of dimensions. However, the ability to categorize messages that populate a display is a powerful concept, related in a reverse way to the ontological analysis of documents. This is an important theoretical takeaway.

It would be very neat, and yet untrue, to say that there was a single grand principle behind the TICCIT design from the start that unfolded inevitably. On the contrary, as each part of the TICCIT design unfolded, it was through the discovery of a way forward for one part of the design, and that almost always opened the way for another important discovery. The base frame innovation came early because it was required by the programmers in order to meet their development schedules. The strategic innovation came as the extension of Dave Merrill's research until the pieces fell into place with Dave's aha-moment.

It would also be neat theoretically to be able to say that once the pieces fell into place the grand concept of design languages, sub-function interfaces, and abstract layers of the design (Gibbons, 2014) emerged immediately in everyone's mind. This would also be an exaggeration. The serendipity that led a creative team out of the wilderness was delivered a little at a time, and only the perspective of over 40 years is bringing the bigger picture into focus.

Most of all, what the TICCIT system represents to those who experienced its design is boldness. The designers of the system moved on to instructional design positions in industry and eventually to universities and research laboratories. Their views of instruction changed, but the TICCIT experience had revealed to them that there is value in radical innovation and that everyone is empowered to have bold ideas. This knowledge is a gift that the team members received from the visionaries who initiated the project, dealt with its enormous demands, and led it to a successful conclusion. Just as we need more researchers and designers today, we need more visionaries to challenge our thinking and show us new ways ahead.

References

Alderman, D. L. (1978). *Evaluation of the TICCIT computer-assisted instructional system in the community college. Final report.* Volume I. Washington, DC: ERIC Clearinghouse [ERIC ED167 606].

Alderman, D. L., Appel, L. R., & Murray, R. T. (1978). PLATO and TICCIT. *Educational Technology, 18*(4), 40–45.

Anderson, R. C. (1961). The role of the educational engineer. *Journal of Educational Sociology, 34*(8), 377–381.

Atkinson, R., & Wilson, H. (1969). Computer-assisted instruction. In R. Atkinson & H. Wilson (Eds.), *Computer-assisted instruction: A book of readings* (pp. 3–14). New York: Academic Press.

Baldwin, C., & Clark, K. (2000). *Design rules: The power of modularity.* Cambridge, MA: MIT Press.

Bitzer, D. L., & Johnson, R. L. (1971). PLATO: A computer-based system used in the engineering of education. *Proceedings of the IEEE, 59*(6), 960–968.

Bloom, B. S., Engelhart, M. D., Furst, E. J., Hill, W. H., & Krathwohl, D. R. (1956). *Taxonomy of educational objectives: The classification of educational goals. Handbook I: Cognitive domain.* New York: David McKay Company.

Bransford, J., Brown, A., & Cocking R. (2000). *How people learn: Brain, mind, experience, and school: Expanded edition.* Washington, DC: National Academies Press.

Branson, R. K., Rayner, G. T., Cox, J. L., Furman, J. P., King, F. J., & Hannum, W. J. (1975). *Interservice procedures for instructional systems development* (5 vols) (TRADOC Pam 350–30, NTIS Nos. AD-A019 4860, AD-A019 490). Ft. Monroe, VA: U.S. Army Training and Doctrine Command.

Briggs, L. J. (1967). *Instructional media: A procedure for the design of multi-media instruction, a critical review of research, and suggestions for future research.* Washington, DC: American Institutes for Research. (Preceded by Briggs, L. J., Campeau, P. L., Gagné, R. M., & May, M. A. (1966). *A procedure for the design of multimedia instruction* (abbreviated title). Pittsburg, PA: American Institutes of Research.)

Briggs, L. J. (1970). *Handbook of procedures for the design of instruction* (Monograph No. 4.). Washington, DC: American Institutes for Research.

Bruner, J. S. (1964). Some theorems on instruction illustrated with reference to mathematics. In E. R. Hilgard (Ed.), *Theories of learning and instruction: The sixty-third yearbook of the society for the study of education* (pp. 306–335). Chicago, IL: National Society for the Study of Education.

Bruner, J. S. (1966). *Toward a theory of instruction.* New York: Norton.

Bruner, J., Goodnow, J., & Austin, G. (1956). *A study of thinking.* New York: Wiley.

Bucciarelli, L. L. (1994). *Designing engineers.* Cambridge, MA: MIT Press.

Bunderson, C. V. (2008). Reflections on TICCIT. In M. Allen (Ed.), *Michael Allen's e-learning annual, 2008* (pp. 1–30). San Francisco, CA: Pfeiffer.

Bunderson, C. V., Gibbons, A. S., Olsen, J. B., & Kearsley, G. P. (1981). Work Models: Beyond instructional objectives. *Instructional Science, 10,* 205–215.

Burton, R. R., Brown, J. S., & Fischer, G. (1984). Skiing as a model of instruction. In B. Rogoff and J. Lave (Eds.), *Everyday cognition: Its development in social context* (pp. 139–150). Cambridge, MA: Harvard University Press.

Byerly, G. (1978). CAI in college English. *Computers and the Humanities, 12*(3), 281–285.

Dubberly, H., & Evenson, S. (2010). Design as learning—or "knowledge creation"—the SECI model. *Interactions, 18*(1), 75–79.

Gagné, R. M. (Ed.) (1965). *Psychological principles in system development.* New York: Holt, Rinehart, & Winston.

Gagné, R. M. (1968). Learning hierarchies. *Educational Psychologist, 6,* 1–9.

Gagné, R. M. (1977). Types and capabilities of learning hierarchies in instructional design. *Journal of Instructional Development, 1*(1), 8–10.

Gagné, R. (1985). *The conditions of learning* (4th edn). New York: Holt, Rinehart, & Winston.

Gibbons, A. S. (2014). *An architectural approach to instructional design.* New York: Routledge.

Gibbons, A., & Fairweather, P. (1998). *Computer-assisted instruction: Design and development.* Englewood Cliffs, NJ: Educational Technology Publications.

Gibbons, A. S., & Rogers, P. C. (2009). The architecture of instructional theory. In C. M. Reigeluth & A. Carr-Chellman (Eds.), *Instructional-design models and theory: Volume III, Building a common knowledge base*. New York: Routledge.

Gibbons, A. S., Bunderson, C. V., Olsen, J. B., & Robertson, J. (1995). Work models: Still beyond instructional objectives. *Machine-mediated learning*, 5(3&4), 221–236.

Glaser, R., & Resnick, L. B. (1972). Instructional psychology. *Annual Review of Psychology*, 23, 207–276.

Koedinger, K. R., Corbett, A. T., & Perfetti, C. (2012). The knowledge-learning-instruction framework: Bridging the science–practice chasm to enhance robust student learning. *Cognitive Science*, 36(5), 757–798.

Lave, J., & Wenger, E. (1991). *Situated learning: Legitimate peripheral participation*. Cambridge: Cambridge University Press.

Markle, S. M. (1964). *Good frames and bad: A grammar of frame writing*. New York: Wiley.

McWilliams, E. (1974). *Hard core CAI: TICCIT system progress report on field testing*. Retrieved on May 20, 2014 from www.atariarchives.org/bcc1/showpage.php?page=33.

Merrill, M. D. (1983). Component display theory. In C. Reigeluth (ed.), *Instructional-design theories and models: An overview of their status* (pp. 397–424). Hillsdale, NJ: Erlbaum Associates.

Merrill, M. D. (2008). Reflections on a four-decade search for effective, efficient, and engaging instruction. In M. Allen (Ed.), *Michael Allen's e-learning annual, 2008* (pp. 141–169). San Francisco, CA: Pfeiffer.

Merrill, M. D., & Twitchell, D. G. (Eds.) (1994). *Instructional design theory*. Englewood Cliffs, NJ: Educational Technology Publications.

Merrill, M. D., Schneider, E. W., & Fletcher, K. A. (1980). *TICCIT* (Instructional Design Library, Vol. 40). Englewood Cliffs, NJ: Educational Technology Publications.

Merrill, M. D., Tennyson, R. D., & Posey, L. O. (1992). *Teaching concepts: An instructional design guide* (2nd edn). Englewood Cliffs, NJ: Educational Technology Publications.

Mitchell, W. J. (1990). *The logic of architecture: Design, computation, and cognition*. Cambridge, MA: MIT Press.

Neisser, U. (1967). *Cognitive psychology*. Englewood Cliffs, NJ: Prentice-Hall.

Pedersen, E. L. (1985). TICCIT will gladly learn and gladly teach composition skills. *Computers and Composition*, 4(SI), 233–241.

Reigeluth, C. M. (1983). *Instructional-design theories and models*. Hillsdale, NJ: Lawrence Erlbaum Associates.

Reigeluth, C. M. (1987). *Instructional theories in action: Lessons illustrating theories and models*. Hillsdale, NJ: Lawrence Erlbaum Associates.

Reigeluth, C. M. (1999). *Instructional-design theories and models, Volume II: A new paradigm of instructional theory*. Mahwah, NJ: Lawrence Erlbaum Associates.

Reigeluth, C. M. (1999). The elaboration theory: Guidance for scope and sequence decisions. In C. M. Reigeluth (Ed.), *Instructional-design theories and models, Volume II: A new paradigm of instructional theory*. Mahwah, NJ: Lawrence Erlbaum Associates.

Reigeluth, C. M., & Carr-Chellman, A. (2009). *Instructional-design theories and models, Volume III: Building a common knowledge base*. New York: Routledge.

Rheinfrank, J., & Evenson, S. (1986). On the semiology of object, space and behavior: The design of strategic design languages. In *Proceedings of the Human Factors and Ergonomics Society 30th Annual Meeting* (pp. 1059–1062).

Rheinfrank, J., & Evenson, S. (1996). Design languages. In T. Winograd (Ed.), *Bringing design to software* (pp. 63–85). Reading, MA: Addison-Wesley.

Richey, R., Klein, J., & Tracey, M. (2010). *The instructional design knowledge base: Theory, research, and practice*. New York: Routledge.

Simon, H. (1969). *The sciences of the artificial* (1st edn). Cambridge, MA: MIT Press.
Simon, H. (1999). *The sciences of the artificial* (3rd edn). Cambridge, MA: MIT Press.
Simon, H. A., & Newell, A. (1971). Human problem solving: The state of the theory in 1970. *American Psychologist, 26*(2), 145–159.
Snelbecker, G. (1974). *Learning theory, instructional theory, and psychoeducational design.* New York: McGraw-Hill.
Snow, R. (1977). Individual differences and instructional theory. *Educational Researcher, 6*(10), 11–15.
Stokes, P. (2005). *Creativity from constraints: The psychology of breakthrough.* New York: Springer.
Stolurow, L. M. (1969). Some factors in the design of systems for computer-assisted instruction. In R. Atkinson & H. Wilson (Eds.), *Computer-assisted instruction: A book of readings* (pp. 65–94). New York: Academic Press.
Suppes, P. (1969). Computer technology and the future of education. In R. Atkinson & H. Wilson (Eds.), *Computer-assisted instruction: A book of readings* (pp. 41–48). New York: Academic Press.
Suppes, P. (1979). Current trends in computer-assisted instruction. In M. C. Yovits (Ed.), *Advances in computers, Vol. 18* (pp. 173–229). New York: Academic Press.
Tennyson, R. D., Wooley, R. R., & Merrill, M. D. (1972). Exemplar and non exemplar variables which produce correct classification errors. *Journal of Educational Psychology, 63,* 144–152.
Tyler, R. W. (1949). *Basic principles of curriculum and instruction.* Chicago, IL: University of Chicago Press.
Vincenti, W. (1990). *What engineers know and how they know it: Analytical studies from aeronautical history.* Baltimore, MD: Johns Hopkins University Press.
Vygotsky, L. S. (1978). *Mind in society: The development of higher psychological processes.* Cambridge, MA: Harvard University Press.
Wenger, E. (1987). *Artificial intelligence and tutoring systems: Computational and cognitive approaches to the communication of knowledge.* Los Altos, CA: Morgan Kaufmann Publishers.
Womack, J., & Jones, D. (2003). *Lean thinking: Banish waste and create wealth in your corporation.* New York: Productivity Press.

12

BRIDGE[1]

A Cross Culture African American Reading Program (1975–1977)

Patricia A. Young

Introduction

The design of educational technologies produced by and for African Americans has a long and rarely explored history. This chapter provides an analysis of the design, designers, and dormancy of *Bridge: A Cross Culture Reading Program* (hereafter, *Bridge*). *Bridge* was developed as an intervention reading program to improve the reading levels of black junior and senior high school students in America's public schools. The program was normed for inner-city black students in grades 7 to 12 who read between second- and fourth-grade levels. The curriculum included: reading Booklets One through Five, Study Books One through Five, a teacher's edition of the study books, six audio recordings, and a teacher's guide. The findings from *Bridge* revealed a skills-based reading program that under controlled conditions resulted in reading gains for African American youth at 6.2 months for 4.0 months of instruction compared to a control group that earned 1.6 months for 4.0 months of instruction. Teachers reported improvements in student behavior and an increase in students' motivation to learn with the *Bridge* materials (Simpkins, 2002).

This is the story of *Bridge's* design, designers, and dormancy. The design of *Bridge* is explored through a text and context analysis of the reading program. Excerpts from interviews with the designers of *Bridge* provide insight into the design process and designers. The dormancy of *Bridge* begins with public opinion on one side and the designers and publishers on the other. The reasons for this dormancy are further explored.

Bridge is analyzed and discussed as a living document that exists in the present day. A comprehensive analysis of *Bridge* can be found in Young (1999).

Discovering *Bridge*

As a graduate student, I found out about *Bridge* through a conversation with an African American scholar. I informed her of my interests in instructional materials designed by and for African Americans and she directed me to *Bridge*. I obtained copies of *Bridge* from a library. Then, I set out to locate the authors of the curriculum series as I explored similar instructional materials as part of my dissertation research. My interest was to disclose the product and process involved in creating this educational technology. The research questions included: How does technology influence the design and media of instruction?; How do instructional materials disclose their nature, and how is this nature culturally and/or linguistically specific?; How do macro and micro social, political, cultural, and economic issues mediate the text and context of a document?; and What elements of the design are believed to improve the education of the African American learner?

Gary A. Simpkins, Charlesetta Stalling (formerly Charlesetta Simpkins), and Grace Holt designed *Bridge*. After several conversations with the two living authors in 1999, I interviewed Gary Simpkins via telephone. Charlesetta Stalling invited me over for dinner in her California home, and I interviewed her thereafter. It was simply that these designers had a story to tell and finally someone wanted to listen.

The Designers of *Bridge*

The designers of *Bridge* were African Americans: a psychologist, reading specialist, and linguist, respectively.

Gary A. Simpkins (1943–2009) earned his Doctor of Education (1976) degree from the University of Massachusetts in the area of Humanistic Applications of Social and Behavioral Sciences (Figure 12.1). He entitled his dissertation "A cross-cultural approach to reading" (1976). Simpkins acquired a Master of Education degree from Harvard University in Psychology and a Bachelor of Arts from California State University Los Angeles in Psychology. During his career he was a student activist, college professor, and mental health psychologist. Simpkins was born in Buffalo, New York, but he grew up in Los Angeles, California.

188   Patricia A. Young

FIGURE 12.1   Dr. Gary A. Simpkins.

Charlesetta Stalling received her Doctor of Education (1977) degree from the University of Massachusetts in the area of Human Services and Applied Behavioral Science with an emphasis in curriculum development, teacher training, and micro counseling (Figure 12.2). She entitled her dissertation "Effects of the cultural context of language on the cognitive performance of Black students" (1977).

FIGURE 12.2 Dr. Charlesetta Stalling.

Stalling acquired a Master of Education (1972) degree from Harvard University in Education with an emphasis in Reading and a Bachelor of Arts (1969) from California State University Los Angeles in Language Arts. Her career enabled her to be a student activist, educational administrator, educator (K-12 and adult), and educational consultant. Stalling was born in San Diego, California and has spent most of her life in California.

Grace S. Holt (1922–1991) graduated from Spelman College in 1942 and acquired a teaching certificate from the University of Chicago. She earned a Master of Education in Inner City Studies (1969) from Northeastern Illinois State College. She entitled her Master thesis "A method of teaching Standard English as a second dialect to Black English speakers in elementary schools." Grace Holt was a public school elementary teacher, college professor, and administrator in Chicago, Illinois.

The Origins of *Bridge*

Bridge was a spin-off of a program model called the Cross-Cultural Approach to Reading developed through Technomics Research and Analysis Corporation, a scientific corporation based in Los Angeles. Simpkins was hired as a consultant on an instructional project that sought to address the massive reading failure of black high school age youth in "urban ghettos" (Simpkins, 1976, p. 135). Around 1969, Dr. Burton R. Wolin, Vice President of Research at Technomics, and Simpkins created reading and writing instructional materials that focused on the language and social experiences of this population (Simpkins, 1976). They wanted to provide these youth with reading experiences using Black English that paralleled their social and linguistic worlds and then guide students into the social and linguistic world associated with Standard English. The term "Black English" will be used throughout this chapter to denote the language of African American people; however, references to Black English have been termed Ebonics, Black Dialect, African American English, Black Vernacular, and Black/African American Language (Smitherman, 1994). The results of their tests on the preliminary and revised version of *Bridge* indicated that the materials were effective in improving the reading skills of black youth; however, further research and development were needed (Simpkins, 1976).

By 1973, Houghton Mifflin Publishing Company had formed an Urban Programs Department in their Educational Division; they sought to publish instructional materials for minority populations. Simpkins was approached by the Urban Programs Department because they heard of the success of his previous reading program. Thereafter, Simpkins agreed to develop an extensive reading program under two conditions. First, he must be allowed to choose his own team of writers; and second, Houghton Mifflin Publishing Company must field test the program in public schools. Further, if the field tests indicated that the program was not an effective tool for teaching reading to black youth, it would not be marketed. *Bridge: A Cross-Culture Reading Program* (Figure 12.3) was the product of Simpkins' efforts with Houghton Mifflin Company. The program was extensively tested in Chicago, Illinois; Phoenix, Arizona; Washington, DC; Memphis, Tennessee; and Macon County, Alabama (Simpkins, 1976).

Design Thinking Behind *Bridge*

In these interview excerpts, Simpkins discussed the process involved in developing *Bridge*. He began with his preliminary research and then shifted to how they

Bridge (1975–1977) **191**

FIGURE 12.3   Book One.
Source: Simpkins et al., 1977d.

sought to fill the gaps in student learning. This is an account of the design thinking involved in creating *Bridge*.

> [In] the preliminary research I went around talking to black kids. "Why can't you read my man. I mean you seem smart, you obviously have great language facility, you know." "Ain't got a damn thing I want to read." "Okay, I'll buy that." But they didn't have any materials that interested them in reading. Also they had gaps in their learning. They were bright kids, but there were gaps in their learning that prevented them from putting the reading skills together. And that's what we aimed the Bridge program at, to fill those gaps in their learning. We knew we were going to get data from this population that was good. Because these kids have learned a great deal about reading, but they just haven't put it together. They have been sitting in class all these years and [have] not learn[ed] … about reading Standard English. What the kids lacked was code switching ability. That is, … they didn't know when … their dialect stopped and Standard English began so the [language] populations blended together and gave them a lot of problems.

And we kept trying to hammer it home [that] … we are not trying to hammer the kids into Black English. In fact, we want to move them from Black English to Standard English, but we don't want to devalue Black English. Because we think that it is really important that the kids be bidialectal. We don't want to take anything from the kids. We want to add on to what they have. We want our kids to be able to go to Harvard and be articulate. And go in the middle of Harlem you know and also be articulate you know in the dialect. So we want our kids to have those code switching abilities.…And from a natural point of view, they should not be having these problems, because these kids have high language facility to carry on. These kids are highly verbal and know how to manipulate the language metaphorically and everything else in the language but somehow it doesn't carry over to Standard English. And so that's what Associative Bridging was about to take the strength of their language and carry it over to Standard English. To show them that these are two separate populations, they can blend together, we can pull them apart. Here's where one starts. Here's where one begins. And also show them that here are the skills for instance. I want the kids to learn about metaphors. So I give them a nice white metaphor like "Oh trees we die at the top." They sit there and look at me like I'm crazy and what the hell is he talking about metaphors and similes … and all that. But if I … tell them about the beauty of metaphors, how rich the language [is]. And let's look at some metaphors. "Hey just take a chill pill" you know some of their metaphors let them be aware that they simultaneously create metaphors their language is rich in metaphors. And this is what enhances their writing and things like that. Kids grasp it immediately you know. Let them get the skills on their own bases and then they can transfer those skills over to Standard English you know. What happens is the kids sit there. The teacher is teaching in Standard English and many things are passing by. So they get those gaps in their learning. So this is an attempt to fill those gaps for the kids.

(personal communication, 1999)

For Simpkins, the process of developing *Bridge* began by learning as much as he could about his target population. He engaged in ethnographic analyses to begin the design process.

The Cross-Cultural Approach

Bridge was founded on the Cross-Cultural Approach to Education; it was a pedagogical approach designed by Simpkins "to accommodate the culture and language of Black non-mainstream" learners (Simpkins, 2002, p. 73). The Cross-Cultural Approach to Education bridged the void in learning between home and school. In this methodology, language was viewed as the nexus between what learners knew and were expected to learn. Thereby, instructional content began with the phonetic, syntactical, lexical, and cultural familiarity to the learners' language. The familiarity to the learners' language formed the cultural context for learning (Simpkins, 1976, 2002).

Associative Bridging and Peer Control were two teaching and learning strategies associated with the Cross-Cultural Approach to Education that became integrated into *Bridge*. The Associative Bridging strategy used cultural and linguistic knowledge to take the learner from the familiar to the less familiar. In the case of *Bridge*, Black English and non-mainstream culture would be the familiar and Standard English and mainstream culture would be less familiar. The Peer Control strategy was an "oral reading procedure" designed to provide learners with "control over the learning process" (Simpkins, 2002, p. 83).

An Analysis of *Bridge*

To evaluate the design of *Bridge*, a text and context analysis was conducted. Excerpts from this evaluation are included here with a more comprehensive analysis in Young (1999). Thomas N. Huckin's approach to critical discourse analysis, as it relates to written text, formed the text and context analysis of *Bridge*. The text analysis provided an overview of *Bridge* in terms of its Genre, Framing, Omission and Backgrounding, Foregrounding, and Visual Representations. The context analysis provided a sociocultural analysis of the instructional materials (Huckin, 1995, 2002).

This section offers an examination of *Bridge* in terms of the product and the process taken to create this educational technology. This analysis includes all materials except for the teacher's edition of the study books. Excerpts from interviews with Simpkins and Stalling provide accounts of the development process.

Text Analysis

Genre

Genre represented "text types" and these text types "manifest[ed] a characteristic set of formal features serving a characteristic purpose" (Huckin, 1995, p. 98). *Bridge* could be characterized as a curriculum unit or instructional materials because it included: (1) reading Booklets One through Five, (2) Study Books One through

194 Patricia A. Young

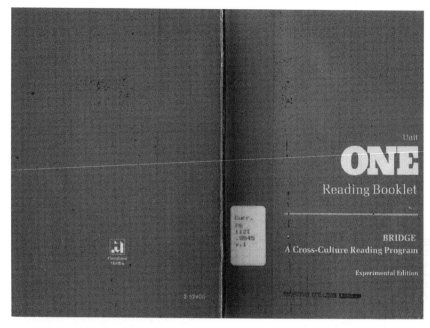

FIGURE 12.4 Reading Booklet One.
Source: Simpkins et al., 1977d.

Five, (3) a teacher's edition of the study books, (4) six audio recordings, and (5) a teacher's guide. The reading booklets have blue cardboard covers (Figure 12.4), and the inside pages are printed on white paper. All other instructional materials are printed on 8 1/2" × 11" paper.

Framing

Framing referred to the presentation of the content and its angle or slant (Huckin, 1995). The slant of *Bridge* appeared to be its design as a program specifically for inner-city black youth who failed academically in reading. For example, the teacher's guide opened with commentary on the Coleman Report and responded to the report's focus on the academic failure of black students across the country. The text stated:

> Today it is not at all uncommon for seventh and eighth grade black inner-city students to score at the second and third grade level on standardized reading tests. Nor is it unusual for black inner-city students to finish high school reading below the fifth grade level. Because the students lack the functional reading skills expected of young adults in our society, the likelihood of their being able to compete successfully for

further education, job training, and employment is low. Regardless of their intelligence, these students frequently are considered—or consider themselves to be dull, ignorant, and backward. The urgent question ... is "What can be done?"... Bridge is one possible solution. It is designed to intervene in the pattern of failure shown by black junior and senior high school students in this country's public school systems.

(Simpkins et al., 1977b, p. v)

Stalling's thoughts, from the interview, on framing *Bridge* with a focus on the needs of black youth, were:

[W]e looked at how black inner city children learn. We know they're intelligent. We know they're smart. We know they like to rhyme. Just like kids nowadays kids like to rap; before then it was playing the dozens. So we know that we like to shuck and jive and rhyme. Have the metaphors the similes and all that.... So yeah we wanted to meet the needs of kids. We wanted to let them know well that no one language or dialect is superior to another except in people's minds. That's why we start with that premise that you're smart. You're capable. You're intelligent; therefore we're going to build off of what you already know. That was the genesis. Build from what you know. Then people are more comfortable with it ... and then without putting down your language or culture we're going to Bridge you to the Standard English which is very obvious that's not hidden. But in a process whereby you know the similarities and differences because quite a few of our kids don't know the differences.... Teachers don't know the similarities and differences. So in a way we were educating teachers at the same time we were trying to educate the students to let them know its okay. And it's up to you to decide when and where to use Black English. So yeah it was meeting their needs, making them proud of who they are.

(personal communication, 1999)

The designers' frame captured an instructional spin specific to "inner-city" black youth's heritage, language, culture, experiences, and interests (Simpkins, 1976). The plan was to acknowledge and respect black youth's intelligence, build their self-esteem, and teach them Standard English.

Omission and Backgrounding

Huckin (1995) defined omission as the best form of backgrounding because what lies in the background is what has been intentionally or unintentionally omitted. Stalling commented that she could not:

> think of any [intentional] omissions and as a writer you always think well did I include everything I should.... I think we were ahead of our times when we actually published it. And maybe now people ... [are] more ready for it. At this point, I can't think off-hand what I would change.

Stalling identified one thing that destroyed sales and ultimately the program—public opinion. The public was not ready for a reading program that incorporated Black English; its academic content proved inconsequential. Further, the public was not ready to acknowledge their own fears about Black English and speakers of this dialect. They reacted out of naiveté versus knowledge. The designers could not predict the general public's reaction.

Since *Bridge* was produced for student consumption on a national basis, there was a need to prepare the public. Rickford and Rickford (1995) suggested measuring the public's response to dialect readers. An evaluation of the public's reaction was unintentionally omitted in the design of the product. This indicated that the design of a product, for profit or for public consumption, must also consider the public's reactions and actions towards that product. Public reaction was a major concern for linguists in 1969 when dialect readers were introduced (Stewart, 1969; Wolfram & Fasold, 1969). Therefore, the design of a product must consider internal and external analyses (e.g., field tests, public opinion surveys, media trouble-shooting).

Foregrounding

Foregrounding focused on emphasizing specific concepts and de-emphasizing other concepts (Huckin, 1995). In *Bridge*, there proved to be conflicting views as to what was foregrounded. The public saw a program that focused on Black English, and the designers saw a skills-based reading program. Simpkins described the situation as follows:

> [W]hen people look at the program all they see is that it has Black English in it. But if you really look at the program you'll see that it is a

well constructed skills based, theory based reading program ... for the kids. Black English is just a part of it. In fact, Jean Chall who was Harvard's expert on reading said she suspects that the gains came from other things in the program than Black English, and I told her she was right. Because people overlooked that it was a very well constructed reading program.

(personal communication, 1999)

Evidence to support Simpkins' contention that *Bridge* was a "well constructed reading program" and emphasized throughout the text can be found in the teacher's manual. For example, it read:

> Bridge: A Cross-Culture Reading Program ... is based on a synthesis of insights generated both from the authors' experiences with inner-city students and from the new directions indicated by research in dialectology, linguistics, reading, cultural anthropology, and learning theory. Bridge places primary emphasis on language skills already in the student's repertoires, using materials representative of the student's cultural experiences.
>
> Educators believe almost universally in the John Dewey axiom "Start where the child is." Many of today's linguists echo this axiom with the charge "Build on the child's cultural-linguistic knowledge." The validity of this pedagogical position has long been accepted by some teachers, but in the case of inner-city children it has been seriously ignored. Bridge draws upon both these precepts by starting with the students' primary language skills as a foundation upon which to build and motivate the acquisition of reading skills.
>
> *(Simpkins et al., 1977b, p. 1)*

On the other hand, the public reacted and emphasized what was "black" about the program instead of what was instructional. Blackness has been associated with negativity throughout much of contemporary history. In the interview with Stalling, she cited a book entitled *Grandpa, Is Everything Black Bad?* (Holman & Kometiani, 1995) to exemplify the tendency to associate black people with bad things. Although the designers sought to emphasize a skills-based program and de-emphasize that it included Black English, public opinion directed the program's perceived outcome.

Visual Representations

Visual representations also assisted in the framing of text (Huckin, 1995). In *Bridge*, photographs and sketches served as backdrops in Reading Booklets One through Five. The artists involved in creating these visual representations were hired by Houghton Mifflin Publishing Company. Most of the black-and-white photographs and sketches depicted black men, women, and children in the garb of the 1970s. In particular, the men and women sport afros—a popular hairstyle—and bellbottoms (pants that flare below the shins). Plaid clothing in the form of pants and jackets was also worn by people in the photographs. Visually these photographs and sketches set the mood of the stories and helped students visualize a scene or the stories' theme.

The text analysis revealed *Bridge* as a curriculum unit focused on the development of black youth's intellectual growth, self-esteem, and command of the English language. Unintentionally, Black English became emphasized more than the skills-based reading program. The visual representations assisted in the cultural context indicative of the 1970s.

Context Analysis

The final stage in approaching the text involved analyzing the context to identify the social, political (Van Dijk, 1993), or economic occurrences within the text. In this case, the instructional materials emulated the time period and they vicariously represented black life and language.

The designers of *Bridge* included what they knew about black youth and incorporated research from areas such as learning theory, dialectology, linguistics, cultural anthropology, and reading (Simpkins et al., 1977b). The fictional stories and exercises were written in the "verbal, imagistic style of good Black English rappers" (Smitherman, 1977, p. 224). The materials tap the "orality of the black cultural experience and the interactive, tonal dynamics of black communication" (Smitherman, 1977, p. 224). If read today, the grammar and phonology reflect Black English; however, the vocabulary and idioms sound dated. For example, idioms like "hip you to that" or "dig on" are outdated, but other idioms like "cool" and "check this out" are currently used, though infrequently (Labov, 1995, p. 54).

Stalling talked candidly about her conceptual goals for *Bridge*:

> Start where the kids are. Take them where they need to go in order to be successful. Start with the familiar. Schema. The metacognition type of activities. Bridging. We do modeling in it. When we first do the peer control reading the teacher models initially so the kids can see it. And then eventually they take over. The other thing we wanted

to do was to give kids more self control, in that whenever possible we tried to organize the materials so that it's based on some of Coleman's [1966] studies—sense of control, sense of locus in that whenever possible we let the students actually control the situation and let the teachers serve as facilitators or managers so that eventually we work ourselves out of a job. That was the other thing we wanted students to feel EMPOWERED—to know that they didn't need us. Once they underst[ood] the concepts and learned different things they could do it on their own.

(personal communication, 1999)

The design of *Bridge* was interdisciplinary and student-centered. The designers incorporated everything they knew and what research could tell them about educating black youth. They used Associative Bridging, a teaching-learning strategy, that allowed students to begin with the "familiar" (Black English) and then move into the "less familiar" (Standard English). Their theoretical perspective argued that Associative Bridging represents John Dewey's axiom "Start where the child is" (Simpkins et al., 1977b, p. 2).

Reading Booklets

In Simpkins' view, a central theme flowed throughout most of the reading booklets. He stated:

[S]ome of the stories had subliminal themes—why learn to read… because we found that the students didn't have good reasons for why [they should] learn to read. They were told to learn to read at a different time and a different place [and] you can be successful. You can be a doctor, lawyer…. So, we tried to put [in] themes [like] learn to read because its functional now to your life and your community.

(personal communication, 1999)

The theme "why learn to read" connected to the political and social climate surrounding the education of black youth in the late 1960s. In particular, President Lyndon B. Johnson's War on Poverty placed the lives and education of black youth under the microscope of the government's hegemonic control. The extensive academic failure of black youth in America's public schools was at issue. Johnson's sociopolitical programs sought to dissect the lives of inner-city black youth; however, this surgery left dismembered theories about deficits and deficiencies that continued to disease the educational progress of black youth. *Bridge* sought to provide an intermediary cure to the language-learning needs of African American youth. This reading program challenged the status quo curriculum and the politics of publishing instructional materials for public schools. *Bridge* answered the call to help re-educate black youth and refute the dismembered theories.

There were 5 initial reading booklets with a total of 14 stories. Only four stories will be reviewed in this chapter. All the stories featured black characters that were either labeled as such in the story or their racial identity was revealed in the story. Many of the stories sought to develop a positive self-image in black youth. Stalling stated the following in this regard: "if we feel better about ourselves, we have a better self-image ... so when we feel better about ourselves we do better" (personal communication, 1999).

BOOK ONE

Book One contains four stories, each written in Black English; they include *Shine, Stagolee, The Organizer,* and *The Ghost* (Figures 12.5 to 12.8). *Shine, Stagolee,* and *The Ghost* appear based on black folklore. The black folklore used in *Bridge* has been known as "oral epic poetry" or "toasts." This collection of folklore remains a product of African folklore meshing with the New World, the slavery experience, "the aftermath of slavery," and the "urbanization" of black people (Simpkins, 1976, p. 138). Smitherman (1977) defines toasts as "a variation on the trickster, bad nigguh theme done in poetic form" (p. 157). In Simpkins' interview he recalled that the toasts began "historically when blacks were in prison—jail and they had time on their hands to sit around and write these toasts." *Shine* was one of the most popular stories for children and adults according to Simpkins.

FIGURE 12.5 *Shine* from Book One.
Source: Simpkins et al., 1977d.

FIGURE 12.6 *The Organizer* from Book One.
Source: Simpkins et al., 1977d.

202 Patricia A. Young

FIGURE 12.7 *Stagolee* from Book One.
Source: Simpkins et al., 1977d.

FIGURE 12.8 *The Ghost* from Book One

Source: Simpkins et al., 1977b.

These toasts held a cultural and linguistic significance for Simpkins. First, the stories represented the oral tradition experienced by him in his youth, and second, they were a part of his heritage. He explained in the interview that:

> the original stories of Shine are filled with "mother fucker this"—"mother fucker that" and so we had to clean them up and make them presentable. When I grew up, we knew all these stories. We use to tell them to each other. But as time went by, black kids today lost their connection with the oral type of tradition—of black culture.
>
> *(personal communication, 1999)*

In the story *Shine*, Shine is a black man and a stoker on a ship called the *Titanic*. As a stoker, he shovels coal into the ship's furnace. Shine warns the captain several times that the ship is sinking. However, the captain refuses to listen, and the ship begins to sink. Shine jumps off the boat and saves himself. From the deck, various people on the boat beg Shine to save them; however, Shine is the only survivor. The story begins with this introduction:

> This story come from Black folklore, you understand. Black folklore is stories that Black folk have told and sung for a whole lot of years. This here story is all about Shine, a strong Black man! Maybe you heard other stories about Shine. Now come here and check out mine.
> *(Simpkins et al., 1977d, p. 1)*

The introduction and the story are written in Black English and include idiomatic expressions used in some black communities. For example, the story begins:

> You ever hear of the Titanic? Yeah, that's right. It was one of them big ships. The kind they call a ocean liner. Now this here ship was the biggest and the baddest ship ever to sail the sea. You understand? It was suppose to be unsinkable. Wind, storm, ice-berg—nothing could get next to it. It was a superbad ship, the meanest thing on the water. It could move like four Bloods in tennis shoes. It was out of sight!
>
> But you know what? The very first time this here ship put out to sea, it got sunk. Can you get ready for that? On its first trip, this here bad, superbad ship got sunk. Now ain't that something?
>
> Well, anyway, this here bad, superbad ship went under. Word was, there was very few survivors. Just about everybody got drown. But quiet as it's kept, they say that the one dude who got away was a Blood. Yeah, can you get ready for that? He was a big, Black strong Brother by the name of Shine.
> *(Simpkins et al., 1977d, pp. 1–2)*

Shine seems to fit Smitherman's (1977) definition of a toast with a "bad nigguh theme done in poetic form" (p. 157). Shine was so "bad" (meaning good in Black English and culture) that he was the only person to survive the sinking of the *Titanic*. He was so smart; he was "superbad."

The idiomatic expressions evident in *Shine* include phrases such as "blood," "superbad," and, "out of sight." These expressions emulate those represented in the 1970s by many black people. The manipulation of language is an inherent part of black peoples' linguistic and cultural expression.

With text written in Black English, the black youth's reading task is just decoding. If these stories were written in Standard English their task would be to decode and translate (Baratz, 1969). These stories remain consistent with Baratz's argument that black youth should learn how to read in their own language and then be taught to read in Standard English. Baratz proposes that a dialect reading program would require Black English texts and transition readers. Transition means that a story is written in Black English and Standard English (Simpkins et al., 1977b). The stories in Book Two fit the Transition criteria.

BOOK TWO

Book Two consists of two stories: *Old But Not Defenseless* and *What I Got To Be Proud Of* (Figures 12.9 and 12.10). These stories are written in Black English and Transition versions. *Old But Not Defenseless* is Stalling's version of *Little Red Riding Hood*. In the Black English version, Geraldine takes the park route to get to her grandmother's house with sweet bread in hand; she runs into a strange fellow who wants to walk with her. Geraldine refuses his offer. At her grandmother's house, Geraldine's grandmother tells her how to defend herself.

In the Transition version of *Old But Not Defenseless*, Geraldine wears a dashiki and carries a bottle of wine to her grandmother's house. Geraldine has also been followed home by a man who poses as an insurance salesman; however, he just wants the bottle of homemade wine that she carries to her grandmother's house. (According to the designers, the wine was used in the Transition version because it was a move towards an American cultural norm—that is, bringing alcohol as a social gift). In terms of written texts, Black English reading materials should present authentic representations of the spoken language (Stewart, 1969). Thereby, authentic representations of black life and language could bring youth to accept and connect to the content area.

According to Stalling, these stories signified the importance of our elders and listening to one's parents. Geraldine's mother told her to go straight to her grandmother's house. It is part of black culture to speak when spoken to but "keep stepping," stated Stalling. This cultural fact is exemplified in the Transition version of *Old But Not Defenseless*:

> It was so hot Geraldine decided to take a short cut through the park where it was cool. Geraldine mother didn't like her to go through the park. Geraldine could hear her mother talking now. "Weird characters be hanging out in the park. If you gotta go through it, go with a couple of other people. And step fast, child. If some guy say something to you, say 'Hello,' but keep on stepping in the direction you going. It's always better to speak than not to speak. 'Cause if you don't, they'll curse you out or go upside your head."
>
> *(Simpkins et al., 1977e, pp. 5–6)*

206 Patricia A. Young

FIGURE 12.9 *Old But Not Defenseless* from Book Two.

Source: Simpkins et al., 1977e.

FIGURE 12.10 *What I Got To Be Proud Of* from Book Two.
Source: Simpkins et al., 1977e.

This excerpt includes linguistic features consistent with Black English. In Black English "be" is used with adjectives to indicate an extended or continuous state of action as exemplified in the sentence "Weird characters be hanging out in the park" (Smitherman, 1994; Stewart, 1969). A second example is a word that omits the prefix; that is, "'Cause if you don't" in Black English for Standard English "Because if you don't" (Stewart, 1969).

Old But Not Defenseless and *What I Got To Be Proud Of* exemplify Transition readers that move the child from Black English to Standard English (Baratz, 1969). These Transition stories proved to be closer to the basilect (Black English) than the acrolect (Standard English). They include more features of Black English and focus on the "orality of the black cultural experience and the interactive, tonal dynamics of black communication" (Smitherman, 1977, p. 224).

BOOK THREE

Two stories are included in Book Three: *Dreamy Mae* and *A Friend in Need* (Figures 12.11 and 12.12). There are three versions of these stories (Black English, Transition, and Standard English).

Stalling wrote *Dreamy Mae*. In the Black English version of *Dreamy Mae*, Mae daydreams that she is a princess with long golden hair; later a friend styles Mae's hair and demonstrates the beauty of her natural hair. *Dreamy Mae*, in the Transition version, daydreams about having long golden hair. A school friend shows her a book about a black princess with natural hair, and Mae begins to realize the beauty of her own hair. The Standard English version of *Dreamy Mae* portrays Mae daydreaming that her hair is golden, and then dreaming that her hair is different colors (e.g., purple, green). In school, Mae is read a story by the teacher about a black princess and again she realizes the natural beauty of her hair.

208 Patricia A. Young

FIGURE 12.11 *Dreamy Mae* from Book Three.

Source: Simpkins et al., 1977f.

FIGURE 12.12 *A Friend in Need* from Book Three.

Source: Simpkins, et al., 1977f.

For Stalling the story had a social and personal meaning. She stated:

> With Dreamy Mae. My mother is a beautician. My mother in law is a beautician and to them (whispering) straight hair is good hair. And I had always told my mother that nappy hair is good hair. We as black folks have the most versatile hair.... You can talk to any beautician and they will tell you. We can straighten it. We can perm it. We can go ... nappy. We can braid it. We can do so many things with our hair and I truly wanted to show in that story two things. One, that our hair is versatile and good ... and two that we come from a long line of proud black people.
>
> *(personal communication, 1999)*

Dreamy Mae represents the cultural stigma of kinky hair. Kinky hair is viewed negatively in some black communities. *Dreamy Mae*'s message promotes pride in one's self-image, culture, and hair. For example, in this excerpt of the Transition version Mae meets a new friend, Barbara, and they sit down on a bench to eat lunch:

> The two girls started to talk. "You know what I really want more than anything else?" Mae said to Barbara.
> "No, what?"
> "I want some long golden hair."
> "What you want that for? asked Barbara.
> "I read a story about a princess who had long golden hair. I saw her picture, and she was more beautiful than anything I ever did see."
> "That's silly," said Barbara. "Golden hair wouldn't look right on you no way. It wouldn't look right on no Black people. You ever see a Black princess with long golden hair?"
> "No, I ain't seen no Black princess at all."
> Barbara had a small book about Africa with her. She opened it to a picture of a Black princess. Mae stared at the picture. She shook her head.
> "That ain't no princess," said Mae. "She got nappy hair."
> "She is too a princess," said Barbara. "Look at the book. It say so right here. Anyway, nappy hair is good hair. That's what my mama told me."
> Mae was confused. She had never heard that nappy hair was good hair. It sure sounded strange, like "nappy" and "good" just didn't go together.
> *(Simpkins et al., 1977f, pp. 21–22)*

Dreamy Mae maintains a strong focus on Black English in the dialogue and Standard English in the narration. For example, the sentence "No, I ain't seen no Black princess at all" demonstrates negation in Black English (Green, 2011). In Standard English, this sentence could be translated as "I have never seen a Black princess." The narration emulates Standard English as illustrated in the sentences: "Mae was confused. She had never heard that nappy hair was good hair."

In Book Three, the two stories *A Friend In Need* and *Dreamy Mae* are written in the three versions. These variations help students understand the relationship between their oral language and the written language of the text. Students begin to distinguish between their spoken language and Standard English without the stigma of inferior or superior language forms (Leaverton, 1973).

BOOK FOUR

In Book Four, there are two stories: *Vibration Cornbread* and *Little Big Man* (Figures 12.13 and 12.14). Each story represents the black experience as written in Transition and Standard English versions.

FIGURE 12.13 *Vibration Cornbread* from Book Four.
Source: Simpkins et al., 1977g.

FIGURE 12.14 *Little Big Man* from Book Four.
Source: Simpkins et al., 1977g.

The economic realities of black families are represented in both versions of *Vibration Cornbread*. In the story, two children cook dinner before their mother gets home from work. They are alone and managing the business of the house. This story held true for Stalling in her own childhood. She stated in her interview:

> Vibration corn bread—latchkey kids. I remember ... this [is] one that I wrote. It wasn't based on any other stories ... other than my history. And my mother use to tell me. "I want you to bake a chicken. I don't want you to mess with that chicken. I just want you to put some salt and some pepper on it." Because I hate to do the same thing the same way. I like to be creative about doing things. So then my mother is a vibration cook in that even when I cook now I don't measure anything. I just dump it on whatever seems right. When I make something, it's never the same way. And I have friends who say, "why don't you write down your recipes." And so this is vibration cornbread.
>
> *(personal communication, 1999)*

Stalling's experience as a latchkey kid was exemplified by the manner in which her mother organized their day. She stated:

> [W]hat I started telling you about this story was my mother when she would go to work. She would set 3 clocks for us. One was to get up. One was for us to leave. And the third clock, we'd better be home before it went off, because we were supposed to be home from school, in the house and have called her. So we had three clocks to respond to a day.... Three clocks.... I'd call her at the beauty shop and let her know we were at home.
>
> *(personal communication, 1999)*

Vibration Cornbread oozes the cultural tradition of vibration cooking. Good cooking has been a cultural norm passed down for generations in some black families. In this fictional youth story the children are learning this tradition, and they are learning to be responsible. The children have to assume the responsibility of managing the home until their mother arrives. Latchkey kids became so out of necessity because many parents could not financially afford baby-sitters or childcare centers.

The text of *Vibration Cornbread* parallels that of *Little Big Man* in that Black English moves closer along the continuum to Standard English. In this example of the transition version of *Vibration Cornbread*, Becky is cooking the way her mother taught her:

> Becky added the corn meal. Then she added the milk and egg to the bowl and stirred it well. After looking at the mixture, she decided that it

needed more milk. "Mama say use your own judgment when cooking. Add a little bit less or a little bit more, depending on how you feel. Mama calls it vibration cooking."
"Scottie, how's this look to you?"
"I don't know. I have to taste it."
"Here, try a little taste." Becky waited for her brother to say something.
"It taste OK. When it's done, it should taste good?" said Scottie.

(Simpkins et al., 1977g, p. 12)

Book Four exemplifies clearly that "there are two dialects in the education complex of black children" (Baratz, 1969, p. 111). In addition, these dialects can be blended in various ways when constructing the written text of dialect readers.

BOOK FIVE

Book Five contains four stories all written in Standard English: *I'll Always Remember*, *City Folks*, *Dig And Be Dug*, and *What Folks Call Politics* (Figures 12.15 to 12.18). Each story is prefaced with a list of six to nine vocabulary words relating to the story. The content in the Standard English version parallels those in the previous booklets in that these stories reflect black people's lives and communities. For example, in *I'll Always Remember*, Shannon, a young woman, is conned into handing over her wallet to a "city slicker." The story rang true for Stalling. She stated that sometimes people from the country come to the city and might say:

> "Oh I'm so glad to get away from this hick town" [yet be] ... very vulnerable and very open to being ripped off. Because we have different mentalities—you know trusting people. Speaking to everyone you meet and then coming to the city and people misinterpreting it.
>
> *(personal communication, 1999)*

In certain parts of the world where many black people reside, one may notice that greeting people is a part of the culture. These greetings may be exhibited as a smile, nod, or verbal expression. This cordial behavior is commonplace. However, when exhibiting this familiar behavior in a large city, a person may become a vulnerable target.

Bridge (1975–1977) **215**

FIGURE 12.15 *I'll Always Remember* from Book Five.
Source: Simpkins et al., 1977h.

FIGURE 12.16 *City Folks* from Book Five.

Source: Simpkins et al., 1977h.

FIGURE 12.17 *Dig And Be Dug* from Book Five.
Source: Simpkins et al., 1977h.

218 Patricia A. Young

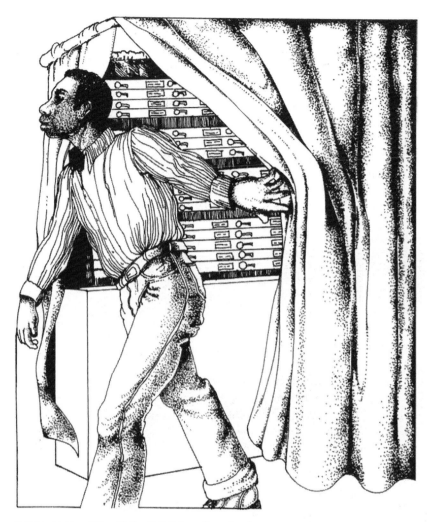

FIGURE 12.18 *What Folks Call Politics* from Book Five.
Source: Simpkins et al., 1977h.

The transition to a total Standard English version is exemplified in *I'll Always Remember*:

> Shannon got off the train. She walked to the baggage-claim section where people were pushing, shoving and pulling. She waited until everyone else had picked up their baggage. Then she put her coat over her arm and claimed her two bags. She walked outside to the taxi stand. There were no taxis in sight. Shannon sat on one of her bags while she waited. In this strange new city she felt very small.

A well-dressed man in his late twenties walked up to her. "Good morning. My name is William Henry," he said.
"Hello, my name is Shannon Simms."
"Please to meet you, Shannon. If you're waiting for a taxi, you'll have a long wait. They've all left for the city."
"Oh, my!" said Shannon.
"It's quicker and cheaper to take the subway," said William Henry.
"It is?"
"Yes! It's called the poor man's taxi," said Mr. Henry. "Where are you going?"
"To the Bronx."
"I'm going there, too," said Mr. Henry. "I'll be happy to show you the way."

(Simpkins et al., 1977h, p. 2)

Here the grammatical structure is consistent with Standard English. The research supports that by the time young people reach the Standard English version of dialect readers they should understand the relationship between their oral language and the written language of Standard English text (Leaverton, 1973).

Books One through Five demonstrate Stewart's (1969) model for the design of dialect readers. Stewart (1969) envisioned readers that transitioned from Black English to Standard English. Although *Bridge* does not reflect Stewart's vision of stories written solely by a linguist, it parallels his overall structure of using stages. Stewart saw the role of linguist as one who strictly controlled the grammatical structure in each version (i.e., each version would specifically focus on one aspect of Black English; for example, the copula—am, is, are).

Study Books One through Five: Activities

The Study Books (Figures 12.19 and 12.20) support the reading booklets by offering instruction in reading skills and practice activities. The activities include story questions, skills lessons, and word-bridging lessons. Then, students assess themselves using the feedback records.

Story Questions

Each story contains questions that correspond to the version (Black English, Transition, or Standard English). Story questions test students' understanding of story topics and details. The three versions present different information on the same story. Questions are similar for each story but may yield a different answer. For example, the correct answer to the question, "How much money did John receive?" might be "a whole lot of money," in the Black English version,

FIGURE 12.19 Study Book Three—Teacher's Edition.

Source: Simpkins et al., 1977a.

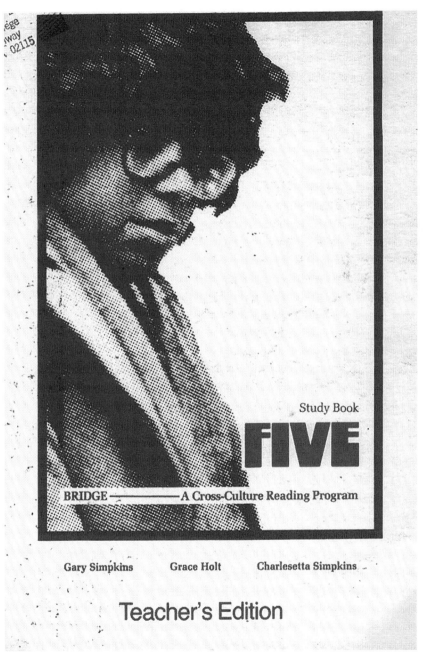

FIGURE 12.20 Study Book Five—Teacher's Edition.

Source: Simpkins et al., 1977a.

"750 dollars" in the Transition version, and "500 dollars" in the Standard English version (Simpkins et al., 1977b, p. 5). There is a cultural significance to the change in the dollar amounts. In the Black English version, it is the norm in most African American cultures to keep personal business to oneself. In this case, the term "whole lot of money" brings with it the undertone that it is none of anyone's concern or business how much money John received. In the Standard English version, responding with the answer "500 dollars" mirrors the dominant culture's expectations that if someone asks you a question you should respond in the affirmative.

All story questions are preceded by audio- and text-based directions that seek to convey value and respect for the students' culture. For example, the directions to the story *Shine* begins:

> Go for what you know about the story "Shine." Check out each sentence down below. Circle the letter of the correct answer (a, b, c or d). There ain't but one right answer to each question so don't be picking out two."
>
> *(Simpkins et al., 1977c, p. 1)*

This statement suggests that students should use their schema (prior knowledge) to comprehend questions and responses related to the story. Further, these words, written in dialect, bring equity and affirmation to Black English in its written form.

In the area of curriculum development and textbook publication, Black English has not been accepted, respected, or legitimized. Black English has only been accepted when the "dialect is presented within a work of fiction, especially when authors frame the representation of dialect by prose that demonstrates their command of Standard English" (Labov, 1995, p. 55). Dialect is accepted in mainstream literature but not in educational technologies. Delegitimizing Black English delegitimizes the people who speak the language.

Skills Lessons

The skills lessons, similarly, represent Black English and culture. These lessons assist students with their comprehension and application of reading skills (Simpkins et al., 1977b). The designers identified nine skills that plagued students; they included cause and effect, inference, figures of speech, key meaning words, main idea, meaning from context, time order, word order, and word parts. These reading skills are "retaught, extended and refined" in the three versions (Simpkins et al., 1977b, p. 6).

The designers stressed the importance of the "searching process" built into the skills lessons. This search process they believed to be more important than obtaining the correct answer. Students are provided with a limited number of questions (four) to enable this process (Simpkins et al., 1977b). Thereby, students are allowed time to find answers. This searching process is usually not valued in higher grade levels and students are often rushed to find the correct answer. If students are allowed the opportunity to relearn this process, they can redevelop fluency in reading. Students who read slowly or take longer to comprehend are perceived to be slow learners and thereby deficient. *Bridge* allows students to relearn how to read in a supportive social environment. The curriculum supports students where they are and provides an environment conducive to learning.

The words and phrases used repeatedly in the Black English lessons reflect the language, experiences, and norms of black communities in the 1970s. This is exemplified through the Skills Lesson for Shine entitled "Digging on Figures of Speech":

> What you gonna learn from this: To dig on words that say more than what the words really mean. Check this out: You got a figure of speech when you come across a word, or some words, that ain't really saying what it seem to be saying. To understand this here figure-of-speech thing, to really get it together, you got to use a little taste of imagination. You can't be using the exact meaning of the words. What you got to do is trip on the picture that the words paint for you.
>
> *(Simpkins et al., 1977c, p. 5)*

This excerpt demonstrates the incorporation of idioms and black linguistic norms. In the first sentence, the word "dig" means "understand." Later in the paragraph, the word "trip" means "to think about." An example of a skills lesson question that followed the above directions states:

> Shine was a stone swimmer.
> (a) Shine was a very poor swimmer;
> (b) Shine was a very good swimmer;
> (c) Shine was a stone.
>
> *(Simpkins et al., 1977c, p. 6)*

These linguistic excerpts exemplify what Smitherman and Quartey-Annan (2011) describe as "language constructed as it would be used in a natural language environment" (p. 264). The designers of *Bridge* sought to replicate the African American cultural experience throughout these instructional materials.

The same excerpt as the one above written in a Standard English version of *Dreamy Mae* begins: "Understanding Figures of Speech." It read:

> What you will learn: To understand words that mean more than what they seem to say.
>
> Study the explanation: You have a figure of speech when the words don't really mean what they seem to say. You can't use the exact meaning of the words. To understand the meaning of these words, you have to use your imagination. What you have to do is understand the picture that the words paint for you.
>
> *(Simpkins et al., 1977c, p. 125)*

The Standard English version of the directions present a more formal tone conducive to written Standard English texts. The use of directions in Standard English suggests the written text structure students must master (Baratz, 1969). Except for the contractions, this example represents the linguistic patterns of written Standard English; however, the language is still more informal than formal. The use of the pronoun "you" personalizes the directions; thus the student may have felt that the writer is speaking directly to him or her. This affirms the designers' goal of valuing the students' language and culture.

Word-bridging Lessons

The word-bridging lessons provide students with activities to improve their vocabulary and translate word meaning between Black English and Standard English. In these lessons, students compare the word usage in Black English and Standard English; the stories aid students in defining word meanings in both dialects. For example, students might define the word "good" in Black English, based on the context of the story, to mean "bad" or "good." However, in Standard English the word "good" only means "good" (Simpkins et al., 1977b). The Black English meaning of "bad" is demonstrated in the stories *Shine* and *Stagolee*. Shine is "bad" as in "good"; he is a good hero. Stagolee is "bad" as in a person who is bad in behavior. Further, he is "bad" as in "good," because he is a good legendary character.

Word bridging parallels words and phrases in Black English to Standard English synonyms. Through this strategy, students begin to learn semantic patterns and systems of language use. This switching from one language to another might be described as "dialect shifting" (Green, 2011, p. 8); dialect shifting or code switching has been perceived as a positive correlation in the reading achievement of African American students (Craig & Washington, 2006).

Feedback Records

Feedback records provide students with an individualized self-assessment tool. Students compete with themselves versus other students. Their relearning process is allowed to redevelop. The feedback records monitor student responses to the story questions and the skills lessons. (These are separate feedback record sheets.) For example, a student tracks their progress in the Story Questions by completing a set of ten questions related to the story *Shine*. The teacher corrects their answers and the number of correct answers is indicated on a sheet (Figure 12.21). The teacher circles the number of correct responses and students monitor their achievement by acknowledging the higher numbered scores (Simpkins et al., 1977a).

The feedback record can be considered a self-monitoring system for students. It provides students with an internal record of their academic progress without penalty.

Teacher's Guide

The teacher's guide covers the role of the teacher and Peer Control Reading. The designers sought to get students' attention, create interaction, limit direct instruction, and establish a personal relationship between students and teacher (as learning consultant).

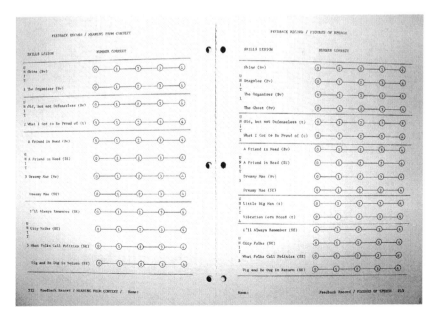

FIGURE 12.21 Feedback Records, Study Book.

Source: Simpkins et al., 1977c, p. 213.

226   Patricia A. Young

The Teacher's Role

In *Bridge*, the teacher's role is clearly defined and specific to the learning needs of students. The teacher is identified as "manager of classroom behavior, manager of materials and individual learning consultant" (Simpkins et al., 1977b, p. 18).

As manager of classroom behavior, the teacher directs the establishment of a positive environment for learning and an atmosphere for success and, as much as possible, ignores inappropriate behavior. The teacher contributes to the development of positive self-images by "consistently and exclusively" following two techniques: "(1) rule setting and (2) positive reinforcement of successful behavior" (Simpkins et al., 1977b, p. 18). The rule setting sets up a pattern that students consistently follow and the teacher consistently reinforces. Positive reinforcement is viewed as the teacher praising or rewarding any and all accomplishments of all her students. This reinforcement improves students' self-image and motivates them to complete assignments (Simpkins et al., 1977b).

The teacher as manager of materials maintains an organized sequence of the reading program. She consistently manages the location of the materials throughout the day and monitors student progress.

Finally, the teacher as individual learning consultant provides individualized instruction, support, reinforcement, or encouragement to students as she circulates the room. The teacher consults with students as learning issues arise (Simpkins et al., 1977b).

The designers worked to provide a reading program that was "teacher proof." Simpkins clarified these beliefs:

> Now what do I mean by teacher proof. I meant that I wanted the program where teachers couldn't FUCK IT UP! Okay. So this program is designed for any teacher who could read. You don't have to have any special instructions, background or training. If you can read, follow the instructions, you can teach the program. Okay. We encouraged them to not deviate from the program but to follow it to the letter. And that's what we encouraged all the teachers to do—no special instructions just follow the program. And it worked out really good. So we changed the teacher's role from the teacher who hovers over the class, who also talks too much, who doesn't distribute reinforcement equally to a manager of materials, a dispenser of reinforcements, so the teacher's role now is an

individual learning consultant. The teacher roams around the class. She never addresses the entire group.... she gives them instruction on how to run the program—how to stay on track. She individually helps kids with problems.... We emphasize that we want a distribution of reinforcement. You know every time you use three negatives we want you to use 3 positives. And part of it is, if this kid only stays in his seat for 5 minutes, seek him out when he stays in for 6 minutes and reinforce him for that 6 minutes.

(personal communication, 1999)

Teacher-proofing instructional materials can be a difficult task; however, *Bridge* sought to limit teacher bias, attitudes, and prejudices. The designers attempted to control human interference that often hinders learning for black youth; thereby creating autonomous learners.

Peer Control Reading

Peer Control Reading exemplifies another skills-based component to the design of *Bridge*. The stories in Peer Control Reading differ from those in Reading Booklets One through Four, and they are also written in the three versions—Black English, Transition, and Standard English. In Peer Control Reading, groups of students "reinforce each other for desired oral reading responses" (Simpkins et al., 1977b, p. 26). Groups are chosen based on reading ability and then randomly selected to read. One person is the "Reader," and the others in the group are the "Correctors." The Reader reads a number of sentences. Then, the Reader is stopped if they make any "oral reading errors" (i.e., omissions, substitutions, mistakes in word recognition) and given a chance to identify and correct the error (Simpkins et al., 1977b, p. 28). If an error is made, the Reader continues reading a few more sentences until the oral reading errors are flawless. In addition, during the Peer Control Reading, the Reader is asked to talk about what they read. The Correctors stop the Reader at errors in comprehension and assist the Reader in understanding the passage (Simpkins et al., 1977b).

Peer Control Reading provides a social environment for students to learn. Students work collaboratively, interact socially, and support each other. It draws upon the "call and response—oral tradition in the black community" (Simpkins, 1976, p. 61). Simpkins stated in his interview: "teachers told us that the peer control group was so much fun that it was hard for them to resist getting into the groups themselves." Peer Control Reading provides a format for the execution of a culture-specific instructional strategy and implementation. The oral tradition of "call and response" can be experienced in Black churches today; thereby the instructional strategy is authenticated by this culture-specific tradition.

Audio Recordings

The audio recordings launch the program, introduce a story, narrate an entire story, or review a skills lesson. The introduction to each section begins with a flighty and fun musical arrangement. The narrator is male; however, some transitions and stories present a female narrator. All the content in the audio recordings, spoken in Black English, connects to the social, cultural, and linguistic traditions in many black communities. The narrator begins the program with an enticing introduction:

> What's happening, Brothers and Sisters! I want to tell you about this here program call Bridge: A Cross-Culture Reading Program. Now I know you thinking that this is just another one of them jive reading programs and that I won't be needing no reading program, but dig it. This here reading program is really kinda different. It was done by a Brother and two Sisters, soul folk you know, and they put sumpin extra in it for ya. They put a little taste of soul. As a matter of fact, a lotta soul. No jive, that's what they put in it. A little bit of soul, something you can relate to.
>
> *(Simpkins et al., 1977b, p. 47)*

In this excerpt, the narrator welcomes the students with a communal greeting, "what's happening." Then the narrator addresses the students as "Brothers and Sisters" thereby signifying that they are members of the same community—the same family. This clues students into listening, because they hear familiar greetings that are used socially in their community. Further, the narrator's intonations and style of speaking are characteristic of some black communities in the 1970s.

Immediately, the narrator addresses student concerns about the reading program and offers the assurance that this program is different from their traditional reading materials. The narrator acknowledges that the program was created by black people like themselves. Usually students do not know the creators of the instructional materials they read. For most students, this was probably their first time reading something written in Black English, and it was highly likely that these students never interacted with instructional materials made by and for black people. The narrator offers the learner something they have never received in instructional materials or even at school before: "a little taste of soul." They define soul as "referring to Blacks and their culture: a way to describe such cultural conventions as food, music, dance, and [a] world view of Blacks" (Simpkins et al., 1977b, p. 57). The students' culture is affirmed and supported.

The program introduction continues:

> Now, I know what you gonna say: "I don't need to be reading no better. I get by. I don't dig no reading and there ain't nothing I wanna be reading no how." But dig. I know where you been and I know where you coming from too. When you were just starting school, reading got on your case, didn't it? Got down on you. Hurt your feelings. Then the second grade, reading just smack you all upside your head and dared you to do something about it. In the third grade (mmmm!) reading got into your chest, knock you down, drag you through the mud, sent you home crying to your mama. Now, by the time you got to the fourth grade, you just about had enough of messing around with this here reading thing, and you say to yourself, "I ain't gonna be messing with this old bad boy no more." You just hung it up.
>
> *(Simpkins et al., 1977b, p. 47)*

In this excerpt of the program introduction, the designers have given a scenario of what happens in the structure of schools and schooling. Schools have always been political institutions, because they control what people know and how much they know. The statement "When you were just starting school, reading got on your case, didn't it? Got down on you. Hurt your feelings" alludes to the fact that academic failure and loss of motivation for learning begins in the early grades. According to Labov (1995), "it is not accidental that the person addressed is in the fourth grade (though the program ... was first tested in grades 7 to 12), since as noted above it is in the fourth grade that resistance to school instruction is first solidified by adolescent peer groups" (p. 51). Then, as it is now, public schools remain paralyzed in a battle to educate the poor and disenfranchised.

This last excerpt addresses the language needs of black youth, who communicate in their homes and community using Black English, and then moves into an explanation of Standard English.

> [I]n this here program, you start off with what we call soul talk. You know, the way you hear a lot of Bloods talk. We call this talk Black Vernacular. You got that? Soul talk and Black Vernacular is the same thing. And you end up in Standard English. Now you know what Standard English is don't you? That's what you see in them textbooks, what you hear on radio and TV, and the way you hear the teacher talk, and stuff like that. You know?
>
> *(Simpkins et al., 1977b, pp. 47–48)*

In this example, the learner is made aware of the learning goals of the program. They are informed that there is a distinction between what they speak at home (everyday talk), school (school talk) (Leaverton, 1973), and the dialects heard in the media.

Bridge is based on the premise that language should be learned in its social and cultural context. A child must be able to see and understand the grammatical structure in their own language to make an easy transition to Standard English. Only through explicit written text and oral communication can students determine how Standard English differs from the dialects they use at home, school, or work, and when writing, reading, or speaking.

Bridge's Dormancy

Reactions to *Bridge* varied across audiences. According to linguist Geneva Smitherman, "the vociferous denunciation of *Bridge* (which included letters and calls to the publisher) by Black school superintendents and other members of the Black middle class pounded the nail into the coffin of the series" (Alim, 2012, p. 373). Those people who had the opportunity to talk with the designers or interact with the program had positive experiences, and those who did not have these experiences but who heard the words "Black English" responded negatively. Simpkins stated that *Newsweek* magazine responded positively to the experimental version of the program (Sheils & Manning, 1976) and wrote an article that hailed *Bridge* as:

> a major break through for black inner city kids in reading ... Anyway, after Newsweek came out with the article everybody and their brother responded to it, that Black English should not be used in the schools. [They stated that] it was a conspiracy—we were trying to keep the kids backwards. And it had no place in education and so on and so forth. And as a result many of the schools backed out from ordering the program. And the sales were lousy because it had so much negative publicity.
>
> *(personal communication, 1999)*

The stigma associated with Black English and speakers of Black English (Dillard, 1972) roared across the black community and the country. In 1969, linguists anticipated this negative outcry and thereby curtailed further development of dialect readers (Stewart, 1969; Wolfram & Fasold, 1969). Other notions on the development of dialect readers proposed the need to test public opinion before bringing dialect readers into instructional designs (Rickford & Rickford, 1995).

In Simpkins' interview he recalled the following:

[W]hat was most discouraging was to hear from blacks who obviously knew little about language and much less about children—to quote Labov. As they sprouted on and on about the evils of using Black English because they have a concept of Black English that is the street black who is hip and all of that sprouting out hip clichés which when we talk about Black English we include the whole population. Black English is the way my grandmother talked, the way my mama talked. It's the way many of the teachers talk when they get a few drinks in them at a party or something. [Laughing.] You know, so Black English covered the whole realm of black people not just a small segment of hip little gangsters in the street or anything like that.

I have talked to parents all over the country in terms of community. I've yet to talk to any community of parents that did not wholehardly support the program in the effort once they knew what the program was about. You know, when we talk to community people and we explain to them what it's about, they become big advocates of the program. And so there is no resistance on the community level. The resistance that we were running into was more on the black middle class—upper class levels, but that's the black professionals who because of their own up bringing and their... perceived need to escape from lower level culture have certain attitudes about the language.

But the thing is I went around the country and talked to some of the kids that were in the program, in the schools (with conviction) and the kids loved the program. For the first time in their lives, they were interested in reading. They found it to be fun.

(personal communication, 1999)

The reactions of the black middle-class community, the coverage of indifferent publicity, and negative comments by officials in education dampened the marketability of *Bridge*. Williams (1976) argued that it has been the black middle class who have "attempted to define the Black experience in terms of ... Black street culture" (p. 15). Blacks who are ashamed or antagonistic about Black English may prevent its use in the school curriculum, as was the case with *Bridge*.

The lack of knowledge about the program's goal and objectives of the designers harmed the success of this reading program. People were not knowledgeable about the language and learning needs of young people, and in particular of black youth. They were fearful of what Black English symbolized and sought no explanation. "The publishers received enough objections from parents and teachers to the use of AAVE [African American Vernacular English] in the classroom that they ceased promoting it [*Bridge*], and further development was shelved" (Labov, 1995, p. 52).

The Future of *Bridge*

Houghton Mifflin field-tested *Bridge* in 1975 at schools in Chicago, Illinois; Phoenix. Arizona; Washington, DC; Memphis, Tennessee and Macon County, Alabama. *Bridge* replaced a previously planned remedial reading program. The participants included 540 students of which 520 were Black and were enrolled in 27 classes. The same teacher taught the experimental and control group. The Iowa Test of Basic Skills in Reading Comprehension measured pre- and post-reading scores. In the seventh to twelfth grades, the experimental groups exhibited a mean gain in grade equivalency scores at 6.2 months for 4.0 months of instruction compared to control groups that earned 1.6 months for 4.0 months of instruction (Simpkins, 2002). Questionnaires of participating teachers revealed the following responses: "Even my chronic trouble-makers are willing to listen to directions and remain on task" and "The stories reminded students of their families" (Simpkins, 1976, p. 130). Student interest was sustained in reading the three different versions; however, teachers were mixed about whether there should be three versions (i.e., Black English, Transition, Standard English).

In 2001, Brookline Books, a private publishing company, revived the series as *Bridge 2: A Cross-Cultural Reading Program*. This version updated the stories from *Bridge* and expanded the cross-cultural approach (Simpkins, 2002). The authors of this version included Gary Simpkins, Geneva Smitherman, and Charlesetta Stalling. *Bridge 2* was never distributed or produced widely. It remains dormant.

Conclusion

Examinations of educational technologies must be presented within their historical, political, and social contexts. *Bridge* was designed by and for African Americans at a time when Black power and liberation were at the forefront of people's thoughts, words, and deeds. Subsequently, other instructional materials designed during this time emanated out of circumstance, condition, or just simple competition. By example, the Education Study Center in Washington, DC under the direction of William Stewart and Joan Baratz produced three experimental readers—*Ollie, Friends,* and *Old Tales* (Wolfram & Fasold, 1969)—that contained Black English and Standard English versions. Although the integration of black dialect into instructional materials was uncommon, authentic examples of educational technologies that represented the black experience in K-12 education were being produced by publishers such as The Free Press (NY) and Afro-American Publishing (IL).

Bridge represents a unique effort in the history of African American educational technologies. This exemplifies a culture-specific design (Young, 2008, 2009) that sought to intervene in the academic future of African American youth. It is a testament to the continuing fact that the value of educating African American youth remains unbalanced.

Acknowledgments

I would like to thank the creators of *Bridge* for permission to use their accomplishments in this publication. Specifically, I thank Frank Simpkins for allowing access to Gary's interview and work. Charlesetta Stallings graciously allowed access to her interview, and Geneva Smitherman provided resources related to her work on *Bridge*.

Note

1 This chapter contains audio material accessible by scanning the individual QR codes for each segment.

References

Alim, H. S. (2012). Interview with Geneva Smitherman. *Journal of English Linguistics, 40*(4), 357–377.

Baratz, J. C. (1969). Teaching reading in an urban Negro school system. In J. C. Baratz & R. W. Shuy (Eds.), *Teaching Black children to read* (pp. 92–116). Washington, DC: Center for Applied Linguistics.

Craig, H., & Washington, J. (2006). *Malik goes to school: Examining the language skills of African American students from preschool–5th grade*. Mahwah, NJ: Lawrence Erlbaum Associates.

Dillard, J. L. (1972). *Black English: Its history and usage in the United States*. New York: Vintage Books.

Green, L. J. (2011). *Language and the African American child*. Cambridge, MA: Cambridge University Press.

Holman, S. L., & Kometiani, L. (1995). *Grandpa, is everything black bad?* Davis, CA: Cultural Cooperative.

Huckin, T. N. (1995). Critical discourse analysis. Functional approaches to written text: Classroom applications. *TESOL-France Journal, 2*(2), 95–111.

Huckin, T. (2002). Critical discourse analysis and the discourse of condescension. In E. Barton & G. Stygall (Eds.), *Discourse studies in composition* (pp. 155–176). Cresskill, NJ: Hampton Press.

Labov, W. (1995). Can reading failure be reversed: A linguistic approach to the question. In V. L. Gadsden & D. A. Wagner (Eds.), *Literacy among African-American youth* (pp. 39–68). Cresskill, NJ: Hampton Press.

Leaverton, L. (1973). Dialectal readers: Rationale, use and value. In J. L. Laffey & R. Shuy (Eds.), *Language differences: Do they interfere?* (pp. 114–126). Newark, DE: International Reading Association.

Rickford, J. R., & Rickford, A. E. (1995). Dialect readers revisited. *Linguistics and Education, 7,* 107–128.

Sheils, M., & Manning, R. (1976, December 20). Bridge talk. *Newsweek,* 68–69.

Simpkins, G. A. (1976). "The cross-cultural approach to reading." Unpublished doctoral dissertation, University of Massachusetts, Amherst, MA.

Simpkins, G. (2002). *The throwaway kids.* Brookline, MA: Brookline Books.

Simpkins, G., Holt, G., & Simpkins, C. (1977a). *Bridge: A cross-culture reading program.* New York: Houghton Mifflin.

Simpkins, G., Holt, G., & Simpkins, C. (1977b). *Bridge: A cross-culture reading program/Teacher's Guide.* Boston, MA: Houghton Mifflin.

Simpkins, G., Holt, G., & Simpkins, C. (1977c). *Bridge: A cross-culture reading program/Study guide.* Boston, MA: Houghton Mifflin.

Simpkins, G., Holt, G., & Simpkins, C. (1977d). *Bridge: A cross-culture reading program/Reading booklet 1.* Boston, MA: Houghton Mifflin.

Simpkins, G., Holt, G., & Simpkins, C. (1977e). *Bridge: A cross-culture reading program/Reading booklet 2.* Boston, MA: Houghton Mifflin.

Simpkins, G., Holt, G., & Simpkins, C. (1977f). *Bridge: A cross-culture reading program/Reading booklet 3.* Boston, MA: Houghton Mifflin.

Simpkins, G., Holt, G., & Simpkins, C. (1977g). *Bridge: A cross-culture reading program/Reading booklet 4.* Boston, MA: Houghton Mifflin.

Simpkins, G., Holt, G., & Simpkins, C. (1977h). *Bridge: A cross-culture reading program/Reading booklet 5.* Boston, MA: Houghton Mifflin.

Smitherman, G. (1977). *Talkin and testifyin: The language of black America.* Boston, MA: Houghton Mifflin.

Smitherman, G. (1994). *Black talk: Words and phrases from the hood to the amen corner.* Boston, MA: Houghton Mifflin.

Smitherman, G., & Quartey-Annan, M. (2011). African American language and education: How far have we come? In M. Adams & A. Curzan (Eds.), *Contours of English and English language studies* (pp. 254–277). Ann Arbor, MI: University of Michigan Press.

Stalling, C. (1976). "Effects of the cultural context of language on the cognitive performance of Black students." Unpublished doctoral dissertation, University of Massachusetts, Amherst, MA.

Stewart, W. A. (1969). On the use of Negro dialect in the teaching of reading. In J. C. Baratz & R. W. Shuy (Eds.), *Teaching Black children to read* (pp. 156–219). Washington, DC: Center for Applied Linguistics.

Van Dijk, T. A. (1993). Analyzing racism through discourse analysis: Some methodological reflections. In J. H. Stanfield & R. M. Dennis (Eds.), *Race and ethnicity in research methods* (pp. 92–134). Newbury Park, CA: Sage.

Williams, R. (1976). The anguish of definition: Toward a new concept of blackness. In D. S. Harrison & T. Trabasso (Eds.), *Black English: A seminar* (pp. 9–24). Hillsdale, NJ: Lawrence Erlbaum Associates.

Wolfram, W. A., & Fasold, R. W. (1969). Toward reading materials for speakers of Black English: Three linguistically appropriate passages. In J. C. Baratz & R. W. Shuy (Eds.), *Teaching Black children to read* (pp. 138–155). Washington, DC: Center for Applied Linguistics.

Young, P. A. (1999). "Roads to travel: A historical look at African American contributions to instructional technology." Unpublished doctoral dissertation, University of California Berkeley, Berkeley, CA.

Young, P. A. (2008). Integrating culture in the design of ICTs. *British Journal of Educational Technology, 39*(1), 6–17.

Young, P. A. (2009). *Instructional design frameworks and intercultural models*. Hershey, PA: IGI Global/Information Science Publishing.

13

CREATING MINIMALIST INSTRUCTION (1979–PRESENT)

John M. Carroll

Introduction

As our society charges into an age of notebook and smartphone computers, it is interesting to revisit the micro-computer revolution that occurred in the decade surrounding the year 1980, and its consequences for the design of user interfaces and of user training and instruction.

In 1976, I joined IBM's Research Division in Yorktown Heights, New York. As a new PhD in psycholinguistics, I became involved in studies of software design understood as human problem-solving, and of names and naming in the context of command languages and personal files and directories (they were not called "folders" yet!). In 1979, I served on a corporate task force to identify emerging needs and opportunities with respect to users and usability.

This was eye opening; 1979 was the year that the Cognitive Science Society was founded and had its first meeting. One original theme differentiating cognitive science from cognitive psychology was its commitment to complex application domains, and not merely to simplified laboratory models of human behavior and experience. The articulation of this commitment in the context of early graphical user interface work at the Xerox Palo Alto Research Center (PARC) led directly to the formation of human–computer interaction.

At IBM, new projects and areas began to form. I joined Clayton Lewis and Robert Mack to begin an investigation of learning through self-instruction. Through the first decades of computing, training was typically quite personalized. Computers were huge and expensive, operated by teams of expensive professionals. Face-to-face training courses, and other field support, were typically bundled into the pricing of such systems. However, as IBM and other companies moved towards much smaller machines, and ultimately to personal computers, training and other field support could not be delivered face-to-face; such services would cost much more than the systems themselves. This was the original motivation for self-instruction designs.

Our investigation continued through the 1980s, though many of our key insights and our most influential designs were developed in the first few years. Thus, in this chapter, I am looking back more than 30 years. Our design cases were directly inspired by empirical studies of self-instruction, and by a particular interpretation of what those studies meant; I turn to those studies and their interpretation in the following section. I will then briefly present two of our early designs: the Minimal Manual and the Training Wheels Displaywriter.

Because these are "historical" design cases, I have had a lot of time to ponder what they mean, and honestly, to reconstruct what they might mean. These reflections are separate from the design work itself, which had its own validity and impact at a particular time, but which is now "just" history. Here I will address three reflections; first, I think our work on minimalist design succeeded to the extent it did because we adopted a "positive design" perspective with respect to human learning; we tried to amplify evident strengths of human learning as much as to mitigate problems. Second, this work ultimately convinced me that designs are a key medium for codifying and developing applied understanding, that they are more than just products of knowledge, and should be regarded as expressions of knowledge. Finally, somewhat painfully, designs disappear almost immediately; by the time I wrote my first book on minimalist instruction, none of our original designs could even be run; indeed, the original Displaywriter, a focus for much of our early work, was re-embodied as a program for the IBM PC in 1984. Traces of designs can live on; IBM's Displaywrite PC software incorporated many of our ideas. At the remove of 30 years, the traces grow faint; I am asked regularly how to design minimalist information for the Web! I call these three points reconstructions of minimalism because at the time we did the original analysis and design work I did not understand our work in this way.

Instruction and the Active User

Our work on minimalist instruction did not start out as a design project. Our initial goal was to understand how self-instruction actually worked so that we could inform and guide IBM designers. We were interested in the characteristics-in-use of the self-instruction model, and examples of it in IBM instructional products. This first generation of self-study tutorials employed hierarchical decomposition and drill-and-practice regimes (Gagné & Briggs, 1979). A basic skill like "typing a short document" was decomposed into subskills (such as navigating to the Typing Menu), which were then successively decomposed (selecting, pressing Enter). Users were expected to recognize, understand, and execute lower level skills, subskills, and basic skills until they were fluent.

We focused our study on clerical workers, people who were expert at typing and other office tasks. We configured our laboratory to look like office space, and asked our participants to use the self-instruction materials, to verbalize their thoughts and experiences as much as possible (to "think aloud"), and to try to ignore us as we watched them (Mack et al., 1983).

It was not pretty. For the first few moments, it often resembled Figure 13.1, an image from IBM's public archive depicting a user of the Displaywriter. Our participants were excited; after all, they were office professionals, and we were paying them to learn new and relevant skills. But quite quickly, people tended to get off track. They noticed and worried about small details that were not addressed in their manuals, and whose primary consequence was to confuse them, frustrate them, and often lead them to draw incorrect conclusions and make errors. Conversely, they missed noticing equally tiny details in the manual and in the user interface that were absolutely critical to what they were trying to do, or worse, were critical to something they would later do, often at such a remove that they were never able to disentangle the problem and make further progress.

For example, in the Displaywriter, successfully queuing a document for printing caused the system to display the system's root menu. The design intent was to

FIGURE 13.1 Model using the IBM Displaywriter.

Source: Courtesy of IBM Archives, IBM Displaywriter, n.d..

convey to the user that the system is ready for another task. However, some users struggled to make sense of the root menu as feedback specific to printing; they looked for clues. Others interpreted this menu transition as evidence that they had failed to print, and repeated the procedure, queuing a second print job. Engaged and creative interpretations and actions often led to frustrating and confusing problems.

Displaywriter stored documents on floppy disks, called work diskettes (Figure 13.2). In creating documents, users were prompted to specify the work diskette on which the document would be stored. If the user mistyped the work diskette name and pressed Enter, the system would prompt the user to insert the diskette with the mistyped name. This was a common error, but there was no simple or obvious remedy for it. From the users' point of view this is a tiny detail that is also a show-stopper. Understandable and mundane errors nonetheless piled up, error upon error.

In an episode I cannot forget, an expert clerical worker became snarled in a tangle of confusions and actual errors. She was generating plausible ideas and interpretations at a ferocious rate, but they were mostly all wrong. Suddenly, she started to flush. Stammering apologies to a colleague and I, she collected her coat and handbag, and began to move quickly towards the door. We had planned a protocol for this situation. We expressed our thanks, apologized for the difficulties with the technology, emphasized that she would still be paid fully for her participation, and escorted her out of the building. I cannot forget her because I have never seen another person so defeated. Unfortunately, I have seen many close seconds, and many of them were in this study.

FIGURE 13.2 IBM Displaywriter (dual diskette drive on the right, printer partially visible on the left).

Source: Image courtesy of We Look 4 Things, n.d..

Guided Exploration

For several years, my colleagues and I informed and guided IBM designers and others. We were popular speakers about user miseries, but we wanted to do more than describe what was happening. We wanted to change it. We were inspired by user interface design work at PARC and later at Apple, though none of it fundamentally addressed the specific problems of self-instruction (Carroll & Mazur, 1986).

In 1982, we started a project on guided exploration; our idea was to replace comprehensive self-instruction with modular and deliberately incomplete resources to encourage and support self-initiated learning. For example, the card in Figure 13.3 addresses the user concern with typing. It presents four brief hints

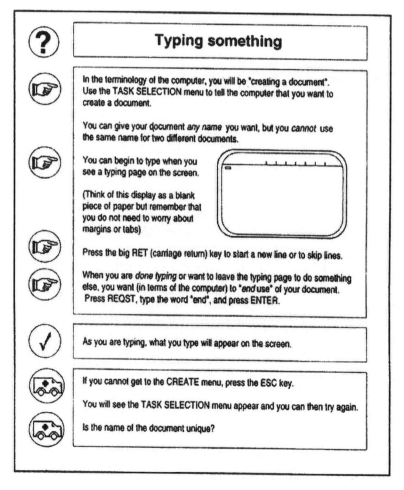

FIGURE 13.3   Guided Exploration card addressing a basic user concern, with a set of hints, a checkpoint, and error information.

focused on things to do towards the concern: name a document, display the typing page, keys to try to move the cursor, and end the document. It presents a simple checkpoint (text appears), and error recognition and recovery information.

The guided exploration cards were more a design probe than a design. We wanted to confront the primary design commitments of self-instruction as a way of further studying them, and of beginning to imagine alternatives. The fatuous instruction DO NOT DO ANYTHING UNTIL AFTER YOU HAVE READ EVERYTHING was our touchstone. Despite the caps, we had never seen anyone follow this instruction. In contrast, the cards conveyed to users that they could get started immediately, engage their own reasoning and improvising, integrate planning and acting, and make progress in goals meaningful to them. Importantly, the cards, in their form and emphasis, conveyed that errors and error recovery are standard and routine, not failures or crises.

We designed 25 guided exploration cards addressing the content of about 100 manual pages. We carried out a study contrasting clerical works learning with the manual or the cards. We found that participants made more progress in less time, and that participants spent a smaller proportion of their time reading cards versus working with the system. We also looked in detail at specific characteristics of the learning experience. Cards learners engaged in exploration far more than manual learners, and with far greater success. They also recognized errors better and recovered from them more often and more rapidly (Carroll et al., 1985).

The Minimal Manual

Although the guided exploration project was inspiring and successful, the cards also raised new issues. For example, learners free to pursue their own meaningful goals occasionally pursued goals that were unwise or impossible to achieve. Some learners were uncomfortable with the extreme lack of structure in a "deck" of cards. We felt that an appropriate challenge would be to investigate whether our ideas could be directly incorporated into the genre of self-instruction manuals, and not just embodied as a design probe to deconstruct that genre.

We created the Minimal Manual as a self-instruction manual, incorporating many of the design concepts of the cards. Thus, in Figure 13.4, the user is given rather general directions for exploring cursor keys and deletion, emphasizing doing things independently, and seeing their effect on the display. The objective, as for the cards, was to encourage and support learners to reason, improvise, plan, act, and think about goals. Instead of telling them exactly where to move the cursor or what to delete, we emphasized that that was their choice to make. Relying on user initiative and sense-making, rather than extensive step-by-step instructions, allowed our Minimal Manual to be 45 pages long; less than a quarter of the official manual.

As with typical self-instruction manuals, prior topics and skills are leveraged in subsequent presentations; thus, the deletion exercise in Figure 13.4 utilizes the

Topic 4: 2

MOVING THE CURSOR

The four cursor-movement keys have arrows on them (they are located on the right of the keyboard).

PRESS THE ↓ CURSOR KEY SEVERAL TIMES AND WATCH THE CURSOR MOVE DOWN THE SCREEN.

The ↑, ←, and → cursor keys work analogously. Try them and see.

If you move the cursor all the way to the bottom of the screen, or all the way to the right, the display "shifts" so that you can see more of your document. By moving the cursor all the way up and to the left, you can bring the document back to where it started.

DELETING TEXT

USE THE CURSOR KEYS TO MOVE THE CURSOR UNDER THE FIRST r IN THE WORD regular.

PRESS THE DEL KEY

The DEL key is located up and to the right of the keyboard keys. Is the Displaywriter prompting you?: **Delete what?**

▶ If you make a mistake at this point, use CODE + CANCL and start the deletion again.

USING THE → KEY, MOVE THE CURSOR THROUGH THE MATERIAL TO BE DELETED, THE WORD regular.

The word is highlighted: you can see exactly what is going to be deleted before it actually is deleted

▶ If the wrong characters are highlighted use CODE + CANCL and start the deletion again.

FIGURE 13.4 The Minimal Manual incorporated design concepts from Guided Exploration cards but embodied them in a standard self-instruction manual design.

cursor movement skill introduced immediately before. Unlike standard manuals of that time, error recognition, diagnosis, and recovery was emphasized. Also, unlike standard manuals of that time, each topic in our manual included open-ended suggestions of small projects users could try on their own. Apparently, our manual was a convincing alternative version for the original IBM manuals; the manual we wrote is the one most easily accessed on the Web as the IBM Displaywriter training manual (IBM Displaywriter System Operator Training, n.d.).

As was the case with the cards, our Minimal Manual produced better instructional outcomes; participants got started faster, spent more time coordinating the manual with user interface interaction, were more successful in referring back to earlier sections of the manual as they progressed through the training, made fewer errors overall, and used error-recovery methods more and more effectively. Overall, they learned more in less time. They were also more successful in applying their learning of the basics in further learning (where all participants used the name manual; a so-called transfer effect). See Carroll et al., 1987.

An extremely important aspect of the Minimal Manual project was that most of the testing work was carried out at IBM's Austin Development Laboratory, the home of the Displaywriter product. There is always a concern, of course, whenever design and evaluation are carried out by the same group, and this collaboration allowed us to bring in disinterested partners, and to replicate and extend our findings. Our small group could never have afforded a study involving transfer effects for advanced Displaywriter functions; the Austin study involved participants in a real office work environment for three full days. Perhaps even more importantly, this collaboration helped our colleagues in Austin to become familiar with our design and its consequences for users. This kind of connection is invaluable since it facilitates the most difficult step in design innovation: getting someone else to understand and adopt a new design.

Training Wheels

A complementary design direction for realizing minimalist instruction was the user interface itself. Online self-instruction also emerged in the 1980s, and some argued that the combination of new graphical user interfaces and online self-instruction would address various problems of procedure following, coordinating the system and instruction, error and error recovery, etc. We studied the Apple Lisa in 1983 and found no basis for this hope. Indeed, graphical user interfaces were still novel and less intuitive than their designers expected, and online tutorials often required manuals and added new coordination problems (Carroll & Mazur, 1986).

Our approach to online self-instruction was again inspired by guided exploration: we started by asking what complexities, and therefore what risks for error and misinterpretation, we could eliminate or mitigate while still providing an instructional experience anchored in the system software. Our training wheels concept is simple and general: we edited the Displaywriter system software to block the execution of functions unnecessary to beginners and functions we had found to trigger difficult or distracting errors. Here again, our relationship with the IBM Austin Lab was critical: a Displaywriter system programmer created the Training Wheels Displaywriter for us, modifying the actual Displaywriter system code.

Figure 13.5 illustrates our approach. A common error was mistyping the Work Diskette name. This should have been a trivial slip but recovering from it required system functions that were not introduced at the beginner level. In the Training Wheels Displaywriter, mistyping the name of the Work Diskette (specified as

244 John M. Carroll

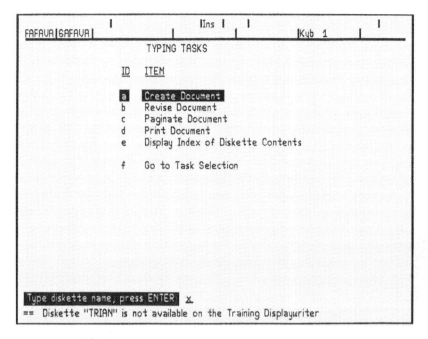

FIGURE 13.5 The Training Wheels Displaywriter blocked the execution of advanced and problematic functions, producing a feedback message without changing system state.

TRAIN in the self-instruction manual) elicits a message rejecting the name, and leaving the user in exactly the same system state as before the typo. This is the key design idea: when the user requests advanced functions, or makes a recognizable error, the Training Wheel software rejects the command, and explains to the user that that function is not available in the training system.

Our rationale for this design was that this intervention would allow users to engage in reasoning and improvising but suffer fewer consequences with respect to error recovery. We indeed found that users were able to progress more rapidly and successfully through initial self-instruction. They did better on final performance and comprehension tests, and they felt better about the experience. They spent far less time in error recovery.

Although error recovery activity can itself be a powerful occasion for learning, tangles of cascading error could lead to confusion, as we had seen in our original studies. The Training Wheels design did not eliminate error recovery; only certain errors were intercepted. Indeed, we found that participants using the Training Wheels and the full system made comparable numbers of non-blocked errors. We found, however, that for non-blocked errors the Training Wheel participants improved their recovery times dramatically as they progressed relative to those using the full system (Carroll & Carrithers, 1984).

We hypothesized that initial self-instruction with Training Wheels would not penalize users when they subsequently transferred to the full system (near transfer). We also hypothesized that seeing how the advanced and problematic functions were accessed, and receiving confirmation about how they were accessed, would be useful to users later when they were able to articulate goals that really required these functions (that is, in far-transfer to the full Displaywriter system). We found that, in both cases, Training Wheels participants did better than those whose original self-instruction experiences were in the full system (Catrambone & Carroll, 1987).

Adoption and Generalization

The success of our minimalist instruction design work in the early 1980s required significant immersion in the word-processing systems of that time, Displaywriter especially. This is unavoidable in that we could not have understood how to reshape Displaywriter manuals and software without such immersion. But it is also self-limiting; by the time our project concluded, Displaywriter was making way for PC-word-processor programs, including Displaywrite. Our work had some immediate impact on these successors, but we wanted broader and more lasting impact than that.

Our original goal was to inform and guide IBM designers. Our collaborations with the IBM Austin Lab, and other interactions with product development organizations in IBM, were critical to advancing this goal. However, in retrospect, an equally significant path to adoption was publication. Because our group was located in the Research Division, external publication was regarded as important evidence of the soundness and impact of contributions. Our early publications on minimalist instruction were appropriated by many other research groups, and by product development groups outside IBM.

Figure 13.6 shows a guided exploration card developed and shipped by Northern Telecom in the mid-1980s. Xerox, Hewlett-Packard, and many other companies adopted ideas from minimalist instruction (Carroll, 1990). During 1985 to 1993 (I left IBM in January 1994), I received many calls from IBM product managers who wanted to consult with us on instructional designs after encountering implementations of minimalist instruction in competitive products. This sounds ironic, and I am not in a position to assess the business case, but I do know that valuable connections among IBM professionals were created that were originally mediated by the external research literature.

Adoption greatly facilitates generalization. We did not think our ideas were specific to word processing, or to office work, but the only meaningful test of generality is through diverse research and implementation. The many product adoptions inside and outside IBM were critical to making this case. In 1996, I organized a workshop for the Society for Technical Communication on minimalism beyond the Nurnberg Funnel, trying to clearly signal that I knew much more could be done than I could ever do (Carroll, 1998).

Introduction	Your Norstar M7310 Phone offers the simplicity of a standard telephone plus the versatility of many special features. This card will help you to use your new Norstar phone and to customize some of its features. When using your phone refer to the detachable Feature List and the Receiver Card under the receiver for quick reference.	
Telephone Buttons	[Rls]	To release a call or a feature press this button.
	[Hold]	To put a call on hold press this button.
	[Feature]	To use a feature press this button and then enter a feature code.
	[dialpad]	Press the dialpad to make a call or to enter feature codes.
	[🔊] [🔊]	When using the receiver, handsfree speaker or headset, press this button to adjust the volume.
Adjusting Ring Volume	Try using some of these buttons now to set the volume of your phone's ring. 1 To make your phone ring press [Feature] [*] [8] [0]. 2 To reach desired volume press [🔊] [🔊] repeatedly	
Display and Display buttons	**Display** The top line shows you the time and date, and call information. The display helps you use Norstar features. Follow the instructions. **Display buttons** Function-names for the three display buttons appear on the second line of the display.	
Selecting Ring Type	Now select a distinctive ring to help you distinguish between your phone and others nearby. 1 Press [Feature] [*] [6]. 2 Press the [Next] display button until you hear the ring type you want. 3 Press [OK] display button to finish.	

FIGURE 13.6 Guided Exploration cards for a telephone system.

Source: Used with permission of Northern Telecom.

   In our own technical work, we deliberately moved on to domains of value at IBM different from document preparation, for example, database systems and object-oriented programming environments. We designed a programming environment called View Matcher that displayed multiple coordinated views of a Smalltalk program as it executed. We focused on this problem because in the

Minimalist Instruction (1979–Present)

late 1980s IBM had many experienced procedural programmers who wanted to adopt the object-oriented programming paradigm, and IBM had entered into a relationship with Digitalk with regard to its Smalltalk/V, and later Smalltalk/VPM, products.

Figure 13.7 shows a View Matcher analysis of a program that plays blackjack: In the upper right is the game; in the upper left is the stack of Smalltalk methods currently executing—the program has been halted at the execution of the takeCard: method; in the lower left are panes reporting variable values (the card the player has just drawn is the four of clubs) and below those the commentary pane presenting documentation about what the program is doing at this point; in the lower right are the several panes composing the class hierarchy browser, a key system tool, displaying the code that implements the takeCard: method—including the halt message. The user can step through the program execution by selecting methods in the execution stack and manually analyze how the program carries out its computations (Carroll et al., 1990).

Our users in this project were again experts. Where before we had worked with expert clerical workers, in this project we worked with experts in procedural programming languages like PL/I. As we had with the word processing work, we tried to leverage user expertise in our design. We expected that expert programmers

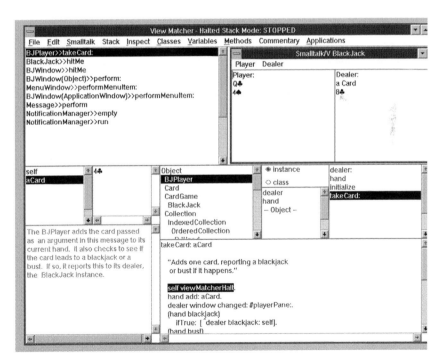

FIGURE 13.7 The View Matcher presenting coordinated views of the halted execution of a blackjack game.

would be able to leverage this expertise to analyze communication among Smalltalk objects through the execution stack, even though the software design concepts of object-oriented programming might be somewhat new to them.

We designed the blackjack game to have an intriguing quirk; it occasionally cheated by taking two turns. We hoped that this sort of software misbehavior would appeal to people who were professional programmers and had debugged many programs. We developed a minimalist self-instruction package around the View Matcher (Rosson et al., 1990); the package guided users to encounter basic software structures of the game at different levels of analysis; again, we hoped, building upon their professional capabilities to help them quickly see the key paradigmatic differences between procedural programming and object-oriented programming. The View Matcher provided a customized bundling of standard Smalltalk tools with documentation we created (the commentary pane, and the halts we placed in the code), but it was completely integrated with Smalltalk, and users were free to break out whenever they wanted, and to continue learning Smalltalk on their own.

I have never stopped generalizing and further exploring minimalist instruction. In 1994, I became a professor at Virginia Tech. Among other things, professors teach and write textbooks. Mary Beth Rosson and I (2002) wrote a text on scenario-based usability engineering and created a set of online cases (Figure 13.8) illustrating the use of the concepts and techniques in our book. Students can browse these

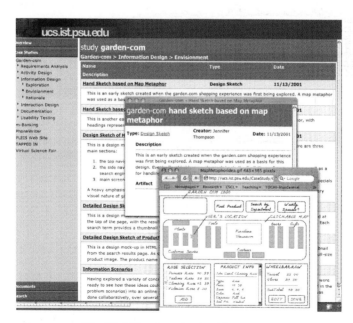

FIGURE 13.8 The Usability Case Studies library presents structured cases that can be analyzed and contrasted.

cases in any order; they can examine how specific designs emerged from analysis and fieldwork; they pose their own inquiries, such as why one project used prototyping differently than another (Carroll & Rosson, 2005, 2006).

I am quite sure I can never escape minimalist instruction, though now it seems less a topic on its own and more a general requirement for information design. Every semester I teach a new class; I am more or less continually developing systems and methods to enable minimalist instruction within my teaching (Carroll, 2014). My research over the past decade has focused on mobile and social computing, and both of these areas demand minimalist designs: mobile devices are small, and people expect to pick them up and use them immediately. There is little space and less time to burden users with instructions that are not obviously relevant to the user's current meaningful activity. Social media and web-based services in general are similarly expected to be transparent, and immediately useful.

The Integrity of Activity

As mentioned in the Introduction, I have had three decades to reflect upon minimalist instruction and upon the designs we developed, and that I continue to develop. I think a key factor in the trajectory of minimalist instruction was that we viewed learner activity positively. This is to say, we saw what people were doing with self-instruction as indicating strengths that needed to be encouraged, facilitated, better supported, and further strengthened by designs. We observed quite terrible consequences of the misfit between the spontaneous actions and interpretations of our participants and the design intent of the self-instruction materials. But we nevertheless concluded that the materials needed to change to fit expectations and propensities of the users. This is what led us initially to create guided exploration instead of working out more effective ways to constrain the interpretations and improvisations we observed. I am not arguing that the latter approach is wrong, just that it is different and would have led to different projects and insights.

For us, this positive orientation came about because my colleagues and I were fundamentally engaged by what people do and what human learning is like. It simply seemed obvious to us that pursuing those issues and articulating what people naturally and spontaneously do and want would enable better designs. Recently, these attitudes have been codified in the positive design movement (Avital et al., 2008). As I see this now, our early work on minimalist instruction was an inchoate example of positive design (Carroll et al., 2009).

Artifacts as Theories

A second conclusion I came to through the course of this work is that designed artifacts should be regarded as more than merely products. They are complex embodiments of understanding, so complex that extracting meaning from them is always incomplete. For example, a rather simple artifact like the guided exploration card in Figure 13.3 raises myriad issues about how people perceive and interpret information, how they coordinate action with information, how they make sense of events and sequences of events, and how they learn. The card itself is a couple of hundred words and a couple of small images, but the design rationale for the card, if it were to be made completely explicit, would surely run to a book or more. I have written more than 100 pages myself, and I am certain I have not fully explained the cards, their use, and their consequences for users.

There are two different but related points here. One is the point that designs embody various sorts of meaning. Thus, Winner (1980) famously suggested that artifacts have political meanings. Based on examples discussed here, and others, we argued that artifacts embody psychological theories (Carroll & Campbell, 1989). We suggested further that human–computer interaction designs are not merely examples of knowledge applied, but that they codify and develop applied knowledge in ways that are superior to conventional symbolic theories.

Thus, the second point is that symbolic theorizing of designs is inherently limited. Our minimalist designs embody ideas from cognitive (Bruner, Piaget) and cultural (Dewey, Vygotsky) learning theories (Carroll, 1990, 1998), but it is critical to note that the hierarchical decomposition and drill-and-practice designs we reacted to were also inspired by these theories. Even for the simple guided exploration card, one can perhaps never capture all the relevant nuance and consequence of experience. This reflection led me to investigate heuristic design representations and design rationale (Carroll, 1995, 2000; Burge et al., 2008). I think the project of curating design cases, in the sense of IJDL, is another constructive reaction to the centrality of artifacts in practical inquiry.

Designs Disappear

My colleagues and I were drawn to create minimalist instruction in order to transform the awful instructional experiences we studied in the early 1980s. Changing the world sounds a little preposterous, but of course people do it all the time. As I have explained, working towards this objective required us to immerse ourselves in the design milieu of self-instruction, and ultimately in our own designs. But there is a painful consequence of immersion in the world and in design: to the extent you succeed, you may very well disappear.

As I mentioned earlier in alluding to my own current work on mobility and social computing, many of the main ideas we discovered and developed in our designs in the early 1980s are now not only obvious, they are invisible. I think this just comes with the territory. People today do not really "see" graphical user interfaces; how could user interfaces be otherwise? But in 1980, user interfaces in general and graphical user interfaces in particular were very visible; they were shocking.

This overarching phenomenon of disappearance by being transformed into a cultural norm is complemented by a lower level of disappearance: historical design work depends on infrastructures of various sorts, and these are also constantly being transformed, or just abandoned. Many historical designs can no longer be used or experienced at all; they no longer exist in the sense that the infrastructures they depended on are now gone. For example, the Displaywriter, once an office system innovation, is now a museum piece. I kept one in my lab at the IBM Watson Research Center until 1994, when I moved to Virginia Tech. I believe I still have the program diskettes with the system code for the Training Wheels Displaywriter in the back of a file cabinet somewhere, but I should paste them into a scrapbook: I don't have access to a machine that could run that code.

As I look back, I understand better now that part of what was going on in our investigation of self-instruction designs was a major transformation of the technological infrastructure for office work. In 1981, I watched a participant balk at the instruction "Backspace to erase." She knew what backspace was (on a typewriter), and she knew very well that it did not erase anything. Today, there may well be no one alive who would have this problem, no expert typists to be confused by design metaphors that only partially match. The transformation of office work has left us with no typists in that sense; today there are only users. We—my colleagues and I, and our hapless participants—were too close to what was going on in 1981 to fully realize what we were part of.

Acknowledgments

Our original work on minimalist instruction was supported by the IBM Corporation. Subsequent work has been supported by the Society for Technical Communication, the US National Science Foundation, and the US Department of Education. I am most grateful to Clayton Lewis and Robert Mack, my close collaborators at the start, and to Sandra Mazur and Mary Beth Rosson who helped develop this work subsequently. I thank the editors and reviewers for organizing this special issue, and for their feedback and encouragement.

References

Avital, M., Boland, R. J., & Cooperrider, D. (Eds.) (2008). *Designing information and organizations with a positive lens: Advances in appreciative inquiry* (Vol. 2). Oxford: Elsevier Science.

Burge, J., Carroll, J. M., McCall, R., & Mistrik, I. (2008). *Rationale-based software engineering*. Berlin: Springer.

Carroll, J. M. (1990). *The Nurnberg funnel: Designing minimalist instruction for practical computer skill*. Cambridge, MA: MIT Press.

Carroll, J. M. (Ed.) (1995). *Scenario-based design: Envisioning work and technology in system development*. New York: John Wiley & Sons.

Carroll, J. M. (Ed.) (1998). *Minimalism beyond the Nurnberg funnel*. Cambridge, MA: MIT Press.

Carroll, J. M. (2000). *Making use: Scenario-based design of human–computer interactions*. Cambridge, MA: MIT Press.

Carroll, J. M. (Ed.) (2014). *Innovative practices in teaching information sciences and technology: Experience reports and reflections.* New York: Springer.

Carroll, J. M., & Campbell, R. L. (1989). Artifacts as psychological theories: The case of human–computer interaction. *Behaviour and Information Technology, 8*(4), 247–256.

Carroll, J. M., & Carrithers, C. (1984). Training wheels in a user interface. *Communications of the Association for Computing Machinery, 27*(8), 800–806.

Carroll, J. M., & Mazur, S. A. (1986). LisaLearning. *IEEE Computer, 19*(11), 35–49.

Carroll, J. M., & Rosson, M. B. (2005). A case library for teaching usability engineering: Design rationale, development, and classroom experience. *ACM Journal of Educational Resources in Computing, 5*(1), Article 3, 1–22.

Carroll, J. M., & Rosson, M. B. (2006). Cases as minimalist information. *IEEE Transactions on Professional Communication, 49*(4), 297–310.

Carroll, J. M., Rosson, M. B., Farooq, U., & Xiao, L. (2009). Beyond being aware. *Information and Organizations, 19*(3), 162–185.

Carroll, J. M., Singer, J. A., Bellamy, R. K. E., & Alpert, S. R. (1990). A view matcher for learning Smalltalk. In *Proceedings of CHI90: Human Factors in Computing Systems* (pp. 431–437). New York: ACM Press.

Carroll, J. M., Smith-Kerker, P. S., Ford, J. R., & Mazur-Rimetz, S. A. (1987). The minimal manual. *Human–Computer Interaction, 3*(2), 123–153.

Carroll, J. M., Mack, R. L., Lewis, C. H., Grischkowsky, N. L., & Robertson, S. R. (1985). Exploring exploring a word processor. *Human–Computer Interaction, 1*(3), 283–307.

Catrambone, R., & Carroll, J. M. (1987). Learning a word processing system with guided exploration and training wheels. In *Proceedings of CHI+GI87 Human Factors in Computing Systems and Graphics Interface* (pp. 169–174). New York: ACM Press.

Gagné, R. L., & Briggs, L. J. (1979). *Principles of instructional design.* New York: Holt, Rinehart, & Winston.

IBM Displaywriter. (n.d.). *IBM Archives.* Retrieved June 7, 2014 from www.ibm.com/ibm/history/exhibits/pc/pc_8.html.

IBM Displaywriter System Operator Training (n.d.). *Bitsavers' PDF Document Archive.* Retrieved June 16, 2014 from http://bitsavers.trailing-edge.com/pdf/ibm/6580_Displaywriter/Displaywriter_Operator_Training_Book_1.pdf.

Mack, R. L., Lewis, C. H., & Carroll, J. M. (1983). Learning to use office systems: Problems and prospects. *ACM Transactions on Office Information Systems, 1*, 254–271.

Rosson, M. B., & Carroll, J. M. (2002). *Usability engineering: Scenario-based development of human–computer interaction.* San Francisco, CA: Morgan-Kaufmann.

Rosson, M. B., Carroll, J. M., & Bellamy, R. K. E. (1990). Smalltalk scaffolding: A minimalist curriculum. In *Proceedings of CHI90: Human Factors in Computing Systems* (pp. 423–437). New York: ACM Press.

We Look 4 Things. (n.d.). Retrieved June 7, 2014 from www.welook4things.com/sub_displaywriter_imgs.html.

Winner, L. (1980). Do artifacts have politics? *Daedalus, 109*(1), 121–136.

14

EXPERTS IN A BOX

Expert Systems and Knowledge-Based Engineering (1984–1991)

Jo Ann Oravec

Introduction

Consider the following statement from a noted expert systems pioneer:

> To build expert systems is to attempt to capture rare or important expertise and embody it in computer programs.... In one sense building expert systems is a form of intellectual cloning. Expert system builders, the knowledge engineers, find out from experts what they know and how they use their knowledge to solve problems. Once this debriefing is done, the expert system builders incorporate the knowledge and expertise in computer programs, making the knowledge and expertise easily replicated, readily distributed, and essentially immortal.
> *(Davis, 1984, p. 18)*

Declarations such as the one above (with phrases akin to "intellectual cloning") were commonplace in research agendas and grant applications during the period 1984 to 1991 (Oravec & Travis, 1992). Social and historical perspectives on expert systems and knowledge-based engineering (KBE) during this period can provide insights for current research and development directions in instructional systems, especially when placed in contrast with contemporary focuses that are collaborative and responsive to context (generally more in keeping with Internet-related affordances). As outlined in the sections to follow, problematic perspectives reflected in such phrases as "essentially immortal" expertise (found in the above quotation) may indeed have skewed research directions and otherwise derailed system development projects, whatever technological considerations were involved.

As a part of artificial intelligence (AI), expert system and KBE strategies attracted considerable academic, corporate, and military attention in the 1980s and early 1990s (Oravec & Plant, 1992; Waterman, 1986; Winston & Prendergast, 1984). Some analysts describe the period as having a "bandwagon" or "bubble" quality (Leith, 2010). After analyzing an assortment of definitions, O'Leary construes "expert systems" as having the following characteristics:

- a rule-based approach is used to model decision making knowledge, and that those rules may include some kind of factor, to capture uncertainty
- interacts with a user from whom it gathers environmental assessments, through an interactive consultation (not always present)
- designed to help facilitate solution of a particular task, typically narrow in scope
- generally performs at the level of an informed analyst.

(O'Leary, 2008, p. 9)

The term "expert system" was reportedly coined for some early system initiatives in 1968 by Edward Feigenbaum of Stanford University (Feigenbaum, 1992), and an assortment of systems were developed over the following decade (Duda & Shortliffe, 1983). Although expert systems and KBE research and development efforts have continued to this day, the 1980s through early 1990s were especially salient in terms of academic and commercial research agenda-setting as well as the establishment of funding sources. I was involved with expert system research and artificial intelligence instruction at the University of Wisconsin during this period and was able to witness as well as participate in some of the KBE bandwagon-style phenomena, including international teleconferences and promotional videos (Oravec, 1988). Linkages of more recent knowledge management approaches with the pioneering expert systems and KBE initiatives described in this chapter are often problematic: some researchers have worked actively to distance themselves from the early "outrageous" claims for the future of expert systems and KBE research (Leith, 2010; Stafford, 2001; Vaux, 2001). The assertions that expert systems would soon displace many human experts were certainly off-putting to many computer professionals who were seeking appropriate technology applications for their systems rather than the production of "black boxes" in which something labeled as "knowledge" would be stored (Perrolle, 1991).

Many of the founding knowledge-elicitation strategies focused on the capture of the expertise of individuals. Some of these initiatives were literally labeled "expert in a box" (as described in O'Leary, 2008). In contrast, many of today's knowledge-related and instructional efforts emphasize collaborative knowledge such as that obtained through various networking platforms and social media (including recommendation systems and wikis), made popular with the rise of the Internet. Emphasis on the context of knowledge production has also increased in recent years (Anderson & Dron, 2010). The more recent focuses on collaboration and context have strong ties to the ubiquitous availability of the Internet as a platform, a presence that was just emerging as a widespread societal force in the 1980s. However, the emotionally involving discourse in academic and popular culture arenas generated in this seminal era concerning whether expert systems could "think," as well as the prospect of replacing human experts with expert systems, still has implications for instructional system efforts, especially those supported by agencies and corporations with long legacies of expert system and KBE initiatives. For example, Stanford Research Institute (SRI) in Menlo Park, California is still often linked with its pioneering "Prospector" expert system designed to assist geologists in mineral exploration (Waterman, 1986).

Visions Guiding Early Expert System Development

Dreams and visions related to particular technologies can indeed be emboldening; for example, dreams of manned space flight to Mars have stimulated efforts to build rockets and proceed with space-related initiatives (Lambright, 2014). A large amount of early research and development in expert systems technology was explicitly framed with the guiding notion of replacing human experts after their knowledge had been "mined." Consider this ambitious research projection for expert systems research efforts in the 1970s:

> For an expert system to be truly useful, it should be able to learn what human experts know, so that it can perform as well as they do, understand the points of departure among the views of human experts who disagree, keep its knowledge up to date as human experts do (by reading, asking questions, and learning from experience), and present its reasoning to its human users in much the way that human experts would (justifying, clarifying, explaining and even tutoring).
>
> (Barr and Feigenbaum, 1982, p. 80)

A 1986 cartoon from *Popular Science* provided a sense of how easily and unproblematically human expertise was to be transferred to expert system format via floppy disk (Hawkins, 1986, p. 83).

Early expert systems and KBE efforts had strong parallels with Tayloristic perspectives and the routinization of human expertise (Perrolle, 1991; Stafford, 2001), decreasing reliance on particular human beings rather than enhancing individuals' abilities using instructional systems and other intellectual support technologies. Frederick Taylor, a pioneer in industrial engineering and scientific management in the early part of the twentieth century, worked to streamline and commodify human labor in an assortment of workplace settings, especially industrial ones. Leith (2010) describes the linkages of Taylorism to expert systems in economic terms: "The promise being made in the 1980s was that cheap, good quality advice would allow us to discard the need for expensive experts." The contrast with perspectives in later decades on knowledge is dramatic, as evidenced by the following definition in a prominent knowledge-themed text of the late 1990s:

> Knowledge is a fluid mix of framed experience, values, contextual information, and expert insight that provides a framework for evaluating and incorporating new experiences and information. It originates and is applied in the minds of knowers. In organizations, it often becomes embedded not only in documents or repositories but also in organizational routines, processes, practices, and norms.
>
> (Davenport and Prusak, 1998, p. 4)

A number of computing efforts in the early 1980s involved the beginning stages of popularly accessible networking capabilities (Hall, 2009). Many industrialized nations were on the verge of the widespread Internet dissemination of the 1990s, but computer networking was still a factor largely in business and research contexts and not in everyday household and community applications. The considerable influx of expertise and attention provided when Internet capabilities were disseminated across wide spectrums of society served to alter many computing strategies (including knowledge-based ones), supporting the notion of collaborative knowledge generation rather than the mining of specific individuals' expertise.

Expert systems and KBE approaches are strongly linked to artificial intelligence (AI), although they expanded beyond AI to cognitive science, knowledge management, and various other information technology emphases (McCarthy, 2007). International perspectives provide some insight into why the US and Japan initiated so much expert systems research. Artificial intelligence had a number of research successes from the 1970s and 1980s, but early support came largely in the US and Japan rather than the United Kingdom. The UK's Lighthill Report of 1974 was a devastating attack on artificial intelligence research that directly resulted in the nearly "complete dismantling" of AI research in England (Crevier, 1993). The exaggerated claims made for AI were a part of this backlash in the UK, as well as the competing demands of other areas of computer research. In the early 1980s in the US, AI as a research and development area was just beginning to emerge from a period of relative neglect, with fields such as computer networking and database design attracting attention and funding. In efforts to move beyond this stage, commercialization of expert systems and KBE became more of an imperative in order to attract new research talent and funding: "With the expert system boom in full swing, epistemology was brought into public view and was shown to have commercial value" (Stafford, 2001). Hellström and Raman (2001) write in comparable terms about the "commodification" of epistemology through these technologies. Artificial intelligence researchers and professors were searching for ways to make their research more useful in a practical sense, thus attracting industrial and governmental dollars. Following the early successes of expert systems, textbooks such as those written by Hayes-Roth et al. (1984) and Waterman (1986) made expert system and knowledge-based engineering strategies more accessible to students as well as to industry practitioners.

The book *The Fifth Generation: Artificial Intelligence and Japan's Computer Challenge to the World* disseminated KBE approaches and drew in strong corporate support (Feigenbaum & McCorduck, 1984), in part because it asserted that Japan was seeking to be the first to explore and exploit expert system technologies for commercial gain. The popularly distributed paperback *The First Artificial Intelligence Coloring Book* was intended to demonstrate the simplicity of notions behind expert systems (Cohen et al., 1983); supposedly, even children could understand basic ideas behind computer-supported knowledge distillation and packaging. As a faculty member in computing and artificial intelligence during this period, I can attest to the intense interest students had in these books and related materials. Students along with many faculty and staff were motivated by discourse that linked philosophical ideas about computers and the human mind with practical applications, with bold rhetoric about the future of artificial intelligence often appreciated as much as subtle nuances. The late ethnographer and computer scientist Diana Forsythe documented some of the animated discourse that emerged in Stanford University and the University of Pittsburgh during this period, particularly concerning the interactions between culture (including user experience) and knowledge (Forsythe, 2001; Oravec, 2004).

Following on from the notion of human beings being displaced by computers, the label of "engineer" (rather than that of "interviewer" or another soft term) became associated with many expert systems practitioners:

> A "knowledge engineer" interviews experts in a certain domain and tries to embody their knowledge in a computer program for carrying out some task. How well this works depends on whether the intellectual mechanisms required for the task are within the present state of AI. When this turned out not to be so, there were many disappointing results. One of the first expert systems was MYCIN in 1974, which diagnosed bacterial infections of the blood and suggested treatments. It did better than medical students or practicing doctors, provided its limitations were observed.... Its interactions depended on a single patient being considered. Since the experts consulted by the knowledge engineers knew about patients, doctors, death, recovery, etc., it is clear that the knowledge engineers forced what the experts told them into a predetermined framework ... the usefulness of current expert systems depends on their users having common sense.
>
> (McCarthy, 2007, para #5)

In the above selection, McCarthy describes an engineering mindset that potentially excludes some relevant human factors, although many of today's engineers are apparently far more sensitive and responsive to context and user concerns. An assortment of academic programs and courses explicitly labeled as "knowledge engineering" arose in higher education institutions in several Western nations in the 1980s and early 1990s (Liebowitz, 1993), such as in the University of Maryland at College Park. A number of the individuals selected by universities and corporations for training in knowledge engineering had backgrounds in the humanities and social sciences, at least temporarily infusing needed ethnographic talent and insight into knowledge-related pursuits (Mykytyn et al., 1994).

A number of influential books that were highly critical of artificial intelligence levied specific attacks on the claims and projections delivered by many expert systems researchers. Works by these authors "occupied the center stage of a heated debate" among many computer scientists about the nature and limits of AI (Brey, 2001, p. 38). Titles of some of these books reveal their approaches: *Mind over Machine: The Power of Human Intuition and Expertise in the Era of the Computer* (Dreyfus & Dreyfus, 1986) and *Computer Power and Human Reason: From Judgment To Calculation* (Weizenbaum, 1976). Winograd and Flores sought to steer artificial intelligence research away from an expert systems and KBE emphasis and towards a more biologically inspired basis in *Understanding Computers and Cognition: A New Foundation for Design* (1987). The authors of these books all had a considerable background in cognitive science and AI, with Joseph Weizenbaum a noted professor of AI at the Massachusetts Institute of Technology (MIT) and Terry Winograd at Stanford; however, they were all inspired to protest what they considered to be the more outlandish claims of AI and expert systems proponents.

Development Infrastructure of Expert Systems

The era in which expert systems blossomed was one of great growth for knowledge-related considerations as a whole. Marc Porat's (1976) identification and cataloguing of various knowledge professions (following the work of economist Fritz Machlup) stimulated interest in the "knowledge economy" and awareness of its economic dimensions. Some philosophers added their input, as did economists. Artificial intelligence pioneer John McCarthy's overview of AI research included an adaptation of T. H. Huxley's quotation about the couplings of philosophy and science: "Extinguished philosophies lie about the cradle of every science as the strangled snakes beside that of Hercules" (McCarthy, 2007). Identifying "knowledge" as consisting of sets of rules (however sophisticated the knowledge "engine" that served as a shell) does not in itself constitute a philosophy, although it was apparently significant in energizing a number of artificial intelligence developers.

The programs Dendral and Mycin are generally considered as the first expert systems (Waterman, 1986), although there is some controversy here. Dendral served to automate the decision-making procedures of experts in organic chemistry. Its name reportedly stems from the phrase "Dendritic Algorithm." Stanford University provided the environment and support for computer scientists Ed Feigenbaum and Bruce Buchanan, along with subject matter experts Joshua Lederberg and Carl Djerassi, to develop Dendral in the mid-1960s. In the early 1970s, Mycin (another early system) was developed at Stanford as part of the doctoral dissertation by Edward Shortliffe. Expert system projects have indeed retained some popularity as dissertation initiatives in a number of fields, providing a way for dissertators to demonstrate their tenacity and inventiveness within a structured technological framework. Mycin identified bacteria related to severe infections and often recommend specific antibiotics. Many antibiotics have the suffix "mycin" (so the name "Mycin" was deemed appropriate). Stanford was also the scene of a great deal of research on AI, so synergies between and among researchers developed.

The notion of the "knowledge engineer" emerged in the late 1970s, with Stanford University the site of much of this effort. Edward Feigenbaum's Heuristic Programming Project Memo 77–25, entitled *The Art of Artificial Intelligence*, states that "the knowledge engineer practices the art of bringing the principles and tools of AI research to bear on difficult applications problems requiring experts" (1977, p. 1). By the mid-1980s, knowledge engineering had evolved into a larger initiative, sometimes even given the status of a "profession." Clancey (1987) asserted that "people who are naturally quick learners are attracted to this profession (and there are some dilettantes), the knowledge engineering process is a skill that can be taught." However, librarians provided some early resistance to the notion that knowledge engineers somehow "invented" the basic notions behind knowledge elicitation, arguing that they had been doing the kinds of knowledge elicitation that knowledge engineers were doing for decades if not centuries (Molholt, 1986). With the increasing availability of expert system "shells," knowledge acquisition and processing was declared to be liberated from the domain of professionals and placed in the hands of the people (Feigenbaum & McCorduck, 1984). The shell structure, with its separation of the knowledge base from the inference engine or other processing unit, was a salient aspect of many early expert systems approaches (in contrast to those structures in which knowledge and inference elements would be intertwined). Some of these shells were made available commercially for personal computers (PCs), spurring the development of a number of AI and PC-themed magazines, journals, and related conferences. The "AI Business" began to be lucrative (Winston & Prendergast, 1984), drawing many AI professionals away from academic life and into start-up organizations or larger industry settings. In 1985, Allen Newell, a noted AI theorist, labeled expert systems as the "major advance" in artificial intelligence for the past decade:

> The emergence of expert systems has transformed the enterprise of AI, not only because it has been the main driver of the current wave of

commercialization of AI, but because it has set the major scientific problems for AI for the next few years.

(quoted in Bobrow & Hayes, 1985, p. 385)

Examples of discourse on the "hype" and "hubris" associated with expert systems efforts abound (Oravec, 2019). Blair (1985, 2002) discusses the "gold rush" in which expert system developers were engaged. Davenport and Prusak (1998) declare that "The field of knowledge technology has suffered from overly high expectations and excessive levels of hype, particularly with regard to expert systems" (p. 126) and note the "limited success" of these early efforts. The "knowledge engineering bottleneck," the difficulty of codifying knowledge from real-world situations, became a critical factor that derailed a number of real-world expert systems projects. Knowledge acquisition has remained a labor-intensive aspect of expert system development, with some researchers developing specialized systems just for this purpose (Rafea et al., 2003). Demonstration projects and academic theses in which individuals could work non-stop on creating and refining rule bases for their projects may have been temporarily successful in showcasing some of the positive aspects of expert systems (such as the dissertation work by Edward Shortliffe), but projects in which volatile contexts and reluctant experts were involved were far less successful. This unfortunate situation was documented in cases provided in the special issue of the *Journal of Systems and Software* on expert system failures that I co-edited with Robert Plant of the University of Miami (Oravec & Plant, 1992).

Real-World Applications of Expert Systems: Campbell Soup

In the advent of expert systems and KBE, artificial intelligence research was moved from the laboratory and framed as ready for practical application, such as in the Campbell Soup example described in this section. Duda and Shortliffe declared in *Science* (1983) that "some consultation programs, although limited in versatility, have achieved levels of performance rivaling those of human experts" (p. 261). Duda and Shortliffe followed with the notion that a "collateral benefit of this work is the systematization of previously unformalized knowledge in areas such as medical diagnosis and geology" (p. 261), thus linking expert system initiatives with larger efforts in information organization and retrieval. Buchanan (1986) listed 60 expert system ventures that were currently in service or able to be placed in practical contexts, and declared: "the quantity of AI research may decline as a result unless the applied systems are experimented with and analyzed" (p. 32).

One of the early exemplars of a "successful" expert system in practical industry application was developed for the US Campbell Soup Company in 1985 by Dr. Richard Herrod of Texas Instruments (Herrod & Smith, 1986). The Campbell expert system was widely promoted in expert systems books and lectures as a triumph, however limited its application and untimely its retirement. The system was designed to gauge how long to cook its products (Mans, 1995). One of the experts assigned to this effort (Aldo Cimino) was retiring after 44 years of service, and the system was reportedly designed to replace him rather than make efforts to train skilled human apprentices. Below is a description of this initiative:

> Campbell's maintenance person, Aldo Cimino, had 44 years of experience on the giant hydrostatic cookers that sterilize soup and other canned products. He knew more than anyone in the company about these complex pieces of equipment and was called in to consult at plants around the world.
>
> *(Mans, 1995, p. 16)*

Herrod of Texas Instruments (TI) endeavored for more than a year to locate the kind of application that would make a suitable showcase for the TI "Personal Consultant" expert system shell (Herrod & Smith, 1986). As outlined in Bobrow et al. (1986), choice of problem for expert system treatment was perceived as critical: if the problem relied on too much contextual information, the system would have needed to have so many rules that updating and fine-tuning the system would have been prohibitive. Herod is quoted as stating: "You build an expert system when you have a significant specialized knowledge that exists only in a few people's heads and is acquired through years of experience" (UPI, 1989). The specific rationale for eliciting Aldo Cimino's knowledge through expert system applications rather than training an intern or apprentice is not entirely clear, but was reportedly in keeping with Campbell Soup's overall corporate perspective during this period (Sidorick, 2009). The following account provides a narrative of what transpired in early interactions concerning the system:

> One day his boss woke up and realized that Aldo was going to retire soon, and then who would answer the tough questions? He called in Dr. Herrod and his group to capture Aldo's expertise. The project took six months and endless man-hours, but resulted in an expert system capable of answering most of the problems as well as Aldo could.
>
> *(Mans, 1995, p. 16)*

The Campbell Soup design experience underscored some of the affective aspects of expert system development and installation. Aldo Cimino is quoted as stating:

> At first I thought, "Oh my God, they're going to get rid of me." ... But then I realized that I was 64 years old and getting ready to go anyway. They just wanted to save some of what I knew. It felt weird at first, but I got used to it. It's like I left a piece of myself at that plant.
>
> *(UPI, 1989)*

Experts who are associated with these systems have reported a sense of personal connection with them, making issues involving their use and ultimate termination more problematic (Feigenbaum & McCorduck, 1986). The Campbell Soup system was originally named "Cooker Advisor," and later "Aldo on a Disk," the word "disk" relating to the large floppy disk upon which the system was stored and with which the system was often portrayed in rhetorical terms. The system was eventually renamed "Simon," in honor of Herbert Simon, 1986 National Medal of Science recipient and also a Nobel Laureate, one of the early pioneers of artificial intelligence (Ambrosio, 1990).

The notion that expert systems provide a kind of "canned knowledge" was in some ways literally true in capturing information about how to cook soup at Campbell Soup Company. Mistakes in the large-scale food preparation arena are costly, wasteful, and potentially dangerous to human health: the Campbell Soup sterilizers involved were 72 feet high and heated 68,000 cans of soup to 250 degrees. The system that resulted from the efforts of Herrod and Cimino (along with Texas Instruments' knowledge engineer Michael Smith) took over a year to develop and included approximately 150 rules (Graubard, 1988), many of which had to be rewritten during the productive life of the system. Through using the system, Campbell Soup reportedly saved up to $2 million a year (Day & Rostosky, 1994). The system was retired in the mid-1990s, in part because experts were still required for difficult cases. As related in an interview with computer scientist Dorothy Leonard, the Campbell Soup system "was very helpful to people, no question; but did it capture all of the expert's knowledge? No way! The deep smarts we're talking about, and the pattern recognition, will not be captured through rule and rule-based logic" (Ubiquity Staff, 2005, para 51). Subsequent expert system efforts at Campbell Soup were initiated in different areas of food production, but none were put into extensive service, making expert system ventures successful in this organizational context at a demonstration level but not in terms of technological concept proliferation.

Brittleness (inability of the system to adapt to changing conditions and input, thus producing nonsensical results) and "knowledge engineering bottlenecks" (previously discussed) were two of the more popular explanations why early expert system strategies have failed in application (Guerlain et al., 1995; O'Leary, 2008). Reluctance of users to invest time and effort to work to overcome these and related technological problems (in part perhaps because of the expert system rhetoric discussed in this chapter) is also a critical factor (Gill, 1995; Oravec & Plant, 1992). In 1988, I presented and published a paper on how "dependence" on these emerging expert system applications could inhibit the intellectual growth of potential new expertise. The dependence theme was indeed relevant to many kinds of computer technologies but was not as salient as I projected in regard to expert systems that had barely left the lab (Oravec, 1988). However, attributing the specific reasons for failures or success of any particular system is a complex process requiring detailed analysis, so only the broadest of generalizations can be made along these lines.

As intriguing narratives about expert systems such as Campbell Soup's emerged from the 1980s, Gary Hochron, Director of the Knowledge Engineering Group at AGS Information Services, advised US businesses to "Capture That Information on an Expert System" (1990, p. 11) in the *Journal of Business Strategy*. However, initiatives to use expert systems in everyday business efforts often failed, extending only into the 1990s at Famous Footwear ("Hype is gone," 1995); few other major businesses publicized related projects with substantial lifespans during that period.

Expert System Linkages with Instructional Design

During the 1984 to 1991 time frame, expert system development in instructional design was not as active as in financial, commercial, and manufacturing arenas. Although Feigenbaum and McCorduck (1984) and other expert system promoters projected that the systems would revolutionize education, there were relatively few tested and implemented projects other than Master's degree initiatives and doctoral dissertations. According to Pollock and Grabinger (1991), expert system development was difficult owing to the lack of skilled technical talent available to educational institutions at the time. Many talented individuals migrated to business and governmental arenas in which they could achieve higher salaries. Some prototype systems were construed as useful exercises for outlining and clarifying expert knowledge within a certain context, but few fully tested and implemented system efforts materialized. Romiszowski (1991) projected that teacher anxieties about the implementations of expert systems in the classroom, and their possible "role-threatening" positions, could affect their eventual use in educational contexts. However, he countered that "maybe they [teachers] will perceive the potential educational benefits and see themselves in full control as managers of the resources at their disposal" (p. 24).

Another of the problems noted by Pollock and Grabinger was that many of the existing expert system development approaches were rooted in the mining of expertise of a single expert. Expertise from multiple sources is often needed, especially in instructional design arenas and curricular development initiatives: "ideally, the reasoning of several experts should be encoded to give consensus solutions" (Pollock & Grabinger, 1991, p. 104). An assortment of expert system initiatives have intentionally endeavored to integrate the expertise of multiple experts (Abdullah et al., 2006), which provides considerable strategic and technical difficulties for developers. In 1991, Pollack and Grabinger provided the following "knowledge base example" as an exemplar of the kind of activity needed for expert system development, efforts that generally involve some differences in opinion and perspective (Figure 14.1).

It may be difficult for today's instructional system designers to understand the appeal of the early expert system research agendas, such as those encapsulated in the following statement: "The goal of expert systems is to solve specific problems

Figure 1

Knowledge Base Example

Facts
A book is a medium.
A slide/tape is a medium.
Computer-assisted instruction is a medium.
Video tape is a medium.

Low is a level of learner control.
Moderate is a level of learner control.
High is a level of learner control.

Verbal abstraction is a type of instructional message.
Simulation is a type of instructional message.

Individual is a group size.
Small group is a group size.
Large group is a group size.

Rules
1. If content is primarily verbal abstractions
    and high level of learner control is necessary
    and group size is small
  Then appropriate medium is a book.

2. If a moderate level of learner control is desired
    and group size is large
    or group size is small
    or group size is individual
  Then appropriate medium is slide/tape.

3. If a high level of learner control is desired
    or a moderate level of user control is desired
    and instructional method is simulation
    and group size is individual
  Then appropriate medium is CAI.

4. If a high degree of learner control is desired
    and group size is individual
  Then the appropriate medium is CAI.

FIGURE 14.1 Knowledge base example from Pollack & Grabinger (1991, p. 100).

Source: Used with approval from Lawrence Lipsitz ©.

and present and 'explain' the solution in terms comprehensible to humans" (Madni, 1988, p. 395). Some expert systems developers worked to moderate this overall goal so as to make expert systems approaches more in keeping with larger information systems trends towards context sensitivity and user personalization (Leith, 2010). However, the notion that the energies behind these research undertakings were solely fueled by unappealing motives may miss some of the more altruistic efforts associated with expert systems research. For example, two decades ago, a research report from India described potential uses of expert systems for developing regions of the world in the following terms:

> To make use of the knowledge and skill of specialists and experts in various fields gained over a long period of time, to have "canned knowledge" or

"canned expertise," computer programs called "Expert Systems" have been developed in many fields, particularly for medical diagnosis. These enable persons with much less knowledge and experience than the specialist in a field to operate at a much greater level of efficiency and knowledge as if they are experts.

(Pandalai, 1994, p. 28)

In regions where expertise was not as commonly available, the promise of expert systems to convey needed expertise in a portable form indeed may have provided hope for many in dire circumstances.

Expert system and KBE research agendas have indeed continued to this day (Suhasini et al., 2011). These research efforts generated considerable discourse on the nature of expertise as well as on cognitive science itself, which in the 1980s was emerging as a force in computer science (Gardner, 1985). However, in the 1990s, research and development emphases shifted away from the expert contexts and towards instructional designs that are more supportive of exploration and problem-"finding" as well as the solving of specific, delimited problems. Expert systems are still being developed for specialized purposes in a number of instructional arenas. An example here is Engin et al.'s (2014) rule-based expert system designed to support students in making certain decisions concerning university course selection. However, most of these recent systems are designed to work along with professionals (such as academic advisors) and not to directly and entirely replace human expertise.

Conclusions and Reflections

The period during which expert systems and KBE approaches emerged as a considerable influence in information technology (from the 1980s to the early 1990s) provides insight into the power of assumptions and perspectives to shape how research is conducted. This era was followed by an assortment of efforts to moderate and fine-tune the initial goals of KBE so as to make it more suitable for instructional technology systems and other application areas. Economic and social aspects of knowledge technologies are critical to consider along with philosophical perspectives (Bolisani, 2008; Kling, 1991; Oravec, 1996). Through the many failures of expert systems and KBE research to fulfill practical application objectives, knowledge-management proponents acquired more adequate (and possibly less arrogant) ways of framing their activities (Oravec & Travis, 1992). Early strategies were often linked to the basic model of the "mining" of the know-how of experts and the creation of rule bases for subsequent processing in expert system shells. The notion of the refinement of knowledge "nuggets" has been a legacy of some early expert systems and KBE efforts (Geisler, 2006). Expert systems and KBE also inspired a great deal of investigation into the question of what constitutes human expertise (Perrolle, 1991), although some of this early research aimed to simplify and distill know-how rather than understand the nature of expertise. Many of the early initiatives were ultimately deemed as failures and no longer utilized. However, as outlined by Howard (2011), the analyses of such failures may serve as important roles for individuals "who share common dilemmas, constraints, goals or contexts" (p. 50).

The "thinking machine" notion served to energize a great deal of early expert systems and KBE research (O'Leary, 2008; Oravec, 2019). However, the fear that automated systems would soon displace or undervalue computer programmers (Kraft, 1977), librarians (Molholt, 1986), lawyers (Leith, 2010), and other knowledge professionals was indeed a force in constraining and delimiting the applications of expert systems rather than expanding their domains. Reluctance to work with knowledge engineers or otherwise contribute to expert systems projects may have halted some otherwise interesting efforts, giving KBE technologies less potential than anticipated (as described in Subramanian et al., 1997). Today's learner-centered approaches and social media advances have injected more collaborative dimensions into knowledge elicitation efforts as well as expanded the role of context, although the idea of mining individual expertise still persists in a number of formulations to this day (as in the logistics and supply chain management expert system efforts of Gunasekaran and Ngai, 2014).

Donald Norman's notion of "disruptive technologies" in *The Invisible Computer* (1999) has some applicability to expert systems and KBE efforts. Norman construes disruptive technologies as those that have the ability to change everyday life as well as the course of their respective industries; he also describes the initial, strong resistance to many of these technologies. In effect, expert systems and KBE efforts have often extended beyond Norman's disruptive levels to be "disconcerting" technologies. They were often directly linked in theme and approach to the displacement of human professionals and potentially even to the undermining of the value of human intelligence, both salient topics that involve economic concerns about the unemployment (or underemployment) of a number of highly skilled and well-educated individuals. Expert system failures sent a powerful message to knowledge and information researchers about the importance of intense and continuing human involvement in system design and implementation (Oravec & Travis, 1992).

Artificial intelligence research has indeed had some remarkable successes: for example, chess-playing computers can defeat grand masters, as predicted by a number of AI pioneers. The success of computers in chess has apparently not stopped chess players enjoying their activities and benefitting from them (Miller, 1992). Many individuals also enjoy acquiring and using information even though computer systems can also do so (albeit in distinctly different modes). Today, collaborative initiatives are often given more emphasis in knowledge-related research; however, in future decades, more individual-centered approaches (such as those found in early expert systems development) may well emerge in some "retro" form in an assortment of applications. Analysis of the historical and technological trends that made expert systems research less of a success than predicted (such as the outlandish claims of many of its researchers, the systems' tendencies towards brittleness, as well as the knowledge engineering bottleneck) can be of help in assisting today's instructional designers in side-stepping comparable obstacles.

References

Abdullah, M. S., Kimble, C., Benest, I., & Paige, R. (2006). Knowledge-based systems: A re-evaluation. *Journal of Knowledge Management, 10*(3), 127–142.

Ambrosio, J. (1990, September 17). Simon says soup is good food. *Computerworld, 24*(38), 33.

Anderson, T., & Dron, J. (2010). Three generations of distance education pedagogy. *The International Review of Research in Open and Distance Learning, 12*(3), 80–97.

Barr, A., & Feigenbaum, E. A. (1982). *Handbook of artificial intelligence* (Vol. 2). Reading, MA: Addison-Wesley.

Blair, D. C. (1985). E-systems: The new gold rush? *Proceedings of ASIS Mid-Year Meeting*. Ann Arbor, Michigan.

Blair, D. C. (2002). Knowledge management: Hype, hope, or help? *Journal of the American Society for Information Science & Technology, 53*(12), 1019–1028.

Bobrow, D. G., & Hayes, P. J. (1985). Artificial Intelligence—Where are we? *Artificial Intelligence, 25*(3), 375–415.

Bobrow, D. G., Mittal, S., & Stefik, M. J. (1986). Expert systems: Perils and promise. *Communications of the ACM, 29*(9), 880–894.

Bolisani, E. (2008). Knowledge transfer on the net: Useful lessons from the knowledge economy. In E. Bolisani (Ed.), *Building the knowledge society on the Internet: Sharing and exchanging knowledge in networked environments* (pp. 110–128). Hershey, PA: IGI Global. http://dx.doi.org/10.4018/978-1-59904-816-1.

Brey, P. (2001). Hubert Dreyfus—Human versus machine. In H. Achterhuis (Ed.), *American philosophy of technology: The empirical turn* (pp. 37–63). Bloomington, IN: Indiana University Press.

Buchanan, B. G. (1986). Expert systems: Working systems and the research literature. *Expert Systems, 3*(1), 32–50. http://dx.doi.org/10.1111/j.1468-0394.1986.tb00192.x.

Clancey, W. J. (1987). The knowledge engineer as student: Metacognitive bases for asking good questions. Stanford University Department of Computer Science. Accession no. ADA186995. http://handle.dtic.mil/100.2/ADA186995.

Cohen, H., Cohen, B., & Nii, P. (1983). *The first artificial intelligence coloring book*. Reading, MA: Addison-Wesley.

Crevier, D. (1993). *AI: The tumultuous search for artificial intelligence*. New York: Basic Books.

Davenport, T. H., & Prusak, L. (1998). *Working knowledge: How organizations manage what they know*. Boston, MA: Harvard Business School Press.

Davis, R. (1984). Amplifying expertise with expert systems. In P. H. Winston & K. A. Prendergast (Eds.), *The AI business: Commercial uses of artificial intelligence* (pp. 17–40). Cambridge, MA: MIT Press.

Day, W. B., & Rostosky, M. J. (1994). Diagnostic expert systems for PLC controlled manufacturing equipment. *International Journal of Computer Integrated Manufacturing, 7*(2), 116–122.

Dreyfus, H., & Dreyfus, S. (1986). *Mind over machine: The power of human intuition and expertise in the era of the computer*. New York: Macmillan.

Duda, R. O., & Shortliffe, E. H. (1983). Expert systems research. *Science, 220*(4594), 261–268. http://dx.doi.org/10.1126/science.6340198.

Engin, G., Aksoyer, B., Avdagic, M., Bozanlı, D., Hanay, U., Maden, D., & Ertek, G. (2014). Rule-based expert systems for supporting university students. *Procedia Computer Science, 31*, 22–31.

Feigenbaum, E. A. (1977). *The art of artificial intelligence.* Heuristic Programming Project Memo 77–25, Stanford University.

Feigenbaum, E. A. (1992). A personal view of expert systems: Looking back and looking ahead. *Expert Systems with Applications, 5*(3), 193–201.

Feigenbaum, E. A., & McCorduck, P. (1984). *The fifth generation: Artificial intelligence and Japan's computer challenge.* New York: Signet.

Forsythe, D. (2001). *Studying those who study us: An anthropologist in the world of artificial intelligence.* Stanford, CA: Stanford University Press.

Gardner, H. (1985). *The mind's new science.* New York: Basic Books.

Geisler, E. (2006). A taxonomy and proposed codification of knowledge and knowledge systems in organizations. *Knowledge and Process Management, 13*(4), 285–296. http://dx.doi.org/10.1002/kpm.265.

Gill, T. G. (1995). Early expert systems: Where are they now? *MIS Quarterly, 19*(1), 51–81.

Graubard, S. R. (1988). *The artificial intelligence debate.* Cambridge, MA: MIT Press.

Guerlain, S. A., Smith, P. J., Obradovich, J. H., Rudmann, S., Strohm, P., Smith, J. W., & Svirbely, J. (1995). Dealing with brittleness in the design of expert systems for immunohematology. *Immunohematology, 12*(3), 101–107.

Gunasekaran, A., & Ngai, E. W. (2014). Expert systems and artificial intelligence in the 21st century logistics and supply chain management. *Expert Systems with Applications, 41*(1), 1–4.

Hall, J. G. (2009, February). 1983 and all that. *Expert Systems, 1–2.* http://dx.doi.org/10.1111/j.1468-0394.2009.00514.x.

Hawkins, W. J. (1986). Expert systems promise supersmart PCs. *Popular Science, 228*(3), 83–85.

Hayes-Roth, F., Waterman, D., & Lenat, D. (1984). *Building expert systems.* Reading, MA: Addison-Wesley.

Hellström, T., & Raman, S. (2001). The commodification of knowledge about knowledge: Knowledge management and the reification of epistemology. *Social Epistemology, 15*(3), 139–154.

Herrod, R., & Smith, M. (1986). The Campbell Soup story: An application of AI in the food industry. *Texas Instruments Engineering Journal, 3*(1), 16–19.

Hochron, G. (1990). Capture that information on an expert system. *Journal of Business Strategy, 11*(1), 11–15.

Howard, C. D. (2011). Writing and rewriting the instructional design case: A view from two sides. *International Journal of Designs for Learning, 2*(1), 40–55.

"Hype is gone, but job of expert systems remains." (1995). *Chain Store Age, 71*(10), 66.

Kling, R. (1991). Computerization and social transformation. *Science, Technology and Human Values, 17*, 342–367.

Kraft, P. (1977). *Programmers and managers: The routinization of computer programming in the United States.* New York: Springer Verlag.

Lambright, W. H. (2014). *Why Mars: NASA and the politics of space exploration.* Baltimore, MD: JHU Press.

Leith, P. (2010). The rise and fall of the legal expert system. *European Journal of Law and Technology, 1*, 179–201.

Liebowitz, J. (1993, March). Educating knowledge engineers on knowledge acquisition. In *Developing and Managing Intelligent System Projects IEEE International Conference* (pp. 110–117). New York: IEEE Press.

Madni, A. (1988). The role of human factors in expert systems design and acceptance. *Human Factors: The Journal of the Human Factors and Ergonomics Society, 30*(4), 395–414.

Mans, J. (1995, April). The new experts. *Dairy Foods,* 15–20.

McCarthy, J. (2007, November 12). Applications of AI. In *What is artificial intelligence?* Stanford, CA: Computer Science Department, Stanford University.

Miller, A. (1992). Check and mate: The ancient game meets modern times. *Compute!, 14*(9), 91.

Molholt, P. (1986). The information machine: A new challenge for librarians. *Library Journal, 111*(16), 47.

Mykytyn, P. P., Mykytyn, K., & Raja, M. K. (1994). Knowledge acquisition skills and traits: A self-assessment of knowledge engineers. *Information & Management, 26*(2), 95–104.

Norman, D. A. (1999). *The invisible computer: Why good products can fail, the personal computer is so complex, and information appliances are the solution.* Cambridge, MA: MIT Press.

O'Leary, D. E. (2008). Expert systems. In *Wiley encyclopedia of computer science and engineering* (pp. 1–10). Hoboken, NJ: John Wiley. http://dx.doi.org/10.1002/9780470050118.ecse146.

Oravec, J. (1988). Dependence upon expert systems: The dangers of the computer as an intellectual crutch. In *Directions and Implications of Advanced Computing Symposium Proceedings, Computer Professionals for Social Responsibility (CPSR).* University of Minnesota.

Oravec, J. (1996). *Virtual individuals, virtual groups: Human dimensions of groupware and computer networking.* New York: Cambridge University Press.

Oravec, J. (2004). Examining the examined career: Diana Forsythe as ethnographer and participant in computing research. *Science and Public Policy, 31*(2), 159–163.

Oravec, J. (2019). Artificial intelligence, automation, and social welfare: Some ethical and historical perspectives on technological overstatement and hyperbole. *Ethics and Social Welfare, 13*(1), 18–32.

Oravec, J., & Plant, R. (1992). Guest editors' introduction. *Journal of Systems and Software, 19*(2), 111.

Oravec J., & Travis, L. (1992). If we could do it over, we'd. ... Learning from less-than-successful expert system projects. *Journal of Systems and Software, 19*(2), 113–122.

Pandalai, K. A. V. (1994). *DRDO Monograph Series: The other side of science.* Madras Defense Research & Development Organization, Ministry of Defence, Govt of India, New Delhi-110 011.

Perrolle, J. A. (1991). Expert enhancement and replacement in computerized mental labor. *Science, Technology, & Human Values, 16*(2), 195–207.

Pollock, J., & Grabinger, R. (1991). Expert systems: Instructional design potential. In *Expert systems and intelligent computer-aided instruction* (Vol. 2) (pp. 100–104). Englewood Cliffs, NJ: Educational Technology Publications.

Porat, M. (1977). *The information economy.* Washington, DC: US Department of Commerce.

Rafea, A., Hassen, H., & Hazman, M. (2003). Automatic knowledge acquisition tool for irrigation and fertilization expert systems. *Expert Systems with Applications, 24*(1), 49.

Romiszowski, A. J. (1991). Expert systems in education and training: Automated job aids or sophisticated instructional media. In *Expert systems and intelligent computer-aided instruction* (Vol. 2) (pp. 17–25). Englewood Cliffs, NJ: Educational Technology Publications.

Sidorick, D. (2009). *Condensed capitalism: Campbell Soup and the pursuit of cheap production in the twentieth century.* Ithaca, NY: Cornell University Press.

Stafford, S. P. (2001). Epistemology for sale. *Social Epistemology*, *15*(3), 215–230. http://dx.doi.org/10.1080/02691720110076549.

Subramanian, G., Yaverbaum, G., & Brandt, S. (1997). An empirical evaluation of factors influencing expert systems effectiveness. *Journal of Systems and Software*, *38*(3), 255–261. http://dx.doi.org/10.1016/S0164-1212(96)00155-0.

Suhasini, A., Palanivel, S., & Ramalingam, V. (2011). Multimodal decision support system for library problem. *Expert Systems with Applications*, *38*(5), 4990–4997. http://dx.doi.org/10.1016/j.eswa.2010.09.152.

Ubiquity Staff (Association for Computing Machinery). (2005). Leonard and Swap on "Deep Smarts." *Ubiquity*, *6*(6). http://dx.doi.org/10.1145/1066328.1066329.

UPI (United Press International). (1989, November 7). *Expert system picks key workers' brains: From airport gate-scheduling to trouble-shooting, technology allows companies to store key employees' know-how on floppy disks*. Retrieved on August 22, 2014 from http://articles.latimes.com/1989-11-07/business/fi-1112_1_expert-system.

Vaux, J. (2001). From expert systems to knowledge-based companies: How the AI industry negotiated a market for knowledge. *Social Epistemology*, *15*(3), 231–245. http://dx.doi.org/10.1080/02691720110076558.

Waterman, D. (1986). *A guide to expert systems*. Reading, MA: Addison-Wesley.

Weizenbaum, J. (1976). *Computer power and human reason: From judgment to calculation*. San Francisco, CA: WH Freeman.

Winograd, T., & Flores, F. (1987). *Understanding computers and cognition: A new foundation for design*. Reading, MA: Addison-Wesley.

Winston, P. H., & Prendergast, K. A. (1984). *The AI business. The commercial uses of artificial intelligence*. Cambridge, MA: MIT Press.

15

"MAKING ALCATRAZ AMAZING"[1]

The Alcatraz Cellhouse Tour (1987–1995)

Elizabeth Boling

Introduction

Museum tours and tours of historic sites are, broadly speaking, designs for learning. A visitor may not walk away from such a tour with specific facts to be recalled later on, so much as with an enriched appreciation for what she has seen. That appreciation is arguably as important as facts, if not more so—and it is almost certainly tougher to convey via intentional design. With translations in ten languages, listeners in the tens of millions since its inception, and a 98 percent satisfaction rating from those who experience it, the audio tour of Alcatraz, Alcatraz Cellhouse Tour (1987), can be considered a classic of the genre. This short design case focuses on the original tour, and was constructed from four sources:

- An interview with Chris Hardman (Artistic Director and Founder of Antenna Theater and the originator, together with Chris Tellis, of the original audio tour of Alcatraz)
- An interview with Nicki Phelps (Vice President, Visitor Programs and Services for the Golden Gate National Parks Conservancy, project manager for the original tour, and director of development over the subsequent 25 years)
- The author's memory of experiencing the audio tour in 1989 as a tourist on Alcatraz Island
- The author's recent rehearing of the original tour (via the 15-year-old cassette player in her car) and the current tour (via CD import to Apple iTunes™)

Experiencing the Tour

Tickets to board the ferry at Pier 33 in San Francisco for the ride to Alcatraz Island sell out days or weeks in advance, and by a month or more for the night tours. When you can get a ticket, you and about 300 other people ride a mile and a quarter across the San Francisco Bay, chased by gulls and listening to the chatter of other tourists. Disembarking on the island, you join a smaller group led by a National Park Service ranger and begin to climb the hairpin path leading to the cellhouse (Figure 15.1). You and about 600 or 700 people an hour tour the cellhouse interior, and tours take place 14 hours a day all year round. Disembarking from the ferry and listening to the ranger describe the general history of the island as she backs up the hill ahead of your group, you shiver in the wind that whips around the island, even though the day is bright enough to see the city clearly across the water. During this walk you may wonder what your feelings would have been if you had come to the island as a worst-of-the-worst prisoner of the federal penitentiary system between 1934 and 1963. Once you enter the

FIGURE 15.1   View from the bay side of the lighthouse with the celhouse immediately behind. The ferry dock and path bringing park visitors to the cell house are beyond.

Source: Used by permission: alcatrazalumni.org.

dim, chilly interior of the cellhouse and put on headphones to start the free audio tour, you don't wonder—the voices of actual inmates and guards describe those feelings, or at least their memories of feelings, directly to you while you stand in the spaces where they stood decades previously.

In 1989 when I visited the island and was guided through the Alcatraz cellhouse by the audio tour, the experience was memorably different than any park or museum tour I had ever taken before—or since. It was intimate; the voices spoke quietly but clearly just to me, both separating me from the crowd around me and joining me to each individual telling me a story at that moment. Unlike other educational tours I had experienced, it felt immediate—not filtered through the dry, instructional lens of a docent, or exaggerated, however positively, by a guide's enthusiasm for the site. It sounded and almost felt as though I was there in the days when the penitentiary was open. I barely noticed being told where to walk, when to pause, or where to look next, and completely lost the sense of being there with 100 other people. In fact, I lost the sense of listening to an audiotape, and at the end of the tour almost had the impression that I had guided myself through Alcatraz.

All the voices on this tour belong to individuals, guards, and inmates from the active days of the penitentiary. A former correctional officer on Alcatraz, Thomas Donahue, begins by directing you quietly to the physical location where the tour will begin, and telling you where to look so that you know you are in the right place (Segment 1, 0:00–1:32). You begin on the main corridor, "Broadway," which would have smelled of many bodies in close quarters then, but which now smells mainly of cool concrete (Figure 15.2). Every minute or so the guide directs you to another location or tells you where to look next. The guide also works into the narrative some facts about the facility and its history, as heard in Segment 1 and Segment 2 (4:26–5:02). These feel like a conceptual orientation that goes along with the navigational directions you are given.

Almost right away you begin to hear the voices of former inmates (Figure 15.3). You are walking through empty spaces with other tourists all around, but these voices bring the experience of having been here years ago to life. At one point, the time spent walking from one location to another is used to help you understand the kinds of prisoners who served time on Alcatraz (Segment 3, 6:30–6:52). At others they remark on how it felt to be incarcerated on Alcatraz (Segment 4, 2:38–2:53) and how it felt to look across the bay, knowing they couldn't take part in life on the outside (Segment 5, 15:26–15:56).

FIGURE 15.2 "Broadway," the main corridor in cell block D down which a new prisoner walked at intake, and the starting point for the audio tour.

Source: Used by permission: alcatrazalumni.org.

FIGURE 15.3 James Quillen's voice is one of those included in the tour (Segments 3 and 4).

Source: Used by permission: alcatrazalumni.org.

Alcatraz Cellhouse Tour (1987–1995)   **275**

Voices and sound effects add layers to the sense of experiencing life at Alcatraz. As you stand in the mess hall, you hear from inmates and officers about an uprising over the bad spaghetti being served there (although you hear at another time how good the food was most of the time), and even though it is short, this story is rich with the sense of experience (Segment 6, 13:52–14:37). Similarly, a description of the cells you are seeing, entirely bare now, gives you the facts about what was there and what was issued to each prisoner (Segment 7, 8:19–8:40) but then other voices join in to give this information immediacy (Segment 8, 8:40–9:00) and connect it to the emotional dimension of prison life (Segment 9, 9:33–9:56). These voices are no longer young, but the timbre in them as the men recount their memories of Alcatraz allows you to imagine them as they were in this place; the voices make the place come alive.

The tour is immersive. It feels longer than the 30 minutes it actually takes because each physical location in the cellhouse seems to have been made alive, and many stories have been told. Each segment is no longer than 20 to 30 seconds or so, sometimes with several voices included in that short span. But the impact of these stories is high, as when a former inmate explains how he kept himself busy when he was locked up in the dark, soundless cells of solitary confinement (Segment 10, 19:45–20:09). More time is devoted to those narratives visitors are likely to want to hear the most about: Robert Stroud, the "Bird Man" (Segment 11, 18:11–19:17), the famous escape from Alcatraz, and the escape attempt during which several guards and prisoners died. I was sincerely sorry when the tour ended and I had to turn in the cassette player—still running, as

Thomas Donahue instructed near the end of the tape. I wanted to return to Alcatraz, and I did so several times. The place had been made alive for me.

Origin and Inspiration for the Design

In the mid-1980s the National Park Service (NPS) was facing multiple problems managing visits to Alcatraz by the public they serve. Boat tours of 150 visitors at a time taking two and a half hours, each conducted by a regular or seasonal ranger, were neither as compelling nor as affordable as they needed to be. They were also subject to inconsistency due to the effect of media on the accuracy of interpretation by rangers, and to the limitations on numbers of visitors who could move through the site smoothly as a group. They were also, according to Nicki Phelps, "brutal" duty for the park rangers who conducted the tours. In response to these problems, the NPS called for proposals to develop an audio tour for use in the cellhouse, the central attraction of the site.

Audio tours were not brand new in the mid-1980s, although in museum and historical site settings they generally reproduced the face-to-face guide format in which a single voice talent read a script, delivering facts and explanations as the listener moved from one point to another. Among the proposals that came in for the Alcatraz tour was one from Chris Hardman, who had pioneered, and by then had several years of experience using, mobile audio as a form of theater that transformed audience members into "audients": full participants in the dramatic experience. His first show of this type, *High School*, sent audients walking at night through an actual high school, each fitted with a Sony Walkman™, listening to the real voices of high school students telling their stories and encountering actors as characters in these stories along the way. He describes the seminal moment for this use of new technology as being a flight to Europe that he took in about 1980. He had fired up Wagner on his (then novel) Walkman™ prior to take-off as a substitute for the noises of a busy passenger compartment. Wagner's *Ride of the Valkyries* happened to play coincidentally with lift-off (the "gigantic lift force" merging with "Wagner sawing away"), joining "where I was and what I was hearing" into the realization that audio synchronized with experience was a theatrical tool of immense potential.

When the call for proposals from the NPS came out, a traditional script had been written and they were simply looking for a contractor to produce it. From the basis he had built up already in generating immersive audio experiences, Chris envisioned an alternative possibility and played them some audio from another project, including a clip from an actual previous inmate of Alcatraz. This had to have been something of a conceptual leap for Park Service personnel, but a compelling moment as well, because they took a chance and contracted for a tour on the model of Chris's vision. Nicki Phelps joined the project from a different company, also a bidder, as project manager.

Key Decisions and Revisions

The core decision in this design was that it should have a dramatic, rather than an expository, frame. The dramatic frame specified that visitors have the prisoner experience in this physical space for 30 minutes, with some history interspersed. This decision was made possible in part by the site. It is self-contained and, while listeners cross and re-cross their own paths moving through it, it is small enough to be navigated in a reasonable period of time. The cellhouse is approximately 28,000 square feet in total, but much of this is taken up by the cells. In fact, Chris points to the "amazing fit" between the audio format and the site as a factor not present in other places. The drama would also be authentic; every voice heard on the tour would be that of someone who had been incarcerated at Alcatraz or who had worked or lived there when the prison was in operation, not the voice of an actor. Again, the site made this decision possible; its active period of use had ended recently enough that those voices were available.

Even so, getting this frame in place required working through obstacles, first among them the natural inclination on the part of rangers to consider non-experiential information—dates, building materials, statistics—as vital elements in the Alcatraz story. Thirty seconds is considered more than twice as long as the average visitor will usually stand at an exhibit. Rangers, who had considered much of the original expository script to be critical, visited the site to stand at various locations for 15 to 20 seconds and see how long that period of time really is. Some points originally considered non-negotiable could be worked into the script, but many had to be left out and rangers agreed to do so as the dramatic shape of the project emerged. According to Chris Hardman, some strong experiential stories had to be cut as well—and some compelling but potentially distressing stories gathered on tape from former residents of the island were left out. Nicki Phelps explains that this was, in part, because the tour was intended for park visitors that included those as young as 8 or 9 years old.

Many of the design decisions made in structuring the tour were rooted in Chris Hardman's insistence that park visitors experiencing the tour are the movie. The tour is prompting them, sometimes implicitly and sometimes explicitly, to pan, zoom, and dolly. Chris refers to his rules guiding these moves and mentions that he has compiled them into a handbook for producing context-specific audio experiences. As an example, the audio always describes or talks about something a visitor is about to see; never something that has already been passed (Segment 12, 24:49–25:03). This keeps the visitor moving—"walking is good; standing is not."

278 Elizabeth Boling

The focus is also on the reveal: while the visitor is looking at a cell, a dining room, a shower room, or a corridor in the present, "people's voices [on the audio] are creating the scene [from the past]." The audio also has to address obvious features of the location where a visitor is supposed to be at a given time so that she can recognize that she is where she should be (Segment 12).

In the first implementation of the tour an entire segment had to be removed within the first couple of months when rangers discovered that some visitors, out of sight from rangers when they visited the second-floor infirmary, were getting lost, scribbling graffiti on the walls and potentially being exposed to asbestos—"a nightmare!" Later, Chris Hardman watched in puzzlement from where he was located, performing maintenance on the cassette players, as a group of visitors headed up the stairs to the second floor, even though the tour had been revised and they should not have been going that way. Catching up with them, he discovered that a previous visitor to the park had bootlegged copies of the first tour cassette and distributed them to this group in advance of their trip. They were simply following the out-of-date script. This was one of the translated versions of the audio tour; even though the tour is free once visitors have paid for the ferry ride to the island, the group might have had concerns over enough cassettes being available for them when they arrived. This element of the design could likely not be addressed differently until technology could provide a solution.

Over time, at least one experiential moment in the original tour has been recognized to create a preservation problem for the park (Segment 14, 5:35–5:47, and Segment 15, 6:18–6:27). Rather than recite facts about the different metals used for cell bars in the oldest part of the installation and in the newer cells, the tour invited visitors to place their hands directly on the bars and feel the difference in their warmth and their sturdiness (Figure 15.4). Unfortunately, the sweat and oil on thousands of hands over decades deteriorates the metal leading to degradation of the site.

FIGURE 15.4 Visitors peer into a cell, at the same moment of the tour and aware of each other, but each also experiencing it individually.

Source: Used by permission: John Martini.

A different kind of wear and tear, a kind of emotional daze, results from the intense experiential quality of the tour. Moving visitors almost continually gives them no place to decompress. This facet of the design was identified sometime after its initial implementation, and changes in pacing made later were not necessarily viewed positively by Chris Hardman. However, he acknowledges that the voices are still there—the foundational rule that every voice heard in the tour is someone who lived on the island between 1934 and 1963 has remained intact through later revision of the tour—and therefore the tour "radiates the past."

Evolution of the Design

While the original design emerged from a happy confluence of then-recent advances in portable audio, Chris's related inspiration and artistic work, the nature of the Alcatraz site, and the willingness of park service personnel to take a chance on Chris's vision, evolution of the Alcatraz audio tour has proceeded in multiple ways across the subsequent 27 years. Early on, practical revisions were made to accommodate the needs of visitors accompanied by guide dogs and/or requiring tactile markers for orientation during the tour. Translations were also made into several languages (ten in all), necessitating the production decisions and the production effort required to mix the translation over the authentic voices keeping the volume regulated so that the dramatic effect of the originals is not lost. The second version, Doing Time, evolved in response to a number of factors discussed below. Current plans for revision of the tour involve a *charrette*—or collaborative design meeting—to be held at about the time of this writing, and recognition that visitors to the park include both many more elderly people than previously as well as young people who "listen faster" than anyone used to do because media styles have accustomed them to short, rapid audio and visual bursts. Everyone is used to increasingly higher levels of production value now than they were several decades ago.

Some fundamental changes have been carried out over time as those responsible for the tour have continued to build relationships with, and interview, alumni of the island's penitentiary era exploring the differing and sometimes contradictory recollections of their time on Alcatraz. During the decades since 1987 the visiting public has also come to accept, perhaps expect, multiple narratives regarding a complex social institution of the type that Alcatraz Penitentiary had been. As an example, a former inmate may recall being walked down the main corridor of the facility without clothing during his initial intake, while prison personnel assert that this did not happen. The current tour, Doing Time, reflects this expanded base of source material, including three levels of narrative—inmates, correctional officers, and the family members of those officers and administrators who lived on the island with them. The tour also now touches on subjects not addressed in the original, although some, like inmate violence and rape, still do not appear; the lower age limit for the tour is still 8 to 9 years old. Parents are now encouraged to start their own tours 10 to 15 seconds before those of their children in case they want to have the children skip certain segments.

Technology has continued to evolve as well, opening up possibilities for changes to the audio tour. Small, high-grade audio recorders have allowed new material to be gathered from the alumni of Alcatraz Island more easily than was possible in the past. In fact, some material is sought from the Alcatraz alumni with interviews eliciting needed information when possible. While the number of authentic alumni is, of course, shrinking over time, the stockpile of material for inclusion in the tour has grown substantially as a result of the ability for designers to capture high-quality interviews from them anyplace they feel comfortable speaking. As Alcatraz alumni age, their memories and interpretations of those memories can evolve as well, so the underlying narrative of the tour must consider and respect these shifts—and they can be captured relatively easily.

Technology evolution has required other revisions, mainly technical, as the tour has been moved from cassette tape to compact disc to MP3 format. It is now being adapted for specialty hardware that will be easier to maintain in the damp, salt-laden island environment than are consumer-grade players, and that will stand up to the extremely heavy use to which they are subjected daily. Chris Hardman reports standing onsite "cleaning, calibrating, and repairing" the original cassette players; it is clear from Nicki Phelps's description of the technology currently in use that functional issues of maintaining equipment and updating the tour ("changes all have to be made in ten languages and the full script") remain important.

Changes made to how the cellhouse site is organized have also required adjustments to the tour. More space in the cellhouse is devoted to retail, and this has created some crowding, which is distracting to the visitors. Chris Hardman points out that, with an effective audio production, a tour or a theatrical event, people appear zombie-like as they move through the experience and then report later that "it was great!" They need to stay immersed in that experience and not be pulled out of it by navigational complexities, so more direction to the visitor is included, delivered by a former correctional officer (Segment 16, 6:18–6:27).

A Classic Design

During the five years I lived in the San Francisco Bay Area, I visited Alcatraz four times. It was my destination of choice when visitors came from out of state and we were expected to show them the sites. I have to confess that I did tour the cellhouse twice without listening to the tour, but I attribute to the tour much of my fascination with the space and all of my appreciation for its historical (not just its immediate) experiential qualities—even when I explored it sans audio—that I would not have been able to develop without the tour, or through interpretation by a ranger no matter how well informed or enthusiastic that ranger might have been. I am related to two interpretive rangers and respect their face-to-face work highly, but I agree with Chris Hardman that this site presented a unique opportunity for a different form of interpretive experience. That original tour was, I get the positive sense, experimental and handmade. The designers stuck close to their core decisions—authentic voices, cinematic sensibility, and focus on experience over information—which resulted in a robust, flexible design.

It is true, as pointed out recently by S. J. Culver (2012) in *Guernica* magazine, that the voices of the current audio tour—gathered purposefully as they have been, and crafted to provide an immediate, but not an introspective or political, experience of the space—steer clear of larger questions regarding the societal implications of incarceration, thereby allowing visitors to move through Alcatraz without considering those implications either. Specifically, these visitors, most of them unlikely to have been, or ever to be, incarcerated themselves, are not encouraged to consider the current state of the penal system in the United States or their role in tolerating if not perpetuating it.

However, the brief for the original tour, as defined at the entry of Chris Hardman into the project, was clearly focused on moving from a traditional interpreter-led format to one with a direct emotional impact, achieved by making guard and inmate voices actually present. This was an innovative step for the NPS at the time. The core decisions made then are still serving as a strong basis, almost 30 years later, for the experience of Alcatraz carried away from the island by several million visitors a year; and revisions to the tour, now in the works, are moving in the direction of including additional voices and greater acknowledgment of the full experience of incarceration.

Note

1 This chapter contains audio material accessible by scanning the individual QR codes for each segment.

Reference

Culver, S. J. (2012, December 3). *Escape to Alcatraz*. *Guernica: A Magazine of Art & Politics*. Retrieved from www.guernicamag.com/features/escape-to-alcatraz/.

16
SIMCALC
Democratizing Access to Advanced Mathematics (1992–Present)

Deborah Tatar, Jeremy Roschelle, and Stephen Hegedus

Intellectual Background

Backgrounds of the SimCalc Team and Present Authors

The founder and long-time leader of the SimCalc project was James J. Kaput, a mathematician and mathematics educator with a strong vision for the appropriate role of technology in mathematics education. Kaput often shared his vision via an analogy:

> When knowledge was expressed in Latin, very few people could learn by reading; however, as knowledge was re-expressed in the vernacular, many more people could learn by reading. Likewise, when math is expressed in an arcane symbolism, very few people can understand it well; however, as technology allows us to find new ways to represent mathematical ideas, there is the possibility of enabling many more people to deeply learn mathematics.
>
> *(Kaput, personal communication)*

Kaput was gifted not only in developing a vision and themes for his projects but also in pulling together a diverse, multidisciplinary team to execute them. Many kinds of expertise were represented on the team over time (Roschelle et al., 2008a). At the onset, the team included Kaput, a mathematician; Nemirovsky, an expert in child development and mathematics; and Roschelle, one of the co-authors and a computer scientist and learning scientist. Over time, the team expanded and contracted. At various times the team included mathematicians, scientists, teachers, experts in teacher professional development, experts in assessment, computer programmers, experimental psychologists, curriculum designers, and industry experts.

Two of the three authors of this retrospective analysis started their careers working with Logo and Boxer, an important rethinking of Logo that integrated programming, specific microworlds, and hypertext to create a multi-purpose computational medium (DiSessa, 1991, 2000; DiSessa & Abelson, 1986). Based on this preparation, they recognized the great opportunity inherent in SimCalc. The first author, Deborah Tatar, was involved in several projects, primarily from 2000 until 2008, and is currently a professor of computer science with a focus on the design of systems that restructure knowing. The second author, Jeremy Roschelle, brings expertise both in computation and the learning sciences and has the longest history with SimCalc, running from 1994 until the present time and encompassing every aspect of the project from implementation to scaling. The third author, Stephen Hegedus, brought a background in mathematics and mathematics education to bear on the project starting in 2000 and took on the running of the overarching project after Kaput's sudden and untimely death in 2005.

Strands of Research and Development for Technology in Mathematics Education

Approaches to the use of technology in mathematics education can be understood as drawing on three different predominant approaches (Drijvers, 2012). One approach emphasizes productivity, and emphasizes tools that are useful in everyday life, such as rulers, slide-rules, calculators, graphing calculators, spreadsheets, and the like. Another approach emphasizes support for structured practice with feedback and tutorials, and includes self-paced workbooks, drill and practice software, and game-like wrappers that motivate practice of mathematical skills. Today, the orientation to optimal practice of mathematical skills continues in the form of intelligent tutors and adaptive learning systems. A third approach is the subject of this chapter, and concerns students' development of the ability to make sense of mathematics and to develop conceptual understanding. Predominant tools in this category emphasize simulation, visualization, and representation—and often involve tools constructed to support deep learning, even if those tools are not currently used professionally in the way that a spreadsheet is.

Each of these approaches has a past, a present, and a future. Each approach has existed across a range of underlying platforms from timeshare systems through to today's cloud and tablet solutions. Thus, it is not the case that one approach is more "modern" than the others. Further, each approach has applications and evidence of effectiveness. Thus, it is not the case that one approach is "better" than the others. The different approaches have different goals, corresponding to different goals that co-exist in mathematics education. Designs, of course, are successful relative to goals. Consequently, we will not attempt to compare designs across these different approaches. However, we will draw upon examples from different approaches to highlight the contrasting approaches with this specific design and its features.

Logo and the Concept of Microworlds

One of the great promises of computer technology in education has been transformation. Some projects try to change learning by, for example, liberating learning from the classroom; others by liberating learning from teachers; yet others, as in the SimCalc project,[1] have sought to use technology to liberate mathematics learning from arcane, esoteric symbol systems and to render it more readily approachable and understandable.

Historical roots of the Simcalc Mathworlds® approach built upon an early great educational movement that was based on the Logo computer language for children; Logo was promoted and memorialized in Seymour Papert's book *Mindstorms* (1980). Authors Tatar and Roschelle were both deeply involved with the Logo movement. This approach contrasts with a "CAI" (Computer-Assisted Instruction) approach, for example, as represented contemporaneously by PLATO (Hammon, 1972). Logo was built to be learnable along principles influenced by the great Swiss psychologist Jean Piaget; Papert offered the evocative analogy from how he explored the concept of ratio as a child using physical gears to how children could now explore a broader range of mathematical concepts using Logo as "gears for the mind." PLATO, in contrast, automated a traditional instructional approach consisting of providing the student with information, practice tasks, and feedback. Whereas PLATO offered teachers an approach to authoring instruction, Logo sought to offer children opportunities to construct their own computer programs. But Logo was more than a computer language.

The expressive form of *turtle geometry* allowed children to explore a rich panoply of outcomes related to the details of their programs. Programs could control the actions of a physical or virtual turtle, by asking it to, for example, move forward. A physical or virtual pen left a trail, thus allowing the children to at once draw a picture and have a trace of whether the commands had been executed as imagined.

As an educational community developed around Logo, its use moved beyond programming towards the development of constrained, playful environments in which students could explore powerful ideas of mathematics and science. These environments were termed "microworlds," and like Einstein's famous *gedanken* (thought) experiments, rendered technical ideas in a form conducive to playful engagement with fundamental ideas. Important principles (Hoyles & Noss, 1993) included: putting learning into children's hands, that is, treating them as *bricoleurs* (tinkerers) and letting them create; seeking newly accessible ways to render powerful ideas in an experience students could interact with; and "no threshold, no ceiling" environments which were initially simple but allowed engagement, over time, with complex endeavors (Abelson & DiSessa, 1986).

Whereas the design target in CAI systems was usually a course of study, the design of microworlds often began by identifying a foundational concept of science or mathematics which students were not reliably learning in a traditional course. Design work included the identification of foundational concepts and working out exactly how to invite and encourage engagement with those ideas, creating a kind of playground in which the learner would be brought back to them time and again. With these playgrounds, modeling was often a fundamental activity: students were invited to use scientific or mathematical constructs to reproduce a familiar phenomenon or experience. For example, students might use the ability of a turtle to move forward and turn in small increments to model a circle as the limit of a regular polygon with increasingly short sides and small turns. Elements that are now often brought into discussion of learning strategies were taken as foundational, in particular, embodied learning and the use of virtual—and physical—manipulatives.

Over the years, there have been hundreds of implementations of microworlds in different areas of endeavor, ranging from music (Bamberger, 1974, 1986) through to chemistry (Schank & Kozma, 2002) and physics (White, 1993). The direction continues in projects such as those reported in DiSessa's *Changing Minds* (2000), which focuses on bringing children into contact with powerful ideas, and has found new life in a variety of intellectual homes: via the Scratch language (http://scratch.mit.edu/), in Media Computation (http://coweb.cc.gatech.edu/mediaComp-teach, Guzdial, 2003), and Storytelling Alice (Kelleher & Pausch, 2007). Other areas of focus include: manifestations of computationally controllable objects (c.f. Hendrix & Eisenberg, 2006; Weller et al., 2008); complex programming environments such as the parallel, distributed environment of NetLogo (Wilensky & Stroup, 2000) and Agent-Sheets (Repenning & Sumner, 1995); and game design (cf. Nemirovsky, 1994); however, some of the most profound, long-lasting, and widespread have been in the area of mathematics education.

The Context of Mathematical Instruction

In the 1980s, the possibility of new ways of engaging students with mathematical ideas began to intersect with a movement towards reform of mathematical curricula. Just as the launch of Sputnik in the 1960s gave rise to "new math," the influential report "A nation at risk: The imperative for educational reform" (Gardner, 1983) incited a wave of thinking about the future of mathematics education. Whereas in the early years of the twentieth century educators sought to enable all students to master shopkeeper arithmetic, now the focus began to shift to algebra for all—a dramatic increase in instructional challenge. Simultaneously, mathematics educators began to question whether educational goals should be limited to computational and symbol manipulation skill and pushed for mathematical attainment to include conceptual understanding and mathematical practices (such as expressing generalities). Presently, this shift continues with newer curriculum standards that emphasize not just skillful and accurate execution of mathematical calculations and procedures but also focusing on conceptual development and enculturation into mathematical practices (e.g., the Common Core State Standards for Mathematics).

This shift in educational goals was supported by emerging mathematics education research, which was grounded in developmental and cognitive science approaches. Unlike instructional research, which tends to ask: "does this or that teaching strategy produce greater test score gains?", the newly emerging body of mathematics education research studied how individual learners build the next stage of mathematical thinking upon ideas and competencies they already had. This research was represented, for example, by the scholarly society "Psychology in Mathematics Education" and interlinked with the policy prerogatives noted above through the agency of an association of mathematics teachers, the National Council of Teachers of Mathematics. In some sense, this scholarship starts from the ur-question of why it is so difficult for so many people to learn mathematical concepts that are quite plain to those who already know them. The kinds of answers provided have to do with uncovering the detailed hidden entailments of mathematical thinking and the aspects of human psychology that make representations work, or, sometimes, not work for particular learners at particular developmental moments.

This is the perspective most strongly represented by the third author of this account. Hegedus had completed his doctoral work investigating the metacognitive behavior of mathematics undergraduates solving single and multi-variable integrals when he joined the project in 2000, and championed continued thought about representational elements.

Dynamic Representations

SimCalc Mathworlds® (www.kaputcenter.umassd.edu/products/software/) constitutes one of a number of technologies for learning that dovetailed with and elaborated the opportunities for reform of mathematics within the context of a pre-existing body of scholarly thought about mathematics education. Other, similar approaches which emerged at roughly the same time include Geometer Sketchpad (Jackiw, 1987–2007) and Cabri Geometre (LaBoarde, 1984–2007). This class of technology eventually became known for its "dynamic representation" approach. Like Logo, dynamic representations enabled learners to be active, playful, constructive, and expressive in a computer-based medium. But unlike Logo, dynamic representations do not focus on programming. Like microworlds, dynamic representations provide an invented, pedagogical environment that is meant to engage students with fundamental ideas of mathematics, rendered in an interactive and dynamic form. Relevant to the emergent development and cognitive psychology of the time, both microworlds and dynamic representations intend to activate students' prior knowledge and, through the activities of exploring and constructing, allow students to build new knowledge. However, whereas microworlds have somewhat more focus on a fanciful context for mathematical ideas, dynamic representations have more focus on providing interactive mathematical notions and representations.

Democratizing Access to Calculus: The Mathematics of Change and Variation

The overall educational purpose of SimCalc was, in Jim Kaput's (its progenitor's) words, to *democratize access to Calculus*. In 1992, when the project that would be SimCalc started, it was clear that the rate of change, co-variation, accumulation, approximation, continuity, and limits were arguably some of the topics that would be most important to children moving forward. Kaput was fond of arguing that whereas "algebra for all" was a necessary advance in educational goals for society in the twentieth century, "calculus for all" would be a necessary advance in the twenty-first century due to the importance of mathematics in understanding and regulating processes of change. Importantly, Kaput conceptualized Calculus not as a course of study taken at the end of a long sequence of mathematical prerequisites, but rather as a strand of mathematical thinking that could develop beginning as early as elementary school and which could enrich classic middle-school topics, such as proportionality. Thus Kaput used the phrase "mathematics of change and variation" (MCV) to break the mindset of Calculus as a specific course, and to focus instead on how the underlying ideas could develop over a decade or more of a student's mathematical development (Kaput & Roschelle, 1998).

At the heart of the SimCalc approach to MCV is the idea of considering rate as the relative change of two quantities (for example, position and time) which could be represented as the slope of a graph or a parameter in an algebraic expression, or a motion or a set of values in a table. Technology provided a technical affordance for realizing these representations in a dynamic interactive form. Pedagogical and curricular research sought to exploit technology to allow a potential restructuring of when mathematical ideas could be explored by young students as well as upper high school students. Introducing a dynamic, technological medium also allowed young children easy access to touch and manipulate mathematical objects, including moving pieces of graphs and watching the resulting changes to the movement of one to linked actors in a simulation. Later on in the evolution of the SimCalc program of research and development, the affordances of classroom networks were incorporated into the integrated software/curriculum suite of resources to enable students to make personal mathematical constructions that could be shared within the classroom and publicly displayed by the teacher in many different configurations. This allowed some researchers to not only investigate the cognitive dimensions of learning the MCV with diverse populations of students but also affective dimensions of engagement and motivation as the participatory nature of the classroom changed (Dalton & Hegedus, 2013).

The aim of this program of design and research, "democratizing access," diverged from the contemporary emphasis on raising test scores, because Kaput sought to introduce students to concepts which were not commonly measured on tests—and to focus on conceptual understanding, whereas most assessments measure procedural skill. It also diverged from an emphasis on preparing students to use modern workplace tools, such as spreadsheets, by focusing more on mathematical insight than on mathematical applications. "Access" did not mean availability or affordability of technologies or textbooks, but rather access to meaningful opportunities to learn. Operationally, "democratizing" meant an emphasis on the design and development of activities for students who would ordinarily be excluded from reaching a traditional Calculus course by deciding "I'm no good at math" or by not achieving suitable grades in prerequisites.

To achieve democratization of access, Kaput was always committed to the idea that technology and curriculum should be, indeed, *had to be*, co-developed to better build on *learner strengths*. In addition, he was always committed to classroom-based education; classrooms are places where all students can have an opportunity to learn (overcoming, for instance, limitations of the resources available in their homes) and where socialization into a mathematical culture can occur. Emphasizing classroom-based education has consequences. First, it means that design must address the situation of having a teacher together with a group of students as well as the situation of the individual learner. Second, it means that (truly) no learner can be left behind.

These braids of thought, stemming from the potential of the computer, the detailed examination of the cognitive bases of mathematical knowledge, and a commitment to classroom-based education, led to a formulation of the SimCalc research project as one which *restructured knowing* through finding points of possible design action where learners' strengths, representational affordances, and a reorganized curriculum provided the opportunity to understand MVC in a new way. Some of this history has been reported, particularly in Roschelle et al. (2008b), which focuses on the research (rather than the design) trajectory of the project and itself draws upon and summarizes diverse earlier sources, including a number of different studies (Kaput, 2001; Kaput et al., 2001; Nemirovsky et al., 1998a; Nickerson et al., 2001; Nemirovsky et al., 1998b; Roschelle et al., 2000).

Three Descriptions of SimCalc Designs

The issue of how the design of SimCalc technologies is described has depended on the context of the description and on the unfolding of projects that have themselves depended on opportunistic factors such as the particulars of novel technologies, shifts in policy concerns, alignments with school districts, teachers, and curricula, funding opportunities, and the developments of thought about pedagogical leverage. Indeed, we prefer to think of it as a representational infrastructure or set of design principles that are, and could be used, in other mathematics software (Hegedus & Moreno-Armella, 2009; Noss & Hoyles, 1996).

Under this rubric, a wide range of functions have been investigated (including new curricular materials available at www.kaputcenter.umassd.edu/products/curriculum_new/).

Nonetheless, in a major 2010 paper reporting the use of SimCalc in three large-scale randomized trials, the technology is described as follows, with five components:

1   Anchoring students' efforts to make sense of conceptually rich mathematics in their experience of familiar motions, which are portrayed as computer animations
2   Engaging students in activities to make and analyze graphs that control animations
3   Introducing piecewise linear functions as models of everyday situations with changing rates
4   Connecting students' mathematical understanding of rate and proportionality across key mathematical representations (algebraic expressions, tables, graphs) and familiar representations (narrative stories and animations of motion)
5   Structuring pedagogy around a cycle that asks students to make predictions, compare their predictions with mathematical reality, and explain any differences.

(Shechtman et al., 2010 p. 839)

These components are explained as follows:

> The SimCalc MathWorlds software provides a "representational infrastructure" (Kaput et al., 2007; Kaput & Roschelle, 1998) that is central to enabling this approach. Most distinctively, the software presents animations of motion. Students can control the motions of animated characters by building and editing mathematical functions in either graphical or algebraic forms. After editing the functions, students can press a play button to see the corresponding animation. Functions can be displayed in algebraic, graphical, and tabular form, and students are often asked to tell stories that correspond to the functions (and animations).... In addition to proportional and linear functions, students and teachers can make piecewise linear functions, which can be used to model familiar situations.
>
> *(Shechtman et al., 2010, pp. 839–840)*

The components were accompanied by a picture (Figure 16.1).

These five definitional elements were largely present in Kaput's (1994) description of what would become SimCalc:

> Imagine a pair of 12-year old students driving a computer-simulated vehicle that provides a windshield view and a carefully linked user- or

SimCalc (1992–Present) **291**

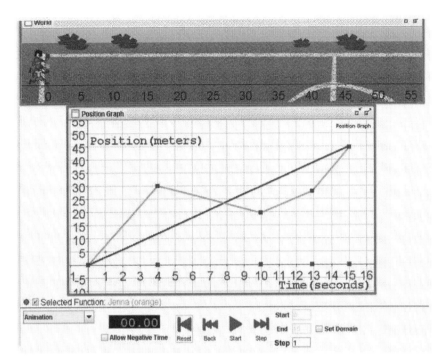

FIGURE 16.1 A picture used to explain a SimCalc Mathworlds microworld in the 2010 article. A position graph is shown related to the simulated situation shown in the "world" portion of the screen. The manipulation and animation functions are set in a window below. Playing the animation causes both the sweeping out of time on the position graph and the animation of the characters in the world. The motion of the character with the orange shirt (and rectangle) is described by the orange line while the motion of the character with the purple shirt (and rectangle) is described by the purple line.

Source: Used with permission.

system-configurable collection of data displays for the dashboard; one set of displays for time, another for velocity, and a third for position. These include sounds for each set (metronome for time, engine pitch for velocity and "echo" when passing roadside objects for position). The dashboard display can include velocity and/or position versus time graphs generated in "real-time" as well as clocks, odometers, tables and so forth. This "MathCars" system is designed to help link the phenomenologically rich everyday experience of motion in a vehicle to more structured and formal representations and to provide exciting and intensely experienced contexts for reasoning about change, accumulation and relations between them.

292 Deborah Tatar et al.

> After some unstructured driving trips, they are now planning to follow a school bus whose (highly variable) velocity has been specified beforehand based on (one-dimensional) velocity data they collected on their own bus trip home the day before.
>
> *(Kaput, 1994, p. 391)*

Aspects of this vision for the design appear in an even earlier picture, as reproduced in Figure 16.2 (Kaput, 1992, p. 540).

The major focus in this view is on authenticity of the motion phenomenon. However, the design focus in the 2010 paper is also mentioned:

> They will also set up and run simulated "ToyCars" on parallel tracks to study relative motion more systematically, describing the motion of each algebraically, confronting such questions as how to describe a later start versus describing a simultaneous start but from different locations.
>
> *(Kaput, 1992, p. 392)*

These two descriptions represent both views of the opportunity space, and perspectives on what constitutes research on learning. In fact, Kaput's (1994)

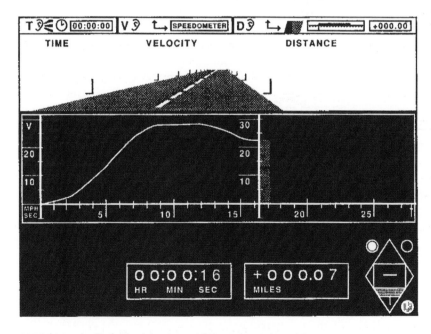

FIGURE 16.2 An Early Envisionment of SimCalc Mathworlds, circa 1992. The "experience" is shown as if through a windshield and the graph shows velocity as it sweeps out over time.

Source: Used with permission, quality as in the original.

article reads like a mathematical proof. It makes arguments for a set of apparently disconnected beliefs and circumstances, taking particular care to unpack the relationship between the child's physical interactions with the world, the child's experience of physical interactions, and the mathematician's formalisms. It then assembles the findings into the vision quoted above. In contrast, the 2010 description is a starting place for exploration of how a particular implementation of "technology + curriculum" fares as it faces the world.

An Important Side-track

Despite the impressive similarities between the 1994 and 2010 presentations, the five definitional elements were *not* obvious at the beginning. Instead, the focus on these five elements evolved and emerged throughout the life of the effort. With hindsight, we can see that the principles are consistent with the earliest designs even if they were not articulated in 1992 or even by 1994.

Kaput was very enthusiastic, in the beginning, about designing features that would engage students' kinesthetic sense, such as the visual sense of the world "zooming by" both sides of the perceptual field. Over time, this design feature was de-emphasized. Likewise, Kaput was interested in supporting motion detectors to measure motion in the physical world and sensors to measure a student's physical motion; these capabilities continued to be supported in the software, but became less important to the classroom experience of most users over time and played a smaller role in design thinking.

On inspection, it might appear that the design process to go from Figure 16.2, the initial vision, to Figure 16.1, the eventual software, was a straightforward elaboration of design principles specified at the onset. This was far from the case. Indeed, as is the case with many educational design processes, the team was distracted by "red herring" design principles which have a nearly ubiquitous presence in public and scholarly discourse about learning technology. Then, as today, "games" were hot, and the team spent much time trying to translate the initial design concept into an educational game. Likewise, there was a belief that students would not pay attention to educational software unless it had the highest quality artwork and animations. In addition, advisors advocated for a rich "narrative" context as necessary to motivate students. Many of these concerns still loom large today as developers design modern software for mathematics learning.

Figure 16.3 illustrates an important path the design team followed for about a year and which turned out to be a dead-end. Figure 16.3 is a screen shot of Alien Elevators, which was the first software designed by the SimCalc project, in 1993 and early 1994. Looking back, Roschelle, one of our authors, said, "what were we thinking?" The two other authors were puzzled by the image: "what is this?" And indeed, the reason this design was abandoned is that students were similarly lost and *not* engaged in productive mathematics. Yet, this design was purposeful, and ultimately led to key insights.

294   Deborah Tatar et al.

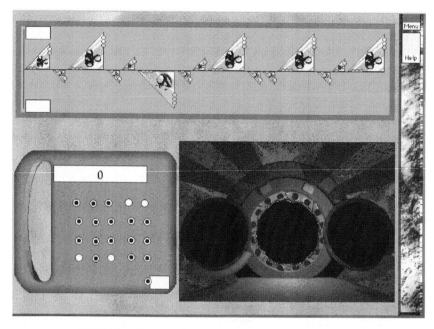

FIGURE 16.3   The "Alien Elevators" 1994 version of SimCalc created an interface that was game-like, based on a narrative, and involved high-quality graphics but which submerged the mathematics. Students were asked to set velocity in one-second increments (bottom left). They could see the alien elevator experience (bottom right). Velocity is shown by the glyphs at the top.

Much work went into an exciting narrative about a journey to a planet where a lost alien society had disappeared, but the elevators were still running, and a mystery had to be resolved. Students would have to learn some mathematics to solve the mystery: on this planet, elevators were controlled not by final destination but rather by setting their velocity in one-second increments. Further, velocity was indicated by a glyph—the strange triangles in the upper portion of the image. Students could experience being "on" the elevator as they traveled the lost alien world to solve the mystery—and the lower right section showed an animation of an elevator door opening and closing like a camera's iris on different floors. The lower left image was a controller which gave access to tools such as more traditional graphs, by which the strange glyphs and the motion of the elevator might be analyzed. Figure 16.4 shows some of these tools in the form of an early design section—these included a velocity graph, a stylized position graph which featured an "elevator" shaft which moved to the right on the horizontal axis with time and a clock.

On reflection, the biggest failure in this design is that the mathematics was obscured by the narrative, game elements, and graphic art. When the SimCalc team

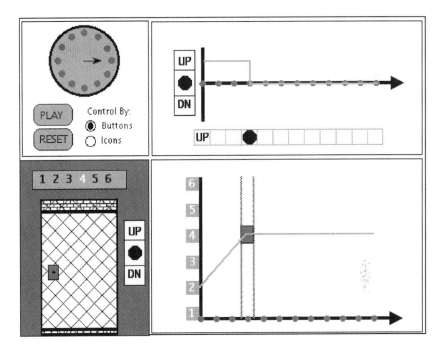

FIGURE 16.4 Controls for the 1994 "Alien Elevator" version of SimCalc included a stylized position graph (bottom right), a velocity graph (top right), a clock, and an elevator. The mathematics was difficult for students to perceive.

turned away from this design thinking, the turn was towards an approach that was deeply mathematical and squarely focused on supports for students to conceptualize mathematics—with a much lighter touch on narrative, gaming, and graphic art.

Enduring Features

Despite the side-track of alien elevators, some key design differences between SimCalc as Kaput first imagined it in 1992 were largely finished by 1997. These changes in SimCalc Mathworlds were realized across five years through a process of considerable design research and included:

- The representation of motion shifted from a first-person ("point of view") perspective to a third-person, flattened perspective. Although the first-person view is experientially compelling, it was hard for students to make connections between distance in a graph and distance in a windshield view.
- The students' opportunity for control shifted from controlling via a gas pedal and brake to controlling by changing the graph itself (as indicated by the

square control points on the graph in Figure 16.1). This followed the realization that by giving students the ability to construct the more mathematical representation (rather than just see it as an output), they could better come to understand what it meant. The output became the movement of the soccer players.
- The nature of the mathematical function changed from a curve to a piecewise linear function. This reflected important growth in understanding about mathematics education. In particular, the project learned that curves were cognitively difficult objects for students to make sense of and that the learning progression could eventually get to curves from piecewise functions by showing how functions made of smaller and smaller pieces could come to approximate curves.
- There is also a noticeable simplification in the number of display elements in the eventual SimCalc Mathworlds design, reflecting the insight that it was essential to focus the learner's attention on a few representations at a time.

There is one contrast between Figures 16.1 and 16.2 that is *not* indicative of a design change: one image shows a velocity graph and the other shows a position graph. SimCalc MathWorlds has always had activities with both velocity and position graphs.

Figures 16.1 and 16.2 present a snapshot of changes; however, the contrast does not adequately explicate the nature of the design. Hence, we now move to a broader overview of the set of SimCalc projects and the design thinking that emerged in them.

Importantly, the *design* principles that constitute the focus of this chapter were complemented by a larger *implementation* principle when SimCalc was introduced into a large number of classrooms between 1997 and 2005. The larger implementation principle is to present teachers with an integrated system of the software, curricular workbooks, and teachers' professional development. The achievement of a stable learning effect when SimCalc is introduced into hundreds of classrooms is importantly *not* due only to software features. Rather, it is also the consequence of carefully designed workbooks that lead teachers and students through a curricular learning progression with the software (including exercises and discussions without the software), and is a consequence of teachers' professional development that encultures teachers into appropriate classroom use of the software.

An Overview of SimCalc Projects

The larger SimCalc project starts from an ideal of improving mathematical teaching and learning, a mechanism, the computer, and a series of perceptions about learning and learners. It developed into a family of projects, each of which explored a facet or aspect of the whole. One history of the effort is given in Roschelle et al. (2008a), with a focus on the process of going from small design studies to larger classroom tests. A graphical timeline appears in Figure 16.5.

SimCalc (1992–Present) **297**

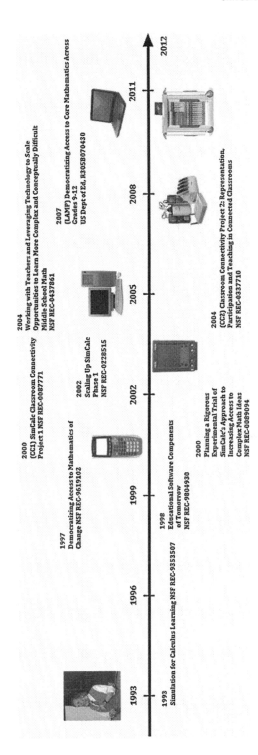

FIGURE 16.5 Timeline of the SimCalc project grants.

Source: Hegedus & Roschelle, 2013. Used with permission.

1992 to 1994: Planning

An initial planning period was concerned with the examination of curriculum, the history of mathematical thought, and a review of the learning sciences. Also during this time, several years were spent conducting the microanalysis of very small numbers of students working with different designs for the representations.

1994 to 1997: First Iteration

The first software design was implemented and then abandoned after less than a year. This design had an overarching narrative concept called "Alien Elevators" and was an extended game in which students would infer rules by which elevators were controlled on an alien planet, where the elevator buttons controlled velocity, not the target floor. This was abandoned because it was found in user testing that the story distracted students from the mathematics and the interface did not yield mathematical insights for students. However, one component of the interface was very productive for students and the project moved forward focused on this element. The element that was retained was a representation of velocity on a graph as a step function, where each step specified a constant velocity for a duration of time.

The work of this time consisted of experiments with a small number of students in a lab, or short teaching experiments in a classroom, each examining how the emerging SimCalc Mathworlds dynamic representations could enable students to develop particular target mathematical understandings.

1997 to 1999: Working with Teachers and Classrooms

This was followed by a second phase, three years spent on curriculum, that involved different educational settings and partners—in Newark, NJ, Syracuse, NY, and San Diego, CA. Notably, sites were chosen to include diverse students who would not ordinarily go on to study Calculus. In addition, tests were conducted with students at different grades, including middle school, high school, and early undergraduate years. At this time—while many of the ideas were beginning to gel but not yet set—there was enough stability to involve teachers and classrooms full of students. However, even after nine years of work and development, measurement of learning outcomes only used research-designed pre-test/post-test assessments, consisting of items as created in response to the special purposes of the particular innovations. These projects resulted in an important diversity of curricular materials, variations of the software, and test questions.

2000 and after: Three Parallel Investigations

At this point, nine years into the project, it split. This split did not reflect a lack of sympathy among project participants, but rather the need to pursue parallel avenues of exploration and therefore to involve people with expertise in those particular areas. There was good reason to believe that the core ideas were solid but it was not clear how they could become widely used. Three avenues were explored: technological, political, and scientific.

Technological Explorations

The technological exploration started from the observation that, although most students had theoretical access to computers, only graphing calculators received widespread, frequent use. Therefore, the research turned to how smaller, less expensive devices could be used to make the key affordances available. The small size of the devices pushed the research to explore distributed, social, networked activities (Hegedus & Kaput, 2003, 2004; Hegedus et al., 2007; Hegedus & Penuel, 2008; Hegedus & Roschelle, 2012; Dalton & Hegedus, 2013; Roschelle et al., 2003; Tatar et al., 2003; Vahey et al., 2004, 2006). Some of this work was supported by Texas Instruments, building on a network infrastructure they were developing and teacher professional development facilities they supported. Work with the graphing calculator was awkward because the screen was small with low resolution and calculator keys had to be repurposed to implement SimCalc Mathworlds functions. Therefore another avenue was also explored: the then novel (and now defunct!) Personal Data Assistant, in particular, Palm Pilot handheld computers. These devices provided infrared beaming, a low-overhead technology nicely suited to classroom communication (Tatar, Roschelle et al., 2003; Vahey et al., 2004, 2006). These projects led to the design of distributed activities that were social and fun but that always drew the student's attention back to important and difficult mathematics.

Political Explorations

The political development had to do with influencing the key state mathematics examinations in Massachusetts. In particular, Kaput's influence over the construction of the high-stakes examinations resulted in a more rational and principled framework. Kaput and Hegedus additionally worked on the construction of SimCalc-based curricula, which they conceived of as a progression throughout middle and high school (www.kaputcenter.umassd.edu/products/curriculum_new/).

Scientific Explorations

The third avenue was scientific demonstration. From 2000 until 2008, culminating in the 2010 paper, the project planned and then conducted a series of large-scale experiments, including randomized trials (Roschelle et al., 2008; Shechtman et al., 2010; Tatar et al., 2008). More than 2000 students, and 150 schools were involved. A pilot plus three different experiments with seventh- and eighth-graders in Texas demonstrated and replicated that SimCalc Mathworlds could produce significant learning gains in important mathematical concepts across a wide range of teaching circumstances.

This level of demonstration was a triumph and should be seen not just as a confirmation of SimCalc Mathworlds itself but also of the design-based research methods used at different scales throughout the early phases of the project. Such methods are necessarily complex, require intense scholarship, and can lead to substantial setbacks, as in the initial implementation; however, they can report real and important learning changes. The success of SimCalc at scale confirms the importance of support for the slow accretion of knowledge about learning and educational change.

Creating the assessments used in these experiments was difficult. It required over $1,000,000 in funding to develop, assessments that were altogether sensitive to the intervention, spoke to teacher and administrator concerns about curriculum, had the right reading and cultural properties, and could be administered within a classroom period. However, none of this development could have happened without pre-existing theories of learning and the roughly 700 test items gleaned from the classroom work over the years (as well as other scholarly studies of algebra learning also primarily supported by the National Science Foundation). The assessments used in these experiments are one example of an element that only worked because of diversity and persistence in the prior work.

The Changing Landscape

In theory, the technological, political, and scientific elements of the project could have been more substantially supplemented by a fourth element: an economic strategy. Indeed, work with Texas Instruments moved in that direction and resulted, in part, in the TI nSpire handheld device. This device does incorporate dynamic representations, particularly for geometry, graphing, and data; however, it stopped short of including SimCalc representations such as motion and editable piecewise graphs. Further, other dynamic representation-based projects, such as The Geometer's Sketchpad, did pursue and succeed as business ventures (for a time); eventually, The Geometer's Sketchpad was undermined by changes in the market and by the availability of a free, open-source clone. Furthermore, at the very time that these projects were attempting to improve and widen instruction in mathematics, policies such as No Child Left Behind (http://www2.ed.gov/nclb/landing.jhtml) were in essence causing teachers and districts to become more risk-averse (Dickey-Kurdziolek & Tatar, 2012). It may well be that economically self-sustaining models of adoption are an unrealistic burden on an intervention aimed at changing so many elements of existing practice at the intimate level of the learning invisible from outside the classroom.

Design Rationale

With this overview of the construction and development of the family of projects up until 2008, we consider the rationale behind, and the implementation of, each element of the 2010 definition. These are the elements that, as the larger project has developed, have become assumptions in research papers. Yet the pedagogic opportunity lies in the details of how these elements are supported by the technologyand understood and utilized in the classroom. These are the elements that each teacher, curriculum designer, assessment creator, and technology designer needs to grapple with.

Anchoring students' efforts to make sense of conceptually rich mathematics in their experience of familiar motions, which are portrayed as computer animations

Kaput approached the ideas that would become SimCalc through historical, curricular and literature analysis. By the end of the 1980s, some kinds of computational environments for learning allowed learners to connect formal algebraic expressions with graphical representations, so that the learner could "follow along." Building on prior work examining mathematical representations, and starting as early as a 1992 publication, Kaput identified the *context of motion* as missing from instruction in Calculus (and algebra).

Although the development of Calculus was historically motivated by the desire to describe motion phenomena, instruction had virtually no relationship to authentic contexts that motivated the work itself. Indeed, often teachers explicitly reject the idea of using motion to introduce algebra or Calculus on the grounds that motion is not mathematics. It is, instead, physics. But motion is not only an academic topic that must be described in formal terms. It is also a universal human experience.

Kaput perceived that integrating familiar aspects of motion into mathematics instruction could benefit students by allowing the redistribution of "sources of structure and action from the mental to the physical realm" (1994, p. 394). However, Kaput's initial thought about how to implement this experience evolved through small group work with children. The elements of realism that featured so vividly in the original description were refined into more strategic and abstracted representations of motion seen in the "world" graphics. Although the earliest work resembled current approaches to games and game-like environments, this was soon dropped. While capturing student interest and engagement is important, and using existing student strengths, such as their experience of the natural world, is crucial, the experiences must not overwhelm or downplay the mathematics to be learned.

The decision to implement motion as animations or depictions in an artificial "world" allowed the scope of inquiry to be simplified to the representation of movement along a line (or, better yet, a number line!). This simplification created a congruence between the portion of motion depicted in the system and what was actually modeled in high school algebra.

Other aspects of the early vision did not make it into the branch of exploration expressed in the 2010 description, albeit for pragmatic rather than pedagogical reasons.[2]

Engaging students in activities to make and analyze graphs that control animations

Using proper notation is a metric of understanding of algebra and Calculus; therefore, use of that notation is usually prioritized in instruction. Yet, arguably, the roots of student understanding lie not in algebra but in the depiction of what is important about the motion phenomena. Graphical representations are less compact than algebraic ones; however, graphs are a more common, everyday representation. For example, one often sees graphs in the newspaper, but hardly ever sees algebra in the newspaper.

In particular, like the motion itself, graphs can be animated over time. Contrast between the depiction of the motion in the "world" and the depiction of the graph helps students learn *how* a graph represents. The graph is an abstraction that, by its nature, draws our attention to certain aspects of motion (change in position over time, change in velocity over time) which we suggest are important.

The context of motion implicitly suggests that time might be an important thing to think about. The everyday description of motion utilizes time. The graphical representation of motion makes time an explicit element. But when we make time an explicit element, we change what we are showing about position, compared to an actual depiction of that motion. Thus, a graph, such as the one in Figure 16.1, does not show a picture of a person going up and down hills but rather a metric of the person's displacement in two dimensions.

This point often seems simple to those who already know algebra, but it is hard to overestimate its importance for large categories of learners. In recent years, research has suggested that people differ in their ability to interpret different kinds of information. Some people, those who prefer linguistic kinds of information, do well with current teaching and learning practices. Others already bring to the project of learning mathematics a tendency to interpret depictions as symbolic. But a subset of students tend to see graphs as pictures (Hegarty & Kozhevnikov, 1999; Kozhevnikov et al., 2005). Even those who are inclined to see graphs as symbolic representations may become confused about the nature of a particular representation.

Engagement with *how a graph represents* was enabled by a core innovation in the SimCalc approach: to *make* and *edit* graphs without having to edit the algebraic notation, and this gave students an easy way into manipulating mathematical representations of motion. Indeed, in the SimCalc approach, students often learn about graphs and tables *before* they encounter algebraic notation. Rather than starting with formal symbolic notations, students' mathematical experiences are gradually formalized.

Animating graphs interacted with design decisions in ways that were not central to the mathematics but that were central to the HCI and pedagogical usability of the system. Drag-and-drop facilities meant that many graphs could be made and their motion consequences easily explored. One key interface element in enabling easy exploration was the implementation of snap-to-grid "hot spots" that allowed students to easily explore integer end-points. This was controversial because it compromised continuity, which is an important mathematical concept. However, pragmatically, trying to make lines do exactly the right thing can be a time-consuming distraction. The downloadable version of SimCalc Mathworlds (www.kaputcenter.umassd.edu/products/software/) allows users to turn off snap-to-grid facilities. Another set of difficult usability issues had to do with the relationship between grabbing and pulling function lines as compared to changing axes or labels in the world's ruler or the Cartesian coordinate plane.

These two elements, namely animation and tying animation to easily manipulated graphical representations, can lead to subtle but important curricular changes. In particular, one place where we lose active cognition among students is in introducing the idea of slope. Most students learn the slope of a line as a calculation of "rise over run," often fixating on the identification of points that make the actual calculation easy. The slope then becomes one calculation among many, a calculation that, for mysterious reasons, is sometimes negative. SimCalc allows the teacher to ground an understanding of slope in a far more sophisticated context, a context in which rate is demonstrated to be instantaneous as it sweeps out, connecting the characters' motions with their positions at a given time. Conceptualizing slope as a description of the relationship between time and position leads towards Calculus without demanding the mastery of algebra and grounds the concept of negative slope as "going backwards."

Another kind of curricular change permitted by SimCalc representations is the more coherent presentation of proportion as a reduced case of rate in which the line just happens to go through 0. Proportion is a major middle-school topic, but is often presented merely as a "calculate the missing quantity" problem, where three numbers are given and the fourth must be calculated using the formula "a/b = c/d." Of course, this formula can be useful in permitting calculations to figure out how much 5 pounds of potatoes will cost if potatoes are $3/2 pounds. However, it is also a mathematical dead-end—it doesn't lead anywhere in further mathematics. SimCalc represents proportion instead as a constant of proportionality, k, in $y = kx$, which is the slope of a line. The analysis of slope as a ratio, $k = y/k$, and a proportional function as a simple case of a linear function, allows a trajectory of mathematical development that continues from middle school through Calculus.

Introducing piecewise linear functions as models of everyday situations with changing rates

Traditional instruction in algebra and Calculus emphasized the definition of a function, and the importance of continuity in the definition of a function. The continuity assumption is key to the ability to calculate inherent in Calculus. But those students who went on to become engineers would go on to use piecewise functions extensively, because many physical systems are best modeled not as one continuous curve but as discontinuous segments that may each be represented as linear (at least well enough for their engineering purposes).

All motion of an object over time is continuous. However, people's experience of motion is not continuous. One of Kaput's major insights from the first iteration was that, by introducing piecewise linear graphs earlier and delaying the introduction of the idea of continuity, many important ideas could be introduced earlier and more effectively into the curriculum to a wider range of students. This notion utilizes the principle of building on existing student strengths, but it is legitimized by engineering practices.

This representation was easy for students to control, by adjusting the height and width of rectangle "chunks" of velocity (where the height was speed, the width was time, and the area represented change-in-position). It also turned out that students could easily understand the area as position change, and this led to interesting mathematical challenges, such as finding different ways to move 6 meters (see Figure 16.6).

Further, the velocity graphs could be related to piecewise position graphs, which were also found to be productive in terms of student insight. Figure 16.7, for example, represents a complex way to get to a final position of 6 meters, but with changing speed and backwards motion.

The introduction and prioritization of graphical experience with piecewise linear models is the cross-cutting computational, pedagogic, and conceptual insight that democratizes access to the math of change and variation. By enabling students to work with piecewise linear functions—that is, functions over a limited domain—we can allow them to explore the descriptive properties of the mathematical language we are introducing first, before showing them that the physical experiences of motion that arise as a consequence of being human are not precisely what Newton was modeling in creating that mathematical language.

A key activity used in conjunction with piecewise linear functions is the "exciting sack race" lesson. This is the more developed form of "driving behind a school bus" from the original concept. The students are given or create one function representing a person who runs a race at a constant speed over some domain (the straight line in Figure 16.1). They then have to create another line, representing a "crazy" race—like a sack race—putting together functions piecewise on the graph. The only rules are that the race must start at time = 0 and end in a tie.

SimCalc (1992–Present) **305**

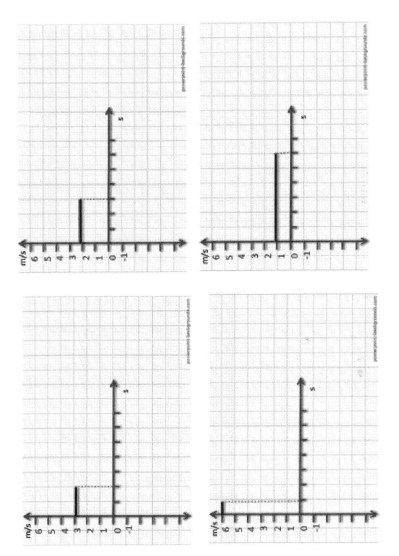

FIGURE 16.6 Changes in velocity: different ways to move six meters.

306 Deborah Tatar et al.

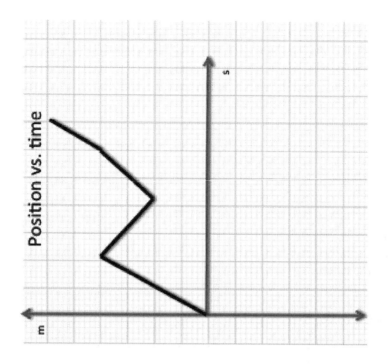

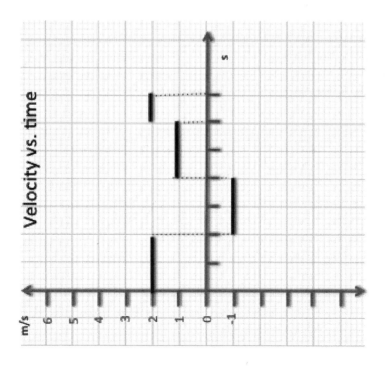

FIGURE 16.7 Piecewise graphs are easier for children to understand than continuous ones.

Subsequently, students are asked to write (in words) the story of the race. Often these stories are on the order of "Jane started really fast, but then she realized that she had forgotten her sunglasses so she ran back to the starting line to get them, but by then she was so exhausted that she couldn't run as fast, so she moved along, but she started staggering and being confused and sometimes went backwards until she finally stopped for a while. That gave her a rest, so she finished really quickly." Some or all students read their stories aloud while the class look at their graphs. Sometimes, teachers ask students to exchange these stories, and ask the new person to draw the function line from just the story. Then the students compare the original and the new lines. This is usually fun, but also motivates the future use of more precise, specialized mathematical language.

In particular, by starting with graphs as compared to algebraic expressions, by tying those graphs to motion phenomenon and finally by allowing the graphs and the motion to model complex motion phenomenon, student learning can be grounded in the desire to represent tractable and interesting problems. This enables complex material to be taught significantly earlier in the curriculum, and indeed elements of the core idea in SimCalc have been taught as early as fifth-grade (9–10 years old).

Both the inclusion of motion phenomenon in mathematics and the emphasis on animating graphs allows changes to the curriculum and changes in emphasis within existing curricula. However, the introduction of piecewise linear functions requires a shift in thought about the core material taught in Calculus. The graphical, piecewise approach *motivates* the more succinct expressions found in algebra and Calculus.

Connecting students' mathematical understanding of rate and proportionality across key mathematical representations (algebraic expressions, tables, graphs) and familiar representations (narrative stories and animations of motion)

SimCalc turns algebra upside down by introducing piecewise functions early and also by introducing graphical interpretations of rate and proportionality, and allowing grounded explorations of slope. Graphical understandings are important in their own right but they are also important in two other ways: as a pathway to other (algebraic) understandings and as a pathway towards understanding the system that compromises the mathematics of change and variation. Each kind of representation—computer models of the "world," graphs, tables, and algebraic expressions, even word-based stories—emphasizes different aspects of the system, some of which are more usefully mathematical. Exercises that ask students to move across different representations develop fluidity and familiarity.

One could say that SimCalc projects a different image of what it means to "know" algebra. In a traditional symbolic approach, knowing algebra is often tantamount to knowing the grammatical transformation rules that correctly rewrite one expression into another form. SimCalc still honors this as important but aligns with an image of "knowing" which has to do with connections among representations. In this view, "knowing" a concept like rate means being able to trace coherently the connections of the concept in different forms—to be able to see rate as an experienced speed, a slope of a graph, covariation in a table of number pairs, and in a symbolic form. For students to build this connected sense of "knowing" algebra, they need tools which help them make the connections. SimCalc is squarely aimed at this connected epistemology.

One of the design challenges associated with this epistemology is that students cannot reasonably make all connections, all at once. Thus, connections among representations must be introduced gradually, which corresponds to giving students access to different visual representations only as the master prior representations. In the early versions of SimCalc Mathworlds, this was handled by developing generic and powerful software which could show all possible representational forms but configuring the software in saved documents. Teachers and students could then load documents in a sequence corresponding to the learning progression in a curricular workbook. More recently, the application/documents approach has been superseded by cloud-based solutions which deliver variant representations to students through activities arranged in a playlist.

Structuring pedagogy around a cycle that asks students to make predictions, compare their predictions with mathematical reality, and explain any differences

This concept was always inherent in SimCalc Mathworlds in that the point draws students' attention to aspects of the world and models they might otherwise overlook. However, the idea of an explicit cycle of comparative prediction centered on the problem at hand developed slowly over time, and in conjunction with other, related theorizing. One highly related pedagogical move is articulated by Schwartz and Bransford (Bransford & Schwartz, 1999; Schwartz & Bransford, 1998) as contrasting cases. The chief idea is that the designer or teacher creates a situation that makes the problem that will eventually be solved in the lesson clear before offering the solution.

The original conception of SimCalc was that the children would explore. Enabling exploration is still a key principle. However, exploration by itself does not necessarily lead to learning—for example, students may get to "solution states" for a particular challenge by exploration but may not know how they got there. The predict–compare–explain cycle is meant to engage students in overt planning and reflection, with an eye towards developing stable explanations of the mathematical representations they are using. Further, the cycle plays into conventional classroom structures, where teachers lead discourse and ask students to make predictions and give explanations as a way to check for and cultivate desired understandings. The commitment to classroom-based instruction means that the technology and related curriculum must respond to the teacher's need to ensure that certain material is encountered.

The predict–compare–explain cycle may be used in whole-class activities. In addition, SimCalc is often used with worksheets that ask students, as individuals or in small groups, to engage in specific activities and record the history of their interaction with the system and the lesson. The cycle is a generally beneficial practice that particularly helps ensure that the student thinks about and processes what she or he is experiencing.

The development and exploration of this principle is a design response of the SimCalc project to the problem of enabling both structured progress and exploration. It is a design response implemented in curriculum and use practices rather than in the technology itself. It is thus aligned with some research on classroom orchestration (Dillenbourg & Jermann, 2010; Dillenbourg et al., 2011), but differs from responses that implement process in the technology itself via scripts and successive disclosure of information (Diziol et al., 2007; Fischer et al., 2007).

Future Exploration

The five elements of the 2010 description and the associated practices are key and enduring pedagogical contributions of the SimCalc project. However, a number of issues have fallen by the wayside, not through any lack of merit.

1. Physically embodied algebra learning. SimCalc long anticipated the importance of embodiment in learning, but with the arrival of the DYI movement, including Raspberry PIs, Arduinos, and really inexpensive sensors and actuators, new opportunities are cropping up that have a chance of having an impact in real K-12 classrooms.
2. Encompassing curriculum. When Jim Kaput passed away suddenly in 2005, he and Stephen Hegedus were in the process of creating an ambitious curriculum that reconceptualized the mathematics of change and variation from sixth- to twelfth-grade. This project was pursued by Hegedus and has to some extent been picked up and continued in the context projects housed at Roschelle's Center for Technology and Learning but suffers from the lack of Kaput's single-minded focus.
3. Restriction of curricular scope. In order to encourage teachers and districts to use SimCalc, exploration has focused primarily on a high-impact setting: that of algebra learning. Algebra is indeed very important. It is the gateway course into four-year colleges in the United States. Enabling children to learn algebra and learn it well is therefore a social justice issue that transcends other aspects of education. But Kaput's vision started with the phrase "democratizing access to the mathematics of change and variation." The project of

creating a development sequence focused on this mathematics that would grow from middle school through college is as yet not complete.

Conclusion: Dynamic Representations and the Problem of Wicked Problems

The fundamental advance in the SimCalc line of work has been to develop a principled design of a dynamic representation system for learning an important and difficult area of mathematics, to conduct research deeply interconnecting that design with cognitive, developmental and pedagogical knowledge bases, and to further expand the work to educational evaluations that show the learning gains achievable in diverse populations at the scale of hundreds of schools and thousands of students. Further, throughout the course of doing this work, the team have been reflective about refining their account of the key principles in the design.

The design story is thus a story of progress, but also a story of how complex the realization of the deep, transformative potential of technology in mathematics learning is. Technology is not a singular, causal factor in promoting learning and design of successful learning experiences but involves interweaving multiple concerns and levels of design.

In his one and only paper, Berkeley architecture professor Horst Rittel (Rittel & Webber, 1973) advanced the idea of the *wicked problem* in design. Wicked problems exist in contrast to *tame problems*. Tame problems (1) have single-valenced solutions, and (2) require only that a person figure the solution out. Wicked problems do not necessarily have solutions. Furthermore, wicked problems are such that the exact formulation of the problem is tied to the types and ranges of solutions we consider.

One lesson from the SimCalc project is that important problems in education are wicked problems (Tatar, 2007). They must simultaneously determine the utility of technology, whose own properties constitute wicked problems, in relationship to curriculum that may be designed in many different ways for promoting learning—which itself remains ultimately mysterious—in the tremendously complex environment of classrooms and schools. To begin to do this, and to keep the difficult exploration going, requires not just devotion and wide-ranging expertise but the garnering of funding from sources with different requirements, expertise in the management of teams, and the ability to focus on the whole and the parts at the same time.

In the end, diffusion of innovation is not simple either. Deeply accepting Kaput's premise of representation change means sometimes *not* addressing today's curricular expectations and end-of-the-year examinations directly—but can result in changing the sequence of learning, so that learning accomplishments occur in different years and time frames than what is conventionally expected. It may also include changing the expected outcomes, which, after curricular changes, may not be fully measured by existing examinations. Kaput aimed his designs at addressing long-term societal change, which can mean that the designs do not tackle short-term desires to increase today's test scores fully—and can result in slow adoption.

And yet, historically we are clearly in the midst of a transformation in what people need to know and be able to do to fully participate in an information age economy. Designs that democratize access to ways of thinking and reasoning that have long-term societal value, such as the ability to reason mathematically about change, have a likelihood of long-term societal impact. The opportunity to design effective dynamic representations—representations which express mathematical meaning through interactive, linked, time-based properties and give a wider range of people the opportunity to learn and master corresponding ways of reasoning mathematically—is a wicked design problem worth solving.

Acknowledgments

Thank you to all the people over many years who have worked on the SimCalc project formally and informally. Thanks to NSF for support: REC-1543022.

Notes

1. We use "SimCalc" to refer to the project and SimCalc Mathworlds® to refer to the implementation.
2. For example, a branch of pedagogical exploration considered collecting real data using motion detectors (ultrasound sensors from cameras), but did not become part of the mainstream project, because it would have introduced another object for schools to purchase. Yet, the exploration of physically embodied phenomena and varieties of mathematical notations, and the use of hybrid physical/cybernetic devices embodying dynamical systems, continued and continue (Brady, C. (2013). "Perspectives in motion." Unpublished doctoral dissertation, University of Massachusetts, Dartmouth, MA).

References

Abelson, H., & DiSessa, A. (1986) *Turtle geometry*. Cambridge, MA: MIT Press.
Bamberger, J. (1974). *Progress report: Logo music project*. Cambridge, MA: Massachusetts Institute of Technology, AI Lab.
Bamberger, J. (1986). *Music logo*. Cambridge, MA: Terrapin Inc.
Bransford, J. D., & Schwartz, D. L. (1999). Rethinking transfer: A simple proposal with multiple implications. *Review of Research in Education*, 24(1), 61–100.
Dalton, S., & Hegedus, S. (2013). Learning and participation in high school classrooms. In S. Hegedus & J. Roschelle (Eds.), *The SimCalc vision and contributions: Democratizing access to important mathematics* (pp. 245–166). Dordrecht, NL: Springer.
Dickey-Kurdziolek, M., and Tatar, D. (2012). "They need to be solid in standard skills first": How standards can become the upper bound. In S. Hegedus & J. Roschelle (Eds.), *The SimCalc vision and contributions: Democratizing access to important mathematics* (pp. 299–318). Dordrecht, NL: Springer.

Dillenbourg, P., & Jermann, P. (2010). Technology for classroom orchestration. In M. S. Khine & I. Saleh (Eds.), *New science of learning* (pp. 525–552). New York: Springer.

Dillenbourg, P., Zufferey, G., Alavi, H., Jermann, P., Do-Lenh, S., Bonnard, Q., ... & Kaplan, F. (2011). Classroom orchestration: The third circle of usability. In *Proceedings of Computer-Supported Collaborative Learning* (pp. 510–517). International Society of the Learning Sciences.

DiSessa, A. A. (1991). An overview of Boxer. *Journal of Mathematical Behavior*, *10*(1), 3–15.

DiSessa, A. (2000). *Changing minds*. Cambridge, MA: MIT Press.

DiSessa, A. A., & Abelson, H. (1986). Boxer: A reconstructible computational medium. *Communications of the ACM*, *29*(9), 859–868.

Diziol, D., Rummel, N., Spada, H., & McLaren, B. M. (2007). Promoting learning in mathematics: Script support for collaborative problem solving with the Cognitive Tutor Algebra. In *Proceedings of the Conference on Computer-Supported Collaborative Learning*. Retrieved from http://repository.cmu.edu/cgi/viewcontent.cgi?article=1139&context=hcii.

Drijvers, P. (2012, July). Digital technology in mathematics education: Why it works (or doesn't). Paper presented at the *12th International Congress on Mathematics Education*, Seoul, Korea.

Fischer, F., Kollar, I., Mandl, H., & Haake, J. M. (2007). *Scripting computer-supported collaborative learning: Cognitive, computational and educational perspectives* (Vol. 6). Dordrecht, NL: Springer.

Gardner, D. P. (1983). *A nation at risk*. Washington, DC: The National Commission on Excellence in Education, US Department of Education.

Guzdial, M. (2003, June). A media computation course for non-majors. *ACM SIGCSE Bulletin*, *35*(3), 104–108.

Hammon, A. L. (1972). Computer-assisted instruction: Two major demonstrations. *Science*, *176*(4039), 1110–1112. Retrieved from http://eric.ed.gov/?id=EJ060645.

Hegarty, M., & Kozhevnikov, M. (1999). Types of visual–spatial representations and mathematical problem solving. *Journal of Educational Psychology*, *91*(4), 684.

Hegedus, S., & Kaput, J. (2003). Exciting new opportunities to make mathematics an expressive classroom activity using newly emerging connectivity technology. In N. A. Pateman, B. J. Dougherty, & J. Zilliox (Eds.), *Proceedings of the 27th Conference of the International Group for the Psychology of Mathematics Education held jointly with the 25th Conference of the North American Chapter of the International Group for the Psychology of Mathematics Education* (Vol. 1, pp. 293). Honolulu, HI: College of Education, University of Hawaii.

Hegedus, S., & Kaput, J. (2004). An introduction to the profound potential of connected algebra activities: Issues of representation, engagement and pedagogy. *Proceedings of the 28th Conference of the International Group for the Psychology of Mathematics Education* (Vol. 3, pp. 129–136). Bergen, NO.

Hegedus, S., & Moreno-Armella, L. (2009). Intersecting representation and communication infrastructures. *ZDM: The International Journal on Mathematics Education: Transforming Mathematics Education through the Use of Dynamic Mathematics Technologies*, *41*(4), 399–412.

Hegedus, S., & Penuel, W. (2008). Studying new forms of participation and classroom identity in mathematics classrooms with integrated communication and representational infrastructures. *Educational Studies in Mathematics*, *68*(2), 171–184.

Hegedus, S. J., & Roschelle, J. (2012). Highly adaptive, interactive instruction: Insights for the networked classroom. In C. Dede & J. Richards (Eds.), *Digital teaching platforms* (pp. 103–115). New York: Teachers College Press.

Hegedus, S., & Roschelle, J. (Eds.) (2013). *Democratizing access to important mathematics through dynamic representations: Contributions and visions from the SimCalc research program*. New York: Springer.

Hegedus, S., Kaput, J., & Lesh, R. (2007). Technology becoming infrastructural in mathematics education. In R. Lesh, E. Hamilton, & J. Kaput (Eds.), *Foundations for the future in mathematics and science* (pp. 172–192). Mahwah, NJ: Lawrence Erlbaum Associates.

Hendrix, S. L., & Eisenberg, M. (2006). Computer-assisted pop-up design for children: Computationally enriched paper engineering. *Advanced Technology for Learning, 3*(2), 119–127.

Hoyles, C., & Noss, R. (1993). Deconstructing microworlds. In D. L. Ferguson (Ed.), *Advanced educational technologies for mathematics and science, NATO ASI Series* (Vol. 107, pp. 415–438). New York: Springer.

Jackiw, N. (1987–2007). *Geometer's Sketchpad®* [Software]. Emeryville, CA: Key Curriculum Press.

Kaput, J. (1992). Technology and mathematics education. In D. Grouws (Ed.), *Handbook on research in mathematics teaching and learning* (pp. 515–556). New York: Macmillan.

Kaput, J. (1994). Democratizing access to Calculus: New routes using old routes. In A. Schoenfeld (Ed.), *Mathematical thinking and problem solving* (pp. 77–156). Hillsdale, NJ: Lawrence Erlbaum Associates.

Kaput, J. (2001). Changing representational infrastructures changes most everything: The case of SimCalc algebra, and Calculus. In *Proceedings of the NAS Symposium on Improving Learning with Informational Technology.* Washington, DC.

Kaput, J., & Roschelle, J. (1998). The mathematics of change and variation from a millennial perspective: New content, new context. In C. Hoyles, C. Morgan, & G. Woodhouse (Eds.), *Rethinking the mathematics curriculum* (pp. 155–170). London: Falmer Press.

Kaput, J., & Schorr, R. (2008). The case of SimCalc, algebra, and Calculus. In G. W. Blume & M. K. Heid (Eds.), *Research on technology and the teaching and learning of mathematics: Cases and perspectives* (Vol. 2). Charlotte, NC: Information Age Publishing.

Kaput, J., Noss, R., & Hoyles, C. (2002). Developing new notations for a learnable mathematics in the computational era. In L. D. Church (ed.), *Handbook of international research in mathematics education* (pp. 51–75). Mahwah, NJ: Lawrence Erlbaum Associates.

Kelleher, C., & Pausch, R. (2007). Using storytelling to motivate programming. *Communications of the ACM, 50*(7), 58–64.

Kozhevnikov, M., Kosslyn, S., & Shephard, J. (2005). Spatial versus object visualizers: A new characterization of visual cognitive style. *Memory & Cognition, 33*(4), 710–726.

Laborde, J-M. (1984–2007). *Cabri-Geometry™* [Software]. Grenoble, FR: CabriLog.

Nemirovsky, R. (1994). On ways of symbolizing: The case of Laura and the Velocity sign. *The Journal of Mathematical Behavior, 13*(4), 389–422.

Nemirovsky, R., Tierney, C., & Wright, T. (1998a). Body motion and graphing. *Cognition and Instruction, 16*(2), 119–172.

Nemirovsky, R., Kaput, J., & Roschelle, J. (1998b). Enlarging mathematical activity from modeling phenomena to generating phenomena. In *Proceedings of the 22nd Psychology of Mathematics Education Conference.*

Nemirovsky, R., Borba, M., Dimattia, C., Arzarello, F., Robutti, O., Schnepp, M., & Scheffer, N. F. (2004). PME Special Issue: Bodily activity and imagination in mathematics learning. *Educational Studies in Mathematics, 57*(3), 303–321.

Nickerson, S. D., Nydam, C., & Bowers, J. S. (2001). Linking algebraic concepts and contexts: Every picture tells a story. *Mathematics Teaching in the Middle School, 6*(2), 92–98.

Noss, R., & Hoyles, C. (1996). *Windows on mathematical meanings: Learning cultures and computers.* Dordrecht, NL: Kluwer Academic Publishers.

Papert, S. (1980). *Mindstorms.* New York: Basic Books.

Repenning, A., & Sumner, T. (1995). Agentsheets: A medium for creating domain-oriented visual languages. *Computer, 28*(3), 17–25.

Rittel, H. W., & Webber, M. M. (1973). Dilemmas in a general theory of planning. *Policy Sciences, 4*(2), 155–169.

Roschelle, J., Kaput, J., & Stroup, W. (2000). SimCalc: Accelerating students' engagement with the mathematics of change. In M. Jacobson & R. Kozma (Eds.), *Educational technology and mathematics and science for the 21st century* (pp. 47–75). Mahwah, NJ: Lawrence Erlbaum Associates.

Roschelle, J., Tatar, D., & Kaput, J. (2008a). Getting to scale with innovations that deeply restructure how students come to know mathematics. In A. E. Kelly, R. Lesh, & J. Y. Baek (Eds.), *Handbook of design research methods in education* (pp. 369–395). New York: Routledge.

Roschelle, J., Tatar, D., Shechtman, N., & Knudsen, J. (2008b). The role of scaling up research in designing for and evaluating robustness. *Educational Studies in Mathematics*, Special Issue on Democratizing Access to Mathematics through Technology: Issues of Design, Theory and Implementation—In Memory of James Kaput (S. Hegedus & R. Lesh, Eds.), *68*(2), 149–170.

Roschelle, J., Vahey, P., Tatar, D., Kaput, J., & Hegedus, S. J. (2003). Five key considerations for networking in a handheld-based mathematics classroom. In N. A. Pateman, B. J. Dougherty, & J. T. Zilliox (Eds.), *Proceedings of the 2003 Joint Meeting of PME and PMENA* (Vol. 4, pp. 71–78). Honolulu, HI: University of Hawaii.

Schank, P., & Kozma, R. (2002). Learning chemistry through the use of a representation-based knowledge building environment. *Journal of Computers in Mathematics and Science Teaching, 21*(3), 253–279.

Shechtman, N., Roschelle, J., Tatar, D., Hegedus, S., Hopkins, B., Empson, S., Knudsen, J., & Gallagher, L. (2010). Integration of teacher training, curriculum and technology for advancing middle school mathematics: Three large-scale studies. *American Educational Research Journal, 47*(4), 833–878.

Schwartz, D. L., & Bransford, J. D. (1998). A time for telling. *Cognition and Instruction, 16*(4), 475–522.

Tatar, D. (2007). The design tensions framework. *Journal of Human–Computer Interaction, 22*(4), 413–451.

Tatar, D., Roschelle, J., Knudsen, J., Shechtman, N., Kaput, J., & Hopkins, B. (2008). Scaling up innovative technology-based math. *Journal of the Learning Sciences, 17*(2), 248–286.

Tatar, D., Roschelle, J., Vahey, P., & Penuel, W. (2003). Handhelds go to school. *IEEE Computer, 36*(9), 30–37.

Vahey, P., Tatar, D., & Roschelle, J. (2004). Leveraging handhelds to increase student learning: Engaging middle school students with the mathematics of change. In *Proceedings of the Sixth International Conference of the Learning Sciences* (pp. 553–560). Los Angeles, CA.

Vahey, P., Tatar, D., & Roschelle, J. (2006). Using handheld technology to move between the private and public in the classroom. In M. A. van't Hooft & K. Swan (Eds.), *Ubiquitous computing: Invisible technology, visible impact* (pp. 187–210). Mahwah, NJ: Lawrence Erlbaum Associates.

Weller, M. P., Do, E. Y-L., & Gross, M. D. (2008). Posey: Instrumenting a poseable hub and strut construction toy. In *Proceedings of Tangible and Embedded Interaction* (pp. 39–46). Bonn, DE.

White, B. Y. (1993). ThinkerTools: Causal models, conceptual change, and science education. *Cognition and Instruction, 10*(1), 1–100.

Wilensky, U., & Stroup, W. (2000). Networked gridlock: Students enacting complex dynamic phenomena with the Hubnet architecture. In *Proceedings of The Fourth Annual International Conference of the Learning Sciences*. Ann Arbor, MI.

17

USING ANALYTICS FOR ACTIVITY AWARENESS IN LEARNING SYSTEMS (2003-2013)

James M. Laffey, Christopher Amelung, and Sean Goggins

History and Perspective

We write this design case to share our experience of designing a system in a university context, which may resonate with many university-based researchers who design pedagogical innovations. The Context-aware Activity Notification System (CANS) was developed over time with the contributions of many colleagues and students. As work at a university, our project began with an integration of academic and practical concerns and was fired along by data and experience which led to dissertation work and eventual external support through a grant. CANS has continued forward as an example and conceptual inspiration for new work on online learning systems. We hope our design experience can help position other researchers/designers who are on the pathway to envisioning and advancing new ways of enabling online learning. CANS is software that augments a learning management system by identifying social behavior, such as when one student reads the discussion post of another, and provides a representation in the interface to help students be aware of such social activity at times and places where such awareness seems appropriate. Quite frankly, as educators who used CANS in our teaching, we miss the activity awareness and social nature of online teaching enabled by CANS and look for next-generation systems that can empower context-aware activity notification in online learning.

As with many stories and designs, CANS began serendipitously. In 1999, we began work on Shadow Networkspace (Laffey & Musser, 2000, 2006; Laffey et al., 2003) that we envisioned as an open source learning management system (LMS) for K-12 schools to match the capabilities that systems, such as WebCT, were beginning to provide to higher education. Along with our goal of developing an open source LMS-type system for K-12, we were developing an interest in social computing (Laffey et al., 2003) and sought ways of making the experience of learning in an LMS more social and engaging. To marry our growing appreciation of the power of social computing with our efforts to develop Shadow, we implemented an Activity Monitor. The Activity Monitor was developed to support social navigation (Laffey & Amelung, 2007; Laffey et al., 2003, 2006). Dourish and Bellotti (1992) defined this form of activity awareness as "an understanding of the activities of others, which provides a context for your own activity" (p. 107). The Activity Monitor appeared on the main interface of Shadow, listing and creating links to the most recent activities in the system, such as posting to the discussion board and uploading a file (Figure 17.1).

As we developed and tested the system, we began to use it in our own online teaching. Almost immediately we, and our students, noticed that the information and functionality of the Activity Monitor was a really interesting part of the learning environment. We nearly always looked to see what had happened and frequently used the links as a way to navigate the course. We recognized that the Activity Monitor met our expectations for social navigation because we could easily follow in the footsteps of others to see what had been produced and to take us to where the action was. In addition, it also created a sense of presence with others in that we could see the social context of our work and workplace by not

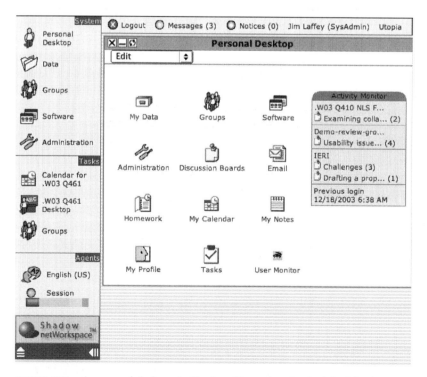

FIGURE 17.1 A personal desktop in Shadow illustrating the Activity Monitor.

only seeing the products of others but also by seeing and experiencing the process of others working. We were eager to have more of this! As we began to envision how the Activity Monitor could be refined and more richly support the social nature of learning in Shadow, we also recognized that the initial implementation would need redesign and reimplementation. Fortunately, we had a doctoral student nearby ready to begin work on his dissertation to take up the challenge of meeting our new vision for activity awareness and social navigation.

The following section is written by Chris Amelung and describes the design work he led as he advanced towards his dissertation and created CANS. This work included moving from our implementation of Shadow, to using the Sakai LMS in our own teaching and the migration of CANS from Shadow to Sakai. Following Chris's implementation and pilot testing we wrote a proposal to the U.S. Department of Education's Fund for the Improvement of Post Secondary Education (FIPSE) and received funding in 2006 to advance CANS. The third section of this article will describe the design work and evolving conceptualization of activity awareness in online learning afforded through the FIPSE funding. In 2013, we shut down CANS because we could not maintain compatibility with new versions of Sakai, and we did not have the resources to address bugs in the user-facing CANS tools which were a major outcome of the FIPSE work. The final section of the chapter is forward-looking in discussing the reimplementation of the CANS design to map to newer forms of LMS and to additional conceptualizations of activity awareness in the context of learning analytics.

Designing CANS

As mentioned in the previous section, with the integration and use of the Activity Monitor in our LMS, we had experienced a hands-on introduction to the potential of awareness information in online learning. This introduction went beyond reading and writing about social learning theory. We actually experienced the benefits and had data to support future work. We saw that our early work in Shadow and with the Activity Monitor positioned us well to advance how we did online learning and how we could learn more about the social nature of this form of learning. Unfortunately, our homegrown LMS was approaching the end of its life cycle and the architecture of our Activity Monitor system needed substantial re-implementation. We could not simply build on what we already had. We needed to start from the ground level and build a new framework on which we could base our next incarnation of social computing in online learning.

Activity Monitor Limitations

Before discussing the work that went into CANS, it is worthwhile briefly explaining why the Activity Monitor needed to be redesigned. The fundamental problem with our activity monitoring and reporting system was that it was too tightly coupled with the LMS. In retrospect, it is easy to see why we ended up this way—we were the authors of our own LMS. We were literally building and evolving Shadow as we were building the Activity Monitor, so it was natural for us to build the Activity Monitor within the LMS. The negative impacts of this design process manifested itself in two ways.

The life expectancy of the Activity Monitor was wholly dependent on the future of the LMS. The Activity Monitor could not exist without Shadow.

The usage of one system inversely affected the performance and effectiveness of the other.

The first point is simple. When designing a new system or feature, such as an Activity Monitor that has the potential for long-term growth and expansion beyond the initial host environment, one should not design the fate of the monitoring system around the future of the host environment.

On the second point, we found in our design of the Activity Monitor that, as activity within Shadow increased, more and more computing power was required to generate the activity notifications. Because these two systems were reliant on the same processing power, the notification generation process began to negatively affect the use of the LMS. Page load times slowed to a crawl and the system became unusable at a modest level of activity. This was certainly not the experience we were designing for!

Influences on the Design

In 2003, I began work on my doctoral dissertation. The purpose of the study was to advance a theoretical framework for development that could be used by programmers to integrate activity notifications into existing computer-supported collaborative environments (CSCE) (Amelung, 2005).

In addition to drawing from our own experiences with the Activity Monitor in Shadow, this research leaned heavily on previous research and existing activity notification design work.

By far the most influential work guiding the design of this new theoretical Framework for Notification was Geraldine Fitzpatrick's past work on the Locales Framework (Fitzpatrick, 1998). The Locales Framework is based on Strauss's Theory of Action, Vygotsky's Activity Theory, and the experience of Fitzpatrick's team on the development and use of their own activity notification system. Through the five aspects of the Locales Framework, Fitzpatrick championed the importance of realizing how the interaction of users occurs within social worlds and users' actions continuously evolve over time because they are influenced by the actions of others (Fitzpatrick, 1998).

Paul Dourish's concept of "embodied interaction" was another great influencer on the design of the Framework for Notification and, consequently, the design of CANS. Dourish (2001) defined embodied interaction as "the creation, manipulation, and sharing of meaning through engaged interaction with artifacts" (p. 126).

In addition to insights provided by Fitzpatrick and Dourish, two existing activity notification systems directly influenced the design of the Framework for Notification and, consequently, the architecture of CANS.

iScent, the InterSubjective Collaborative Event Environment, was built by its authors to be an extremely flexible system through its well-designed distributive architecture (Anderson & Bouvin, 2000). While I did not replicate the extent of iScent's extremely distributed nature for CANS, this system did provide the inspiration and leadership required to decouple CANS from the LMS.

Groove, a desktop notification system built by the founder of Lotus Notes Ray Ozzie, provided the design guidance needed to decouple CANS from the browser and thus gave us the ability to provide activity notifications through any network-enabled device.

Principles of the Framework for Notification

The principles of the Framework for Notification are: Social Context, Awareness in Context, Activity Discovery, Trends in Activity, Meaning of Activity, and Notification Customization (Table 17.1).

The foundational principle behind this Framework is the social context. The social context is "the socially constructed place for user actions and interactions defined by current membership, the collective goals of individuals, recent activity, and the communicative affordances of the technology" (Amelung, 2005, p. 45). The remaining principles of the Framework articulate how aspects of social

TABLE 17.1 The Principles of the Framework for Notification

Principle	Description
Social context	The place where user actions and interactions occur. Social context partially determines the salience of awareness information, the collective goals of individuals, and the recent activity in the context.
Awareness in context	Deliver notifications to users when the notification is relevant to the user's social context.
Activity discovery	Allow the discovery of activity outside the user's current context to promote the formation of new social contexts.
Trends in activity	Maintain activity and notification histories to determine the impact notifications have on user actions and interactions. Trajectory of activity partially determines the salience of awareness information.
Meaning of activity	Provide mechanisms for users to interpret and construct meaning from the activity occurring in a context.
Notification customization	Provide notification customization so the user has the final decision on the notifications received.

Source: Amelung, 2005.

action and information about that action moderate this foundational principle. Details about those principles and the Framework can be found in Amelung (2005, pp. 48–52, and see 2007).

The Framework's Influence on CANS

During the dissertation work, the Framework was tested and evolved through 11 iterations of CANS. The final design of CANS, and how it relates to the Framework for Notification, is presented in Figure 17.2.

After reflection on the types of changes and trajectory of development through the 11 iterations of the design, we have identified some key influences the Framework had on CANS. First, the decision for when a notification should be shared with the user must be based on the user's current social context. This principle helps the designer of future systems keep the focus on the user's current point of view and needs. Second, the Activity Discovery principle guides the developer to realize that even though the current social context has priority for the user, there

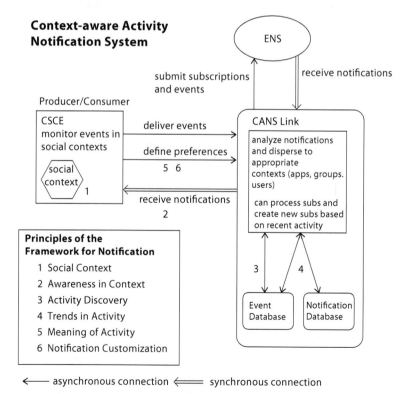

FIGURE 17.2 Framework for Notification and CANS.

Source: Amelung, 2005, p. 101.

are activities and conditions that warrant interruption. These notifications should not by default be obtrusive, but they should be presented in a more peripheral way so that the user has the information needed to adjust their current activity and goals, if they so choose.

Third, the Framework influenced CANS by "identifying how activity is part of a process and how the knowledge of activity through notifications impacts the goals and outcomes of those processes" (Amelung, 2005, p. 104). Defined through the Trends in Activity principle, this concept created perhaps the most long-term value for CANS. Because of this guidance, CANS was created with the ability to record the activity history and the notification history of an LMS. CANS became not only a social computing aid to online learning but more importantly it became a research tool. As will be explained in the section on CANS and Learning Analytics, this design gave researchers the ability to not only influence users' actions and interactions but to record, measure, and analyze those interactions. And, finally, the Meaning in Activity and Notification Customization principles illustrated the need to afford users the ability to configure their own notification preferences because, through that configuration, users are able to develop a better sense of meaning for the notifications when activity occurs.

CANS in Action

All this work and range of influences led to the CANS and Sakai implementation shown in Figure 17.3.

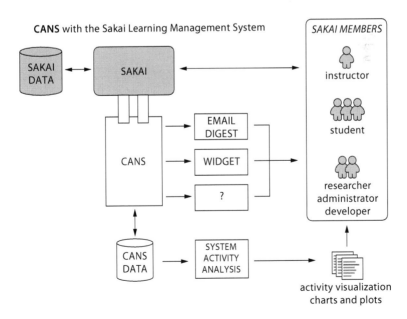

FIGURE 17.3 CANS and Sakai.

This implementation with Sakai allowed us to monitor user activity and record a history of the activity and associated notifications. This functionality provided a basis for envisioning ways to notify users about activity which could impact the sense of presence and co-presence, as well as provide cues for social navigation with the potential to improve teaching and learning. Our first efforts to provide activity notification included e-mail digests and desktop widgets which provided information outside of the LMS and internal to Sakai widgets such as the social comparison widget which would appear on the student's LMS homepage.

E-mail Notification

Figure 17.4 is an example of a standard CANS e-mail notification that an instructor or student would receive once a day. It is a report of the activity that occurred during the previous day. In this example, John Smith is the instructor of a fictional "History of the Internet" course. Robert Jones and Susie Que are two students in that course. From the instructor's perspective, this e-mail notification is a tool for tracking students' activity in the class. The instructor, without ever logging into the actual LMS, can determine who has posted discussion and chat messages or viewed course resources. A student who receives this notification digest can

---

CANS notification digest for Thursday, December 7, 2006

History of the Internet
https://sakai.university.edu/portal/site/history_of_internet

Discussion
John Smith posted "When was the Internet invented?" 18:18:03
Robert Jones posted "What is Internet 2.0?" 15:50:10
Robert Jones posted "Re: When was the Internet invented?" 15:47:52
Susie Que posted "Re: When was the Internet invented?" 15:42:35
Susie Que posted "Re: What is Internet 2.0?" 15:37:03
Robert Jones posted "Re: When was the Internet invented?" 15:36:22

Resource
Robert Jones viewed "Orientation Activity" 18:13:05
John Smith created "Orientation Activity" 17:02:45
Robert Jones viewed "Welcome to the Class" 10:01:35
Susie Que viewed 'Wecome to the Class" 09:35:22
John Smith created "Welcome to the Class" 09:34:29

Chat
Susie Que created 16:16:14
Robert Jones created 16:15:21

This automatic notification message was sent to users of the CANS Email Digest
To unsubscribe, send an email to request-cans@university.edu

FIGURE 17.4   CANS e-mail digest.

quickly scan the e-mail for activity they overlooked and also evaluate their level of activity compared to the other students. Tools like this e-mail digest were very helpful in having students attend to the ongoing progress taking place in their course as well as provide models for how other students were taking on the learning tasks of posting, replying, etc. This form is quite effective in small courses or when not much activity is taking place but quickly becomes overwhelming when lots of student activity is undertaken and reported.

Desktop Awareness Widget

Another form of notification is through a computer's desktop, such as the CANS Desktop Awareness Widget shown in Figure 17.5. A widget is intended to be a small lightweight application that routinely carries out a set of tasks; in this case our widget queries the CANS server for new notification information based on the user's notification preferences. Because the CANS system was designed around the importance of notification customization, the system could be configured, in limited ways, to conform to the user's needs. Users have the option to be notified about new, viewed, edited, and deleted files, discussion and chat messages, assignments, and announcements. The types of notifications are mapped to the types of activity that can take place in the LMS, and ideally CANS would be customized to fit with individual course demands and student preferences.

Social Comparison Digest

CANS was designed to be extensible for data-processing activity based on context and user preferences to generate activity representations, such as the Social Comparison Digest (Figure 17.6). The social comparison widget is an example of how

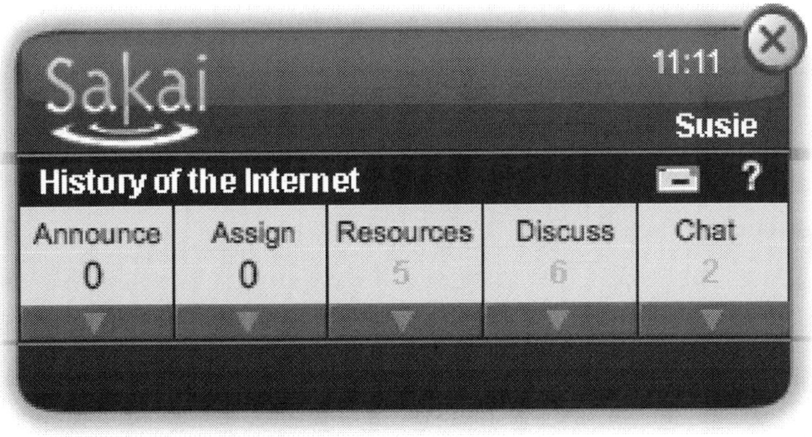

FIGURE 17.5 CANS Desktop Awareness Widget.

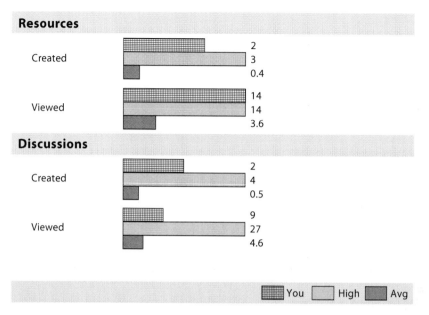

FIGURE 17.6 CANS Social Comparison Digest.

activity information can be condensed and presented to show how a user's level of activity compares to other students in the class. With a glance, a student can see their number of new and viewed resources (files) and discussion messages in a group and compare that amount to the class average and the most active user in the class.

CANS was designed as an activity monitoring and notification system with a high level of potential for customization and configurability. We saw CANS as a powerful notification system that could impact the social nature of online learning. We also envisioned CANS as a data-collection tool for social computing researchers. While discussions of big data and learning analytics were not yet the prevalent conceptualizations that they are today, the potential to use data to predict and shape behavior was beginning to inform our planning.

Extending CANS

In 2006, with partners at the University of Michigan and Virginia Tech, we submitted a proposal to extend CANS by developing: (1) new representations of student activity in online learning which could impact their sense of presence and co-presence as well as support social navigation; (2) activity awareness tools that could assist online instructors; and (3) a notification manager that would allow students and instructors to customize and personalize their awareness representations. Following from the Framework and our experiences using CANS, we identified accountability and meaningfulness as central to our continuing design work. We saw that accountability drove action but we also knew that students did not like the feeling of being watched and that it could be relatively easy to thwart an activity monitoring system by simply doing activities mindlessly. Finding ways to make and help students be accountable to their own expectations became a target for our work. Similarly, information is just noise in the learning process unless it means something to the tasks at hand or the social nature of the experience. Making the information meaningful was the premise behind all the trouble we went through to build in the "context-aware" functionality. However, while we could build in functionality for representing courses, tasks, and members, how to apply that functionality had to be found in a balance of the course structure and the individual needs and interests of students and instructors.

A key to our new thinking about how to improve accountability and meaningfulness in the basic activity awareness tools developed during the dissertation phase of CANS was a project that I (Laffey) had led in 1992 and 1993 at Apple Computer. The project, called LIMB, or Lots of Information Managed Bodaciously, was designed to support the tech support staff who answered customer phone calls needing solutions to technical problems. During that work we had identified "cheat sheets" as a key resource used by all tech support staff. The "sheets" were typically pieces of paper stuffed in a "drawer of knowledge" or tacked to a wall close to their phone and provided tech specs and troubleshooting tips created by their tech support peers. One staff member may have created a spec sheet on printers and at some point he had shared a copy of it with a few colleagues. However, subsequently, the original member may have upgraded the spec sheet four or five times but the colleagues may still be working from the original or other early versions. The documents were extremely valuable because they were created by experts (in a particular domain) to do the type of tasks under the conditions each tech support person faced. To support the sharing and use of up-to-date information and not make the work of the original expert any more difficult, we conceptualized a subscription service so that once a valuable document had been identified, others could subscribe to it and be sure to be kept up to date.

For CANS we reconceptualized the subscription service into a reporter mechanism whereby students and instructors could develop reporters to customize their awareness information. Typically, instructors would start by creating some default reporters for students to use and then students could create custom reporters to monitor the activity of team members or respected classmates, or to be used for one particular assignment that required interdependence. Figure 17.7 shows the Activity Monitor that enabled the creation (1) and management of reporters/notifiers as an application within Sakai and relevant to a specific course. The application design conformed to the style requirements of Sakai but enabled instructors and students to create and manage reporters. They could set which

326   James M. Laffey et al.

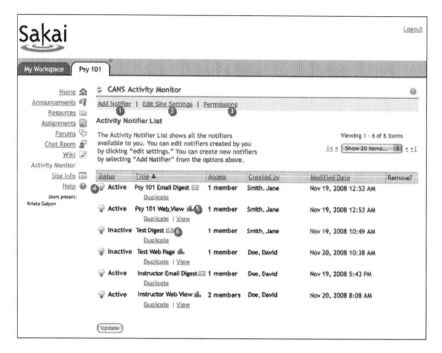

FIGURE 17.7   CANS Activity Monitor.

activities and members to monitor (2) and create permissions for who had access to the reports (3). The list of reporters (4) includes web views (5) as well as digests to be delivered via e-mail (6).

Figure 17.8 shows the result of a request to add a reporter/notifier, and shows the selections available for the type of notifier (1), events to be monitored (4), members to be monitored (5), who to notify (6), and status as active or inactive (7). As we advanced through design stages, some of the concerns we encountered included addressing who had authority to enable monitoring and the granting of permissions and how to simplify the creation process. We developed a tiered system of authority so that university administrators could make decisions about what was possible across all courses and then, within that range of possibilities, course instructors could make decisions about what was enabled for their courses and students. This approach allowed us to address a variety of policies and FERPA concerns across universities as well as allow instructors to be comfortable with the activity awareness practices and customs of their courses. One of the key approaches to simplifying the creation process was to allow members to duplicate and modify reporter/notifiers instead of starting over with each new idea for activity awareness.

Figure 17.9 shows a sample of a new model of a daily e-mail digest. The sample shows the daily activity of the course through a summarization of the key activities

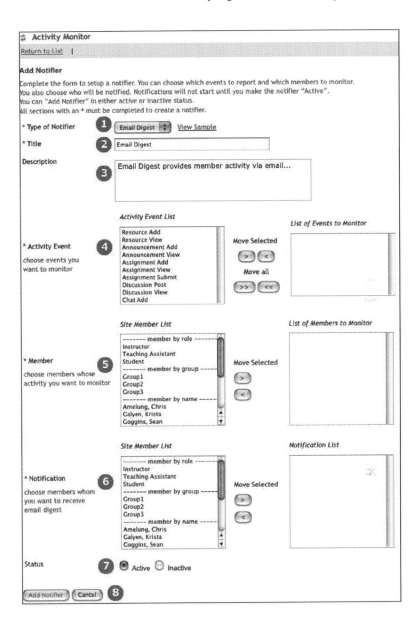

FIGURE 17.8 Form for setting up an activity notifier.

and then lists the resources created and viewed by other students. This view of a digest is based on decisions the teacher and student have made about what is available and presumed useful.

Another view of the same data can be provided through an interactive web page as is shown in Figure 17.10. This page represents a one-day view, the last

From: no-reply@sakia.missouri.edu
Subject: **CANS notification digest for Wednesday, September 23, 2009**
Date: September 24, 2009 6:50:41 AM CDT

CANS Notification Digest for Thursday, September 24, 2009
FIPSE-CANS

Notifier title: JForum email

TOOL	NEW	READ	EDIT
DISCUSSION	0	2	NA
RESOURCES	2	2	0
ASSIGNMENTS	0	0	0
ANNOUNCEMENTS	0	NA	0
CHAT	0	NA	NA

RESOURCES
activityChart_mod3_Team1.png was read by *student name 1*   at 12:59:46
FS09 usability was created by *student name 1*   at 15:29:22
activityMonitor_last_FS09.xls was created by *student name 3*   at 15:30:24
activityChart_mod4_Team2.png was read by *student name 4*   at 13:00:53

FIGURE 17.9   An e-mail digest which can be sent to a student each day for each class.

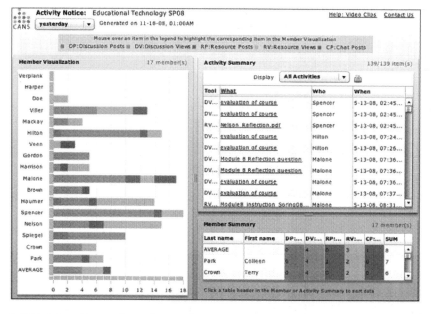

FIGURE 17.10   Interactive web page for examining course activity.

three days' view, or the prior week's view, and is typically of more interest to the instructor than to the students. It allows the instructor to see a visualization of each member's levels of participation in the left column and allows for sorting as well as a mouse-over for more detail. The top-right display currently showing Resource Views can be switched between events such as discussion posts and views so that the instructor can see the actual items the students are posting or accessing as well as being able to click through to the item. These items can also be sorted by title, members, or dates. The bottom-right view provides a numeric summary for each member across each event type. Instructors reported this interactive and summary form of data to be of value for identifying students who may be falling behind or for monitoring how students follow instructions in a lesson.

Figure 17.11 shows a view of data developed for a widget on the home page of the course site in Sakai. The purpose of developing a widget and placing it on the course home page is to make the social information available to the students while they are working on course activities and to put the information in "plain view." The top pane of the widget shows social comparison data from the last seven days of activity and allows the student to see how their level of activity compares with the course average or with the top 10 percent of active students. This is a form of support for accountability in that it allows the student to compare themselves with others in the class and determine if the comparison data indicate a need for changes in activity level on their part. The middle pane allows selection across event types such as discussion and resource posts and views and shows the most recent and popular events for each category. If a student sees an object, such as a discussion board post, that is of interest to them, they can click the name and go directly to the discussion. The bottom pane provides recommendations based on data from the student and peers to suggest potentially relevant and interesting activity.

CANS and Learning Analytics

In the time since the development of CANS, a new community of scholars focused on learning analytics in large-scale course management systems and other learning environments has emerged. Sean Goggins, who was a graduate student in our program following Amelung, experienced CANS in his courses and subsequently used CANS data to formulate an approach to understanding online learning in groups. Goggins is now leading several research projects that take insights from the CANS research as a basis for developing new formulations for learning analytics (Paredes & Chung, 2012; Reynolds & Goggins, 2013; Xing & Goggins, in press; Xing et al., 2014). We believe that the early work on CANS and activity awareness in context, when coupled with new approaches and thinking about learning analytics, serves as a prime example for the kinds of tools that will help instructors manage courses and students to manage their learning.

330 James M. Laffey et al.

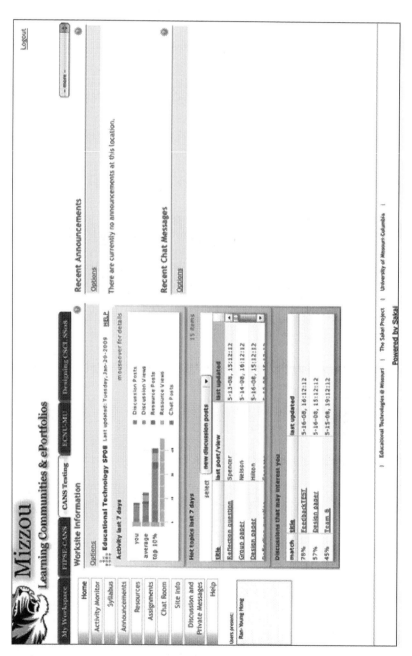

FIGURE 17.11 CANS widget data presentation in Sakai.

We have published a number of articles in the learning analytics and related literature, with Goggins' leadership especially focusing on the use of CANS data to understand small group behavior in completely online learning environments (Goggins et al., 2007, 2009, 2010a, 2010b, 2011, 2013a, 2013b).

The future of tools to support design through learning will include (1) continued advances in awareness for both teachers and students; (2) the design of tools that better support online small group work; and (3) the incorporation of learning indicators (analytics) in those tools. Finally, the sustainability of innovative learning designs will benefit from researchers and institutions of learning embracing open source LMSs such as Instructure Canvas (http://canvas.instructure.com).

Advancing Awareness

Most current LMS systems provide some level of basic awareness of who is posting the most in discussion forums or downloading which course resources. The instrumentation of contribution provides one simple view, but leaves out an important dimension of CANS design: analysis of what we call "read data." In our work studying awareness in CANS, we found that a critical aspect of technical implementation was the gathering and presentation of detailed information about who was reading posts made by others. In fact, we found that higher levels of read behavior in online courses is a significant indicator of the level of knowledge construction present in student posts (Goggins et al., 2010a). Future awareness systems should leverage these findings and carefully study the social influence of read awareness, since it has long been recognized that behaviors change as people gain the ability to compare themselves with others in a social environment (Festinger, 1954).

Tools to Support Group Work

A significant challenge for technology-mediated learning is supporting awareness of both course-level and small group-level activity without overwhelming students and teachers with information. We showed that learning groups interact with each other to varying degrees, and that these differences are indicators of group cohesion and learning performance (Goggins et al., 2011). Using the read data advantage that CANS offers over existing LMS analytics provides useful group awareness indicators, such as how many students are reading a member's posts or how many students have read the assignment. When read data are presented in the student interface, students see that their work is being used by others. They are not just completing assignments but also contributing to group knowledge. Awareness that others are using your work enhances the social nature of the learning experience while also emphasizing the need for quality work because there is an audience for the work other than just the instructor. When the instructor sees read data, she has confirmation that her expectations for social

FIGURE 17.12 Illustration of different levels of group cohesion derived from CANS data.

learning are being met (or not). Figure 17.12 illustrates how groups can be viewed as more or less connected. Four of the six groups in this example from an online course in Sakai are adjacent to each other to varying degrees, and the closeness illustrated in Figure 17.12 corresponds with interviews with participants, and the different perceptions they had of "group cohesion."

Incorporation of Learning Indicators

Work to date focuses on awareness and discovery of how groups connect with each other in online courses. A next stage in the development of LMS awareness systems will focus to some extent on identifying behavioral indicators of learning. To accomplish this, our work suggests that the content of interaction must be analyzed as well as the CANS record that an interaction occurred.

One such indicator is a shift in the topical focus of discourse. Introne and Goggins (2012) developed a topic modeling algorithm that incorporates network analytic techniques as well as topic models to identify shifts in discourse from one topic to another. This kind of analysis emerges from computational examination of the texts within discussion board messages. Figure 17.13 is one example of how our topic-modeling algorithm is able to show changes in topic over time in an online news group. The same approach could be applied in a next-generation version of CANS.

Importance of Open Source LMS Tools

Sustained innovation and the integration of new analytics features into live course management systems remains a difficult challenge. Like Shadow before it, Sakai is now having a difficult time sustaining itself. Our experience was that Sakai was difficult to deploy and challenging to integrate with, as a complex, Java-based technology. More recently, we have begun to experiment with adding learning analytics to Canvas, an open source LMS. Canvas is based on a popular web framework known as Ruby on Rails, and is hosted on a new type of distributed open source software system called GitHub, which enables anyone to fork, modify, and submit changes to the code (Dabbish et al., 2012). Creating an easy path for newcomers to contribute code via GitHub gives LMSs like Canvas a significant advantage for the introduction of awareness and learning analytics tools like CANS. For these reasons, four major universities recently formed a consortium with Canvas-maker Instructure to share in the development of more innovative LMS technology (Instructure, 2014).

Conclusions

In reflecting back on our work of designing CANS we think examining two tensions and areas of failure helps us make sense of our design process and outcomes. The first tension is contrasting design in the academic world (or at least the way we approach design as university researchers) and design in the commercial world. All software product teams confront the same challenges of user models, systems models, human-computer interfaces, process support, effective code, and testing cycles. In the commercial world these tasks are built around product cycles and must yield software products that optimize all aspects of the product model, meet schedules, and map to profit and loss constraints. Typically, the team members are experienced and talented professionals with demonstrated track records for their roles. Failure is not tolerated and leads to negative reviews, possible loss of jobs, and potentially finding a new career better suited to the team member's talents.

In the academic world, the product development process morphs into a research and development agenda. While functional design and working code is

334 James M. Laffey et al.

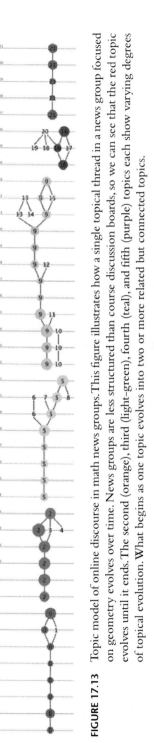

FIGURE 17.13 Topic model of online discourse in math news groups. This figure illustrates how a single topical thread in a news group focused on geometry evolves over time. News groups are less structured than course discussion boards, so we can see that the red topic evolves until it ends. The second (orange), third (light-green), fourth (teal), and fifth (purple) topics each show varying degrees of topical evolution. What begins as one topic evolves into two or more related but connected topics.

needed, the products must optimize the constructs of the research agenda in the sense of making them come to life in innovative ways to impact desired outcomes. Schedules revolve around the academic calendar and are typically seen in years rather than in the weeks and months more common to commercial products. All product development is resource constrained but, rather than following market research models, academic development is based on perceived significance of the development to the interests of the researchers and strength of the case researchers can make to funding agencies regarding the intellectual merits and potential social impacts of the work. Commercial developers usually work from a budget which is set in advance, and although budgets are subject to business conditions in a company they usually form the basis for a complete development process. In the academic world, projects may bounce between fitting it in within your other demands to periods with external funding.

In contrast to a team of experienced professionals, academic progress is usually made through student work. Students are often gifted and resourceful but quite frequently it is their first job as part of a development team and the first time they are using knowledge and skills outside of classroom assignments. Student work can lead to many surprises, both on the plus and minus side. An example of the plus side is the computer science student we hired as an undergraduate who then enrolled in our Masters program and is now a staff member as a lead programmer who mentors the next generation of undergraduate hourly programmers. On the negative side are the numerous students who we hire with great promise and then cannot be found the next semester, or the ones who spend all of their time programming and none of the time needed to pass their other subjects, ending up on probation and unable to be rehired.

Failure is the basis for most progress in design and development. We often talk about "failing fast" in order to get beyond weaker ideas and move to more powerful ones. The initial work referenced in this article of developing ShadowNetworkSpace and the Activity Monitor ended with abandoning those products, but with important insights for new product formulations. CANS iterated through multiple versions until we found the most powerful ways to represent activity in context, including the "read" activity which is now a strong basis for new models for analytics.

The early versions of notifications in CANS were weak and mapped to only a few use cases but they led to activity awareness representations that were more robust and meaningful to student and teacher work. In some ways, failure is more tolerable in the academic world than in the commercial world because it is seen as part of the scientific process. Even if the software is abandoned before it is broadly used or commercialized, the scholarly publications allow for sharing advances in constructs and in the development of new knowledge. Embracing open source LMS systems over proprietary systems creates new possibilities for direct implementation and sustainability of future innovations like CANS into a larger community of developers.

These distinctions between academic and commercial development explain some of the choices we made but they do not obscure the fact that CANS is no longer being used. Failing to attend to key markers of commercial development increases the risk of academic software failure. For example, our failure to account or budget for transitions in technology such as the upgrades to Sakai was a critical error. Similarly, while we conducted needs assessments to understand how our software functionality could be useful, we did not do market research to determine how best to present and package the functionality for adoption. Finally, as researchers we sought ways to optimize the conceptual reification of our framework for activity awareness, but in doing so we may have missed opportunities (as will be discussed in the following section) to meet user needs, which may potentially have led to broader adoption.

The second tension that characterizes the design process for CANS is that social learning, while recognized as desirable, can be hard to achieve in online learning and that efforts to try to support social learning can lead to negative outcomes. Education is a social activity and the ability to engage the social nature of learners is important to teacher–student relationships as well as to support learning through dialogue with others and engaging learners in teamwork that amplifies what can be accomplished in a given time period. The tools for being social in an LMS are relatively limited today and were far worse 15 years ago. So much so that teachers and students often prefer avoiding assignments that call for social interaction—except for the most minimal sort—because coordination, cooperation, and collaboration often lead to frustration and disappointment when they are required parts of online learning assignments. Waiting for others to do their work and not knowing when or whether they will do that work so that you can continue with your part of the work is the most common criticism we hear from students in our online courses. Faculty wishing to avoid having to intervene or hearing student complaints often choose to use assignment types which avoid social interdependence.

Our research showed us that the activity awareness afforded by CANS was perceived to be most valuable when more social interdependence was a required part of learning tasks. Thus, until the tool sets of LMS include mechanisms to support social learning in ways which avoid the pitfalls of frustration and extra work, instructors will be reluctant to include social learning as key components of online learning. But without assignments that require interdependence, instructors and students will not see the benefits of social information nor receive the benefits of social learning. This chicken-and-egg problem contributed to the demise of CANS. The operation of CANS required a parallel server configuration be set up to Sakai and this was expensive in hardware and time; so, without a compelling demand for these services from faculty, few institutions were willing to implement CANS. Perhaps in the future, with lower costs and more common use of virtual servers, a configuration such as CANS would be more viable.

Earlier we discussed how future versions of learning analytics should focus on indicators of learning behavior, not just indicators of behavior. To the extent that CANS could have filtered through activity to identify the behaviors most salient for learning, we would have added more value to instruction and made CANS more valuable to instructors. Hypothetically, learning analytics uses data to identify predictors of learning outcomes but we never achieved sufficiently large numbers of users to meaningfully do predictive analytics. In retrospect we could have approximated some of the benefits of predictive analytics by utilizing instructor expectations for what should happen in their courses as a proxy for the analytics. Mapping behavior against expectations and reporting student performance to the instructor could have been a strong way to make the value and potential of CANS more salient for instructors.

CANS has demonstrated approaches to make online learning more social and we see opportunities for next-generation systems that merge activity awareness with learning analytics for more powerful online, context-aware teaching and learning.

Acknowledgments

Partial support for the advancement of CANS and the work described here has been provided by a grant from the Fund for Improving Post Secondary Education (# P116B06–0045), 2007–2009.

Support for the future vision of learning analytics portion of this chapter was provided by an NSF Grant, "VOSS: Toward a Context Adaptive Theory of the Relationship Between Structural Fluidity and Virtual Organization Performance" and Josh Introne, of Michigan State University.

We would also like to thank the many contributors through design, development, and testing who have helped advance CANS, especially Dale Musser, David Reid, and Ran-Young Hong.

References

Amelung, C. (2005). "A context-aware notification framework for developers of computer supported collaborative environments." Unpublished doctoral dissertation, University of Missouri, Columbia, MO.

Amelung, C. (2007). Using social context and e-learner identity as a framework for an e-learning notification system. *International Journal on E-Learning, 6*(4), 501–517.

Anderson, K. M., & Bouvin, N. O. (2000). Supporting project awareness on the WWW with the iScent framework. *ACM SIGGROUP Bulletin, 21*(3), 16–20. http://dx.doi.org/10.1145/605647.605650.

Dabbish, L., Stuart, C., Tsay, J., & Herbsleb, J. (2012). Social coding in Github: Transparency and collaboration in an open software repository. In *Proceedings of the ACM 2012 Conference on Computer Supported Cooperative Work* (pp. 1277–1286). New York: ACM Press. http://dx.doi.org/10.1145/2145204.2145396.

Dourish, P. (2001). *Where the action is: Foundations of embodied interaction*. Cambridge, MA: MIT Press.

Dourish, P., & Bellotti, V. (1992). Awareness and coordination in shared workspaces. In *Proceedings of the 1992 ACM Conference on Computer-supported Cooperative Work* (pp. 107–114). New York: ACM Press. http://dx.doi.org/10.1145/143457.143468.

Festinger, L. (1954). A theory of social comparison processes. *Human Relations*, 7, 117–140.

Fitzpatrick, G. (1998). "The Locales Framework: Understanding and designing for cooperative work." Unpublished doctoral thesis, The University of Queensland, Brisbane St. Lucia.

Goggins, S., Galyen, K., & Laffey, J. (2010a). Network analysis of trace data for the support of group work: Activity patterns in a completely online course. In *Proceedings of the 16th ACM International Conference on Supporting Group Work* (pp. 107–116). New York: ACM Press. http://dx.doi.org/10.1145/1880071.1880089.

Goggins, S. P., Laffey, J., & Gallagher, M. (2011). Completely online group formation and development: Small groups as socio-technical systems. *Information Technology & People*, 24(2), 104–133. http://dx.doi.org/10.1108/09593841111137322.

Goggins, S., Laffey, J., & Galyen, K. (2009). Social ability in online groups: Representing the quality of interactions in social computing environments. In *Proceedings from IEEE Conference on Computer Science and Engineering* (pp. 667–674). IEEE. http://dx.doi.org/10.1109/CSE.2009.339.

Goggins, S., Laffey, J., & Tsai, I-C. (2007). Cooperation and groupness: Community formation in small online collaborative groups. In *Proceedings of the 2007 International ACM Conference on Supporting Group Work* (pp. 207–216). New York: ACM Press. http://dx.doi.org/10.1145/1316624.1316654.

Goggins, S. P., Mascaro, C., & Valetto, G. (2013a). Group informatics: A methodological approach and ontology for sociotechnical group research. *Journal of the American Society for Information Science and Technology*, 64(3), 516–539. http://dx.doi.org/10.1002/asi.22802.

Goggins, S. P., Laffey, J., Amelung, C., & Gallagher, M. (2010b). Social intelligence in completely online groups. In *Proceedings from IEEE International Conference on Social Computing* (pp. 500–507). IEEE. http://dx.doi.org/10.1109/SocialCom.2010.79.

Goggins, S., Valetto, G., Mascaro, C., & Blincoe, K. (2013b). Creating a model of the dynamics of socio-technical groups. *User Modeling and User-Adapted Interaction*, 23(4), 345–379. http://dx.doi.org/10.1007/s11257-012-9122-3.

Instructure. (2014). *Unizin, a new higher ed consortium, Chooses Canvas by Instructure as its foundational learning platform*. Retrieved from www.instructure.com/press-releases/unizin-chooses-canvas.

Introne, J., & Goggins, S. (2012). Tracing knowledge evolution in online forums. In *Proceedings from ACM Web Science Conference: Words and Networks Workshop*.

Laffey, J., & Amelung, C. (2007). Cues and mechanisms for improving the social nature of online learning. In *Proceedings from World Conference on Educational Multimedia, Hypermedia and Telecommunications* (pp. 1277–1282). Chesapeake, VA: AACE.

Laffey, J., Lin, G.Y., & Lin, Y. (2006). Assessing social ability in online learning environments. *Journal of Interactive Learning Research*, 17(2), 163–177.

Laffey, J. M., & Musser, D. (2000). Shadow netWorkspace learning systems project. In *International Workshop on Advanced Learning Technologies* (pp. 188–189). IEEE. http://dx.doi.org/10.1109/IWALT.2000.890605.

Laffey, J. M., & Musser, D. (2006). Shadow netWorkspace: An open source intranet for learning communities. *Canadian Journal of Learning and Technology/La revue canadienne de l'apprentissage et de la technologie*, 32(1).

Laffey, J. M., Musser, D., Remidez, H., & Gottdenker, J. (2003). Networked systems for schools that learn. *Communications of the ACM*, *46*(9), 192–200. http://dx.doi.org/10.1145/903893.903937.

Paredes, W. C., & Chung, K. S. K. (2012). Modelling learning & performance: A social networks perspective. In *Proceedings of the 2nd International Conference on Learning Analytics and Knowledge* (pp. 34–42). New York: ACM Press. http://dx.doi.org/10.1145/2330601.2330617.

Reynolds, R., & Goggins, S. P. (2013). Designing socio-technical systems to support guided "discovery-based" learning in students: The case of the Globaloria game design initiative. In *Proceedings from International Workshop on Teaching Analytics*, Leuven, Belgium.

Xing, W., & Goggins, S. (in press). A candidate participation based student grade prediction model: Integrating learning analytics, educational data mining and theory through genetic programming. *Computers in Human Behavior*.

Xing, W., Wadholm, B., & Goggins, S. (2014). Learning analytics in CSCL with a focus on assessment: An exploratory study of activity theory-informed cluster analysis. In *Proceedings of the Fourth International Conference on Learning Analytics and Knowledge* (pp. 59–67). New York: ACM Press.

INDEX

Page numbers in **bold** denote tables, those in *italics* denote figures.

active learning *see* Computer Assisted Instruction in Elementary Mathematics; Nicaragua Radio Mathematics Project (NRMP)
activity notification systems *see* Context-aware Activity Notification System (CANS)
African American reading program *see* *Bridge: A Cross-Culture Reading Program*
Afro-American Publishing 233
airborne television instruction *see* Midwest Program on Airborne Television Instruction (MPATI)
Albuquerque Indian School 37, 38, *39*, *43*
Alcatraz Cellhouse Tour 8, 271–282; design decisions 277–279; design evolution and revisions 278, 279–281; experience of 272–276, *272*, *274*, 278–279, *279*; inspiration for design 276–277
Alderman, D. L. 155, 174, 175, 176
Alien Elevators 293–295, *294*, *295*, 298
American Annals of the Deaf 27–28
American Indian schools *see* Carlisle design model for American Indian schools
American Sign Language (ASL) 26, 31, 32–33, 55, 56–59, 60
Anderson, K. M. 319
Anderson, Richard C. 156, 181
Apple Computer 325

artificial intelligence 256–257, 266; *see also* expert systems and knowledge-based engineering
assimilation 3; *see also* Carlisle design model for American Indian schools
Atkinson, R. 153
audio tours 276; *see also* Alcatraz Cellhouse Tour

Baratz, Joan 204–205, 214, 233
Barr, A. 255
behaviorism 4, 5; *see also* Skinnerian teaching machine
Bell, Alexander Graham 22, 23, 55
Bellotti, V. 316
Benjamin, L. T., Jr. 87
bilingual approach to deaf education 32, 33, 57–59, 60
Bilingual-Bicultural education 32, 33
Bitzer, D. L. 157
Bitzer, Donald 154
Black English 190, 196–197, 230–232, 233; *see also Bridge: A Cross-Culture Reading Program*
black folklore 200, 203
Blair, D. C. 260
Bloom, B. S. 158
Bobrow, D. G. 259–260, 261
Bouvin, N. O. 319

Index

branching teaching machines 98–100, *99*, 102
Bridge: A Cross-Culture Reading Program 6, 186–233; Associative Bridging 192, 193, 199; audio recordings 228–230; Book One *191, 194,* 200–205, *201, 202, 203*; Book Two 205–207, *206, 207*; Book Three 207–211, *208, 209*; Book Four 211–214, *211, 212*; Book Five 214–219, *215, 216, 217, 218*; *City Folks* 214, *216*; context analysis 198–199; design thinking 190–192; designers 187–189, *188, 189*; *Dig And Be Dug* 214, *217*; dormancy 230–232; *Dreamy Mae* 207, *208*, 210–211, 224; feedback records 225, *225*; field testing 190, 232; foregrounding 196–197; framing 194–195; *A Friend in Need* 207, *209*, 211; genre 193–194; *The Ghost* 200, *203*; *I'll Always Remember* 214, *215*, 218–219; *Little Big Man* 211, *212*, 213; *Old But Not Defenseless* 205–207, *206*; omission and backgrounding 196; *The Organizer* 200, *201*; origins 189–190; Peer Control Reading 193, 227; public opinion 196, 197, 230–232; *Shine* 200, *201*, 204, 222, 223, 224; skills lessons 222–224; *Stagolee* 200, *202*, 224; story questions 219–222; Study Books 219–225, *220, 221, 225*; teacher's guide 225; teacher's role 226–227; text analysis 193–198; *Vibration Cornbread* 211, *211*, 213; visual representations 197–198; *What Folks Call Politics* 214, *218*; *What I Got To Be Proud Of* 205, 207, *207*; word-bridging lessons 224
Briggs, L. J. 158
Brigham Young University 157, 174, 177–178, 179
Brookline Books 232
Bruner, J. S. 158
Bucciarelli, L. L. 172
Buchanan, B. G. 260
Buchanan, Bruce 259
Bunderson, C. Victor 156, 174, 177, *177*, 178, 180
Bureau of Catholic Indian Missions 41
Bureau of Indian Affairs 36
Burton, R. R. 178
Byerly, G. 175, 177–178

Cabri Geometre 287
calculus *see* SimCalc project
Campbell Soup Company 260–263
Canvas Learning Management System 331, 333
Carlisle design model for American Indian schools 3, 35–47, *37, 43*; academic education 42; context 35–36; corporal punishment 40; daily routine 38–41, *39*; food 40–41; industrial education 42–44; music and sports 40; outing system 44; reasons for failure 44–46; religious instruction 41; student agency 45
Carlisle Indian Industrial School 36
Cawley, J. F. 120
Chiloco Indian School *39*
Cimino, Aldo 261, 262
Civilization Fund (1819) 35
Clancey, W. J. 259
cochlear implants 32
Cognitive Science Society 236
Coleman Report, US 194–195
Commissioner of Indian Affairs 36, 40
Computer Assisted Instruction in Elementary Mathematics 6–7, 134; audio instruction 139–140; context 134–136, 137; design *135*, 138–141, *139, 144*; reasons for failure 149–150; student experience 143–145, *146, 147*
computer-assisted instruction (CAI): costs 152–153; instructional quality 153–154; PLATO system 153–154, 157, 174, 285; *see also* Computer Assisted Instruction in Elementary Mathematics; TICCIT system
Computer-Based Education Research Laboratory (CERL) 154
constructionism 7, 8
constructivism 8
Context-aware Activity Notification System (CANS) 9, 315–337; activity monitor 324–329, *326, 327, 328*; background 315–318, *316*; design 317–324, *320, 321, 322, 323, 324*; desktop awareness widget 323, *323*; e-mail notification 322–323, *322*, 326–327, *328*; extensions to design 324–329, *326, 327, 328, 330*; Framework for Notification 318, 319–321, **319**, *320*; influences on design 318–321, **319**, *320*; learning analytics and 329–333, *332, 334*; reflections on 333–337; social comparison digest 323–324, *324*; tools to support group work 331–332, *332*; topic modeling algorithm 333, *334*

Convention of American Instructors of the Deaf 25, 26, 27
Coombs, Phillip 125
critical discourse analysis 193
Cross-Cultural Approach to Reading 189–190, 193; *see also Bridge: A Cross-Culture Reading Program*
Culver, S. J. 281

Davenport, T. H. 256, 260
Davis, R. 253
Dawes Allotment Act (1887) 35
deaf education: bilingual approach 32, 33, 57–59, 60; oral-only systems 22–25, 31, 55; technology in 32, 56, 57–59; *see also* Rochester Method of deaf education; Tennessee School for the Deaf
Deighton, Lee 114
Dendral 258–259
Dewey, John 199
dialect reading *see Bridge: A Cross-Culture Reading Program*
DiSessa, A. A. 286
Displaywriter 237, 238–245, *238, 239, 244,* 251
disruptive technologies 266
distance education 131–132
Djerassi, Carl 259
Donahue, Thomas 273
Dourish, Paul 316, 318
Dublin, Ohio 128–129
Duda, R. O. 260
dynamic representations 287–288; *see also* SimCalc project

Educational Film Library 65
Educational Testing Service (ETS) 5, 156
elaboration theory 178
embodied interaction 318
embodiment in learning 309
Engin, G. 265
expert systems and knowledge-based engineering 8, 253–267; Campbell Soup example 260–263; development infrastructure 258–260; linkages with instructional design 263–265, *264*; visions guiding early development 255–258

Feigenbaum, Edward 254, 255, 259, 263
Fine, B. 100–101
fingerspelling 55–56; *see also* Rochester Method of deaf education
Fisher, Leonard Everett 114, *117*

Fitzpatrick, Geraldine 318
Flores, F. 258
Florida School for the Deaf 31
"flying classroom" *see* Midwest Program on Airborne Television Instruction (MPATI)
Ford Aerospace 179
Ford Foundation 125, 129
Forsythe, Diana 257
The Free Press 233
Fund for the Improvement of Post Secondary Education (FIPSE) 317

Gagné, Robert 158, 166–167
Gallaudet, Thomas Hopkins 23
Gallaudet University 56, 174
Geometer Sketchpad 287, 300
Gibson, Althea 118, *119*
GitHub 333
Glaser, R. 159
Goodman, R. 98
Grabinger, R. 263, *264*
Grant, Ulysses S. 35
graphical user interfaces *see* minimalist instruction
Groove 319
Guernica magazine 281

Hardman, Chris 271, 276–277, 278, 279, 280, 281
Hayes, P. J. 259–260
Hayes-Roth, F. 257
Hazeltine Corporation 179
hearing aids 32
Hellström, T. 256
Herrod, Richard 260, 261, 262
historical context 1–9, *2*
Hochron, Gary 263
Holland, J. G. 100
Holt, Grace S. 187, 189
Houghton Mifflin Publishing Company 190, 232
Howard, C. D. 266
Huckin, Thomas N. 193, 196
Huxley, T. H. 258

IBM 90, *93*; *see also* minimalist instruction
Indian School Journal, The 39
Indiana University Libraries Moving Image Archive (IULMIA) 63–65, *63*
instructional theory 158–159
instructional training films 5, 62–66, *64*; context of wartime film production 65–66; distribution and archive 63–65, *63*; *see also Supervising Women Workers*

Index **343**

Interactive Radio Instruction (IRI) 134, 137, 148
International Congress on Education of the Deaf, Milan 22–23, 55
International Journal of Designs for Learning 10
Interservice Procedures for Instructional Systems Development (IPISD) 158
Introne, Josh 333
iScent (InterSubjective Collaborative Event Environment) 319

Johnson, Lyndon B. 199–200
Johnson, R. L. 157
Jones, R. L. 120
Journal of Business Strategy 263
Journal of Systems and Software 260

Kaput, James J. 283, 284, 288–289, 290–293, 299, 301, 304, 309, 311
Kellaghan, T. 120
Kerkow, Herbert 65
Klinefelter, C. F. 66
knowledge economy 258
knowledge-based engineering *see* expert systems and knowledge-based engineering
Koedinger, K. R. 176
Krupat, Andrew 40

Labov, W. 222, 229, 232
Larson, L. C. "Ole" 63–65
learning analytics 329–333, *332*, *334*
learning hierarchy analysis 167–168
learning management systems (LMSs): Canvas 331, 333; open source 331, 333, 335; Sakai 317, 321–322, *321*, 325, *326*, 329, *330*, 333, 336; Shadow Networkspace 315–318, *316*, *330*
learning theory 158–159, 167, 198, 250
Lederberg, Joshua 259
Leith, P. 255
Leonard, Dorothy 262
Lewis, Clayton 236
Lighthill Report, UK 256
Lincoln Memorial University 51, *52*
listening technology 32
Locales Framework 318
Logo language 284, 285, 287
Loral 179
Louisiana School for the Deaf 31

McCarthy, John 257, 258
McCorduck, P. 263
Machlup, Fritz 258

Mack, Robert 236
McLaughlin, Clayton 26, 28, 30
McWilliams, E. 155–156
Madni, A. 263–264
Mans, J. 261
Massive Open Online Courses (MOOCs) 134, 137
mathematics education: approaches to use of technology in 284; dynamic representations 287–288; microworlds 285–286, 287–288; *see also* Computer Assisted Instruction in Elementary Mathematics; Nicaragua Radio Mathematics Project (NRMP); SimCalc project
Meredith Publishing 90
Merrill, M. David 156, 163–167, *164*, *165*, *167*, *170*, 174, 182
microworlds 178, 285–286, 287–288; *see also* SimCalc project
Midwest Program on Airborne Television Instruction (MPATI) 6, 123–132, *124*; challenges 130–131; genesis 125–126; program *125*, 126–129, *127*, *128*; student experience 129
Milan Conference 22–23, 55
minimalist instruction 6, 236–251, *238*; adoption and generalization 245–249; Displaywriter 237, 238–245, *238*, *239*, *244*, 251; guided exploration cards 240–241, *240*, 245, *246*; learner frustrations 237–239; Minimal Manual 241–243, *242*; reflections on 237, 249–251; Training Wheels Displaywriter 243–245, *244*; usability case studies 248–249, *248*; View Matcher 246–248, *247*
Mitchell, W. J. 160
MITRE Corporation 156, 157
Montpelier, Indiana 123
museums *see* Alcatraz Cellhouse Tour
Mycin 258, 259

National Native American Boarding School Healing Coalition 46
National Park Service (NPS) 276–277
National Science Foundation (NSF) 154, 155, 156, 157, 174, 175
Native Americans *see* Carlisle design model for American Indian schools
Neisser, U. 158
Newell, A. 158
Newell, Allen 259–260
Newsweek magazine 230

Nicaragua Radio Mathematics Project (NRMP) 134; context 136–137; design 141–143, *142*; reasons for failure 149–151; student experience *138*, 148, *149*
No Child Left Behind policy 300
Noble, Charles 125
Norman, Donald 266
Northern Telecom 245, *246*
Northern Virginia Community College 157, 174
nSpire handheld device 300

O'Leary, D. E. 254
operant conditioning 4, 85–87, 94–97, **94**, 98–100, **101**, 102
oral epic poetry 200
oral-only deaf educational systems 22–25, 31, 55
Ozzie, Ray 319

Pacific Horizons Reading Scheme 114
Palo Alto Research Center (PARC) 236, 240
Pandalai, K. A. V. 264–265
Papert, Seymour 285
Parker, Don H. 110–112, 120
Pedersen, E. L. 174
Phelps, Nicki 271, 276, 277, 280
Phoenix College 157, 174
Piaget, Jean 285
piecewise linear functions 304–307, *305, 306*
Plant, Robert 260
PLATO system 153–154, 157, 174, 285
Pollock, J. 263, *264*
Poore, H. T. 56
Popular Science 255
Porat, Marc 258
Pratt, Richard Henry 36
Pressey, Sidney 87
"Problems in Supervision" training film series *64*, 65; *see also Supervising Women Workers*
programmed instruction 4, 5, 101, 154, 156, 157; *see also* Midwest Program on Airborne Television Instruction (MPATI); Skinnerian teaching machine; SRA Reading Lab
Prusak, L. 256, 260
Purdue University 125

Quartey-Annan, M. 223–224
Quillen, James *274*

radio: Interactive Radio Instruction (IRI) 134, 137, 148; *see also* Nicaragua Radio Mathematics Project (NRMP)
Raman, S. 256
reading programs *see* Bridge: A Cross-Culture Reading Program; SRA Reading Lab
Reel, Estelle 41–42
Reel Course of Study for American Indian schools 41–44
Resnick, L. B. 159
Rheem Manufacturing 90
Rickford, A. E. 196
Rickford, J. R. 196
Rittel, Horst 310
Rochester History 28, 29
Rochester Method of deaf education 3, 22–34, 55–56; context 22–27; details of system 27–31, *27, 29*; influence 32–34; reasons for disappearance 31–32
Romiszowski, A. J. 263
Rosson, Mary Beth 248
Ruby on Rails 333

Sakai Learning Management System 317, 321–322, *321*, 325, *326*, 329, *330*, 333, 336
Santa Fe Indian School 38, 42
satellite television transmission *see* Midwest Program on Airborne Television Instruction (MPATI)
Schlosser, L. 131
Science 260
scientific management 255
Scott, A. 51
Scouten, Edward L. 28, 30
self-instruction *see* minimalist instruction
Shadow Networkspace 315–318, *316, 330*
Shechtman, N. 290
Shortliffe, Edward 259, 260
sign languages: American Sign Language (ASL) 26, 31, 32–33, 55, 56–59, 60; Milan Conference and 22–23, 55; signed English 31, 57
SimCalc project 8, 283–311; Alien Elevators 293–295, *294, 295*, 298; background 283–289; connections across representations 307–308; context of motion 301–302; democratization of access to calculus 288–289; descriptions of designs 289–296, *291, 292*; design rationale 301–309; dynamic representations 287–288, 298, 300, 310–311; future directions 309–310;

graphs 302–303, 307; overview of projects 296–300, *297*; piecewise linear functions 304–307, *305*, *306*; political explorations 299; predict–compare–explain cycle 308–309; scientific explorations 299–300; technological explorations 299; wicked problems 310–311
Simon, H. A. 158, 160
Simon, Herbert 262
Simonson, M. 131
Simpkins, Gary A. 187, *188*, 190–192, 193, 196–197, 199, 200, 203, 204, 226–227, 230, 231, 232
Skinner, B. F. 85–87; *see also* Skinnerian teaching machine
Skinnerian teaching machine 5, 85–102; background 85–87; design 87–90, *88*, *89*, *91*, *92*, **93**, *93*; operant conditioning 85–87, 94–97, **94**, 98–100, **101**, 102; Skinner's critiques of other educational technologies 97–100, *99*; student experience 100–101, **101**
Smalltalk 246–248, *247*
Smith, Michael 262
Smitherman, Geneva 198, 200, 207, 223–224, 230, 232
Society for Technical Communication 245
Socratic teaching 98
speech-only deaf educational systems 22–25, 31, 55
SRA Reading Lab 6, 104–121; complexity 118–120; consumables and coherence 117–118; currency and cultural awareness 118, *119*; design decisions 110–114, *113*, *115*, *116*; effectiveness 112–113, *113*, 120–121; illustrations 114, *117*; physical materials 105–110, *105*, *107*, *108*, *109*, *111*, 113–114
Stalling, Charlesetta 187, 188–189, *189*, 195, 196, 197, 198–199, 200, 205, 207, 210, 213, 232
Stanford University 254, 255, 257, 259; *see also* Computer Assisted Instruction in Elementary Mathematics; Nicaragua Radio Mathematics Project (NRMP)
Stewart, William 219, 233
Stokes, P. 173
Stolurow, L. M. 153
Stratovision 125
Strauss, Anselm 318
Stroud, Robert 275

Supervising Women Workers 5, 65–83; context *63*, *64*, 65–66; design 66–80, *66*, *67*, *69*, *71*, *73*, *74*, *76*, *78*, *80*; design concerns 82–83; drama vs. direct instruction 80–81; human performance technology 82; production design 81
Suppes, Patrick 135, 136, 141, 143, 148, 153, 180
Swafford, Barry 50, 51, 52–60

Taylor, Frederick 255
teaching machines 4, 5, 87; branching 98–100, *99*, 102; *see also* Skinnerian teaching machine
technological theories of design 158–159
Technomics Research and Analysis Corporation 189–190
teletype (TTY) 136–137, 140–141, 143, 145, 152
television: captioning 57–58; Skinner's criticisms of 97; *see also* Midwest Program on Airborne Television Instruction (MPATI); TICCIT system
Tellis, Chris 271
Tennessee Association of the Deaf 54–55, 56, 57
Tennessee School for the Deaf 3, 50–60; bilingual education 57–59, 60; events impacting 54–57; physical spaces 51–54, *52*, *53*, *54*; technology 56, 57–59
Texas Instruments 260, 261, 262, 299, 300
Thorpe, Jim 40
TICCIT system 7, 152–182; authoring 172–173; base frames 160–163, *161*, *162*; component display theory 165–166; context of design practice 157–158; context of design theory 158–159; control system design 168–171, *169*, *170*; design problems 159–167; display type design 165–166, 168–171, *170*; evaluations 174–179, *177*; goals 155–156, 180; implementations 174; instructor effect 175; integration of strategy and logic 171–172; learners benefiting most from 177–178, *177*; learning hierarchy analysis 167–168; logic problem 160–163, *161*, *162*; objective typology 165, 166–167, *167*; objectives hierarchies 167–171, *169*; orientation effect 178; origins 154–156; PRACTICE key 176; stakeholders

TICCIT: *continued*
    156–157; strategy problem 163–167,
    164, 165, 167; WHY? key
    178–179
toasts 200, 203
Total Communication approach to deaf
    education 31, 32
training films *see* instructional training
    films; *Supervising Women Workers*
turtle geometry 285
TUTOR language 154
Tyler, R. W. 158

United States Agency for International
    Development (USAID) 136–137, 150
United States Office of Education 65–66
University of Maryland 258
University of Pittsburgh 257
user interfaces *see* minimalist instruction

View Matcher 246–248, *247*
Vincenti, W. 158
Vygotsky, L. S. 178, 318

War on Poverty 199–200
Waterman, D. 257
Weizenbaum, Joseph 258
Wenger, E. 153
Westervelt, Zenas *24*, 25, 26, 28, 29, 30, 33
Westinghouse Corporation 125
wicked problems 310–311
Williams, R. 232
Wilson, H. 153
Winograd, Terry 258
Wolin, Burton R. 190

Xerox 236, 245

zone of proximal development 178